AFTER THE SHEIKHS

'It is almost forty years since the publication of Fred Halliday's landmark book *Arabia Without Sultans*. Now, in the wake of the Arab spring, another young British academic has written an important account of prospects for the Gulf region … Orientalist special pleading doesn't get a look in. This is an unsentimental story of hard-nosed political calculation, conspicuous consumption, opaque budgets and sovereign wealth funds.'

Ian Black, *The Guardian*

'What is the secret of the Gulf monarchies' survival? There are numerous reasons. The support of Western powers, oil wealth and an effective secret police are among them. But in this exceptionally argued book, Christopher Davidson concentrates on the prime reason: the Gulf monarchies enjoy considerable legitimacy from their populations. … This fine-tuned monarchical resilience, Davidson argues, cannot be sustained for much longer. Immense internal pressures are building up and the pressure-cooker is about to explode. Davidson marshals an impressive array of evidence.'

Ziauddin Sardar, *The Independent*

'Britain and the US are uncritical friends of the hereditary Gulf rulers; but what if they are likely to collapse, as Christopher Davidson convincingly predicts? It would be folly to ignore the writing on the wall for these insatiably greedy elites; Davidson's warning should be on the desk of every Foreign Office Minister.'

Lord Avebury, vice-chair of the All-Party Parliamentary Human Rights Group

'Davidson argues that the Gulf regimes will be gone—at least in their current form—within the next two to five years. This audacious prediction should not be lightly dismissed. The dynamics he analyses and the facts he has gathered, based on long-term observation of the region, provide tantalising clues that profound change may indeed be at close hand.'

Dirk Vandewalle, Associate Professor of Government, Dartmouth College

'*After the Sheikhs* is a book of tremendous value. It applies a rigorously constructed theoretical framework to a rich array of empirical data in order to assess the long-term survivability of some of the world's last authoritarian holdouts. For anyone interested in understanding the post-2011 Middle East, this is essential reading.'

Mehran Kamrava, Director of the Center for International and Regional Studies, Georgetown University, Qatar

'At a time when the Gulf Kingdoms arrogantly boast of having avoided the fate of their neighbours in the revolutions of the Arab Spring, this book provides a convincing counter-narrative and a powerful warning to rulers who treat their countries as personal fiefdoms.'

Waleed Abu Alkair, head of Monitor of Human Rights in Saudi Arabia

'This book must be read by every Western policymaker betting on the status quo in the GCC, by every pro-democracy activist struggling to realise Davidson's predicted outcome, and by every GCC citizen dreaming of a better future but made to fear the worst if change was to come.'

Ala'a Shehabi, writer, pro-democracy activist, founder, Bahrain Watch

CHRISTOPHER M. DAVIDSON

AFTER THE SHEIKHS

The Coming Collapse of the Gulf Monarchies

OXFORD
UNIVERSITY PRESS

OXFORD
UNIVERSITY PRESS

Oxford University Press, Inc., publishes works that further
Oxford University's objective of excellence
in research, scholarship, and education.

Oxford New York
Auckland   Cape Town   Dar es Salaam   Hong Kong   Karachi
Kuala Lumpur   Madrid   Melbourne   Mexico City   Nairobi
New Delhi   Shanghai   Taipei   Toronto

With offices in
Argentina   Austria   Brazil   Chile   Czech Republic   France   Greece
Guatemala   Hungary   Italy   Japan   Poland   Portugal   Singapore
South Korea   Switzerland   Thailand   Turkey   Ukraine   Vietnam

Copyright © 2013 by Oxford University Press

Oxford is a registered trade mark of Oxford University Press in the UK
and certain other countries.

Published by Oxford University Press, Inc
198 Madison Avenue, New York, New York 10016

Published in the United Kingdom in 2013 by C. Hurst & Co. (Publishers) Ltd.

www.oup.com

Oxford is a registered trademark of Oxford University Press

Library of Congress Cataloging-in-Publication Data
Davidson, Christopher M. (Christopher Michael)
After the sheikhs : the coming collapse of the gulf monarchies / Christopher Davidson.
p. cm.
Summary: "Noted Gulf expert Christopher Davidson contends that the collapse of these
kings, emirs, and sultans is going to happen, and was always going to"
— Provided by publisher.
ISBN 978-0-19-933064-5 (hardback)
1. Persian Gulf States—Politics and government—21st century. 2. Saudi Arabia—Politics
and government—21st century. 3. Monarchy—Persian Gulf States. 4. Monarchy—Saudi
Arabia. I. Title.
JQ1840.D38 2013
320.9536—dc23
2013014438

1 3 5 7 9 8 6 4 2

Printed in India
on Acid-Free Paper

CONTENTS

Preface and Acknowledgements   vii
Acronyms   ix

Introduction   1
The revolutions that never came   3
Explaining monarchical survival   5
Further explanations   12

1. State Formation and Economic Development   17
   Origins of the Gulf monarchies   18
   Britain and the early order   22
   Independence and state formation   26
   Economic development trajectories   40

2. Explaining Survival—Domestic Matters   49
   Distributing wealth   50
   National elites   58
   Co-opting expatriates   62
   Cults of personality   66
   Heritage and history   70
   Co-opting religion   72
   Environmental credentials   75

3. Explaining Survival—External Matters   79
   Development assistance and international charity   81
   Active neutrality: peacekeeping and mediation   85
   Soft power in the West: strategic investments and
   development assistance   90

v

CONTENTS

Soft power in the West: cultural institutions   95

Soft power in the West: financing universities and
manipulating research   98

Soft power in the East: China and Japan   104

4. Mounting Internal Pressures   111

Resources, populations, and subsidies   112

Voluntary unemployment   117

Squandering wealth   121

Poverty and real unemployment   129

Discrimination, statelessness, and sectarianism   134

Censorship and limiting expression   145

5. Mounting External Pressures   155

Welcoming foreigners and eroding legitimacy   156

Western bases and armaments   163

Antagonising Iran   169

Israel: the unholy alliance   175

Division and disunity   179

Interference and coups d'état   182

6. The Coming Collapse   191

Evolving opposition   193

Modernising forces   196

Countering the Arab Spring: the wrong side of history   201

Bahrain: rage and revolution   205

Oman: protests and promises   209

Saudi Arabia: the cracks appearing   211

Kuwait: 'The People's Spring'   216

United Arab Emirates: opposition emerges   220

Qatar: champion or charlatan?   226

Conclusion   229

Postscript   239

Notes   245

Bibliography   281

Index   289

PREFACE AND ACKNOWLEDGEMENTS

I began researching and writing *After the Sheikhs: The Coming Collapse of the Gulf Monarchies* in summer 2009 from the confines of my temporary office at Kyoto University. The original idea for the book, however, occurred to me back in 2002, when I was still writing up my PhD. Intrigued by several frank and discreet discussions when living in the UAE's northernmost emirate of Ra's al-Khaimah, I was determined to burrow beneath the hype and gauge the true extent of loyalty to traditional monarchies in such states, especially in communities with less favourable economic circumstances. Since then, much has changed in the region, with oil price shocks, credit crunches, property bubbles, terror campaigns, rampant sectarianism, and of course full blown revolutions on its doorstep. Although largely unforeseen and at first difficult to understand, I found that most of these events and their associated impacts helped to strengthen my thesis and—more importantly—they strengthened my resolve to finish the manuscript as soon as possible. Although the book was never intended to be a crystal ball it is worth noting that the original, 2009 version forecast the collapse of most of the Gulf monarchies within the next decade. In contrast, this final 2012 version contends that most of these regimes—at least in their present form—will be gone *within the next two to five years.*

A very large number of individuals deserve my thanks. Over the past few years they have provided encouragement, fact-checking, fascinating pieces of information, and—on occasion—some necessary criticism. These include academics, human rights and pro-democracy activists, members of several political societies and religious organisations, government employees from all six gulf monarchies and neighbouring states, and of course a small army of concerned citizens and expatriates. I am also very thankful to the following universities for inviting me to give lectures on earlier, prototype versions of this book: the London School of Economics, Oxford, St. Andrews, Yale, Stanford, and Otago. The feedback I received from such well-informed audiences undoubtedly helped me shape my thoughts.

Above all I thank my indefatigable publisher, Michael Dwyer, and all of his team at C. Hurst & Co.

ACRONYMS

ADBIC	Abu Dhabi Basic Industries Corporation
ADEC	Abu Dhabi Executive Council
ADFAD	Abu Dhabi Fund for Arab Development
ADFD	Abu Dhabi Fund for Development
ADFEC	Abu Dhabi Future Energy Company
ADIA	Abu Dhabi Investment Authority
ADNCC	Abu Dhabi National Consultative Council
ADNOC	Abu Dhabi National Oil Company
AQAP	Al-Qaeda on the Arabian Peninsula
Aramco	Arabian American Oil Company
ATP	Association of Tennis Professionals
Bapco	Bahrain Petroleum Company
BCHR	Bahrain Centre for Human Rights
CENTCOM	US Central Command
CEO	chief executive office
CIA	Central Intelligence Agency (of the US)
CNPC	China National Petroleum Corporation
COM	Council of Ministers (of the UAE)
DIC	Dubai International Capital
DIFC	Dubai International Financial Centre
DLF	Dhofar Liberation Front
DPW	Dubai Ports World
EAD	Environmental Agency Abu Dhabi
ECHR	Emirates Centre for Human Rights
EDB	Economic Development Board (of Bahrain)
EMAL	Emirates Aluminium

ENOC	Emirates National Oil Company
EPPCO	Emirates Petroleum Products Company
F1	Formula One
FIFA	Fédération International de Football Association
FNC	Federal National Council (of the UAE)
FTA	free trade agreement
GCC	Co-operation Council for the Arab States of the Gulf
GDP	gross domestic product
HH	his highness
HIV	human immunodeficiency virus
HRH	his royal highness
ICBC	Industrial and Commercial Bank of China
ICC	International Criminal Court
ICD	Investment Corporation of Dubai
IDEX	International Defence Exhibition (of Abu Dhabi)
IMF	International Monetary Fund
IPIC	International Petroleum Investment Company (of Abu Dhabi)
IPC	Iraqi Petroleum Company
IRENA	International Renewable Energy Agency
ISP	internet service provider
JAFZ	Jebel Ali Free Zone (of Dubai)
JETRO	Japan External Trade Organisation
JODCO	Japan Oil Development Company
KAUST	King Abdullah University of Science and Technology
KCIC	Kuwait-China Investment Company
KFAS	Kuwait Foundation for the Advancement of Sciences
KFAED	Kuwait Fund for Arab Economic Development
KIA	Kuwait Investment Authority
KIPCO	Kuwait Projects Company
LSE	London School of Economics and Political Science
NYU	New York University
ODA	official development assistance
OECD	Organisation for Economic Co-operation and Development
OPEC	Organisation of the Petroleum Exporting Countries
P&O	Peninsula and Orient Steam Navigation Company
PDRY	People's Democratic Republic of Yemen

PFLOAP	Popular Front for the Liberation of the Occupied Arabian Gulf
PRC	People's Republic of China
PGA	Professional Golfers Association
PIN	personal identification number
QIA	Qatar Investment Authority
QPC	Qatar Petroleum Company
QSI	Qatar Sports Investments
QE2	Queen Elizabeth 2 cruise liner
RAND	Research and Development Corporation
SABIC	Saudi Arabian Basic Industries Corporation
SCR	Supreme Council of Rulers (of the UAE)
Sinopec	China Petroleum and Chemical Corporation
SMS	short message service
SPC	Supreme Petroleum Council (of the UAE)
TDIC	Tourism and Development Investment Company (of Abu Dhabi)
UAE	United Arab Emirates
UCL	University College London
UK	United Kingdom (of Great Britain and Northern Ireland)
UN	United Nations
UNDP	United Nations Development Programme
UNESCO	United Nations Education, Scientific, and Cultural Organisation
UNICEF	United Nations Children's Fund
UNRWA	United Nations Relief and Works Agency
UNSC	UN Security Council
US	United States (of America)
USSR	Union of Soviet Socialist Republics
VAT	value added tax
WTO	World Trade Organisation
ZCCF	Zayed Centre for Coordination and Follow-Up

INTRODUCTION

Central to the stability of the world's oil and gas industries and home to the birthplace of Islam, Saudi Arabia and its five smaller neighbours—the United Arab Emirates, Kuwait, Qatar, Oman, and Bahrain—have long fascinated scholars, diplomats, and journalists. In recent years international interest in the 'Gulf monarchies' of the Arabian Peninsula has soared. Not only have they played a key role in the War on Terror—on both sides of the conflict—but they also now account for the lion's share of the Arab World's gross domestic product[1] founded on ever-rising trade flows, financial zones, tourism, and even real estate sectors.

Since their formation and in some cases independence in the mid-twentieth century, the Gulf monarchies have remained governed by highly autocratic and—as many have argued—seemingly anachronistic regimes. Nevertheless, their rulers have demonstrated remarkable resilience despite having bloody conflicts on their doorsteps, fast-growing populations, and powerful modernising and globalising forces impacting on largely conservative societies. Obituaries for these traditional polities have frequently been penned—in some cases by leading commentators—but even now, well into the twenty-first century, these absolutist, almost medieval entities still appear to defy their critics. If anything, with the 2011 and 2012 'Arab Spring' revolutions that have been sweeping aside the region's republics and accelerating the fall of other incumbent presidents, the apparently steadfast Gulf monarchies have, at first glance, re-affirmed their status as the Middle East's only real bastion of stability. Even when violence and unrest erupted in some of their cities, this was largely contained, and the integrity of monarchy as a legitimate political system was ostensibly maintained. After all, as the lickspittle spokesmen and legions of public relations consultants employed by the Gulf monarchies are usually quick to point out, these states are somehow different: they are not 'dictatorships' and should thus be immune from precipitate political upheaval.

The near future, however, is far less predictable for the kings, emirs, and sultans currently in power. Serious internal and external pressures have been accumulating in the Gulf monarchies, in some cases long preceding 2011. Although these have had an uneven impact on the region due to significant socio-economic and political disparities, there are nonetheless important patterns and commonalities in these pressures which mean they will soon affect all six states. Indeed, a compelling argument can be made that these regimes are now, more than ever, only as strong as the weakest link in their chain. If an especially brittle monarchy succumbed to a popular revolution or fell into a state of anarchy, then a veritable 'domino effect' could unfold, as the erstwhile illusion of stability or invincibility that has distinguished the Gulf monarchies from the floundering Arab republics would be swiftly dispelled. In this scenario, if one Gulf state failed, then even the wealthiest and most confident of rulers would find their positions, or at least their legitimacy, under threat.

Some of the mounting pressures have clearly been recognised by the Gulf monarchies, but many others have been ignored, inadequately addressed, or left undiagnosed for too long. Thus, after considering the earlier, unsuccessful predictions of monarchical demise and providing an understanding of the emergence, development, and survival of these polities to date, this book's primary purpose will be to identify better these contemporary pressures and demonstrate why they now matter so much. Against this backdrop I will assert that these pressures will soon lead to the collapse of the Gulf monarchies, or at least most of them in their present form. Although I claim that this collapse is inevitable—regardless of the Arab Spring and wider events—an argument is made that the revolutionary movements of 2011 and 2012 in North Africa, Syria, and elsewhere are undeniably going to serve as important, if indirect catalysts for the coming upheaval in the Persian Gulf. Not least because many of the pressures that had been building up in the Arab republics are now also manifest in the Gulf monarchies, even if sometimes below the surface.

The revolutions that never came

By the time the monarchies were all independent states in the early 1970s the threat of some sort of popular, Gamal Abdul Nasser-inspired Arab nationalist revolution reaching the Persian Gulf seemed to have petered out. As discussed later in this book former national front activists, especially in Dubai, Bahrain, and Kuwait, had long since been co-opted by their respective ruling families, often becoming successful businessmen with stakes in fast growing, oil-rich economies.[2] The humiliation of military defeat by Israel in 1967 had also dealt a significant blow to the prestige of the Arab republics and their ability to project nationalist sentiments elsewhere, and the final nationalist revolution—Libya in 1969—served only to clear a path for Muammar Gaddafi's military junta. Moreover, despite their non-revolutionary status and an 'Arab Cold War' between Egypt and Saudi Arabia in the 1960s,[3] by 1971 all of the Gulf monarchies had become full members of the Cairo-based Arab League,[4] and, through their partial participation in the Organisation of the Petroleum Exporting Countries cartel,[5] they were increasingly tolerated by the Arab republics and perceived as playing a reasonably active role in countering Israel and other foreign interests in the region.

Instead, the most acute threat to the Gulf monarchies in the early 1970s was deemed to be some sort of sweeping socialist or Communist revolution, likely supported by the Union of Soviet Socialist Republics or the People's Republic of China. In 1962 restive tribes in Dhofar—the southern province of Oman—had formed a liberation front, which by 1968 had already adopted a Marxist-Leninist stance and had openly begun to receive Soviet and especially Chinese support in a bid to overthrow the British-backed sultan of Muscat.[6] Furthermore, the following year a Marxist-Leninist wing of the South Yemen-based liberation front[7] had seized power, eventually forming a Soviet, Chinese, and Cuban-backed People's Democratic Republic of Yemen—right on the southern flank of Saudi Arabia.

Understandably, much of the scholarship devoted to the region at the time reflected these circumstances, often discussing the likelihood of further Marxist-Leninist rebellions spreading throughout the Arabian Peninsula.[8] After all, the Dhofar Liberation Front had renamed itself the Popular Front for the Liberation of the Occupied Arabian Gulf, and was only finally defeated in 1975 following a series of British-backed counterattacks on behalf of the beleaguered Omani ruling family.[9] Published in 1974, Fred Halliday's *Arabia Without Sultans* was based on extensive fieldwork in Dhofar during the early 1970s and remains one of the best perspectives on this period. Focusing heavily on Oman's underdevelopment and the disenfranchisement of various tribes under the yoke of a traditional monarch supported by an imperial power, the book is vividly optimistic about the prospects of successful armed insurrection in the region. Although not explicitly attacking capitalist structures, Halliday nonetheless painted a grim picture of continuing misery and the deepening exploitation of the region's indigenous population. He argued strongly that increased social conflict was going to be the major impetus for political change in the Gulf monarchies.[10]

But while Dhofar-like Marxist-Leninist rebellions were perceived as acute, short-term threats to the Gulf monarchies by some area specialists, those focusing on other parts of the Middle East were boldly claiming that longer term, intangible 'modernising forces' were also likely to lead to significant shifts in the political and social order, and eventually the demise of traditional ruling systems. Writing in 1958, Daniel Lerner had already predicted in his *Passing of Traditional Society: The Modernizing of the Middle East* that most of the region's societies would pass through a series of distinct phases, beginning with urbanisation, proceeding through literacy and mass communication, and then eventually leading to political participation.[11] By the early 1960s many more scholars had put forward similar arguments for other parts of the developing world, all essentially claiming that a combination of more modern social settings, especially cities, combined with new, modern technologies—especially relating to communications—would inevitably lead to the formation of some sort of educated, conscious, and better-connected middle class, which in turn would become increasingly unwilling to be governed by primitive, non-participatory political structures. Seymour Martin Lipset, for example, in his 1959 article 'Some Social Requisites of Democracy: Economic Development and Political Legitimacy' and a volume that appeared the following year, *Political Man: The Social Bases of Politics*, had asserted that the wealthier a nation became, and the more its population was exposed to modernising forces, then the better was its chances of sustaining democratic institutions.[12] Similarly, the following year Karl Deutsch packaged these forces and processes under his 'theory of social mobilisation', stressing both their cumulative impact and their inevitable or extremely likely capacity to transform political behaviour.[13]

Published in 1968, Samuel Huntington's *Political Order in Changing Societies* took 'modernisation theory' to a higher level. Questioning the smooth predictability of such political changes, he argued that incumbent regimes would resist strongly, often by developing short-term containment strategies, and possibly by resorting to violence. Nevertheless he still subscribed to the inevitability of new, modern social groupings eventually dispensing with traditional polities. And in one particularly celebrated chapter—'The King's Dilemma'—he even singled out traditional monarchs, stating that they would soon have to grapple with the dilemma of either suppressing modernising forces and thus facing mass rebellion, or instead allowing modernisation to occur and thus risk ceding absolute powers to a mobilised middle class.[14] On the latter scenario, his claim that '…the monarchical parent is eventually devoured by its modern progeny'[15] seemed particularly relevant for the Gulf monarchies, even if they were not explicitly mentioned, as at that time all were on the cusp of accelerating socio-economic development. Oil revenues were beginning to flow to fledgling governments, populations were being urbanised as oil boom opportunities abounded in fast-expanding cities, literacy rates were increasing as more and more schools were being established, and mass communications was arriving in the region for the first time in the form of newspapers, transistor radios, and television. Thus, while Huntington would have also probably predicted an 'Arabia without sultans', he would have likely foreseen the demands for political change being led by a restless, newly-created middle class, rather than by Halliday's exploited and insurgent proletariat.

Explaining monarchical survival

As the years and decades went by, it soon became apparent that both sets of predictions were wrong, at least with reference to the Gulf monarchies. Although at first glance seeming to have adopted capitalist modes of production, the Gulf economies never really spawned a proletariat—or at least not one that was interested in overthrowing the classes above it. Equally, although an urban, educated, and mass communications-literate population was undoubtedly emerging in the Persian Gulf—as per Lerner and Lipsets' expectations—it hardly compared with the middle classes of more developed democratic states and nor did it seem keen to press for the kind of greater political participation that Deutsch and Huntington would have expected. This ongoing apathy, or political demobilisation, and the concomitant endurance of traditional monarchies on the Arabian Peninsula, can largely be explained by the region's unusual political economy, specifically the rent-based nature of the economic and political systems that emerged in all six monarchies following their first significant oil exports.

First discussed by Karl Marx in the 1860s, in the context of a decadent class which benefits from profit-income derived from renting out property and thus does not actually produce anything itself,[16] 'rentier capitalism' or 'rentierism' was then expanded in the twentieth century to include discussion of entire 'rentier states'. These were originally understood to be those developed nations that could supply loans to less developed nations and thus charge interest,[17] before Hussein Mahdavy's 1970 article 'The Patterns and Problems of Economic Development in Rentier States' revised the definition to specify those states that received significant rent from 'foreign individuals or concerns'. Moreover, with Shah Muhammad Reza Pahlavi's oil-rich Iran as his case study, he made the explicit connection between hydrocarbon rents accruing to a government, and the formation of a new, rentier elite class.[18]

In 1987 Hazem Beblawi's article 'The Rentier State in the Arab World' brought the debate even closer to the Gulf monarchies. Having also drawn on Marx's views on class formation, Beblawi claimed that a rentier state was a one 'in which only a few are engaged in the generation of the wealth, with the majority being only involved in the distribution or utilisation of it'.[19] With their relatively small indigenous populations—which have themselves sometimes been used as a simplistic explanation for the durability of traditional political systems[20]—and, by this stage, governments with ever-increasing rent from hydrocarbon exports, the Gulf monarchies appeared to have become the quintessential examples of Beblawi's rentier states. Able to distribute rent to their citizens in the form of various economic benefits—whether direct transfers of wealth, services, or public sector jobs—and with vast numbers of expatriate workers being imported to the region to fulfil most labour requirements, the majority of the region's indigenous population was increasingly being distanced from the forces of production and thus sidelined into becoming a rentier class dependent on government subsidies, rather than a distinct proletariat or middle class. In this way political acquiescence was assumed to have been bought, as it seemed that most Gulf nationals would be satisfied as long as they benefited from a mode of production caught somewhere between feudalism and capitalism, in which traditional familial or tribal ties to a ruling family guaranteed access to wealth and economic opportunities. More recent Gulf-specific studies have added much weight to this analysis, with Steffen Hertog's 2010 study on Saudi Arabia's political and economic history, *Princes, Brokers, and Bureaucrats*, providing much evidence to show how oil income has often allowed the state to act independently of demands in society.[21]

A few problems remain, however, with proving the direct connection between rentierism and the survival of traditional political systems. As Michael Ross noted in his 2001 article 'Does Oil Hinder Democracy?', the Middle East was a particularly difficult region on which to test the theory, given that most Arab governments at that time could be considered authoritarian, regardless of their natural resources or rent-based structures.[22] Nevertheless, Ross demonstrated that a 'taxation effect' did exist in the hydrocarbon-rich states, most notably the Gulf monarchies, whereby governments derived such large revenues from oil and gas sales that they became unlikely to tax their population heavily, if at all; in turn the public would be less likely to demand representation or accountability from their rulers.[23] Similarly, Ross illustrated a 'spending effect' in rentier states, whereby wealthy governments could pay for extensive patronage projects to enhance the reputation of rulers, and—through the generous funding of quasi-civil society bodies—could engender a 'group formation effect', weakening the appeal of poorly funded, unlicensed and genuine civil society bodies.[24] Indeed, in young states such as the Gulf monarchies, where a tradition of civil society organisation was noticeable by its absence, it was noted that governments relied primarily on largesse rather than repression to block the formation of powerful social capital.

With hydrocarbon reserves declining in several Gulf monarchies, especially since the 1990s, and with the ability of governments to keep spending or expanding the public sector being challenged, another problem loomed for the rentierism assumption. Nonetheless, the 'new rentierism' described in my 2005 book *The United Arab Emirates: A Study in Survival*, tried to offer an explanation. Dubai—the second largest of the UAE's constituent emirates—had run out of sizeable oil rents some time before, and was thus rapidly diversifying its economic base into tourism, export-processing zones, and real estate opportunities for foreign investors. All three activities were kick-started by the government, which fostered a more liberal investment environment and then distributed hitherto worthless tracts of desert land to powerful indigenous families. In turn these families were able to develop or rent out their land to expatriates, thus reaping rewards from a feudal-capitalist system while still maintaining a certain separation from the wealth creation process.[25] Similarly in Bahrain and Oman, which were also low on hydrocarbon reserves, recent analyses have demonstrated that new, land-related activities managed to shift at least some of their national populations from oil-financed rentier expectations to this post-oil, private sector rentierism. Other research has also revealed how all six Gulf monarchies—even those with very sizeable hydrocarbon reserves—have kept reinvigorating an old sponsorship practice, the *kafala* system.[26] With most businesses being required by law to have a local partner, this has effectively allowed Gulf nationals to market themselves as sponsors to industrious foreign entrepreneurs.[27] Thus even the most minor of Gulf national families have often had the opportunity to transform themselves into 'mini rentiers' courtesy of their nationality and regardless of their closeness to ruling families or access to land. Writing in 2011, Matthew Gray's article 'A Theory of Late Rentierism in the Arab States of the Gulf' pushed some of these ideas a little further forward, arguing that 'late rentier' states have had to become much more entrepreneurial and responsive to markets, even if they remain undemocratic, and have had to open up to globalisation while at the same time keeping strong protectionist elements.[28]

But as central as political economy is in understanding the survival of traditional monarchy on the Arabian Peninsula, several other explanations are worth considering also. These have mostly focused on the region's political culture and are particularly useful for grasping the subtler differences between the six states beyond their self-evident economic and demographic disparities. Especially plausible is the view that some of the most resilient traditional polities in the developing world have been those that have successfully kept reviving and reinventing traditional sources of legitimacy—including cults of personality, tribal heritage, and religion—while simultaneously co-opting and controlling modernising forces such as education and communications wherever possible. In this revised approach to modernisation theory, the most durable regimes are therefore those that approach modernising forces as an opportunity rather than as a threat, and find ways of harnessing rather than suppressing them. Published in 1978, Michael Hudson's *Arab Politics: The Search for Legitimacy* provides an early Middle East-focused example. Although still arguing that no Arab regime could attain lasting legitimacy without implementing full participatory democracy, Hudson acknowledged that several Arab states, especially the Gulf monarchies, appeared to have gained considerable legitimacy from their populations, often by using a range of resources, including personalities and religion. Applying his 'mosaic model', he claimed that these regimes had been able to maintain and perhaps even enhance traditional loyalties, despite a period of intense modernisation.[29] Writing more recently on the Qatar case, Allen Fromherz puts this well: '[the state] should be a boiling stew of problems brought about by the conflict between tradition and modernity, but it is not... Many political scientists, at one time predicting its fall, now predict a long term future... The old political system is usually the first to go after the forces of modernity and tradition have clashed. Yet Qatar remains a monarchy...'[30]

The Gulf monarchies have been particularly skilled at grafting seemingly modern political institutions onto essentially traditional power-bases. Over the past few decades a plethora of ministries, government departments, and other authorities have been created as the size of the state has grown. In some cases consultative councils and even parliaments have even been set up. But for the most part these have remained extremely limited, often being dominated by staff or members who have been autocratically appointed, and with the institutions they represent enjoying only limited powers compared to those of the ruling families. They have nevertheless provided a veneer of credibility and modernity for the regimes, not just to appease international critics, but also for domestic consumption. And as Hisham Sharabi argued in his 1992 study, *Neopatriarchy: A Theory of Distorted Change in Arab Society*, such strategies have allowed regimes to move away from a total reliance on inherited patriarchal authority to a system in which it can be re-introduced and maintained in an apparently modern state.[31]

These strategies can also be connected back to Max Weber's original tripartite classification of authority, first presented in his 1919 lecture 'Politics as a Vocation'. Weber argued that polities would eventually mature from relying on the charismatic, authority of one patriarch and his family, to regimes based on traditional, often feudal authority, before finally progressing to states governed by legal-rational authority where powers were vested in offices rather than office-holders and where the rule of law could be upheld by an independent judiciary.[32] In this light, the hybrid, 'neo-patriarchal' governments that have emerged in the Gulf seem to have allowed the monarchies to arrest or stall Weber's process somewhere between the second and third stages, while also continuing to rely on the initial stage of authority. Writing in 2002, Daniel Brumberg makes a direct connection between such neo-patriarchy and the Gulf monarchies in his article 'The Trap of Liberalized Autocracy'. On discussing Kuwait, which unlike its neighbours had long been experimenting with an elected parliament, he contended that '…the mixtures of guided pluralism, controlled elections, and selective repression… is not just a survival strategy… but rather a type of political system whose institutions, rules, and logic defy any linear model of democratisation'.[33] And of Bahrain and Qatar, which at that time had not yet followed Kuwait's lead, he argued that '…political eclecticism has benefits that rulers are unlikely to forgo' and predicted, with uncanny accuracy, that these regimes '…would soon join the ranks of Arab states dwelling in the gray zone of liberalised autocracy'.[34]

Linking together all of these political economy and political culture explanations, and perhaps providing the best all-round understanding of the resilience of traditional monarchy have been the various attempts to describe the multi-dimensional, socio-economic contracts that seemingly exist between the Gulf's ruling families and their citizens. First applied in the European context, most notably by British and French writers in the seventeenth and eighteenth century, the concept of a 'social contract' was used as an intellectual device to explain the most appropriate relationship between governments and individual citizens. Although Hobbes advocated absolute monarchy as the ideal form of authority, while Locke and Rousseau advocated 'natural rights' and the need for collective sovereignty in the name of the 'general will' of the people, all three were nonetheless agreed on the need for governments to forge agreements with their citizens by guaranteeing certain privileges and protection in exchange for political consent.[35] Best applied to the Middle East context by Mehran Kamrava in *The Modern Middle East: A Political History since the First World War*, first published in 2005, the Hobbesian social contract is rebranded a 'ruling bargain' for the Arab world, where people choose to remain politically acquiescent in return for sufficient stability and services from their governments.[36]

Writing in 2008 and 2009 in *Dubai: The Vulnerability of Success* and *Abu Dhabi: Oil and Beyond*, I examined two different constituent emirates of the UAE—one scarce in oil wealth and one abundant—through the prism of Kamrava's ruling bargain. Although arguing that government-led distribution of rentier wealth and opportunities to its citizens was an important source of legitimacy for rulers, I contended that there were several other, non-economic sources of legitimacy for the UAE's rulers, including cults of personality, tribal heritage, religion, and seemingly modern government institutions. In fact, both books described many of the other sources that a revised modernisation or neo-patriarchy approach would expect to identify. By revealing the full spectrum of legitimacy sources available, it was also demonstrated that each Gulf monarchy's ruling bargain will differ, depending on its unique socioeconomic or historical circumstances. In some, especially those with high economic resources and small populations, it was reasoned that distributed wealth would remain the chief pillar of the system, while in others non-economic legitimacy sources would take precedence. And in those monarchies with rapidly declining or improving economic resources, a certain dynamism would likely be observed, as the relative weighting of the different legitimacy sources would be modified in order to reflect the changing reality and maintain the regimes' resilience. Nevertheless in all cases it was emphasised that the Gulf monarchies' governments, even the poorest, have to keep up the appearance of being distributors of wealth rather than extractors in order for their ruling bargains to function.[37] Moreover, as others have argued, any attempt to collect income tax would significantly undermine the mutual consent that underpins the social contracts.[38]

In these earlier books I also stressed the centrality of citizenship and the promotion of national identity in the Gulf monarchies' ruling bargains, as many of the services and privileges associated with citizenship can only really be sustained if the national populations remain distinct, aloof, and in some cases compact. Often ignored, or in some cases misrepresented as a threat rather than as an opportunity for regimes of the region, the role of the millions of expatriates who work in the Persian Gulf—and who now make up the majority of residents in all of the Gulf monarchies' major cities—was also discussed. Both books argued that as long as their remuneration and other benefits remained higher than in their country of origin, and as long as regimes kept blocking any path to naturalisation, then expatriates would remain mere labour migrants: primarily interested in safe and stable short-term wealth creation before eventually returning home. Thus, they would have no interest in altering the domestic political status quo, and if anything the more influential, wealthy, and skilled expatriates in the Gulf monarchies would become another important supportive or at least silent constituency of the traditional monarchies.[39]

Further explanations

Two other explanations for the survival of Gulf monarchies—and more broadly the survival of monarchy in the Arab world—have circulated over the past fifteen years. Both have been popular and thus also warrant attention. But given that they have often downplayed economic factors and have focused primarily on distinct historical, cultural, or familial circumstances associated with the Arab world that are now rapidly changing, it is likely they will soon fall out of favour. The most nuanced and sophisticated of these further explanations is that monarchical resilience is mostly due to the internal strength of the ruling families themselves. Published in 1999, Michael Herb's *All in the Family: Absolutism, Revolution, and Democracy in the Middle Eastern Monarchies* argued that the evolution of collective action mechanisms and 'bandwagoning' techniques within the contemporary ruling families have reduced some of the divisiveness and factionalism which historically plagued the region's monarchies for much of the last century.

In Herb's terms the result has been the emergence of 'dynastic monarchies', especially in the Persian Gulf. These dynasties, as they continue to expand with an ever-growing number of junior princes and sheikhs, have in some cases become self-regulating proto-institutions,[40] perhaps providing some of the strength and stability normally associated with large-scale single-party political systems, such as those in East Asia. Certainly, as the Gulf monarchies' oil-rich economies have boomed and state functions expanded, more high profile business and governmental positions have been created, and the most prudent Arab monarchs have distributed these as 'consolation prizes' to powerful members of their extended families. In this scenario, it is reasoned, any renegade family member will find it difficult to destabilise the monarchy or launch a *coup d'état*, as most relatives will side with the established authority, preferring not to lose their prominent places within the regime. Backed by case studies from across the region, Herb demonstrated that the more resilient monarchies such as Saudi Arabia, Kuwait, and the UAE had followed these strategies very closely, while other, swiftly deposed, monarchs such as Libya's king[41] had failed to do so.[42]

But given the survival of other, non-dynastic traditional monarchies, most notably Oman—whose ruler[43] has strongly resisted such power-sharing measures[44]—and the dynastic monarchy explanation's lack of emphasis on wealth distribution and social contracts, does it really explain regime longevity? Moreover, the ultimately unsuccessful attempts in Arab republics to implement Gulf-style dynastic rule for themselves also seem to undermine the explanation.[45] After all, Iraq's Saddam Hussein, Egypt's Hosni Mubarak, Syria's Hafez Al-Assad, and Libya's Muammar Gaddafi all sought to position their sons as successors while placating other relatives with important regime posts. But, as the events of 2011 and 2012 have demonstrated, even these 'monarchical presidencies' or *jamlaka* have proven to be very brittle.[46]

The second alternative explanation is much less convincing, although it is still regularly advanced by spokesmen for the Gulf monarchies to explain the latter's continuing lack of meaningful reform. Based on vague notions that international concepts of pluralism and political freedom are inimical to the region, regime mouthpieces usually claim that democracy just won't work, due to special characteristics, or *khususiyya*, such as tribal heritage and religious beliefs. Or they simply state that their countries are too young and thus 'not ready' for such changes. In this manner the Gulf monarchies have usually portrayed themselves as exceptions, thereby encouraging a 're-orientalisation' of the region in the eyes of their observers, critics, and even their own citizens.

Before 2011, when attempts at political reforms or the staging of elections within other authoritarian Middle East states often failed, the most autocratic of the Gulf monarchies were usually quick to alert their populations to the dangers of democracy and the fundamental incompatibility of such systems with the supposed anthropological reality of the Arabian Peninsula. Given its proximity, Iran's various flawed elections and the resulting violence have been useful examples, but even easier to exploit have been Kuwait's troubled experiences with democracy. As the only Gulf monarchy which has a functioning, although very limited parliament, Kuwait's system has long been distrusted by its monarchical neighbours, and the many problems it has faced have often been used to justify autocracy elsewhere in the region and warn against the perils of representative government. Such warnings have usually appeared as commentary pieces in the state-backed media, or even in official governmental statements and speeches. Following an especially problematic period in Kuwaiti politics in April 2010, Dubai's ruler and the UAE's unelected prime minister[47] stated to the media that 'Our leadership does not import ready-made models that may be valid for other societies but are certainly not suitable for our society'.[48] Speaking in December 2011 in an interview with CNN he repeated his argument by stating that 'we have our own democracy; you cannot transport your democracy to us'.[49]

Closely connected to this re-orientalisation explanation, the Gulf monarchies have similarly cautioned that if democracy was to be implanted in the region then certain unsavoury groups—the usual suspects being Islamic fundamentalists—would seize power. In recent years, and especially since 9/11 and subsequent terror threats, this has been a fairly convincing justification of autocratic power, not only for citizens, but also for the international community and above all the United States. In this sense, the Gulf monarchies have been following much the same line as the collapsing Arab republics, which, according to Jean-Pierre Filiu's *The Arab Revolution: Ten Lessons from the Democratic Uprising*, published in 2011, sought to 'spread the idea that the state's mission is to defend the supposedly unified nature of the state and the Islamic community'.[50] Abu Dhabi's crown prince[51] provides a good insight into the strategy, having been recorded in a 2006 US diplomatic cable referencing a meeting with US diplomats as stating that 'if there were an election [in the UAE] tomorrow, the Muslim Brotherhood would take over'.[52]

As much of this book demonstrates, it is unlikely that such justifications will remain effective for much longer, especially if the Gulf monarchies end up being bordered by post-Arab Spring states that hold successful elections and carefully integrate Islamic parties into the democratic process. Even prior to 2011 some Gulf nationals had begun to speak out on this issue, with a Saudi intellectual[53] claiming in 2010 that the autocratic Gulf monarchies would always seek to brand the strongest opposition force, whether made up of Islamists or others, as an obstacle to progress. Moreover, he stated that if Saudi Arabia had held elections forty years ago then the fear-mongering would have focused on 'social-ists and leftists… since that was predominant then. Now it's the Islamists… democracy cannot impose results that it wants. That's another form of dictatorship'. Similarly, writing in 2010 on the UAE's stance, a since imprisoned blogger[54] argued that 'Kuwait is an enlightening exam-ple in the region and it should stay glowing despite the pressure that anti-democracy governments exert on it'.[55]

Nevertheless, up until 2011 the commentarial and scholarly consen-sus on the Gulf monarchies, and the Arab world more broadly, sub-scribed heavily to both the need for re-orientalising the region and an appreciation of the dangers posed by Islamists and opposition groups via the democratic process. Published in 2010, Morten Valbjørn and André Bank's article 'Examining the Post in Post-Democratization: The Future of Middle Eastern Political Rule through Lenses of the Past' serves as a particularly good example. Valbjørn and Bank discuss Hun-tington's predicted 'Third Wave of Democratisation' and how it seemed to peter out in the 1990s, having impacted only on Eastern Europe, Latin America, and parts of Africa, without really reaching the Middle East. They then demonstrate that much of the subsequent literature on Arab politics either ignored the possibility of democracy in the Middle East, or wrote it off as a result of an 'inherently undemocratic Islamic culture' and the region being 'eternally out of step with history'.[56] As the latter parts of this book will demonstrate, for many years this has been a convenient but badly flawed explanatory device for swathes of the aca-demic and diplomatic community, especially when it comes to discuss-ing the Gulf monarchies.

1

STATE FORMATION
AND ECONOMIC DEVELOPMENT

Five of the Gulf monarchies only came into existence, at least as independent states, in the twentieth century, with Saudi Arabia being forged from a powerful hinterland alliance of religious and tribal forces, and with Kuwait and the smaller sheikhdoms emerging from the protection of the British Empire. The Sultanate of Oman, once a modest trading empire with territories stretching from East Africa to South Asia, has a much longer history but nonetheless also one heavily influenced by foreign powers, religion, and tribal politics.

These early interactions with outside forces, especially Britain, were incredibly significant in the shaping of the Gulf monarchies' political and economic structures, many of which remain in place today and were prototypes of the contemporary rentier state. The period of state formation and independence also matters, as the new governing institutions set up at this time were often along the described neo-patriarchal lines. In parallel, the remarkable economic development trajectories of the six states deserve much attention. Especially the fast growth of their oil and gas industries, the emergence of sizeable sovereign wealth funds, and the more recent efforts to diversify their economic bases by establishing manufacturing sectors, export-processing zones, tourism industries, financial hubs, and even real estate markets. Unsurprisingly this has led the Gulf monarchies to pursue a number of different paths, often as a result of varying levels of resources and diverging economic realities.

Origins of the Gulf monarchies

In 1744 an historic pact was made in the interior of the Arabian Peninsula between a powerful tribe from the province of Najd—led by Muhammad bin Saud—and the followers of the influential preacher, Muhammad bin Abd Al-Wahhab. Preaching a more purified brand of Islam—a doctrine of pure monotheism and a return to the fundamental tenets of Islam as laid down by the Koran—the Wahhabis were Unitarians, emphasising the 'centrality of God's unqualified oneness in Sunni Islam'.[1] Seeking to renew the Prophet's golden era of Islam, all who stood in their way were to be swept aside, including Islamic rulers with 'impure' lives, and especially those that collaborated with foreign, non-Islamic powers such as Britain. Ultimately led by the Al-Saud dynasty following Al-Wahhab's death, they had become a 'religio-military confederacy under which the desert people, stirred by a great idea, embarked on a common action',[2] and sought constant expansion in the manner of the original Islamic concept of *dar al-harb* or 'territory of war'—referring to the conquering of non-Islamic lands.[3] Although defeated by an Ottoman-backed Egyptian force in the early nineteenth century,[4] the Saudi-Wahhabi alliance soon returned to power, controlling even more of central Arabia by the end of the century.[5]

In the early twentieth century, having fought off challenges from the Al-Rashid family from the northern province of Hail, the Al-Saud's most celebrated leader—Abdul-Aziz bin Saud—consolidated Saudi-Wahhabi control over Riyadh, the dynasty's capital, and the rest of the Najd province. Soon after, Abdul-Aziz extended his influence to the eastern province of Al-Hasa and eventually the western province of Hejaz, which had formerly been ruled by the British-backed Emir of Mecca, Sharif Hussein—to whom London had earlier promised an independent Arabian kingdom in return for his support for British operations against the Ottomans in the First World War.[6] By 1932, with continuing support from the religious, Wahhabi establishment, Abdul-Aziz was in de facto control of most of the Arabian Peninsula and named his new kingdom—Saudi Arabia—after his own family and ancestors.

Kuwait's history is somewhat different, as religion has played a less prominent role while—as a much smaller territory—relations with foreign powers have been more significant. Nevertheless, as with the Al-Saud dynasty, Kuwait's ruling Al-Sabah family is also very much a product of centuries-old tribal struggles. As a branch of the huge Bani Utub tribal federation, the Al-Sabah had migrated north out of the Arabian interior in the late seventeenth century along with another prominent Bani Utub family, the Al-Khalifa. Both settled in the fishing and trading post of Kuwait, before the latter left for the settlement of Zubarah on the Qatari Peninusla in 1766.[7] By this stage the Al-Sabah were in firm control of Kuwait, and their ruler—Abdullah Al-Sabah—spent the next four decades consolidating his family's supremacy over the sheikhdom's political and economic affairs. In the nineteenth century Kuwait remained autonomous of the Saudi-Wahhabi alliance, mostly due to the Al-Sabah receiving nominal protection from the Ottoman Empire.

Under the rule of Mubarak Al-Sabah, also known as 'Mubarak the Great', Kuwait nevertheless began to move much closer to Britain, eventually signing an agreement in 1899 which guaranteed the sheikhdom British protection in exchange for London's control over its foreign affairs. In part this new relationship was due to Mubarak's troubled succession in 1886: having replaced his assassinated elder brother[8] he needed to counter the Ottoman links still maintained by his predecessor's supporters.[9] On a more macro level the switch in protection was also due to the decline of the Ottoman Empire, and was intended to improve access to British-Indian markets, especially in pearls, which at that time were Kuwait's most lucrative export. In any case, Ottoman influence greatly decreased, although subsequent Al-Sabah rulers briefly tried to use relations with Istanbul during the First World War as leverage over Britain.[10] In the early 1920s, relations with Britain deepened further following a Saudi-Wahhabi attack on Kuwait's Jahra fort[11] which resulted in the deployment of British gunboats and the crafting of a British-backed border agreement between the Al-Sabah, the Al-Saud, and Britain's mandated territory of Iraq.[12]

Like Kuwait, the other small Gulf monarchies had entered into similar protection agreements with Britain, but in most cases they had done so much earlier. This was partly because of the more immediate threat and regular attacks they faced from the Saudi-Wahhabi alliance, and partly because the Ottoman Empire was less relevant to the various sheikhs of the lower Persian Gulf, with its agents making fewer visits there. But more important, at least from the British perspective, was that the British East India Company—which controlled the highly profitable maritime trade routes between Bombay and Basra—had begun complaining towards the end of the eighteenth century of disruptive 'pirate attacks' on their ships. While the authenticity of these complaints remains contested, with some historians contending that the Company was primarily interested in removing local trade rivals,[13] Britain nevertheless responded to the Company's concerns and mounted a series of naval and amphibious attacks in 1809 and 1819 on various ports in the lower Gulf. After the threat of piracy was removed Britain then began offering peace treaties or 'truces' to the several identifiable sheikhdoms in the area. In this way, their respective ruling families became recognised by Britain as the heads of 'Trucial States', having ceded control over their own foreign affairs and guaranteed no further pirate attacks in exchange for imperial protection. After several renewals the treaties were made permanent in 1853 under the Perpetual Maritime Truce: a durable and mutually beneficial arrangement that remained in place for more than a century.

By this stage, the ruling Al-Khalifa family of Bahrain was well established, having not only signed the British treaties but also eventually hosting Britain's regional base—the 'permanent residency'. As descendants of the same Bani Utub clan that had departed from Kuwait in the 1760s, in 1783 they had invaded Bahrain and defeated its Omani-origin ruler of the time.[14] They and their allies then moved their homes from Zubarah to the Bahraini towns of Riffa and Muharraq. Although attacked by the Saudi-Wahhabi alliance at the turn of the century and briefly occupied by Oman in 1802, the Al-Khalifa soon consolidated their hold over the archipelago, with Abdullah bin Ahmed Al-Khalifa and Salman bin Ahmed Al-Khalifa emerging as joint rulers.

In many ways the ruling Al-Thani family of Qatar emerged from the shadow of the Al-Khalifa, with their ancestors having co-habited Zubarah and other parts of the peninsula under nominal Al-Khalifa control until 1867, when a Bahraini force attacked Doha, another Qatari settlement. Given that the attack was seaborne, it meant that the Al-Khalifa had broken the terms of their British peace treaty, prompting Britain to separate Qatar from the Al-Khalifa and offer formal recognition to Muhammad bin Thani, an influential tribal leader who had previously allied himself with the Saudi-Wahhabi movement. Within just four years, however, Muhammad's son and successor, Jassim bin Muhammad Al-Thani, deemed Britain an unsuitable guarantor against renewed threats from Bahrain and moved into an alliance with the Ottomans—a relationship which continued until 1893 when Jassim refused to permit an Ottoman customs house in Qatar. In 1916, with no remaining Ottoman influence in his territories, Jassim's son—Abdullah bin Jassim Al-Thani—finally signed Britain's Perpetual Maritime Truce, thus bringing Qatar into the Trucial States.

The ruling Al-Qasimi family of Ra's Al-Khaimah in many ways bore the brunt of the British attacks in 1809 and 1819. Remaining weakened, they had to cede control of their second town, Sharjah, to a distaff branch of the family in 1869, and between 1900 and 1921 even fell under Sharjah's control. Nevertheless, both Ra's al-Khaimah and Sharjahs' rulers signed the British treaties, and both were recognised as 'gun salute' states,[15] given their strategic position close to British-Indian shipping lanes. Rising in prominence throughout the nineteenth century, in part due to the declining fortunes of the Al-Qasimi, was the ruling Al-Nahyan family of Abu Dhabi. As the dominant clan of the large Bani Yas tribal grouping, the Al-Nahyan had moved from the interior to the island of Abu Dhabi in the late eighteenth century, and—given their relative innocence in the alleged attacks on British shipping—were especially well placed to benefit from British protection. Ruled between 1840 and 1909 by Zayed bin Khalifa Al-Nahyan or 'Zayed the Great', Abu Dhabi was able to fend off repeated Saudi-Wahhabi attacks which allowed the Al-Nahyan to consolidate their control over much of the coastline of the lower Gulf. However, much like Qatar's secession from Bahrain, the Al-Nahyan were soon forced to relinquish control over their second town, the fast-growing fishing and pearling port of Dubai. In 1833, following a significant tribal dispute, Maktoum bin Butti, also of the Bani Yas, and several hundred tribesmen left Abu Dhabi, moving up the coast to settle in Dubai. Sidelining the Al-Nahyan governors[16] and declaring Dubai to be an autonomous sheikhdom, they soon entered into Britain's Perpetual Maritime Truce, thus helping protect the nascent Al-Maktoum dynasty from a number of Abu Dhabi and Sharjah-launched attacks. In the 1880s and 1890s, under Rashid bin Maktoum Al-Maktoum and then Maktoum bin Hasher Al-Maktoum, Dubai's influence expanded greatly as it became an effective free port for the region, attracting large numbers of disgruntled merchant families from other sheikhdoms and even from towns on the Persian coastline.[17]

The other Trucial States, much smaller, existed alongside Abu Dhabi, Dubai, Ra's al-Khaimah, and Sharjah. Some were short-lived, being temporary British-recognised breakaways from their larger neighbours before eventually being reabsorbed as Britain lost interest. Nevertheless, by the beginning of the twentieth century, a number of distinct ruling families had managed to solidify their control of such territories. Ajman and Umm al-Qawain, sandwiched between Sharjah and Ra's al-Khaimah, were ruled respectively by the Al-Nuaimi and Al-Mualla families. While Hamriyyah, also along the lower Gulf coastline, was ruled by the Al-Shamsi tribe, and Dibba, on the Indian Ocean coastline, was ruled by another branch of the Al-Qasimi.

Further down the Indian Ocean coastline, the port city of Muscat had been controlled interchangeably by the Portuguese, the Ottoman Empire, and Persian governors until Abu Hilal Ahmed bin Said was elected as Imam of Muscat in 1744 following the final expulsion of Persian influences. Consolidating his hold over other parts of Oman, Ahmad had effectively founded the Al-Said dynasty, which, under his second successor—Sultan Said bin Sultan Al-Said—assembled a slave-trading empire in the early nineteenth century stretching from the island of Zanzibar off the east coast of Africa to Gwadar, in present day Pakistan. However, following Britain's outlawing of slavery in 1833 the Al-Said's revenues began to decline, as much of Oman's trade was with British colonies. And in 1856, following Sultan's death and a subsequent succession struggle within the family, British mediators intervened, effectively separating the Sultanates of Muscat and Zanzibar in 1861. In 1871 the Al-Said dynasty was again re-shaped by British interests, with London becoming concerned that Sultan's Muscat-based successor, Azzam bin Qais Al-Said, was becoming too powerful after uniting tribes from the interior. Funding his main rival, Turki bin Said Al-Said, Azzam soon lost the struggle, and Turki manoeuvred Oman into a much closer relationship with Britain, with his successors signing a treaty of friendship in 1908.[18]

Britain and the early order

The origins of all the Gulf monarchies were thus to some degree moulded by British interests, or in some cases disinterest. The ruling dynasties of the Trucial States were direct creations, while Kuwait's Al-Sabah and Oman's Al-Said owed much of their survival to British protection. Meanwhile the Al-Saud benefited from the power vacuum in central Arabia resulting from the weakness of the British-backed Emir of Mecca. One of the most important aspects of Britain's control over the region was the political support provided to specific families. This was especially evident in the Trucial States, where the various peace treaties provided rulers with protection from external and internal threats—including rival families and tribes inhabiting the same territory. Moreover, the documents all included clauses requiring the rulers to sign on behalf of their 'future heirs',[19] thus guaranteeing further British support for their dynasties.

By the beginning of the twentieth century Britain's position became even clearer, with the Viceroy of India[20] remarking in 1903 that '…if [internal disputes] occurred, the sheikhs would always find a friend in the British Resident, who would use his influence as he had frequently done in the past, to prevent these dissensions from coming to a head, and to maintain the status quo'.[21] Similarly, in the late 1920s, following a series of fratricides in the region,[22] the Political Resident called for an even stronger British position, claiming that 'Unless and until [the British] are prepared to interfere much more than they have done in the past, and are prepared, if necessary, to bolster up a weak sheikh, however much they might regret it, the only other course will be to continue shaking hands with successful murderers.'[23]

In parallel to this protection, most of the Gulf monarchies were obliged to cede much of their control over foreign policy to Britain. Again, the Trucial States provide the best example, as although they remained 'independent Arab sheikhs in special relations with His Majesty's Government'[24] and had transferred no territorial sovereignty to Britain,[25] they were nonetheless required to sign collectively an 'exclusivity treaty' in 1892. Three clauses were included, forbidding the rulers from entering into agreements with non-British parties, from allowing non-British parties to visit their territories, and from selling or mortgaging any part of the territories unless it was to British agents.[26] In practice, the clauses helped Britain thwart other European powers from gaining a foothold in the Persian Gulf, especially France which had been trying to increase its influence in Oman, and Germany which had begun to construct the Baghdad railway.[27]

Also helping Britain to keep the Gulf monarchies, or at least the Trucial States, within a dependent and sustainable relationship were the new economic structures that began to form, especially in the early twentieth century. Having previously relied on animal husbandry, basic re-export trading and—in the coastal towns—fishing and pearl diving, the various sheikhdoms began to move away from mere subsistence activities in the

1920s, with Britain seeking to channel large sums of 'locational rent'[28] to most of the ruling families with whom it had entered into protection agreements. In particular, rent was provided in return for landing rights for British aircraft en route from Europe to India and the maintenance of British-built airbases in their territories. After building military air-bases in Salalah in southern Oman and on the Omani island of Masirah,[29] a base was also established in Sharjah,[30] and in the early 1930s agreements were signed with both Sharjah and Dubai to allow civilian aircraft to land.[31]

Similarly, oil, or rather oil exploration concessions, provided another means of channelling rent directly to the ruling families. In 1922 fresh agreements between most of the Gulf's rulers and Britain required the former to eschew any oil concessions that were not supported by the British government.[32] And in 1935, after sizeable oil discoveries had already been made in Kuwait and Bahrain, the London-based and British Government-backed Iraqi Petroleum Company (IPC)[33] formed a wholly owned subsidiary, Petroleum Concessions Ltd., which was to be the sole operator of concessions for all of Britain's Gulf protectorates.[34] Unsurprisingly, a British ultimatum was then issued, binding the rulers to deal only with Petroleum Concessions.[35] By the late 1930s, the concessions were providing a very high stream of income for the ruling families, even in those territories where oil had not yet been discovered, a good example being the 1937 concession signed by IPC with the ruler of Dubai. Even though oil was not discovered in the sheikhdom until thirty years later,[36] the ruler nonetheless received an 'advance' lump sum of 60,000 rupees, and was given an annual income of 30,000 rupees. Moreover, he was promised a 200,000 rupee payment upon the discovery of oil, and a further three rupees for each barrel extracted during the prospecting process.[37]

Together, these air landing rights rents and the various oil concession payments were viewed by Britain as strategic subsidies which would help reinforce the status of the Gulf monarchies and thus prolong the self-enforcing, low-cost nature of the peace treaties. On the one hand, the new rents were understood to reduce the likelihood that Britain would have to resort to coercive measures to maintain its relationships. In 1939 the Political Resident even remarked that '...a key reason for the good-will between the British and the rulers was that negotiations over air and oil gave the rulers a square deal which carried a money bag rather than a big stick'.[38] While on the other hand, according to the India Office, the new rents were understood to have provided 'greater protection for the chiefs of tribes who were willing to co-operate… and to protect them from any danger that they might face as a result of their co-operation'.[39] Specifically, the new rents facilitated the setting up of prototype, pre-oil versions of the aforementioned rentier states. Received directly by the ruling families and their governments, the rents were in turn used to distribute some wealth to their populations rather than having to rely on taxation from merchants.

Overall, the new British-influenced political and economic structures that emerged kept most of the region's monarchies in power well into the twentieth century. It is no coincidence, perhaps, that every sheikhdom involved in the British protection treaties was by the 1950s also in receipt of at least one form of British rent payment. Indeed, in much the same way as Britain's earlier political support for breakaway sheikhdoms such as Dubai and Qatar, its intervention on behalf of a favoured member of Oman's ruling family in the 1870s, and its military assistance for Kuwait in the 1920s, the new rents also became an important part of the survival and in some cases creation of Gulf monarchies. In the case of Ajman, for example, the lack of air landing rights or oil concession payments became such a source of concern that the sheikhdom was purposely selected to host a British military base—an agreement which netted Ajman's ruler an annual rent of 10,000 rupees and allowed him to reduce taxation in his sheikhdom.[40] Similarly profiting from British rents was the Sharqiyin tribe of Fujairah—a semi-autonomous Indian Ocean coastline territory nominally controlled by Sharjah. In 1951, concerned that the Sharqiyin were being courted by the American-Saudi oil giant, Aramco, Britain moved to lock the area into another IPC concession. In 1952 the Shariqin's chief[41] was duly upgraded to the status of the other Trucial States' rulers: this allowed the IPC to begin payments, and Fujairah was declared to be independent of Sharjah.[42]

Conversely, when sheikhdoms were deemed to be no longer of strategic interest to Britain, or their ruling families were proving problematic, Britain moved to cut payments and in extreme cases facilitated the collapse of dynasties. Hamriyyah and Dibba, for example, were quietly reabsorbed by Sharjah, as without rent payments their respective rulers were in no position to maintain sufficient loyalty from resident tribes. Similarly, the Indian Ocean coastline town of Kalba, which in 1936 had been recognised by Britain as a sheikhdom with its ruling family receiving rent for air landing rights, was reabsorbed by Sharjah in 1951. Britain had already ceased payments after failing to build an airbase and had chosen not to intervene following a series of fratricidal killings within its fragmented ruling family.[43] Other examples included the Al-Kaabi family of Mahadha, close to Oman. Despite repeatedly presenting his case to Britain in the late 1950s for both recognition and the need for rent payments in return for providing soldiers to help guard oil exploration parties, he was refused and Britain allowed Mahadha to fall under the control of Muscat's Al-Said.[44]

Independence and state formation

By the time of Abdul-Aziz bin Saud's death in 1953, Saudi Arabia had already become an internationally recognised state[45] with rulership having been handed on to his eldest sons, albeit with some turbulence. The first to take over was Saud bin Abdul-Aziz, who then abdicated in 1964 in favour of his more reform-focused younger brother, Faisal bin Abdul-Aziz. Following Faisal's 1975 assassination at the hands of a younger relative,[46] he was succeeded by Khalid bin Abdul-Aziz, who was then succeeded in 1982 by Fahd bin Abdul-Aziz. Since Fahd's death in 2005 another of Abdul-Aziz's sons, Abdullah bin Abdul-Aziz, has been king, having already effectively ruled Saudi Arabia as Fahd's crown prince and regent since 1996.[47] In parallel to the now very elderly Abdullah, and underscoring the ongoing centrality of the original Saudi-Wahhabi pact to the Saudi state, the religious community continues to be led by the Al-Sheikh family—the direct descendants of Muhammad bin Abd Al-Wahhab.[48] Presently led by the one-eyed Abdul-Aziz bin Abdullah Al-Sheikh, the Al-Sheikh remain in control of key positions in government, especially in justice and education, and maintain close family ties to the Al-Saud through intermarriage.[49] Together with other relatives and allies they also continue to dominate a number of state-backed bodies such as the Council of Senior Religious Scholars, thus forming the official religious establishment in Saudi Arabia.

Since Saud's accession, Saudi Arabia's government has been run by a Council of Ministers. Established by charter, it has served as both the executive and the legislative body of the Saudi state, with all of its members being appointed by royal decree.[50] In 1992, after a number of demands and petitions made to the ruling family by both liberal and conservative opponents in the wake of the Kuwait crisis[51] and the return of western troops (including female soldiers) to the region, Fahd instigated a number of reforms aimed at appeasing the religious community while also providing the state with a greater veneer of accountability.[52] Collectively, the new 'Basic System of Governance' or 'Basic Law' re-confirmed Islamic *Sharia* law as the basis for all legislation in the state, while also establishing new regulatory bodies to monitor government performance and separate the judiciary from other parts of the government—albeit with judges still being appointed by the king. To provide a greater degree of stability for the ruling family and to guard against internecine disputes or coups d'état, the 1992 reforms also clarified that succession would be limited to male descendants of Abdul-Aziz.[53] In this way, Fahd sought to enshrine in law some of the stabilisation mechanisms later observed by Michael Herb in his aforementioned work on dynastic monarchies.[54] In 1993, in a further effort to promote accountability, Fahd established a new Consultative Council or *majlis al-shura*. Although, as with the Saudi judges, all involved were appointed by the king.[55]

Under Abdullah, little has changed. The Consultative Council now stands at 150 members, but each is still appointed, sitting for four-year terms. Its powers remain weak, with its ability to call ministers to question or launch investigations into governmental affairs being very limited, despite supposedly being allowed to propose legislation.[56] The only significant development in recent years was an election in 2005 for municipal councils. But this too was severely restricted, with only half of the seats being elected, with only male candidates and voters being permitted, and with councillors enjoying little power as central ministries continued to dictate regional and municipal policies.[57] Fresh elections should have been staged in 2009, but these were cancelled on the grounds that the government needed time to study how best to 'expand the electorate and the possibility of allowing women to vote'. Although elections were eventually staged in late 2011, seemingly as a concession to the Arab Spring movements elsewhere in the region, the same restrictions remained in place with no women being involved and with only half of the seats being elected.[58]

As with Fahd, Abdullah has also tried to address the succession issue and strengthen the Al-Saud as a dynastic monarchy. In 2006 an Allegiance Commission or *Hayat al-Bayah* was set up, ostensibly to allow for some degree of consensus within the family over appointing new rulers and also to facilitate the dismissal of kings by the rest of the family in the event of illness or other problems.[59] Although limiting the powers of Saudi Arabia's religious police in recent years and—in 2007—separating the Supreme Court from the Al-Sheikh-controlled Ministry for Justice,[60] Abdullah has otherwise followed Fahd's strategy of reinforcing the Saudi-Wahhabi alliance. In particular, he has ensured that only the state-appointed, Riyadh-based Council of Senior Religious Scholars has the ability to issue a *fatwa* or Islamic legal pronouncement in Saudi Arabia, thus reducing the influence of religious figures elsewhere in the country.[61]

In 1961 Kuwait joined Saudi Arabia as an independent state, after Britain formally withdrew its control over the increasingly prosperous and autonomous sheikhdom. Abdullah Al-Salim Al-Sabah duly proclaimed himself 'emir' and the United Nations granted recognition to the emirate of Kuwait, while the US had already established a consulate before Britain left, and had even begun to process Kuwaiti visas.[62] Almost immediately, however, British troops had to be re-deployed following Iraqi claims on Kuwait. But by 1963 a new government in Iraq relinquished these claims[63] and over the next two decades the Al-Sabah dynasty consolidated its position. The family has since ruled unopposed, with Jabar Al-Ahmad Al-Jabar Al-Sabah suffering only a brief exile in 1990 following Saddam Hussein's invasion of Kuwait, and being quickly reinstated in 1991 following the US-led multinational Operation Desert Storm which ousted Iraq's forces. Jabar was succeeded in 2006 by his crown prince, Saad Al-Abdullah Al-Sabah, who represented a different branch of the family. But due to Saad's poor health he was peacefully deposed and replaced by another member of Jabar's line, Sabah Al-Ahmad Al-Jabar Al-Sabah, who continues to be Kuwait's emir.

Following independence, Abdullah was quick to draw up a new constitution for Kuwait and to establish a new parliament, the National Assembly. As discussed later in this book, Kuwait's merchant population had long been involved in various consultative institutions, given their relative wealth and political influence, so democratic or rather consultative traditions were much more ingrained in Kuwait than in Saudi Arabia. The first parliamentary elections were staged in 1963, with all literate male Kuwaitis being eligible to stand for the fifty seats.[64] Significantly, and much like the Al-Saud rulers, Abdullah also sought to strengthen the Al-Sabah as a dynastic monarchy by confirming in the constitution that the Al-Sabah were the inviolable rulers of Kuwait, and that future rulers must always be descendants of the long-serving former ruler of Kuwait, Mubarak Al-Sabah. The constitution also required the prime minister to be a member of the ruling family, and allowed the emir to appoint fifteen of the sixteen cabinet positions. Moreover, political parties were banned, and the emir was able to dissolve parliament as he saw fit and to pass emergency laws when parliament was not sitting.[65]

But despite these restrictions, the parliament proved more vibrant than anticipated, with various outspoken blocs forming—including Arab nationalists and Islamists—and with some tribes even holding 'primary elections' to select their preferred parliamentary candidates.[66] Endless debates and controversies—few of which could be resolved given the inherent tension from having elected members of parliament alongside appointed cabinet members—led to unapproved budgets and the stalling of various development projects. While the government tried to boost support for their preferred parliamentary blocs, often by naturalising further tribes in exchange for loyalty, the emir eventually chose to step in and dissolved parliament in 1976.[67] Only after the 1979 Islamic revolution in Iran did the emir re-open parliament, expecting greater government support due to uncertainties over Iran's intentions. Even then, he was prudent to offer loyal parliamentary candidates further advantages: the number of electoral districts was increased from ten to twenty-five, and more naturalisations took place, mostly in the new constituencies. Moreover, in an effort to placate the Islamist blocs and gain their loyalty, the emir called for greater restrictions on alcohol and on the celebrating of Christmas and other non-Islamic events.[68]

By the mid-1980s Kuwait's parliament was again under threat, with the Iran-Iraq War continuing to destabilise the region and with a series of car-bombings and an assassination attempt on the emir. In 1986 Jabar duly dissolved parliament, and it remained closed until after the trauma of invasion and liberation.[69] During this period the only space for political discussion was in the more traditional setting of Kuwait's meeting-houses or *diwaniyas*. Since its reopening in 1991 the parliament has remained a source of controversy, having been closed down on several more occasions by the current emir. Such closures have usually been in order to prevent uncomfortable questioning of the prime minister—up until recently Nasser bin Muhammad Al-Sabah. Thus its powers are still very limited, with the ruling family and its 'sovereign' appointees continuing to dominate the emirate's executive, in something of a neo-patriarchal model. Nonetheless, despite weariness, declining voter turnouts,[70] and general disillusionment with the system, elections have continued, having last been staged in early 2012. And on some occasions parliamentary opposition has managed to push through key reforms, notably the 2006 'Orange Movement' decision to reduce the number of electoral districts down to just five—an effort to tackle the corruption and vote-rigging which was alleged to be taking place in many of the smaller electoral districts.[71]

Much like the Al-Saud and the Al-Sabah, the ruling families of the former Trucial States have also ruled unopposed since their independence. In Bahrain's case, Isa bin Salman Al-Khalifa ruled from 1961 until his death in 1999 when he was peacefully succeeded by his eldest son, Hamad bin Isa Al-Khalifa, who continues to rule. Succession in Qatar has, by contrast, been much more complicated, with Ahmad bin Ali Al-Thani being deposed in 1972, one year after Qatar's independence, by his cousin Khalifa bin Hamad Al-Thani. Then, in 1995 Khalifa was dramatically deposed by his second wife's eldest son, Hamad bin Khalifa Al-Thani. Nevertheless, the overall authority of the Al-Thani dynasty has never come under serious question, with the family remaining in tight control of Qatar. In Abu Dhabi, after succeeding his unpopular older brother with some degree of British assistance in 1966,[72] Zayed bin Sultan Al-Nahyan enjoyed a long and relatively untroubled reign. His death in 2004 was closely followed by the succession of his eldest son and long-serving crown prince, Khalifa bin Zayed Al-Nahyan. But following a secret family agreement reached in 1999 which saw Khalifa's ambitious younger half-brother, Muhammad bin Zayed Al-Nahyan, being appointed as deputy crown prince,[73] Muhammad was then immediately upgraded to crown prince following their father's death—despite Khalifa having two adult sons. Since then, Muhammad has risen to become one of the most powerful members of the Al-Nahyan family, controlling most key policy areas in the emirate. In neighbouring Dubai, the Al-Maktoum family had a similarly long-serving patriarch, with Rashid bin Said Al-Maktoum ruling from 1958 until his death in 1990. Survived by four sons, his eldest—Maktoum bin Rashid Al-Maktoum—duly succeeded. However, and as something of a precursor to the Al-Nahyan succession arrangements, he appointed one of his younger brothers—Muhammad bin Rashid Al-Maktoum—as crown prince in 1995, rather than one of his own sons. Between then and 2006, when Maktoum died, Muhammad was Dubai's de facto ruler, and thus his eventual succession in 2006 was little more than a formality.

The ruling families of the smaller former Trucial States have, like Qatar, been a little more prone to internecine disputes and 'palace coups'. In Sharjah's case, only a year after independence its ruler Khalid bin Muhammad Al-Qasimi was assassinated by an exiled former ruler, Saqr bin Sultan Al-Qasimi. Turning to Khalid's most educated younger brother, the ruling family appointed Sultan bin Muhammad Al-Qasimi as ruler. In 1987 Sultan's passed-over elder brother, Abdul-Aziz bin Muhammad Al-Qasimi, briefly seized power before Sultan was able to reassert control.[74] Similarly, in Ra's al-Khaimah the succession process has been bumpy, although the ruling Al-Qasimi family's authority has never been directly contested. As discussed later in this book, the emirate's long-serving ruler, Saqr bin Muhammad Al-Qasimi, had appointed his eldest son, Khalid bin Saqr Al-Qasimi, as crown prince in 1961. But in 2003 the aging Saqr had switched crown princes, choosing one of his younger sons, Saud bin Saqr Al-Qasimi.[75] Although Khalid was forced into exile, his return to Ra's al-Khaimah following Saqr's death in 2010 prompted a brief crisis before Saud was eventually confirmed as the new ruler.

The period immediately before and after the Trucial States' independence from Britain in 1971 deserves special attention, as it has had important ramifications for these monarchies' subsequent state formation process. In 1968 the British government announced that within just three years it would dismantle all of its bases and treaties 'east of Aden', in an effort to cut imperial expenditure and focus more resources on Britain's struggling domestic welfare system. The ruling families of the Trucial States were so alarmed by the prospect of their protector's departure that they even offered to subsidise the deployment of British troops in the region after independence was granted.[76] Britain's solution, however, was to encourage the various rulers to form a cohesive federation that would provide their sheikhdoms with at least some degree of collective security.

Various meetings and negotiations took place, but it quickly became apparent that Bahrain and Qatar were unwilling to form a state with their less developed neighbours,[77] with both declaring themselves independent emirates in summer 1971. To make matters worse, Ra's al-Khaimah was also baulking at joining the federation, as it too held ambitions to become an independent state. Moreover, on 1 December 1971—the day before Britain's official withdrawal—Iran had seized three contested islands belonging to Sharjah and Ra's al-Khaimah, thus further alarming the remaining Trucial States rulers. Nonetheless, the following day a six member federation of United Arab Emirates was inaugurated,[78] and the next month Ra's al-Khaimah reluctantly agreed to join. Given that Abu Dhabi commanded the bulk of the UAE's oil reserves it became the federal capital and its ruler, Zayed, was installed as the UAE's first president with Dubai's ruler, Rashid, as vice president.[79]

Much like Kuwait, Bahrain began its period of independence with an attempt at building a parliament as the ruling family sought to involve the influential merchant community. A constitution was drawn up detailing a fully elected body with an all-male electorate, and the first ballots were cast in 1973. Political parties were forbidden and the unelected prime minister—Khalifa bin Salman Al-Khalifa—was a member of the ruling family. Nonetheless some political blocs did form, and a brief period of vibrant debate ensued. But within just two years the emir moved to dissolve the parliament. Members had begun to dispute the Al-Khalifa family's enthusiasm for an American military presence in Bahrain and were frustrated over the lack of land reform, with the Al-Khalifa continuing to own most of the island's territory. Moreover, parliament had crossed another red line by calling for a more transparent state budget as oil revenues boomed.[80] Thus, for most of the 1980s the only spaces for political discussion in Bahrain were in more traditional settings, in particular the *majalis* for Sunni citizens, and the 'mourning houses,' or *mataams* for Shia citizens.[81] By the early 1990s, with deepening security ties between the Al-Khalifa and the US, and with rising unemployment and falling incomes, hundreds of Bahrainis petitioned the emir for a reinstatement of the 1973 parliament, but only an appointed advisory council was established. Further opposition and fresh demands in the 1990s—detailed later in this book—were similarly unsuccessful, with the emir refusing to re-open parliament.

By 2001, however, the ruling family chose to return to earlier neopatriarchal strategies by holding a referendum on a 'National Action Charter' that would supposedly transform Bahrain into a constitutional monarchy. In 2002 a new constitution was duly implemented on the basis of the charter which promised the creation of a bicameral, half-elected parliament, the abolishing of much maligned 'security courts', and a new requirement that half of all judges were to be elected. In 2006 'political societies' were even approved,[82] bringing Bahrain the closest of all Gulf monarchies to accepting political parties. However, the charter also re-designated the emir as 'king' with Bahrain becoming a kingdom rather than an emirate, and the king remained in control of all key appointments, including the prime minister and all of the cabinet ministers. Crucially, he also retained the power of approving or rejecting all proposed legislation.[83] But interestingly, in parallel to the Khalifa bin Salman-controlled government, the king also set up a new Economic Development Board (EDB), which was gradually assigned more and more control over Bahrain's economy. Given that the EDB is chaired by the king's eldest son and crown prince, Salman bin Hamad Al-Khalifa, and given that—until recently at least—Khalifa bin Salman's ministers had to answer to the EDB,[84] Bahrain provides a good example of how state formation in the Gulf monarchies has often been manipulated in order to manage ruling family divisions. Broadly speaking, the Al-Khalifa dynasty has become factionalised into conservatives led by the prime minister and a number of key members of the royal court, and reformists, led by the crown prince. The king, rather precariously, has had to sit somewhere in the middle.

Although having shared a similar imperial history to Bahrain, Qatar's post-independence state formation process has been quite different and much more autocratic, mostly due to its smaller population and—as discussed in the following chapter—the ruling family's greater ability to distribute wealth and resources. A 'Basic Law of Qatar' had already been drafted in 1970, a year before Britain's departure, and this went on to become a provisional constitution in 1972. Although designed to be as flexible as possible, so as to reflect the transitional nature of the Qatari state,[85] it nonetheless provided the basis for setting up an appointed Council of Ministers and a twenty-member Advisory Council or *Majlis Al-Shura*. Although the latter was also appointed, some concessions were made to electoral politics, with Qatar being divided into ten tribal districts, the leaders of which could each nominate four members, two of whom would then be selected by the emir.[86] In 1975 the Advisory Council was expanded to thirty-five members, but it remained under the full control of the Al-Thani family, with the emir able to re-appoint its members indefinitely and to block or ratify all proposed legislation.[87]

Much like the Kuwaiti constitution and the second Bahraini constitution, Qatar's provisional constitution also sought to combine patriarchal authority with legal-rational authority by slipping in a clause aimed at establishing the permanency of the ruling family. This required all Qatari citizens to '...pledge their loyalty and absolute obedience to the Ruler in the fear of God'. Moreover, in another attempt to strengthen the dynasty and prevent unwanted succession disputes the constitution described the need for consensus between ruling family members, although without outlining procedures or specifics.[88]

Upon his succession in 1995, Hamad bin Khalifa Al-Thani made a number of promises to reform Qatar's political institutions and several decrees were duly signed. Three years later the first elections were held for Qatar's Chamber of Commerce and Industry; and in 1999 the first elections were held for Qatar's twenty-nine member Municipal Council, with over 22,000 men and women voting. In 2007 a second round of elections were held, with about 50 per cent of the electorate voting.[89] Much like the Saudi elections though, these were only for an institution with very limited powers, and no influence on Qatar's central government. In 2003 a referendum had already taken place on the subject of a new, permanent constitution to replace the original 1972 provisional constitution. Significantly the new constitution—approved by 97 per cent of Qataris—committed the state to becoming 'democratic' and called for a new, elected Advisory Council as opposed to the original appointed body. The council was to be expanded to forty-five members, thirty of whom would be elected; it would sit for four year terms and its recommendations would still require the emir's approval.[90] Elections were promised for 2005 but never materialised, as was also the case in 2010. The council thus continues to be fully appointed and is increasingly criticised for its ineffective role and limited scope. Indeed, it only meets for eight months a year, and only sits for two hours a week.[91] Nevertheless in late 2011 another announcement was made that the promised reforms would still take place, with elections due to be held in 2013 for thirty of the forty-five positions.[92]

The UAE's state formation has been more complicated, not least due to the existence of a federal government that came into being following independence in 1971, and the continuing existence of various emirate-level governments answering to their respective ruling families. Originally envisaged as a loose confederation, with only limited powers being transferred to federal ministries, a provisional constitution was signed by the six founding rulers in late 1971, and then by the ruler of Ra's al-Khaimah in early 1972. Given that Abu Dhabi, as discussed, was in control of most of the UAE's oil reserves and had become the UAE's capital, most of the new ministries were located there. But neither defence nor oil policies were transferred to the federal government, as it was felt that too rapid centralisation of such key matters would harm the status and prestige of the poorer emirates' governments, thus risking friction and instability. Indeed, when Abu Dhabi attempted to unify the different emirate-level armed forces in the late 1970s both Dubai and Ra's al-Khaimah threatened their withdrawal from the union, prompting a constitutional crisis. Only in 1996 was the constitution made permanent with a unified UAE Armed Forces being established under Abu Dhabi's umbrella. By this stage Dubai and most of the other emirates were pressing ahead with costly infrastructure projects in efforts to build up more diverse economic bases, and preferred to transfer as many costly services as possible to Abu Dhabi and the federal government.[93]

Overseeing the federal government since 1971 has been the Supreme Council of Rulers, which is made up of the seven hereditary rulers of each emirate and, on occasion, their respective crown princes. While the constitution allows for an SCR presidential election to take place every five years,[94] in practice the rulership of Abu Dhabi remains synonymous with the presidency of the UAE, not least because of Abu Dhabi's single-handed financing of most federal development projects. The SCR also reflects Dubai's elevated status in the UAE by awarding only the rulers of Abu Dhabi and Dubai veto power in its meetings—as per an article of the constitution,[95]—and by always appointing the ruler of Dubai as the UAE's vice president. In support of the SCR, or more specifically the president, there exists a presidential office and a presidential court with its own staff. However, given the ruler of Abu Dhabi's similar emirate-level institutions it is unclear if the two function independently.

Responsible for most of the federal government's decision-making is the Council of Ministers. Since its establishment in 1972 its composition has always reflected the relative power and influence of the member emirates. Although originally made up of eleven ministers in addition to a prime minister, the COM soon expanded to nineteen positions as the other emirates began to supply their contingents of appointees.[96] The premiership was transferred to the crown prince of Dubai, before the above-mentioned constitutional crisis persuaded the ruler of Dubai to become prime minister as well as vice president. Abu Dhabi has always held the lion's share of COM positions including the deputy premiership and ministerial posts for the interior, higher education, and public works. Today, the COM's membership has increased to twenty ministers and four ministers of state, including four women. But it remains equally in favour of Abu Dhabi, with members of its ruling family now also controlling the Ministry for Foreign Affairs and the Ministry for Presidential Affairs among other portfolios. In total, there are now five members of the Al-Nahyan family serving as ministers while other Abu Dhabi nationals serve as the ministers for justice,[97] the economy,[98] and energy.[99] Moreover, at least two further ministers are de facto members of the Abu Dhabi contingent given their close ties to the emirate.

Operating beneath the COM, the Federal National Council is a consultative body made up of contingents from each emirate. Comprising forty members, including an internally elected speaker and two deputies, this chamber sits for sessions of two years at a time, and has several sub-committees. Much like the COM, the more powerful emirates dominate,[100] with Abu Dhabi and Dubai each supplying eight members, while Sharjah and Ra's al-Khaimah supply six, and the other three emirates supply just four.[101] These contingents, which were originally all appointed, were often made up of senior representatives of non-ruling tribes or sections, and they now include women. As with the Qatari Advisory Council, in recent years there has been mounting criticism of the FNC, with many of its members and other citizens claiming it is largely ineffective. While it has been successful in petitioning ministers on rather banal subjects,[102] it has been incapable of making more substantive interventions,[103] and has often failed to elicit responses from ministers.[104] In 2006 elections were held for half of the FNC positions, but these were widely ridiculed as only a few thousand UAE nationals were eligible to vote. A second round of elections should have taken place in late 2010 but were delayed until late 2011. As with Saudi Arabia's 2011 Municipal Council elections, the latest FNC elections seem to have been used as a concession to the Arab Spring, as the size of the electorate was expanded to 80,000. Yet this still represented only a small proportion of UAE nationals—about 12 per cent[105]—and the FNC's powers have remained very limited.[106] Embarrassingly for the UAE's president—who had publicly called for a high voter turnout—fewer than 30 per cent of eligible voters actually participated.[107]

At the apex of the emirate-level governments are the private offices and courts of both the rulers and crown princes. Given Abu Dhabi's much greater geographic size, it also has ruler's representatives in both its eastern and western regions, and these also have their own private offices and courts. While it remains possible for unilateral decisions to be made by the rulers' offices and then issued as decrees, as in other Gulf monarchies, in practise only Abu Dhabi and Dubai's rulers still exercise this privilege, with most legislation now being crafted by the federal COM. Abu Dhabi, Dubai, and Sharjah all have emirate-level executive councils, which tend to deal with most domestic matters. In many ways the Abu Dhabi Executive Council—founded in early 1971, before the creation of the UAE— is more powerful than the COM, as it presides over several Abu Dhabi-specific government entities including the influential Supreme Petroleum Council, three municipalities and three police forces (one for the capital and one for each of its two outlying regions), along with a score of recently established Abu Dhabi specific bodies including an education council, an environmental agency, and a tourism authority.

Sharjah's executive council, although much smaller, operates along similar lines, but it is noteworthy that Dubai's executive council is far less formal, with its meetings being arranged on a more ad hoc basis, often in the conference suites of business hotels. In some ways, the nature of Dubai's council is supposed to reflect the emirate's history as a dynamic business hub, with it often being referred to as 'Dubai Inc'. Also at the emirate-level, at least in Abu Dhabi and Sharjah, are national consultative councils which are supposed to operate in a similar manner to the FNC and have faced similar criticisms. The Abu Dhabi National Consultative Council's usefulness is particularly questionable given that the Abu Dhabi Executive Council is not required to consider the recommendations that it receives. Moreover, after more than forty years of operation the ADNCC remains entirely appointive, and—incredibly—only three of its current members were first appointed in the last twenty years. None of the members are female, in contrast with the Sharjah National Consultative Council which now has 17 per cent female membership.[108]

In contrast to Bahrain, Qatar, and the UAE's constituent emirates, which were the last of the Gulf monarchies to achieve independence, Oman is actually the oldest independent Arab state. But by the mid-twentieth century its politics were almost equally dominated by Britain, which was not only instrumental in Oman ceding its Gwadar province to Pakistan in 1958 and putting down the aforementioned Dhofar rebellion in the mid-1970s, but also played a central role in installing Oman's current sultan, Qaboos bin Said Al-Said, in the midst of the conflict. With Qaboos' father, Said bin Taimur Al-Said, struggling to unite the country, prevent mass emigration, and placate the rebels, Britain judged Qaboos to be the ruling family's best hope. Thus, in 1970 a British-backed arrest team—claiming the consensus of the rest of the Al-Said dynasty—detained Said and, in something of a repeat of the arrest and removal of Abu Dhabi's ruler in 1966, he was forced into exile in favour of his younger rival. Since then Qaboos has not faced a direct challenge, or at least not from other members of the ruling family, and after Muammar Gaddafi's ousting and death in 2011, he is now the Gulf's longest serving head of state.

After the 1970 coup, which is commonly referred to as Oman's 'awakening' or Renaissance Day,[109] the country's state formation is best understood as a congerie of the strategies employed by its northerly neighbours. An initial attempt was made by Qaboos to share some degree of power following the appointment of his uncle, Tariq bin Taimur Al-Said, as Oman's prime minister later in the year. However, unlike the rulers of Kuwait, Bahrain, and more recently Qatar—which all seem to have found benefit in institutionalising the position of prime minister—Qaboos soon took fright at the prospect of any co-existing authority and removed the office in 1971. Since then, in addition to being Oman's undisputed ruler, Qaboos has been concurrently holding the positions of minister for foreign affairs, minister for defence, director of the Central Bank of Oman, and chief of staff of the armed forces.[110] This meant that Qaboos' royal court or *diwan* quickly became something of a 'super ministry' in Oman—responsible for most governmental matters connected directly to the national interest.[111] Nevertheless, other ministries continued to exist under the umbrella of a Council of Ministers, and an appointed State Consultative Council was established, ostensibly to advise the government.

In 1990 an appointed Consultative Council or *Majlis Al-Shura* replaced the existing State Consultative Council. Each of Oman's fifty-nine tribal districts or *wilayat* were to nominate three representatives to the council, one of which would be appointed by the sultan himself. And between 1993 and 1997 the system was refined further so that larger *wilayat* could nominate two candidates each (including women), while the smaller *wilayat* nominated one candidate. By 2000, with the sultan seemingly recognising the usefulness of having an institution which provided an appearance of representative government without actually having legislative powers, the electorate was greatly expanded. About 25 per cent of the adult population—approximately 175,000 Omanis—were eligible to vote. In 2003 it was expanded again, with full suffrage, and in 2007 another round of elections was conducted for its eighty-three seats. However, as with most of the other Gulf monarchies' parliaments, the council has remained largely toothless, with its president still being appointed by the sultan, with an executive bureau overseeing its agenda and the activities of its five permanent committees, and with its members remaining unable to compel ministers to respond to questions.[112] Moreover, since 1996 there has also been a State Council or *Majlis Al-Dawla*, which is supposed to operate in parallel to the Consultative Council and perform much the same duties. Its seventy-three members are entirely appointed by the sultan for four year terms, with most being retired senior government figures, military commanders, judges, and 'anyone that His Majesty the Sultan deems fit'.[113] As such, it effectively serves as a powerful counterweight to the elected body.

Perhaps the biggest distinction between Oman and the other Gulf monarchies is that Qaboos has never publicly named a crown prince or successor. Nonetheless, as with his neighbouring rulers, he has tried to use the state's constitution to ensure the Al-Said's dynastic longevity after his own death. An article of the constitution[114] stipulates that a Ruling Family Council will be responsible for choosing as successor in the event of the throne becoming vacant, while a decree in 1975 clarified that the sultan is the 'source of all laws'; since then all of the government's legislation has been styled as a royal decree. This included the 1996 Basic Law of Oman, which not only specified that Arabic is Oman's official language and that *Sharia* law constitutes the basis of all legislation, but also stated that Oman's system of government should be that of a 'hereditary sultanate… based on justice, consultation, and equity'. The 1996 law also provided further clarification on the sultan's position, describing the post-holder as being Oman's 'symbol of national unity, as well as its guardian and defender', and stated that 'respecting him is a national duty and that his orders must be obeyed'.[115]

Economic development trajectories

Since independence, or in Saudi Arabia and Oman's case their modern state formation, oil and gas exports have undoubtedly played the leading role in the economic development trajectories of all six Gulf monarchies, albeit with some important variations. In Saudi Arabia's case, oil was first discovered in 1938 in Dammam, close to the town of Dhahran. Given that the kingdom was, as described, beyond British control, the Al-Saud had been able to offer early concessions to American companies, with Standard Oil of California and the Texas Oil Company being joined by Standard Oil of New Jersey and Socony-Vacuum Oil in the 1940s to form the Arabian American Oil Company or Aramco. Significantly, unlike the Arab nationalist republics, the Al-Saud were careful not to nationalise fully their oil industry in the 1950s and 1960s, preferring to maintain a close relationship with their American partners and benefit from the latest technologies and market access. Nevertheless, by 1973 the Al-Saud were under pressure within the region to change their stance, given the America's support for Israel in the Yom Kippur War. A 25 per cent government stake in Aramco was duly taken, before full nationalisation in 1980 and a rebranding of the company in 1988 as 'Saudi Aramco'.

Kuwait's first oil discoveries were also in 1938, although it was a British-backed company—the Kuwait Oil Company—that won the first concession. Further discoveries were made throughout the 1940s and 1950s, and in the years after independence oil exports massively increased. Similarly keen to avoid oil industry nationalisation, the Al-Sabah nevertheless also came under pressure, and in the 1970s terminated the British concessions and granted the Kuwaiti government full ownership of the Kuwait Oil Company. Of the Trucial States, Bahrain was the first to discover oil, with the wells at Jebel Dhukan being opened in 1934. Notwithstanding the Al-Khalifa's various treaty relationships with Britain and their hosting of the British Political Resident, the Bahrain concession was initially awarded to Standard Oil of California, which had established the Bahrain Petroleum Company or Bapco some years earlier. Although the Bahraini government did take a 60 per cent stake in Bapco in the early 1980s, 40 per cent remained with the American firm Caltex— the successor company to Standard Oil. Significantly, at this time a new Supreme Council for Oil was established to oversee Bahrain's hydrocarbon industry, with the prime minister, Khalifa bin Salman Al-Khalifa, unsurprisingly assuming its chairmanship.

As with Kuwait, Qatar was closely tied to British oil concessions following the first drilling in 1939. Later offshore concessions in the 1940s were however granted to the American company Superior Oil and Central Mining and Investment, and in the 1950s to Royal Dutch Shell. In 1973, closely mirroring the Al-Saud's decision to part-nationalise, the newly independent Qatari government took a 25 per cent stake in the country's oil industry before choosing fully to nationalise the new Qatar Petroleum Company in 1976. In recent years, gas has become much more important to Qatar than oil, with the government-owned Qatargas being established in 1984. Following major discoveries, most of which were located in the massive offshore North Field shared with Iran, exports of liquefied natural gas commenced in 1997, and in 2001 a second government-owned gas company, Rasgas, was established.

The development of the UAE's hydrocarbon industry is a little more complex to understand, much like its state formation. Given that most of the original concessions were signed before the UAE came into being, the two principal oil-producing emirates of Abu Dhabi and Dubai had already entered into agreements with different companies. In Abu Dhabi's case, following the discovery of oil at Umm Shaif in 1958, the original British concessions were mostly renewed, with the granting of concessions to British Petroleum. Many other concessions were granted though, with Campagnie Française des Petroles, Royal Dutch Shell, Exxon-Mobil, Total, and the Japan Oil Development Company all winning sizeable stakes, most of which have been renewed. Since independence in 1971 a national oil company—the Abu Dhabi National Oil Company (ADNOC)—has always held controlling stakes in the various concessions, but these have never exceeded 60 per cent.[116] Similarly, Abu Dhabi's gas industry has only been part-nationalised, with ADNOC holding stakes of 68 per cent and 70 per cent in the emirate's two main gas concessions, while the remainder has been shared between British, American, and Japanese companies.[117]

With oil discoveries in the early 1960s, Dubai followed a similar pattern to its neighbour with the government-owned Dubai Petroleum Company managing several international concessions from Britain, the US, Spain, France, and Germany. Production increased greatly in the 1980s before peaking in 1991. Since then, Dubai's oil industry has been described as simply 'ticking over', with Abu Dhabi having accounted for over 90 per cent of the UAE's oil exports over the past decade.[118] After oil was discovered in the western province of Oman in 1964, the Omani government pursued much the same model as Abu Dhabi and Dubai, with its wholly owned Petroleum Development Oman taking a 60 per cent stake in the industry and granting concessions to Royal Dutch Shell, Campagnie Française des Petroles, and Partex. Production increased greatly throughout the 1970s, and eventually reached its peak in 2000, at the same time that Oman opened its first major gas plant at the port of Sur.

Today, the Gulf monarchies produce a combined total of about 16.6 million barrels of crude oil per day,[119] about 19 per cent of the global total, with the bulk being produced by Saudi Arabia, Kuwait, and the UAE—or more specifically Abu Dhabi. The six states also produce about 232 billion cubic metres of natural gas per year,[120] about 8 per cent of the global total, with the bulk being produced by Qatar, Saudi Arabia, and the UAE. More importantly, perhaps, the Gulf monarchies account for 37 per cent of all known crude oil reserves and 25 per cent of all known natural gas reserves,[121] with Saudi Arabia alone accounting for 25 per cent of global oil reserves[122] and with Qatar accounting for at least 15 per cent of global gas reserves.[123] As discussed later in this book, an important disparity between the six states has thus emerged, with a hydrocarbon-rich group—namely Saudi Arabia, the UAE, Kuwait, and Qatar—all of which have at least a few decades of supply remaining, and with a much poorer group consisting of Oman and Bahrain, the latter of which now has to import most of its oil given the depletion of domestic reserves.[124]

Closely connected to the region's hydrocarbon industry has been the channelling of surplus oil and gas revenues into long-term overseas investments by many Gulf monarchies. Conceived as a means of cushioning their domestic economies should the international oil industry falter, most of these sovereign wealth investments have been made through a handful of government owned authorities or companies. Today, their combined assets are thought to be in excess of $1.7 trillion,[125] and were generating some 10 per cent in interest per year prior to the 2008 credit crunch.[126] Although their operations remain fairly secretive, it is thought that they have historically favoured index-linked blue chip investments in the developed world along with mature western real estate.[127] Following the Dubai Ports crisis of 2006, when a government-owned Dubai company that had already purchased Britain's Peninsula and Orient Steam Navigation Company unsuccessfully attempted to take over operations in several P&O managed ports in the US, most of the Gulf monarchies' sovereign wealth funds have been careful to keep their stakes in western companies and multinationals relatively small in order to assuage fears that their investments are being used to gain political influence, and to avoid future xenophobic backlashes. As discussed later in this book, it appears that the funds have now branched out significantly into emerging markets and Pacific Asia, with Kuwaiti and Saudi Arabian funds in particular having poured billions of dollars into China. Soon it is likely that the value of these Pacific Asian investments will exceed those in Western Europe and North America.[128]

By far the largest of the funds is the Abu Dhabi Investment Authority (ADIA). Founded in 1976, it had accumulated $100 billion in overseas assets by the mid-1990s[129] and about $360 billion by 2005.[130] Now symbolically housed in the tallest building in Abu Dhabi, it was estimated that ADIA controlled nearly $900 billion in assets in early 2008[131] and now it probably has about $600 billion following some losses, especially in the US.[132] The second largest and the eldest of the region's funds is Saudi Arabia's SAMA Foreign Holdings. Founded in 1960, it now holds over $400 billion in assets. The Kuwait Investment Authority (KIA), founded in 1963, was for many years the largest of the funds, but after the 1990 Iraqi invasion of Kuwait and the subsequent costly rebuilding programme a number of its assets were sold. Nevertheless it still stands at over $200 billion, making it the region's third largest fund.

The other Gulf monarchies have more modest funds, reflecting their smaller hydrocarbon surpluses. The Investment Corporation of Dubai for example, may have about $20 billion in assets,[133] but this is unclear given some of the below-mentioned controversies regarding the Dubai government's ability to make debt repayments. Bahrain's Mumtalakat Holding Company and Oman's State General Reserve Fund are even smaller, perhaps less than $12 billion[134]—and with depleting oil reserves they are unlikely to grow much further. Instead, the fastest growing funds are likely to be the more recently established Qatar Investment Authority—founded in 2006 and now controlling about $60 billion in assets given its access to substantial gas export revenues—and the numerous other sovereign wealth funds in Abu Dhabi that seem to operate in parallel to ADIA. Notable among these are the Mubadala Development Company, which was founded in 2002 under the umbrella of the emirate's crown prince and which now controls about $15 billion in assets, and the much older International Petroleum Investment Company (IPIC), which has recently been rejuvenated under the stewardship of one of the crown prince's brothers[135] and now controls about $14 billion in assets.[136]

Nonetheless, despite these substantial overseas investments, there has been a keen awareness in the Gulf monarchies of the need to diversify their economic bases, not only in an effort to reduce their vulnerability to the vagaries of the international oil markets, but also to generate employment opportunities for their fast-growing indigenous populations and to cope with some of the other mounting pressures discussed below. Initially most of the diversification efforts were concentrated on building up heavy, energy-reliant export-oriented industries, all of which relied on the competitive advantage of having cheap abundant energy supplied by the state. Unsurprisingly, it has been the resource-rich states, notably Saudi Arabia, Kuwait, Qatar, and the UAE's Abu Dhabi that have led the way, often by developing petrochemicals, metals, fertilisers and plastics industries. In Saudi Arabia's case the biggest player has been the Saudi Arabian Basic Industries Corporation (SABIC), which was established in 1976 to produce polymers and chemicals. Today it is one of the world's largest exporters of such products, and is also the region's largest producer of steel.[137] Established in 1997, Saudi Arabia's Maaden was originally focused on developing the country's gold mines, but has since diversified into the manufacture and exporting of aluminium and phosphate.[138] Six new 'economic cities' have been inaugurated too, the largest being the King Abdullah Economic City on the Red Sea coast. Containing both a seaport and industrial zone, it is intended to become an attractive, integrated hub for foreign direct investment in Saudi Arabia's manufacturing sector.[139]

Since the founding of the Shuaiba Industrial Zone in 1962, Kuwait's heavy industries have followed a similar pattern of development.[140] Most have concentrated on the exporting of petrochemicals, with others focusing on the production of ammonia, fertilisers, and cement.[141] Some of these industrial projects have either stalled or collapsed, often as a result of the aforementioned vibrancy of debate within Kuwait's parliament. Most notably, in 2008 a multibillion dollar joint venture between Kuwait's

Petrochemical Industries and the American Dow Chemicals—expected to position Kuwait as the world's greatest producer of polyethylene—was cancelled.[142] Qatar's heavy industries have likewise concentrated on petrochemicals, fertilisers, and steel, with most activity taking place close to the main gas-exporting centres of Ras Laffan and Mesaieed. Most production is in the hands of Qatar Steel, the Qatar Primary Material Company, and Industries Qatar—which are second in the region only to SABIC. Abu Dhabi's most prominent downstream industrial companies are Fertil (established in 1980 and co-owned by ADNOC and Total),[143] the Abu Dhabi Polymers Company (established in 1998),[144] and Emirates Aluminium (EMAL). The latter now operates the world's largest aluminium processing facility on Abu Dhabi's manmade Taweelah island.[145] Over the next few years the sector is set to expand further, with both Mubadala and the Abu Dhabi Basic Industries Corporation (ADBIC) planning to build massive new aluminium plants.[146] And by 2013 Abu Dhabi's IPIC will have built a new Chemicals Industrial City: capable of producing 7 million tonnes per year of aromatics and ammonia derivatives, it will be the world's largest such complex.[147] The government has put its full weight behind these developments, having increased spending on industrial infrastructure by over 400 per cent over the past decade. By the end of 2012 it promises the completion of the $7 billion Khalifa Port and Industrial Zone on Taweelah[148] and has committed a further $8 billion for other sector-specific infrastructure projects. A new unit—ZonesCorp[149]—has been set up to administer these new districts, provide organisational support, and build residential camps for labourers.[150] Combined, it is expected that the new projects will account for 15 per cent of Abu Dhabi's GDP by 2030.[151]

In parallel to these heavy, energy-related industries, many export-processing zones have been set up in the region. Again there has been significant variation, with most being in the Gulf monarchies which no longer have the competitive advantage of abundant hydrocarbon resources. By providing integrated industrial zones, mostly geared towards small manufacturers and branches of foreign companies, these states have sought to attract foreign direct investment and kick-start import-substitution industries while also creating diverse employment opportunities for their citizens that are not directly tied to oil, sovereign wealth funds, or government services. Crucially, as specially designated 'free zones' in most cases they have allowed companies to circumvent the described *kafala* sponsorship system, and have thus proved popular with multinationals seeking bases in the region unrestricted by domestic legislation. The pioneer of this strategy is Dubai, which launched its Jebel Ali Free Zone in 1985. Within a few years the zone had attracted several hundred companies, many of them from Europe, North America, and Asia. In 2007 it even became the primary headquarters of the formerly Texas-based multinational, Halliburton. Since then Dubai has set up other zones, many of which have been sector-specific and similarly popular. In 2000 the Dubai Internet City and Dubai Media City were launched, respectively for IT and media-related companies. And in 2003 Dubai Healthcare City was set up to serve as a base for foreign medical companies and services, including the Harvard Medical School,[152] while Dubai Knowledge Village was established to house branches of several international universities, most of which concentrate on offering postgraduate degrees to the emirate's substantial expatriate population. Other UAE emirates, including Sharjah and Ra's al-Khaimah, have followed Dubai's lead, having established smaller versions of Jebel Ali. And elsewhere in the Gulf there has been the Bahrain Logistics Zone, the Salalah Free Zone in Oman, and the Qatar Science and Technology Park, among others.

Similarly pioneered by the more energy-scarce Gulf monarchies have been the region's tourism, financial, and real estate industries. With regards to tourism, Dubai was again the frontrunner, with dozens of luxury hotels having been built over the past fifteen years, including the iconic, seven star Burj Al-Arab. Since then millions of tourists have been attracted to the emirate, most of whom have favoured the winter sun, tax-free shopping festivals, and a range of sports and music events—many of which are world-class. In 2010 the government claimed that nearly nine million visitors had stayed in the emirate's hotels.[153] Some other Gulf monarchies have followed suit, notably Oman, Bahrain, Qatar, and Abu Dhabi, the latter having opened its lavish Emirates Palace hotel in 2005 and claiming to have hosted nearly two million tourists in 2010.[154] Although Kuwait was the first Gulf state to develop a significant financial sector, it was really Bahrain that set up the region's first international financial centre—now housed in Manama's Financial Harbour. Established in 2004, the Dubai International Financial Centre signalled the UAE's first major attempt to challenge Bahrain's position. Envisaged as a potential bridge between the time zones of other leading financial centres such as London, Hong Kong, and Singapore, the DIFC has also served as something of a free zone, with multinational financial companies locating their Middle East branches within its jurisdiction. More recently, recognising the economic benefits and prestige associated with hosting such centres, other Gulf monarchies have also attempted to develop financial hubs, albeit along more limited lines. In 2005 the Qatar Financial Centre was set up, primarily to provide a link between energy-based companies and global financial markets. And in the near future Abu Dhabi's presently modest financial centre will move to a much larger Mubadala-constructed campus on Sowwah Island.

More problematic has been the nascent real estate sector. For some years it was a major contributor to the non-oil related GDP of several Gulf monarchies, but following the 2008 credit crunch the sector contracted sharply due to limited credit and considerable oversupply. As the pioneer, having allowed foreign nationals to purchase real estate since 1997 on the murky basis of long leases and then ill-defined freehold status,[155] Dubai has since experienced the greatest reversal of fortunes, with its over-extended real estate sector and more than $170 billion in cancelled projects[156] now likely to hamper the emirate's economic development for years to come. The tipping point came in late 2009, when its largest real estate developer—Nakheel—was unable to service substantial debts. This led to plummeting international confidence in the government of Dubai's ability to rescue state-backed developers, with the situation only stabilising following a substantial $20 billion loan package from Abu Dhabi.[157] Symbolically, Abu Dhabi's assistance appeared to be delivered with political strings attached, as when Dubai's much vaunted Burj Dubai—the world's tallest skyscraper—was finally opened in early 2010, its name was abruptly changed to Burj Khalifa to honour Abu Dhabi's ruler, Khalifa bin Zayed Al-Nahyan. Recent indications are that Dubai remains in trouble, with even the ruling family-backed Dubai Holdings having had to restructure $2.5 billion of debt in early 2012.[158] Meanwhile other Gulf monarchies have also experimented with real estate, although on a much smaller scale, with both Bahrain and Qatar launching projects in recent years, Oman seems to have gone furthest in supporting full freehold ownership for foreigners, following fresh legislation in 2006.[159]

As with the variance in hydrocarbon exports and sovereign wealth funds, the numerous diversification efforts and their relative performances have further underlined the important economic differences that now exist between the Gulf monarchies. The non-oil sector in resource-scarce Bahrain now accounts for nearly 90 per cent of its GDP,[160] while in the UAE's case it is approximately 70 per cent, mostly as a result of Dubai's efforts.[161] In contrast, the non-oil sectors in Saudi Arabia and Oman account for about 55 per cent of GDP,[162] and in both Kuwait and Qatar the non-oil sectors account for less than 50 per cent of GDP.[163] The varying levels of foreign direct investment in the Gulf monarchies also reflect the differing approaches to diversification, with Saudi Arabia's economic cities and other developments being responsible for attracting close to $193 billion in investments in recent years, and with the UAE's various projects—again mostly in Dubai—having attracted $76 billion. In comparison, both Qatar and Bahrain have attracted less than $20 billion in foreign direct investment, while Kuwait—again encumbered by political instability—has only managed $130 million in investments.[164]

Overall, the significant economic differences between the six states are clearly reflected by the widening gap in GDP per capita in the region. With a total population of less than one million and with substantial gas exports and sovereign wealth, Qatar's GDP per capita now stands at $179,000—the highest in the world. Although more modest, with a population of about five million, the wealthy UAE also has a high GDP per capita of about $50,000, which is about the same as Kuwait, which has a population of just over 2.5 million. At the lower end of the scale, resource-scarce Bahrain, with a population of 1.2 million, has a GDP per capita of $40,000, while Oman, with a larger population of three million only has a GDP per capita of $25,000. Despite its sizeable hydrocarbon revenues and large sovereign wealth funds, Saudi Arabia's GDP per capita is now actually the lowest in the region—$24,000—mostly due to its considerably larger population of 27 million.[165] This means that the Gulf monarchies, despite so many obvious similarities, are becoming an increasingly unusual cluster of countries with half of the group being well within the world's top ten—in terms of GDP per capita—while other members remain firmly outside the top fifty, and can at best be considered middle income economies.

2

EXPLAINING SURVIVAL—DOMESTIC MATTERS

The survival of the Gulf monarchies to date—at least on a domestic level—has been predicated on the unwritten, unspoken ruling bargains or social contracts that exist between the ruling families and their populations. Together with the neo-patriarchal governments that have formed, these bargains and their constituent strategies have usually been enough to placate most citizens, satisfy the needs of resident expatriates and guarantee some degree of political acquiescence from the population, thereby allowing the monarchies to avoid repression or coercive 'maintenance of the polity'.[1]

Given the economic and demographic disparities between the six Gulf monarchies, these ruling bargain components differ from state to state and, as circumstances have changed; new components have been added while others have been withdrawn. Nevertheless within all of these highly dynamic bargains there are readily identifiable patterns and much common ground.

All of the Gulf monarchies have emphasised the state being first and foremost a distributor of wealth rather than an extractor, and arguably this remains the central pillar of monarchical survival. Drawn mostly from revenues derived from the region's hydrocarbon concessions or from rent generated by more recent post-oil activities, the largesse of these modern day rentier states has undoubtedly provided their ruling families and governments with considerable 'eudemonic legitimacy'—that is, legitimacy derived from economic well-being and the provision of social welfare.² Closely connected to this component has been the ability of these states to boost massively the national identity and social status of their citizens or 'locals'—immediately identifying them as recipients of distributed wealth and often positioning them in advantageous business positions. In the wealthiest monarchies, this automatically elevates citizens above all other sections of the population. Although technically not part of this 'rentier elite', the millions of expatriates living and working in the Gulf states are often similarly satisfied, as most are able to enjoy a competitive, tax-free income, and usually plan on returning home after a few years. Those that do not conform can easily be suppressed and deported.

Non-economic components of the ruling bargains also matter greatly, especially in those monarchies with a declining ability to distribute wealth. In many cases, rulers and their heirs have invested much time and effort in cultivating personal resources or even perpetuating personality cults; often based on sporting prowess, scholarly achievements, or celebrity status. The aim, it seems, has been to sustain an air of traditional authority for these individuals to keep governing their people. Connected to this has been the generous funding and support for museums and other projects that emphasise the Gulf monarchies' tribal heritage and pre-oil history, often serving as 'living memories' of how the incumbents can trace their lineage back to key founding fathers. Similarly important, especially in Saudi Arabia, but apparent in all six states, has been the exploitation and co-option of religion, mostly—but not exclusively—Islam. Ruling families have worked hard to generate an image of piety, while their governments have carefully funded and controlled most parts of the clerical establishment, thus heading off religious opposition. Other components have also recently been experimented with, often with mixed results. Projects and initiatives focusing on the environment or green energy, for example, have recently been proving popular. Despite the region's massive hydrocarbon production and extremely high carbon footprint per capita, they have served to win favourable headlines for the dignitaries involved.

Distributing wealth

Since the 1960s the traditional system of tribal leaders giving gifts to their subjects, friends, and enemies in exchange for loyalty or faithful service has been massively advanced. The verbal instructions or small chits of paper issued by sheikhs or their secretaries to grateful petitioners were quickly replaced by official documents drawn up by rulers' courts or new bureaucrats as hydrocarbon revenues allowed the nascent states to transfer wealth directly to their citizens and establish the most generous welfare states in the developing world, underpinned by subsidised utilities, fuel, and foodstuffs. One of the more visible benefits for citizens was the provision of government housing. Although fairly modest in the 1960s and 1970s, the free dwellings nonetheless allowed for air-conditioning and the connection of refrigerators, televisions, and other appliances. In the poorest parts of the region, especially in Saudi Arabia and Oman, the effect was to transform the lives of thousands. Many older Omanis today, for example, often state that 'before Qaboos there was nothing', referring to the poverty and lack of basic amenities prior to Qaboos bin Said Al-Said's succession in 1970. In more recent years, the quality of free housing, especially in the smaller, richer Gulf monarchies, has dramatically improved, while expatriates have often moved into the original government housing. Recipients in these states can now expect sizeable apartments and villas, usually with one bedroom for every child. In some cases, utilities are also provided for free, as are telephones.[3]

In Qatar, for example, the Barwa Housing Project has provided hundreds of families with reasonably high quality free accommodation complete with parks and playgrounds. The housing is available only to Qatari citizens, but allows for a relatively high monthly income threshold of $4,400.[4] Similarly, and more extensively in the UAE, the Sheikh Zayed Housing Programme provides 'deserving UAE national families' with three choices: either a government-provided house, an interest free loan to buy a new house, or a grant to refurbish or maintain an existing residence. Most of the government-provided houses are of good quality, especially in the wealthiest emirate of Abu Dhabi, and the quality of free houses in the poorer, northern emirates, has been improving of late. In 2008 the programme's annual budget was increased to $350 million, and an announcement was made that over 40,000 new villas would be constructed for UAE nationals over the next four years at a cost of $4 billion.[5] In parallel Dubai now has its own such housing scheme, unsurprisingly named after its ruler—the Muhammad bin Rashid Housing Programme—and in early 2011 more than 700 new homes were allocated to UAE nationals at a cost of over $250 million. Aiming to 'offer appropriate accommodation to Emiratis of all social classes and meeting their basic needs, especially a dignified housing' the programme has little in common with government housing in other parts of the world, as the units are of nine designs ranging from three to five bedrooms and have façades in different architectural styles including Islamic and Andalusian. Moreover, the beneficiaries have been receiving text message construction updates direct from the developer.[6]

Significantly, despite all of these new Gulf homes being part of official government spending, the keys are usually handed out to recipients in a more traditional setting—often by a ruling family member at some sort of cultural gathering. An incident heavily reported in the UAE's state-backed media provides a particularly good example: in 2008 the ruler of Dubai was apparently touring the eastern province of Abu Dhabi in his role as UAE prime minister when he came across a 99 year old UAE national. Upon seeing cracks in the walls of the man's house Muhammad asked him if he needed anything. Replying simply that he 'wished for a long and happy life', Muhammad reportedly replied 'here we will build for you a very comfortable home' before ordering the construction of a new villa for the man, and new accommodation for all the man's grandsons. Three years later, in 2011, the local reaction to Muhammad's earlier visit was understandably positive, with the elderly man explaining that 'there are no words to describe the generosity and care [Muhammad] shows towards his people' and with the district's governor being similarly enamoured of the sheikh.[7]

As well as houses, the government-led granting of land for agricultural and commercial use to citizens has also proved popular—a straightforward resource for many Gulf monarchies to exploit given that in most cases the state or even the ruler himself owns all land unless specifically re-assigned. For citizens still dwelling in rural or hinterland areas, many have been provided with plots of land to develop into working farms. And in the wealthier Gulf monarchies, especially Abu Dhabi—where Zayed bin Sultan Al-Nahyan had a particular keenness for 'greening' the emirate with trees and vegetation—many nationals have been provided with grants to purchase the necessary farming equipment and hire expatriate workers. Alternatively, and sometimes in addition to agricultural land, citizens have also been provided with plots of land in urban or industrial areas—either to be developed as retail outlets, workshops, or simply to build blocks of apartments to then rent out to expatriates. In some instances these plots of land have never been developed, serving simply as car parks or rest areas for lorries—but either way, they still generate rent for their respective landlords. As with the allocation of houses, the process is usually linked directly to key members of ruling families, despite being a part of official government spending. In Abu Dhabi, for example, the Khalifa Committee for Social Services and Commercial Buildings—named after and chaired by Zayed's eldest son and Abu Dhabi's current ruler, Khalifa bin Zayed Al-Nahyan—has dispensed over $10 billion in such property or grants since its inception in 1981.[8] Undoubtedly its popularity helped bolster Khalifa's status as Abu Dhabi's long-serving crown prince. Similarly in Qatar, all citizens are eligible to receive a plot of land ranging from 700 to 1,500 square metres, and an interet-free loan of about $250,000 towards its development. In order to claim these plots an application must be made directly to the ruler's court—a process through which 'the Emir's patronage is reinforced both symbolically and practically'.[9]

In addition to social security benefits for unemployed citizens—which are very generous, about $3,000 per month in the wealthier Gulf monarchies,[10] and modest in all but the poorest Gulf monarchies of Bahrain and Oman—the welfare states that have been set up since the 1970s also include free healthcare and education. Again there is marked disparity between the quality of services offered in the wealthiest and poorest of the six states. In Qatar, for example, a new $2.4 billion hospital is being established in co-operation with Cornell University,[11] while the state-sponsored Qatar University is believed to operate with a massive endowment. In the UAE and Kuwait, similarly well-equipped hospitals have been in place for years, and students at state sector schools and universities can usually expect to receive free textbooks and in some circumstances even free laptop computers. In Saudi Arabia, a new public research university—the King Abdullah University of Science and Technology—was launched in 2009 at great expense. Comprising eleven faculties and already educating several hundred students, the university even offers stipends of several thousand dollars per year to its students. While Bahraini and Omani state sector hospitals, schools, and universities clearly lack the same level of attention and funding as in their neighbours, they are nevertheless far in advance of facilities available elsewhere in the developing world and are still easily among the best facilities available in the Arab world. Oman's Sultan Qaboos University—established in 1986—

enjoys a long and distinguished history in the region, as did Bahrain's Salmaniya Hospital until recently.

Another important and highly visible feature of the Gulf monarchies' allocative states has been the provision of public sector employment to most citizens, provided that they meet the most basic of qualifications. In the 1970s and 1980s almost all citizens who graduated from university were guaranteed jobs in the civil service, in ministries, or in other government departments. Moreover, citizens invariably enjoyed higher salaries than their expatriate counterparts, along with generous pensions, relaxed working hours, and good promotion prospects. Although something of a taboo subject in the region, it remains fair to say that citizens—especially at this period—were not required to work to international standards, with very few ever being fired from their positions. Put politely, with reference to Saudi Arabia '...royals have on many occasions used their fiscal authority to...employ veritable armies of idle bureaucratic clients'.[12]

In recent years it has become harder for the Gulf monarchies, especially those with declining resources or larger populations such as Bahrain, Oman, and Saudi Arabia, to keep creating and funding such generously paid and well-protected jobs. But in the smaller, wealthier monarchies it undoubtedly remains a central strategy, with public sector salary increases usually being tied to important political events. In the UAE, for example, within days of Khalifa bin Zayed's succession as Abu Dhabi ruler and UAE president in late 2004 it was announced that all nationals working in the public sector would receive an immediate 25 per cent pay increase: understandably a popular decision.[13] Even more dramatically, in December 2009—just days after Dubai's economic crash was reported in the international media and many UAE nationals were questioning their real estate investments in the emirate—the federal government announced that all citizens in the public sector would receive a 70 per cent pay rise, including all staff employed by the giant ministries for health and education. Emiratis interviewed by state-backed newspapers were understandably impressed, with one remarking 'I would like to thank the Government for making it easier for Emiratis to live in the city, and for helping provide for their future plans,' while another claimed 'this increase will help me live more comfortably, buy property, and increase the limit on my spending'.[14] Significantly, as with most such salary hikes in the region, expatriates were excluded.

As discussed later in this book, in those Gulf monarchies where public sector employment can no longer be guaranteed for citizens, it has been harder for the ruling families and governments to rely continuously on salary increases to boost popularity. Nevertheless, steps have been taken to make sure that those who end up working in the private sector can still benefit from their nationality. In Saudi Arabia and Kuwait, for example, many jobs that appear to be in the private sector are very often in large, government-backed parastatals such as the Saudi Basic Industries Corporation or the Kuwait Projects Company (KIPCO). In this sense, employment conditions for citizens differ very little from those working in ministries or government departments. Similarly, in Abu Dhabi, which has recently streamlined the number of civil service jobs from 65,000 to 28,000, and has plans to trim the number to 8,000,[15] many new pseudo-public sector jobs have been created by giant government-backed companies and the many joint ventures they have sponsored. The aforementioned Mubadala Development Company is particularly noteworthy, as together with its many offshoot projects it now employs thousands of young UAE nationals.

Where genuine private sector employment opportunities for nationals do exist, for example in Bahrain and Dubai's export-processing free zones it is far more difficult to earmark jobs for citizens or to offer them different rewards from expatriates. Nevertheless, efforts have been made—though not always successfully—by some Gulf monarchies to encourage companies to help indigenise the labour force, either by imposing quotas or by introducing legislation that offers citizens greater job protection or better working hours than their expatriate peers. In 2004, a report conducted by Tanmia—the UAE's National Human Resource Development and Employment Authority—recommended that the 'system introduced by the Government of applying minimum quotas for employment of UAE nationals needs to be applied to more economic sectors to ensure jobs for nationals' and that private sector firms should contemplate introducing training programmes specifically for citizens.[16] Moreover, in late 2009, with concerns over the credit crunch growing, the UAE's federal government resorted to blatant protectionism, announcing that it would be illegal for employers to make UAE nationals redundant from their jobs, except in the most extreme cases.[17]

Other aspects of the wealth distribution strategy of the Gulf monarchies include the regular cancelling of debts, and the dispensing of 'government charity' to the minority of indigent citizens who somehow slip through the free housing and welfare state net. The former mechanism, much like the periodic public sector salary increases, tends to be deployed during economic or political crises as a means of reinforcing the loyalty of citizens. Kuwait provides the best example of this, with the government having revoked most personal debts and stock market losses following the 1982 Souq al-Manakh crash—named after the informal, unregulated bourse that had been set up in an air-conditioned garage. Thousands of Kuwaiti nationals had bought into the market, in many cases their first experience of personal investments, before having their stocks wiped out. In 1991, following Kuwait's liberation from Iraq, the government again moved to abrogate most personal debts, allowing citizens more quickly to resume their pre-war lifestyles. And in 2008 the government set up an $18 billion emergency fund, specifically to assist Kuwaiti nationals with debt problems. As the effects of the credit crunch on Kuwait's economy intensified, this was extended in 2009 following the government's purchasing of over $23.3 billion of consumer loans—this being financed from the annual interest accrued on foreign assets held by the Kuwait Investment Authority.[18] As discussed later in this book, widespread debt cancellation has re-emerged in Kuwait 2011 and in many other Gulf monarchies, as all grapple with the aftermath of the Arab Spring.

With regards to 'government charity', much like the free housing projects, the organisations involved tend to remain very closely tied to the state and are invariably patronised or very publicly subsidised by key members of the ruling families. In the UAE for example, there exists the Khalifa bin Zayed Al-Nahyan Foundation in Abu Dhabi which donates to a wide range of causes, and the Emirates Foundation which is chaired by the crown prince and has recently focused on distributing grants for nationals with special needs. In Dubai and the other emirates there exist similar, albeit less well-endowed, bodies. Qatar also provides a good example of this strategy, with its largest domestic charitable body—Qatar Charity—providing a range of funds to help less well off Qatari families and to support Qatari orphans. Crucially, although it styles itself as a non-governmental organisation and is headed by a general manager,[19] rather than a member of the Al-Thani ruling family, Qatar Charity is nonetheless inextricably linked to the establishment. It receives financial and logistical support from government bodies including the Ministries for Civil Service Affairs and for Housing, Foreign Affairs, Finance, Economy and Trade, Islamic Affairs, and Education. It is also assisted by the Supreme Council for Family Affairs and the Planning Council—both of which are key social policy vehicles for the Qatari government. As such, it has been argued that Qatar Charity's various efforts are fully in line with state policies and objectives.[20] Ironically, it is now difficult for citizens of Gulf monarchies to give money directly to the poor and thereby bypass such state-sanctioned charities. And in some cases such private charitable acts are frowned upon by the establishment. In recent years in the UAE, for example, in advance of Ramadan—the holy month during which all practising Muslims have a duty to be charitable—the Ministry for Interior has been issuing statements that beggars should not be tolerated, and that those caught would be arrested, deported, and blacklisted from returning to the UAE, meeting the cost of the deportation themselves. In 2007 it was reported that over seventy such beggars, mostly of Arab origin, were arrested and deported in this manner, with any nationals caught having been directed to official charities and threatened with punishment if they repeated their behaviour in the future.[21]

An important corollary of the Gulf monarchies' allocative states is the visible lack of taxation, or at least any obvious extractive practices. It is often assumed that the region has no real history of tax, and that hydrocarbon exports and the resulting rentier structures have allowed states to avoid such unpopular measures. This is partly true, as there has never been a system of direct taxation in any of the Gulf monarchies. However, prior to the oil era there were a substantial number of indirect taxes, licence fees, and other charges levied by the old, traditional governments. Taxes were levied on the size and quality of pearls that merchants attempted to sell and sales of camels, dates, and fish were taxed too. Payments also had to be made to sheikhs for all fishing or trading vessels that were moored in their ports. In some cases these indirect taxes—or more modern variations—have been reintroduced, especially in those Gulf monarchies that have faced declining hydrocarbon resources. In Dubai there are now significant charges levied for parking cars, crossing bridges, purchasing alcohol, and waste removal. Government fees have also been added to utility bills. In the near future value added taxes may start to appear in the Gulf monarchies, but it is far from certain. In 2008 all six of the Gulf monarchies began planning to introduce a modest VAT, but despite IMF recommendations to press ahead,[22] in late 2011 the plans were delayed until at least 2013 given the tense political situation in the region.[23] Nevertheless, there remain no plans to introduce income tax in any of these states, as this continues to be regarded as deeply unpopular among citizens and thus politically unpalatable for the ruling families and their governments. A recent study on Saudi Arabia puts this well, describing the 'large-scale fiscal obligations' owed by the state to its 'various clients in society', and demonstrating that 'over time this paternal largesse has proved difficult to reverse'.[24]

National elites

Given that most aspects of the welfare state and the various wealth distribution mechanisms in the Gulf monarchies are geared primarily towards citizens, it has become increasingly important for these states to develop carefully a sense of national identity. On a basic level, governments need to control exactly which of their residents are entitled to the many privileges and benefits of the rentier state and, especially in the more resource-scarce monarchies, there is a need to make sure that the national wealth never has to be too thinly spread. More subtly, the building of a clear social divide between citizens and expatriates, especially in those Gulf monarchies such as Qatar, the UAE, and Kuwait—where the majority of residents are now expatriates—has also created a readily identifiable elite status for nationals. Put simply, in these monarchies almost any citizen, regardless of background or education, can automatically assume a relatively high social standing, courtesy of their passport or identity papers.[25] For many years—and this is often still the case—this meant in practice that citizens could queue-jump expatriates, win arguments with the police (especially if the police were expatriates), and in general enjoy preferential treatment in public. While this obvious social stratification is now becoming a little blurred—notably in those monarchies such as Bahrain and Oman that have sought foreign direct investment or have established tourism industries—there nevertheless lingers an atmosphere of favouritism and state-sponsored social inequity. Either way, from a ruling family's perspective any awkwardness or resentfulness from expatriates is massively outweighed by the political benefits of having a national population that not only enjoys distributed wealth but also de facto elite status.

Although not an example of wealth distribution as such, the aforementioned sponsorship or *kafala* system is also heavily dependent on this elite status and the distinction between citizens and expatriates. While some of the more resource-scarce Gulf monarchies, notably Bahrain and Dubai, have gone to great lengths to liberalise their economies and create a more equitable competitive environment for foreign entrepreneurs and investors—either by removing the *kafala* requirement in the free zones or by allowing ministries rather than individuals to serve as sponsors—most Gulf states have shied away from abolishing the system, given the significant economic benefits it brings to many citizens. In the most straightforward examples, well placed nationals can essentially sell their status as a citizen to foreign partners who need to conform to existing legislation (such as having a sponsor control at least 51 per cent of the company's stock)[26] and seek a local partner. In these situations it is not uncommon to find that the local partner is effectively a 'sleeping partner', with the foreigner doing most of the work. As mentioned, this allows citizens to enjoy another stream of rent often above and beyond any land or property they may have acquired with the help of the state.

One important mechanism for guarding and preserving the narrow and distinct social base entitled to these privileges has been the control over citizens' marriages by using a mixture of formal and informal methods. Although there are many exceptions, and some significant variances between the different Gulf monarchies, it is generally the case that national women must marry national men. The usual explanation for this social requirement is that women marrying foreign men will erode cultural values, religious values, and the use of Arabic by their children. However, for an increasingly vocal younger generation of Gulf national women, this is becoming harder to make sense of, as their male counterparts have always been able to marry whomsoever they wish, regardless of nationality, race, or even religion. Moreover, earlier generations of Gulf women, especially in the pre-oil era, were much freer, with many marrying Muslim Arabs from neighbouring sheikhdoms or even further afield. After all, there is no Koranic requirement for a woman to marry a man from her own country.

At the family level, a system of stigmatisation remains in place for women who marry foreigners, and many such women are effectively ostracised from their families if they press ahead with these unions. While no laws exist in the Gulf monarchies to prevent such occurrences, there is little doubt that pressure continues to be exerted from the top—with rumours and discussion of 'unpublished decrees' still frequently circulating that are rarely scotched by officials. What policies are in place are highly discriminatory, with Gulf national women generally being unable to pass on their passport to any offspring from such unions or—most crucially—both their husbands and offspring being ineligible to receive any of the rentier state benefits. A recent exception to this is the UAE, which in late 2011 announced that such children could apply for passports at the age of eighteen.[27] But it remained unclear exactly what benefits they would be entitled to before that age. Moreover, there is still no doubt that the offspring of UAE national men and foreign mothers—even those born and brought up in different countries, or out of wedlock—enjoy much better rights. In 2009, a UAE committee even visited Egypt and Syria to identify such children who might be eligible for UAE citizenship. A six-month Ministry for Interior programme was announced for these 'would-be UAE citizens to go under a series of educational, social and health orientation programmes to learn UAE customs, traditions, heritage and values that will smooth their integration into UAE society'.[28]

Also at the policy level, for those Gulf monarchies that provide 'marriage funds' to young male citizens—another wealth distribution mechanism, ostensibly to defray the rising cost of wedding ceremonies—payments will only usually be made to men who are betrothed to fellow nationals. In other words, there now exists a significant financial incentive for many men to marry compatriots rather than foreigners. An oft-cited example is the Sheikh Zayed Marriage Fund which began in Abu Dhabi in 1990, before later being made accessible across the entire UAE. In its first decade over 60,000 youths benefited from the scheme, which dispensed more than $630 million in grants.[29] Today, on average, it offers grants of $19,000 to each eligible applicant.[30] Similarly narrow incentives exist in Qatar, where the housing allowances are doubled for Qatari men if their wives are also Qatari.[31] And across the region ruling family-sponsored mass weddings for such marriages remain highly popular, often costing millions of dollars and involving giant feasts for hundreds or thousands of guests.[32]

Another prominent mechanism for guarding and preserving the social base of national elites in the Gulf monarchies has been the adoption of a 'national dress' code. There are significant variations across the region, with men and women in Oman, Saudi Arabia, and Kuwait wearing several different styles of garments, and with the younger generations in all six Gulf monarchies increasingly wearing western clothes during their leisure time. For the most part the older generations in all these countries, and most citizens—young and old—in the wealthiest of the Gulf monarchies tend to wear a fairly strict uniform of white *thobes* or *dishdashas* (men) or black *abayas* (women). Such quotidian sartorial choices allow the observer to differentiate instantly between a citizen and an expatriate, which helps the former to access the aforementioned privileges associated with citizenship and the concomitant elevated social status they bring. In those monarchies such as Qatar or the UAE where the material rewards of citizenship are the greatest and where the expatriate component of the total resident population is the highest, adherence to the dress code is most prevalent. As one recent study put it, 'it is no mere fashion that leads all Qatar national men to wear their traditional *thob* at all times… the emir and his government have perpetuated these neo-traditional myths of authenticity, allowing the creation of a citizen autocracy'.[33] Certainly, it is very important to note that this dress code is primarily a product of the oil era and the rentier state: although sometimes referred to as 'traditional dress' or even 'Islamic dress' by foreigners, the current national dress code in these Gulf monarchies has few roots in tradition or religion, with early pre-oil photographs from the region demonstrating that the indigenous populations once wore a variety of colours and styles.

Further connected to the dress code, it is also notable how in recent years some male ruling family members have increasingly adopted different colours for their *dishdashas*, especially when making public appearances. This often results in formal events or occasions where the most senior sheikh present is dressed in black, brown, or blue, while other nationals wear white. In this manner the patron distinguishes himself from the regular citizenry by being visibly superior. Also of interest, and reinforcing the argument that dress code marks elite status and those benefiting from distributed wealth, is the reaction to expatriates who adopt national dress. While little attention is paid to tourists buying and trying on such clothes, to Caucasian-origin western expatriates, or to prostitutes (who regularly wear national dress in order to move discreetly between locations), there is generally a negative reaction to Arab, South Asian, or African expatriates (or any person who could be confused with a citizen) who may try to wear such dress. These attempts are usually viewed as an encroachment on the entitlement of nationals, and on some occasions even lead to police intervention. From another angle, it is also interesting that some of the indigenous Gulf communities who seemingly have the least to gain from the survival of the current regimes choose not to adopt national dress. Notably, the Shia population of Bahrain (and increasingly the Shia population of Saudi Arabia's restive Eastern Province) now infrequently wear national dress. And since the onset of the Bahrain revolution in February 2011 it has become commonplace for protestors to burn effigies of white *dishdashas*—representing the Al-Khalifa ruling family and their supporters—from washing lines in their back yards.

Co-opting expatriates

For decades the Gulf monarchies have relied on substantial expatriate workforces, not only because of the small size of their indigenous populations relative to the enormous development opportunities that have arisen since the first oil booms, but also because of the benefits and privileges enjoyed by citizens and their subsequent preference for public sector employment. Today, there are now several million foreigners employed in these states, working across all sectors, and from all parts of the world. While accurate figures are difficult to come by, given the obvious sensitivities of governments admitting to such demographic breakdowns, it is still possible to make useful generalisations. Most of the region's unskilled labour force (usually housed in worker camps outside the main cities) is made up of South or East Asians, while most of the retail and service sectors are made up of South Asians, or non-Gulf Arabs. Westerners, Australians, and South Africans, along with educated non-Gulf Arabs make up a significant proportion of the region's professional class and white collar private sector workforce.

In Saudi Arabia there are now nearly eight million expatriates—nearly a quarter of the total population.[34] In the more resource-scarce Oman, where there are fewer economic opportunities, there are unsurprisingly fewer expatriates. Nevertheless, as of 2011 there were still more than 600,000 foreigners living there, accounting for 17 per cent of the total population.[35] Meanwhile in Bahrain about 550,000 or nearly half of the island's population were thought to be expatriates—at least before the 2011 uprisings began.[36] The most dramatic examples are, however, in the more resource-rich small monarchies. In Kuwait, over 1.1 million expatriates account for nearly 70 per cent of the total population,[37] while in the UAE expatriates now seem to make up 90 per cent of population.[38] The latter figure is based on official UAE government data claiming that the total population has risen to 9 million[39]—this has been widely disputed and can be put down to the UAE's historic rivalry with the much larger Saudi Arabia. Qatar, now the fastest growing Gulf economy with the smallest number of citizens—only 290,000—will soon catch up with the UAE. Already the population comprises 80 per cent expatriates, and with a staggering annual population growth rate of nearly 60 per cent their proportion will increase dramatically.[40]

The presence of substantial expatriate populations has profound socio-economic consequences but in terms of political stability they may have greatly contributed to the survival of the Gulf monarchies. Most expatriates in the region are there to make money and eventually return to their home countries relatively better off. Indeed, most only stay in these states for two to five years, with very few regarding their host country as a real home or a retirement destination. In this regard they differ greatly from immigrants who arrive in 'melting pot' countries such as the US, Canada, and Australia—many of whom intend to spend their whole lives there and help shape their adopted nations. Gulf expatriates are thus better viewed as strictly temporary economic migrants. Although not entitled to the full benefits of the rentier state, they nevertheless enjoy a tax free salary which is usually better than that they could expect in their country of origin. Often they have no real interest in the politics of their host country, and certainly never revolutionary politics. In many ways they become a loyal, silent support base for the ruling families, as the latter usually portray themselves as the guardians of stable, fairly apolitical states where money can be made safely and smoothly. The Al-Maktoum ruling family of Dubai perhaps provide the best example of this. Styling his make-shift government as 'Dubai Inc'., the ruler's aim has been to portray himself as the chief executive officer of a corporation, rather than as an autocrat presiding over an unelected government. As the emirate's indigenous population has continued to shrink, relative to the influx of hundreds of thousands of expatriates each year, the government has regularly announced new initiatives to hold the situation in check. But in many ways it has suited the ruler's interests well—even if it has alarmed the citizenry—to govern over a city made up of temporary migrants.

For the minority of expatriates who remain in the Gulf monarchies longer, the formula needs to be a little different. There are communities of Palestinians in Kuwait, communities of Iranians and Indians in Dubai, and other substantial foreign populations in the region that have spent decades living and working there, sometimes even having been born and brought up in its cities. A tiny minority can expect naturalisation, but this is controversial with the genuine indigenous populations and—as discussed later—has now become a major issue for some opposition movements. Instead, the governments prefer to create an atmosphere of sanctuary or unofficial asylum for these communities, even if it is illusory. Very often these expatriates are from underdeveloped or war-torn regions, many of whom either cannot return home or—in the case of Kuwait's hundreds of thousands of Palestinians (or at least those who were not expelled following the emirate's liberation in 1991)[41]—have no valid travel documentation. While most are aware that their livelihoods are at the whim of their hosts (many other nationalities apart from Palestinians also have been deported from Gulf monarchies due to political disputes), there is a general acceptance of the status quo. Thus, as with the more temporary migrants, most of these expatriates prefer to keep their heads down or try to save up enough to buy citizenship elsewhere.

Much international media attention focuses on the plight of the huge population of unskilled expatriates. In particular, the appalling living conditions in some of the workers' camps—some of which have no basic facilities or even sewerage—are routinely portrayed as a manifestation of evil, immoral, slave-based economies. There is certainly much truth to this, with 'workers' often viewed as somehow sub-human by citizens and skilled expatriates alike, and usually discriminated against by apartheid-like regulations (for example, not being allowed to enter shopping malls, parks, or museums). But in many ways the outrage is the result of having a First World society occupying the same uncomfortably small spaces as a developing world society. Very few of the workers can be considered slaves, as most have not made a step into the unknown. In many cases these men have followed their fathers, brothers, or other male relatives who have worked there before, usually with the same conditions. Most are still separated from their passports upon arrival, driven around on cattle trucks, and work punishingly long hours. Sometimes they do not return home for two or three years at a time. But this is usually expected and known to the new arrivals, and most are there—just like the skilled expatriates—to make more money than they could at home. Indeed, an independent survey published in 2009 claimed that the majority of foreign construction workers in the Gulf monarchies considered their current conditions to be better than those in their native countries.[42]

In this light the workers are best viewed as the dark side of a tragic, remittance-based economic system where South and East Asian countries sell their labour in exchange for salary transfers and investments from the Gulf states into their impoverished communities. When riots do break out in the worker camps the roots causes are only very occasionally political,[43] and the disturbances pose little threat to the survival of the Gulf monarchies. Usually, they are the result of workers not having been paid by an unscrupulous employer or perhaps an unsafe workplace or some other labour-specific complaint. Sometimes the government will move fast to address the problem and deport a few of the ringleaders. But not always, as the workers' embassies usually remain silent in the Gulf monarchies—unwilling to champion the interests of their countrymen lest they jeopardise the flow of remittance wealth.

The region's most violent labour camp episodes have taken place in Saudi Arabia and the UAE, in the latter's case especially since 2009 following the collapse of many property developers and construction companies in the wake of Dubai's real estate slowdown. In May 2010, for example, at the same time that over 500 Syrian and Egyptian labourers went on strike in Mecca due to unpaid wages,[44] over 100 Vietnamese construction workers were arrested in and deported from Dubai. Apparently owed several months' wages—totalling less than $1,400 each—the men had marched to the UAE Ministry for Labour to demand their rights.[45] In early January 2011 it was the turn of Nepalese labourers, this time striking over the assault of one of their number by five Egyptian security guards—a confrontation which had apparently been sparked by complaints about the absence of sanitary facilities.[46] And later that month more than seventy Bangladeshi workers were deported from Dubai—part of a bigger strike of about 5,000 men. The protestors claimed they had not been paid their overtime, and were asking for an increase in their weekly wage of barely $55. When asked for a response, the Bangladeshi consul-general in Dubai was unsurprisingly cautious, agreeing that the UAE authorities had the right to break up the strike because it was 'illegal' and stating that the company in question '…had not breached the contract in paying the salaries… if the workers had problems, they should have solved it through a dialogue with the employer'.[47] Overall, Pakistani construction workers are most likely to face imprisonment, followed by deportation from the Gulf monarchies, not least because they out-number other nationalities in most worker camps. In early 2011 the Pakistani minister of state for foreign affairs estimated that over 4,000 Pakistani nationals were being detained in Middle East states, almost all of them in the Gulf monarchies with nearly 1,800 in Saudi Arabia and over 1,600 in the UAE. He also clarified that a special government department had been set up to provide one-way tickets home for these destitute prisoners.[48]

The most unfortunate cases seem to be those workers who have sim-ply become marooned in the Gulf monarchies. With bankrupt or non-existent sponsors, they are often unable to leave their host countries and have remained in a state of limbo, often having to take out loans in order to survive until they can afford their return flights. As a spokesperson for Human Rights Watch described in 2010 '...because of the layoffs and the fact that some of these workers are stranded, we are seeing an increase in suicides, where some workers feel the only way out is to kill them-selves, hoping that the people who have lent them money will avoid going after their families or their houses back in India and other locations in South Asia... unfortunately, that is not the case; the creditors still go after the families even after the death of migrant workers'. Furthermore, he claimed that the governments involved have not '...committed to fun-damentally changing the way that migrant workers are brought in and the way that migrant workers are treated, so I think it is a problem that is going to be here for a while, especially given the economic downturn'. Similarly, the founder of a rare, Sharjah-based NGO committed to help-ing such labourers—Adopt-a-Camp[49]—described how her work used to be '...heart-warming—it used to be English classes for labourers, hygiene workshops ... and care packages, and seeing wonderful stuff and doing wonderful stuff and the men's smiles'. But then her work changed, becom-ing '...heartbreaking because rather than teaching men and enlighten-ing them and expanding their horizons here, and trying to give them a good experience, it becomes like a man who is starving. The top priority for me becomes getting him food, getting him water, and seeing men in those conditions is heartbreaking'.[50]

Cults of personality

Of the non-economic components of the Gulf monarchies' ruling bar-gains, the most visible is the extensive personal image-building undertaken by select members of the ruling families. Much like other Arab authoritarian regimes, large portraits of rulers and their key brothers or crown princes adorn street corners, the walls of government departments, banks, and even most private sector companies. The aim is usually to portray the men in question in a soft or flattering manner. As such, most portraits feature beaming smiles, wrinkle-free faces, white teeth, and generally avuncular expressions. Almost all depict national dress, helping observers make the visual connection between their rulers and the country's history and heritage. A few portraits, however, also display the rulers as 'hard men', with more serious expressions and often sporting large sunglasses or occasionally military uniforms. Crucially, these are a minority, and are always in close proximity to more gentle portraits. The aim here, it seems is to demonstrate to the population that the rulers should be both loved and feared, and certainly never crossed. Further to this, in many Gulf monarchies rumours and urban legends of rulers and their sons' involvement in violent acts also abound—often connected to familial disputes or business deals that have turned sour. These are often widely and publicly discussed, but rarely with any substance, and never suppressed—likely because they provide the subjects with a certain cachet and machismo.

In most Gulf monarchies the public portraits are usually triptychs, often with the centre figure's portrait being raised slightly higher than those on the left and right. In Kuwait, for example, the emir is at the centre, with his crown prince to the left, and the prime minister to the right. The recently deposed Nasser bin Muhammad Al-Sabah's prime ministerial portrait, for example, usually depicted him as laughing or grinning. Similarly in Bahrain, the triptych usually follows the same pattern, albeit with a king instead of an emir. For many years it has also been common to see solo portraits of Bahrain's powerful unelected prime minister, Khalifa bin Salman Al-Khalifa, clearly reflecting his centrality to the regime. In Qatar the three portraits are again those of the emir, his crown prince, and the unelected prime minister. Recently, however, the emir has often been depicted on his own, wearing western dress and usually representing some historic achievement or victory for Qatar. In 2011–12, for example, large pictures of him holding aloft the soccer World Cup appeared on billboards in recognition of Qatar's 2010 announcement that it would stage the 2022 World Cup. Portrait politics are a little more complicated in the UAE, given the federation and the relationships between and within the various ruling families. In Abu Dhabi, the triptych's centre figure is still usually the once popular and handsome Zayed bin Sultan Al-Nahyan, despite his death over seven years ago. The current ruler— an unassuming-looking character—is displayed on his left, with his image being either heavily enhanced or badly out of date. The powerful crown prince is always on the right. In some cases Zayed is still portrayed on his own, as a younger man on horseback, or sometimes holding a falcon or some other symbol of the country's heritage. The other emirates usually feature their current ruler in the centre, with their crown prince and either a powerful brother or 'deputy crown prince' at their sides. Exceptions include Sharjah, where the ruler is often depicted on his own— likely due to his crown prince not being a son, and a long history of internecine disputes in the emirate. In Dubai there are occasionally solo portraits of Rashid bin Said Al-Maktoum—the father of the current ruler and the man credited with building up Dubai over much of the twentieth century. On major highways and sometimes in federal government buildings it is now common to see dual portraits of the rulers of Abu Dhabi and Dubai, or perhaps a triumvirate of these two along with the crown prince of Abu Dhabi. In Oman and Saudi Arabia triptychs and other public portraits are less common. In the former, as described, the sultan reserved most authority for himself, being reluctant to elevate other ruling family members. As such, where portraits do exist, they are usually of the sultan alone. In Saudi Arabia, despite power being more evenly shared among ruling family members, the king is also usually depicted alone. This is likely due to the large number of similarly aged relatives who rival each other in the succession process, thus allowing the king to be visually depicted as the 'linchpin of the political system',[51] symbolising unity, and taking on the role of supreme mediator.

Titles as well as portraits also matter in terms of personal image-building in the region. Over the years the various ruling families and their principal members have taken on increasingly grandiose titles—usually ones that have no connection to the region's history and which, in some cases, are sacrilegious. Given Saudi Arabia's more autonomous state formation process, the Al-Saud family quickly took on the guise of royalty, adopting a system of titles in the 1940s not dissimilar from Britain's. Notwithstanding a clear emphasis on egalitarianism in Islam, the male descendants of the king became 'His Royal Highness' or 'HRH', while other, lesser, ruling family males became 'His Highness' or 'HH'. Similarly in Oman, it appears that the sultan has taken on the full-blown 'HRH'—a title which no previous sultans have used. The other Gulf monarchies—ruled simply by 'sheikhs' until Britain's departure—also quickly upgraded their titles upon independence. Though most were careful not to antagonise Saudi Arabia or embarrass Britain, with their various rulers settling on the title of emir rather than king, they nonetheless took on the title of 'HH' while lesser members of their families adopted 'His Excellency' or 'HE', despite the title usually being reserved for government ministers or ambassadors. More recently, there have been efforts by these smaller monarchies to further glorify their leaders. Most notably, the aforementioned 2002 Bahraini constitution upgraded the emir to a king, despite the tiny size of the kingdom. While more subtly in the UAE the state-backed media has started to refer to the rulers of Abu Dhabi and Dubai (but not the other emirates) as being HRH, with their families being 'royal' as opposed to merely 'ruling'.

Another interesting phenomenon has been the celebrity status desired and cultivated at great expense by some ruling family members, especially in those states where political mobilisation is most limited—such as Qatar and the UAE.[52] For many years young sheikhs, often those associated with horse-riding, falconry, or other manifestations of sporting prowess or activity linked to tribal heritage have been celebrated and venerated by younger sections of the indigenous populations. With the advent of new internet technologies and communications, this celebrity culture has been taken to an even higher level. No longer are images just built up by the state-backed media or by appearances at large weddings and other traditional events. Instead many ruling family members now have their own websites, Facebook fan pages, and even Twitter feeds. Most put modesty to one side and are dedicated to highlighting their various personal accomplishments, often with extensive accompanying photographs and videos. For many years the best example was the crown prince of Dubai—who became ruler in early 2006. Indeed, Muhammad bin Rashid Al-Maktoum was the first prominent Gulf sheikh to have his own website,[53] and this was used extensively to demonstrate that he was not only an active politician, but also a prolific poet, a rifleman, and a champion horse-rider (winning medals at several international events).

Today, the current crown prince of Dubai—Hamdan bin Muhammad Al-Maktoum—has adopted much the same strategy, although in many ways he—or rather the ruling family's advisors—has taken personal image-building even further. Most of his activities still resonate with tribal heritage, such as horse-riding, falconry, and the writing and reciting of Bedouin-style poetry. But other activities are also featured to demonstrate his relative modernity (such as appearing in rap music videos), his fearlessness, and the tougher side to the personality.[54] In a rare personal interview conducted in 2011 the twenty-nine year-old Hamdan stated that he 'learned to be an effective leader through hobbies from skydiving to poetry' and that 'the hobbies exercised by the Crown Prince of Dubai are the hobbies of leadership in the foundation'. The interviewer summed these up as '…the hobby of parachute-jumping from aircraft to learn the courage and bravery and self-confidence, and the hobby of horse riding to learn leadership and a major focus, along with scuba diving, to learn patience and the search for secrets', before concluding that 'all of these hobbies give Hamdan bin Muhammad a major role in formulation of the outlook for the Emirate of Dubai, and paving the way for development plans in the emirate'. While on the subject of poetry, Hamdan also made clear references to taking on the role of 'philosopher king' having stated that 'I have lived childhood delighted, along with my father and my mother and my brothers and I grew up in an environment that allowed me to get to know the true meaning of life, and meditate on the greatness of the Creator and the natural beauty of the desert, which gives a sense of harmony and consistency with nature, all contributed in building my character poetry since childhood, [and] on the other hand taught me and my father Sheikh Muhammad bin Rashid, from a young age that hard work guarantees conquering the impossible'.[55]

Heritage and history

Helping remind citizens why hereditary monarchies still exist, why some individuals are entitled to build cults of personality and promote localised nationalism, and why these monarchies enjoy special characteristics that somehow exempt them from democratic development, the Gulf ruling families and their governments have expended considerable effort and expense at creating museums, restoring old buildings, and funding other projects connected to tribal heritage and the region's history. While such activities in themselves are not unusual, what is remarkable is the central role they often play in government planning and the vast resources assigned to them—at least compared to elsewhere in the developing world where other priorities usually loom higher. In many cases government authorities responsible for heritage have been set up in Gulf monarchies before even departments for tourism or the environment. And in Oman, the only full minister (apart from the deputy prime minister)[56] who is actually a member of the ruling family is the minister for heritage and culture.[57]

Although there are a few exceptions—especially in Qatar and Abu Dhabi, where more broadly focused museums are being established—most of the museums and cultural projects in the region tend to be quite narrowly focused on the pre-oil past. There is usually an emphasis on the background and history of the ruling families themselves, and it is commonplace to see giant ruling family trees adorning walls in the region's museums. In most cases these provide a quick visual link between centuries-old founding fathers and whoever the current ruler is—the latter usually having his name printed in bold, circled, or with a larger picture than his ancestors. In the case of Qatar, this has been described as 'heritage and history [being] mythologised to support the ruling family. It is in appearing to preserve Qatari heritage… that the legitimacy of the Al-Thani, especially the emir, is assured'.[58]

There is also usually an emphasis on traditional, pre-oil economy activities such as boat-building, rope-making, basket-weaving, pottery, or glass-blowing. Often these are housed in 'heritage villages' which are usually staffed and operated by citizens employed by the responsible government authority. Old forts and watchtowers have been lovingly restored, often at great expense, and many of these look magnificent. Some older looking buildings have, however, been built from scratch—sometimes with breeze blocks behind the façade—including forts on islands, brand new 'old souqs', as in Qatar and Kuwait, and dozens of newly built 'windcatcher' or *barjeel* towers, as seen in Dubai's 2004-built Madinat Jumeirah development. Heritage-focused festivals, competitions, and other events have also been set up in recent years. These have included date-growing tournaments, $250,000 heritage awards sponsored by rulers,[59] falcon-hunting and sword dancing tournaments, the unveiling of world record-breaking 15 metre swords, and the staging of the world's largest *youla* Bedouin dances.[60] Well-funded camel races also take place across the region, but mostly in Oman and the UAE. Much has been written on these races, often demonstrating that they were never a traditional pursuit, and are instead examples of 'invented tradition'[61]—providing a spectacle that can bring together ruling families and their citizens in a pseudo-traditional context, far away from the urban skyscrapers and other evidence of the oil era.

Together, these developments form part of an entire region-wide industry that seems committed to creating 'living memories' of the Gulf monarchies' crucial early period of state formation.[62] Or, as a recent study described of Qatar, they are 'expensive and widely publicised attempts to showcase Qatari and Islamic culture [which] attest to the concern with the preservation of the image of cultural authenticity'.[63] Given that many of the attractions are visited by nationals, expatriates, and tourists alike, the industry is in many ways helping to re-orientalise the region and its population from both inside and out. As discussed, this process has important political benefits for the surviving traditional monarchies. Significantly, the more awkward aspects of the monarchies' state-formation— namely the relationships between the ruling families and Britain, or the region's reaction to Arab nationalism in the 1950s and '60s—feature rarely in these state-sponsored projects. The massive impact of oil wealth on society and the economy also often remains out of focus, although there are notable exceptions, such as the Abu Dhabi Petroleum Exhibition, which has done much to catalogue that emirate's transformation. In general, the school and university curricula in the Gulf monarchies also tend to shy away from these topics: in some cases local or regional history is never taught, or if it is it dwells on the pre-oil era and skirts more sensitive issues. There are, however, some exceptions, such as Qatar University, which recently introduced modules in Gulf history and society. It is likely that more of the region's schools and universities will soon have to follow Qatar's suit, as demand for the subject will probably grow from both young nationals and expatriates. Bahrain is also an interesting case, given the sectarian tensions discussed later in this book. School and university textbooks have been used to promote an official history of the country, which seems to have little bearing on reality. The ruling Al-Khalifa family is usually portrayed as having liberated Bahrain, rather than conquering it, and earlier periods when the island was ruled by Shia dynasties appear to be glossed over.[64]

Co-opting religion

Viewed as a double-edged sword, religion—and most especially Islam— has been considered both a threat and an opportunity for the Gulf monarchies. As will be discussed later, Islamist movements—both intellectual and militant—have frequently questioned the status quo in these states. Most have highlighted the un-Islamic behaviour of the various ruling families, the slide into autocracy, the reliance on non-Islamic foreign powers for security, and rampant corruption among other matters. As such, these groups have often represented a powerful alternative and sometimes dissenting voice on the Arabian Peninsula, and in some cases have even been joined by establishment figures. Indeed, as has been noted, '…because Islam is a transcendent religion that can never be fully co-opted, [even such autocratic] governments must cede some autonomy to state-supported religious institutions or elites, thereby raising the prospect that elements of the religious establishment could defect to the Islamist opposition'.[65]

The Saudi ruling family has always been in the tightest position, given its described alliance with the Wahhabi movement, given the presence of two of Islam's holiest shrines in Mecca and Medina, and given its hosting of millions of Muslim pilgrims each year. Since 1986 the king of Saudi Arabia even changed his official title to 'Custodian of the Two Holy Mosques'[66]—reviving a pious title formerly used by the caliphs, the Ottoman sultans, and Egypt's Mamluk sultans. But the smaller Gulf monarchies, even though none claim such specific religious credentials, are also wary. Much like Saudi Arabia, all rely on non-Islamic powers—namely the US—for their security guarantees, with most also physically hosting such troops on their territory. And since 9/11, and the Anglo-American invasions on nearby Muslim countries—Afghanistan and Iraq—their position has clearly become more precarious.

The strategies for containing and co-opting Islam have varied in each of the monarchies, depending on their circumstances, although there are some common patterns. In a similar manner to the recently deposed leaders of the Arab authoritarian republics, loyal clerics of the Gulf's ruling families have from time to time invoked certain Koranic passages in order to justify absolute power. As per a late-2011 statement by Al-Azhar University on the Arab Spring, this has usually been done by narrowly interpreting a verse[67] which states 'O you who have believed, obey Allah and obey the Messenger and those in authority among you'. The verse has frequently been cited in isolation, but as the Al-Azhar statement contends, it should never have been cited out of context, and especially without considering the preceding verse,[68] which states 'Indeed Allah commands you to render the trusts to whom they are due and when you judge between people to judge with justice'.[69] The Saudi ruling family has probably gone the furthest with this strategy, with the Wahhabi religious establishment and its government representatives claiming that the Al-Saud enjoy 'rightful leadership' or *wali al-ahd* on this very basis.

The smaller Gulf monarchies, notably Qatar and the UAE have instead concentrated on using their resources to police and fund their mosques and domestic religious establishments. Almost all clerics are government employees, and these are quite closely monitored. Most have to carry photo identification cards, and their sermons usually have to be chosen from an official list of approved topics, drawn up by the relevant government body each week. A 2006 cable from the US embassy in Abu Dhabi confirms this practice, describing how 'UAE officials publicly and strongly condemn extremism and terrorist attacks, anti-extremism has been the focus of government-approved Friday sermons in the mosques'.[70] As well as providing generous salaries to clerics, thus slotting them into the rentier state's giant public sector, wealth in these monarchies has also been used to build large and often lavish mosques, religious schools, and other institutions. Unsurprisingly some of the biggest mosques in the world are now in the Gulf monarchies—such as Abu Dhabi's Sheikh Zayed Grand Mosque, which was built by the government and can accommodate 40,000 worshippers. Taking several years to complete, it cost more than $540 million and is the burial place of the late Zayed bin Sultan Al-Nahyan. Although there are some exceptions—such as Qatar's largest mosque, which is simply called 'Qatar Mosque' or 'Fanar',[71] and the proposed new Al-Farooq Mosque in Dubai—most of the largest mosques in the Gulf monarchies usually carry the name of a key ruling family member, despite invariably having been built using state funds. There are of course countless other projects connecting Islam to the largesse of the ruling families or the state, some of them highly innovative and often winning positive headlines for the sponsors. In the UAE, for example, the Dubai International Holy Koran Award Committee has begun planning and designing a holy book collection or *mushaf* named after Abu Dhabi's ruler—the 'Sheikh Khalifa bin Zayed Al-Nahyan Mushaf'. The aim is to produce a million of these volumes which will then be freely distributed 'under orders of the prime minister'.[72] Set on its own island and designed by the same architect as the contemporary section of the Paris Louvre, Qatar's enormous Islamic Arts Museum is another powerful example; one closely associated with the ruler and his high-profile wife Moza bint Nasser Al-Misnad. It opened in late 2008 and has been featured in dozens of international newspapers and magazines.

Also providing ruling families with religious legitimacy, or more accurately allowing rulers to portray themselves as tolerant, benevolent monarchs, there has been much support for other religions in some Gulf monarchies. With the exception of Saudi Arabia—where all other religions are banned—Christianity is booming in the Gulf monarchies, courtesy of substantial Indian and Filipino expatriate populations. Churches for almost all denominations exist in the five smaller Gulf states, including even evangelical chapels. Prime land, usually donated by a ruling family member, continues to be gifted to these churches to aid in their expansion. In Abu Dhabi, an ancient Nestorian Christian monastery which had been discovered on one of the emirate's outlying islands was even opened to the public in 2010 by the government's Tourism and Development Investment Company[73]—thus acknowledging and celebrating the country's pre-Islamic past. Hindu and Sikh temples also exist in some of these states, as does a Zoroastrian tower of silence in Dubai, which has on occasion been the location of Zoroastrian world congresses. Although, as discussed in the following chapter, there remains a nominal boycott on Israel by the Gulf monarchies and synagogues are not permitted in any of these states, there are nonetheless some pockets of tolerance for Jews. In Bahrain for example, there exists a tiny community of Bahraini Jews. Although their number has dwindled from several hundred to just a few dozen, they are reportedly well respected and have served in the upper house of the parliament. In 2008 the king even appointed a Jew as Bahrain's joint ambassador to the US, Canada, and Brazil.[74]

Environmental credentials

The Gulf monarchies rarely conjure an image of being environmentally friendly, given the centrality of hydrocarbons to the region and the various associated heavy industries, most of which rely on abundant fossil fuel. Moreover, the generous public sector salaries, the extensive welfare benefits, and the other trappings of the rentier state also lead to expectations of high consumption lifestyles for many Gulf nationals, including multiple vehicles per household and a heavy reliance on air-conditioning. According to the US Department of Energy's Carbon Dioxide Information Analysis Center, the Gulf monarchies now suffer from some of world's highest per capita carbon dioxide emissions. In 2008 Qatar was the worst ranked country in the world, with 53.5 metric tonnes of carbon dioxide emissions per capita. The UAE was the third worst, with 34.6 metric tonnes, while Bahrain was ranked fifth, with 29 metric tonnes. Kuwait, Saudi Arabia, and Oman were all not far behind, being ranked seventh, thirteenth and fourteenth respectively.[75] Given the rapid development in the region since 2008, especially in Saudi Arabia, Qatar, and the UAE, it is likely that they remain among the world's worst offenders—perhaps having increased their lead. Waste per capita is also believed to be very high in the Gulf monarchies, with a recent study concluding that Abu Dhabi had one of the highest waste per capita rates in the world—some six times greater than Western European countries.[76] Improvements have been made across the region, but most waste is still thought to be dumped in desert landfill sites. Although vehicles per capita is a less useful measure for the Gulf monarchies, given that the rate for citizens is likely to be much higher than that for expatriates, it is noteworthy that Qatar is now firmly in the world top ten according to World Bank figures, with 724 vehicles per thousand residents, while Bahrain and Kuwait are close behind.[77]

Nevertheless, despite the region's poor track record, protection of the environment has recently become a high profile policy in some Gulf monarchies. The UAE and Qatar governments in particular have transformed what was previously a liability for their regional and international reputations into something of a strength. A plethora of projects, institutions, new government departments, and other initiatives have been announced—most of which aim not only to remedy their domestic environmental crises, but also to promote international research and development into cleaner energy and other environmental clauses.[78] In much the same way that wealth distribution strategies to citizens and funding of religious establishments have been closely associated with key members of the ruling families, the same has often been true with these environmental projects. The state-backed media have provided extensive coverage, often publicly linking a specific ruling family member to a development, thus winning him or her favourable domestic headlines. It has also been a policy area which has largely attracted favourable international coverage, with many of the articles being republished for domestic readers.

The new Qatar Environment and Energy Research Institute for example falls directly under the umbrella of the ruler's wife. Aiming to 'mitigate climate change and contaminants harmful to the environment' and focusing on 'Qatar's desert and marine ecologies, plant and animal life, and air quality', it is well financed and has thus far been lauded by the domestic media[79] and further afield. A recent RAND Corporation publication focusing on the institute, for example, begins by stating that 'Qatar's leadership has created a vision of sustainability for the country'.[80] More extensively, Abu Dhabi has set up the new Environmental Agency Abu Dhabi (EAD) and recently commissioned the Stockholm Environmental Institute in Sweden to formulate a rigorous climate policy for the emirate.[81] Since 2009 there has also been the Zayed Future Energy Prize which now presents winning companies or government departments with prizes of over $4 million.[82] All photographs displayed on the prize's official website feature the crown prince in the centre of groups of high profile international dignitaries, while all text descriptions of the prize refer to the 'legacy of Sheikh Zayed'.[83] But by far the most high profile environment-related initiative in the region has been Abu Dhabi's Masdar City. Being built by the Abu Dhabi Future Energy Company (ADFEC), which is a subsidiary of the crown prince's Mubadala Development Company, the plan has been to create a large carbon-neutral development in the emirate's hinterland. The broader aim is for Masdar to provide the infrastructure for a free zone that will allow up to 1,500 renewable energy and other environment-related international companies to base themselves in Abu Dhabi, or at least have their regional headquarters there. Some of these will be focused on carbon capture technologies and it is expected that they will export their services to nearby countries still relying on outdated hydrocarbon extraction technologies.[84] ADFEC is also hoping to attract research and development focused companies to Masdar in an effort to make Abu Dhabi the region's capital for green technologies.[85] Similarly, Mubadala's investment in the Finnish company WinWinD is likely to lead to a wind power joint venture in Masdar.[86] In support of all these companies is a new research centre—the Masdar Institute—and several leading international research bodies are already operating there.[87] Again, there has been extensive coverage by the domestic media, and although there has been some criticism of Masdar in the international media, Mubadala and the crown prince have generally benefited from ADFEC's overall aims.

3

EXPLAINING SURVIVAL—EXTERNAL MATTERS

In parallel to their domestic ruling bargains, there also exist several strategies aimed at securing the survival and raising the status of the Gulf monarchies in the region and internationally. For many years the priority was building strong links with the rest of the Arab world, especially Palestine and those Arab states that refused to acknowledge Israel. This had the twin aims of satisfying pro-Palestinian and anti-Israeli sentiments in their own populations while also allowing the ruling families to sit more comfortably alongside Arab nationalist governments. More recently, and especially since Kuwait's invasion by Iraq and subsequent liberation by a US-led force in 1991, the priority has been gaining influence and good standing in those states perceived as the most reliable security guarantors—namely the Western powers. Rising tensions with Iran, and a seeming impasse over its developing nuclear programme, have meant that such Western-centric efforts have continued to intensify. But there is now also the added dimension of seeking improved relations with the Eastern powers, including China, which have not only become key trading partners but may also soon offer alternative security guarantees. A third, but interconnected priority for the Gulf monarchies has been the need to forge good relations with other Muslim states and communities, including those far beyond the Arab world. Complimenting their efforts at boosting Islamic credentials and heading off domestic Islamist opposition, this strategy is also intended to deflect and counter external Islamist extremist aggression—a threat which became particularly acute following 9/11 and the subsequent al-Qaeda campaign in Saudi Arabia.[1]

To some extent, the Gulf monarchies have employed conventional strategies to achieve these aims: building up military defensive capabilities with equipment primarily sourced from the West; joining regional organisations such as the Arab League; and attempts to build collective security arrangements between themselves—most notably the Gulf Cooperation Council. As will be discussed later, despite much scholarly attention having been paid to these strategies, they have been fraught with risks and their successes remain limited. Instead a number of other, subtler, policies perhaps better explain the external survival of the Gulf monarchies.

First, as a natural extension of the domestic rentier state and their popular wealth distribution strategies, the Gulf monarchies have become increasingly keen to distribute some of their resources to less fortunate neighbours, mostly in the form of development aid, charity, or gifts to other Arab, Muslim, or nearby states. Second, efforts have been made by most Gulf monarchies to use their location and resources to position themselves as useful 'active neutrals'—either by despatching peacekeeping missions or mediating regional disputes. This strategy has usually allowed them to avoid taking sides in nearby conflicts, while also consolidating a reputation of benevolence and peacefulness in less stable or potentially threatening states. Also it has helped deflect broader Arab public opinion away from their difficult-to-disguise dependency on Western military protection. Third, there have been long-running efforts to fund museums, universities, and other cultural projects and institutions in the Western powers—and increasingly their Eastern counterparts—in order to improve recognition and opinion of the Gulf monarchies, and thus help build up their 'soft power' base in these influential states. In some cases even development aid has been channelled into these countries for this purpose. As with the domestic survival strategies, there are again significant divergences in these sets of policies, depending on the individual circumstances of each Gulf monarchy. Nevertheless, a pattern is clearly evident, with at least some aspects of each strategy being visible in each monarchy.

Development assistance and international charity

Since the 1970s the wealthier Gulf monarchies—notably Saudi Arabia, the UAE, and Kuwait—have been among the biggest donors of development aid to the poorer Arab states in the Middle East and North Africa. More recently they have been joined by gas-rich Qatar, and their aid programmes have now reached out much further, with countless donations to communities in East Africa, South Asia, South East Asia, and even Eastern Europe. Most of the aid has been carefully controlled by the Gulf monarchies' respective ministries for foreign affairs or by well-established state-controlled institutions such as the Saudi Fund for Development (set up in 1974), the Abu Dhabi Fund for Development (which dates from 1971 under the name Abu Dhabi Fund for Arab Development),[2] and the Kuwait Fund for Arab Economic Development (established in 1961, making it the first foreign aid vehicle set up by a developing state). However, such official development assistance (ODA) is only part of the story, given the many individual ruling family members and other state-sponsored charities in the Gulf monarchies also involved in such activities. The UAE has probably gone the furthest in trying to organise its various efforts under one umbrella, by setting up an External Aid Liaison Bureau in 2008. This was partly a response to disbelief and criticism from various United Nations representatives following a potentially accurate claim from a UAE minister that 3.6 per cent of GDP was allocated to development aid.[3] Unsurprisingly, given the various rulers' described efforts to boost their personal legitimacy, many of the more tangible results of development assistance (such as hospitals, mosques, and schools) in recipient countries are named after the monarch in question.

Overall, throughout the period 1976–2006 it was estimated that over 4.2 per cent of Saudi Arabia's GDP or about $49 billion was devoted to development aid,[4] while in the UAE, Kuwait, and Qatar it is thought that aid has often been over 3 per cent of GDP. Although this is still much less than the Gulf monarchies spend on military hardware—which is usually between 4 and 11 per cent of GDP[5]—the gap does seem to be narrowing as ODA becomes an increasingly central pillar of foreign policy for these states. It is important to appreciate that Gulf ODA as a percentage of GDP is often higher than in the West, including the United States. In the Arab world, Palestine has unsurprisingly been the oldest and most generously targeted ODA destination. Over the past decade

Saudi Arabia has supplied the Palestinian Authority with nearly $500 million in aid, and in addition has channelled hundreds of millions of dollars to help Palestinian refugees through both the Arab League and the United Nations Relief and Works Agency. Today it is thought that Saudi Arabia alone provides Palestine with between $14 million and $17 million per month.[6] Likewise, the UAE has supplied Palestine with considerable aid over the years and in the past decade it is thought that over $4 billion has been provided, including a $62 million residential complex built in 2004 and named after Abu Dhabi's late ruler, Zayed bin Sultan Al-Nahyan, and the $70 million rebuilding of the Jenin Camp after its destruction in 2002.[7] Crucially, despite Hamas' surprise election victory in 2006, Gulf ODA to Palestine has not slowed. If anything, it has accelerated—perhaps best symbolised by the Sheikh Khalifa bin Zayed Mosque in Bethany, named after Abu Dhabi's current ruler. At a cost of nearly $5 million, the mosque will have the tallest minarets in Palestine when complete.[8] This response contrasts with other donors such as the US—which has been reviewing its aid programme given Hamas' ostensible ties to terror organisations.[9] As such, the Gulf monarchies' role in Palestine's development is now unparalleled.

The Lebanon has been another major Gulf ODA destination, given its similar centrality and relevance to regional politics. After the resolution of the Lebanese civil war in 1990, the UAE injected between $500 and $700 million into the stricken country, and funding was provided for the Lebanese Army to purchase high-tech mine-clearing equipment.[10] Following the 2006 conflict with Israel, the UAE Red Crescent Society provided Lebanon with a further $300 million as part of the Emirates Solidarity Project. Most of the money has been spent on rebuilding physical infrastructure damaged by Israeli bombing and constructing new hospitals and schools.[11] Since then the UAE is believed to have pledged and delivered a further $300 million in aid to Lebanon.[12] In 2006 and 2007 Saudi Arabia provided the Lebanese Central Bank with nearly $2.7 billion, including $500 million to be spent on reconstruction.[13] Qatar has been equally keen to assist, having ploughed an estimated $250 million into rebuilding Bin Jbeil—the most badly damaged Lebanese town in the 2006 war. Much of this money was used to construct 12,000 new houses and repair 470 places of worship—including Sunni and Shia mosques and Christian churches.[14]

Iraq has been a more problematic recipient of aid from the Gulf monarchies, mostly due to Kuwait's insistence that the post-2003 Iraqi government eventually repays about $16 billion of loans—most of which were provided to Saddam Hussein's government by Kuwaiti banks prior to Iraq's invasion of Kuwait in 1990. Nevertheless, in its keenness to head off Iranian encroachment in Iraq, Saudi Arabia's assistance has been very generous, ranging from reconstruction projects to the pledging of billions of dollars of export guarantees and the providing of massive soft loans. The UAE's assistance to Iraq has perhaps been even greater, with several large donations having been made since 2005, including a gift of $215 million for the reconstruction effort,[15] and the UAE Armed Forces' supplying of helicopters and other equipment for the new Iraqi military.[16] In summer 2008 the UAE announced that it would also scrap all of Iraq's outstanding debts to the UAE—amounting to some $7 billion—so as to 'help alleviate the economic burdens endured by the brotherly Iraqi people'.[17]

Many East African countries have benefited from Gulf ODA: originally those with substantial Arab or Muslim populations, but more recently some others have begun to receive assistance. The UAE has been dispensing aid to Somalia since the early 1990s, and in 2008 began supplying medicines and foodstuffs to the Sudan.[18] Saudi Arabia has followed a similar path, having allocated $10 million in aid to the Horn of Africa countries through the World Food Programme and with ruling family member Al-Waleed bin Talal Al-Saud having personally provided a further $1 million of aid, specifically to help Kenya. The latter gift prompted the World Food Programme's Executive Director to claim '… it is exactly the kind of support that these desperate people deserve from both private donors and governments'.[19] Qatar is also getting involved, having recently paid for the reconstruction of the Asmara International Stadium in Eritrea and the building of a new 'Qatari-Eritrean Hall of Friendship' as part of the complex.[20] Although these sums and assistance packages are far smaller than those currently being channelled to the Arab states, it is likely that more Gulf ODA will be sent to East Africa as security in the region deteriorates and it remains open to pirates and terror groups that may target Gulf interests.

For many years South Asian states—primarily India and Pakistan—have received generous aid from the Gulf monarchies, not least due to their shared economic histories and labour migration flows. But over the last decade the value of aid has dramatically increased, mainly as a response to the perceived threat of al-Qaeda and other Afghanistan and

Pakistan-based organisations to the region's security. After the 2005 earthquake in Kashmir, Saudi Arabia immediately donated $3 million to Pakistan and promised a further $570 million in follow-up assistance—the largest package provided by any donor state. A new organisation was set up—the Saudi Public Assistance for Pakistan Earthquake Victims—which set about constructing over 4,000 new houses at a cost of $17 million for some of the homeless Pakistanis.[21] More recently, following the 2010 floods in Pakistan, Saudi Arabia has again been the primary donor to Pakistan's relief efforts, supplying more than $360 million in aid and helping to build two new hospitals.[22] Over the same period it is believed that Saudi Arabia provided Afghanistan with over $200 million in aid. Both Kuwait and the UAE pledged $100 million to Pakistan after the 2005 earthquake,[23] and their collective aid efforts to Afghanistan also amount to several hundred million dollars. Since 9/11 the UAE Red Crescent Society has supplied over $40 million, with a further $30 million having been supplied by other Abu Dhabi-based groups.[24] This has been used to construct a large hospital, six clinics, a public library, eleven schools and even a 6,000 student capacity Zayed University of Afghanistan. A Zayed City is also being built to house over 2000 displaced persons,[25] again named after Abu Dhabi's late ruler.

Development aid has been channelled into other parts of Asia too, especially in countries with either a predominantly Muslim population or a labour supplying relationship with the Gulf monarchies. Although Gulf aid was slow to reach Indonesia and elsewhere in East Asia following the 2004 tsunami, with Saudi Arabia's response being described as 'shameful' by Al-Jazeera and with Kuwait's *Al-Qabas* newspaper urging its government 'to give them more as we are rich',[26] the same mistake is unlikely to be made again. Qatar, for example, now has a new state-sponsored charity—Reach Out to Asia—specifically to provide aid and educational outreach to poorer parts of South East Asia. Chaired by one of the emir's daughters, its significance has been described as 'not being lost on Qatar's large population of South East Asian migrant workers'.[27] The UAE is being similarly proactive, with its aid programme now reaching as far as Mongolia. Commissioned by the new Mongolia-based Zayed bin Sultan Al-Nahyan Charitable and Humanitarian Foundation and supervised by a lesser member of the Abu Dhabi ruling family, a complex containing housing, schools, mosques, and healthcare facilities is being built at a cost of about $1 million. Significantly, the project has been described as being for '…the Mongolian Muslims living in Olgiy… situated in the extreme west of Mongolia and sharing borders with China and Russia'.[28]

Surprising to many, Gulf ODA has also played a major role in Europe, or more specifically the development of Muslim communities in Eastern Europe. Most notable has been the substantial aid that has flowed into Kosovo and other parts of the Balkans since the conflicts of the late 1990s. The government-backed Saudi Joint Committee for the Relief of Kosovo spent $5 million funding housing projects and providing food and medical supplies; it also paid for the building of mosques and the setting up of 'religious programmes',[29] while the Saudi Red Crescent Society despatched medical volunteers to the various refugee camps.[30] The UAE has been equally if not more active in Kosovo, with its total aid programme now believed to have totalled some $30 million. The Muhammad bin Rashid Charitable and Humanitarian Establishment—named after the current ruler of Dubai—ploughed several million dollars into the Kosovo relief effort, and in 1999 the UAE's terrestrial TV stations participated in a charity telethon. The event raised $15 million and then Muhammad doubled this sum, although not anonymously. The money was used to build over fifty new mosques in Kosovo in 2000.[31] Upon visiting Dubai in 2009 to take part in a university graduation ceremony, former US Secretary of State Colin Powell referred to this and other Dubai development assistance in the presence of Muhammad by stating that the 'emirate is now on a par with New York, London, and Paris' and 'praising the humanitarian and charitable campaigns launched by the wise leadership to help people around the world realise the concept of wealth-sharing and achieve social equality among peoples in various communities, especially the poor'.[32]

Active neutrality: peacekeeping and mediation

Closely connected to the dispensing of development assistance and international charity have been the increasingly extensive peace-keeping missions despatched by some Gulf monarchies to regional hotspots—often involving the same countries in receipt of ODA. Although there are some exceptions, in most cases the Gulf deployments have not seen frontline action and have usually been in a supporting role to forces from other states. Nevertheless their activities have often led to favourable regional and international headlines. As a small state with a small indigenous population, the UAE perhaps provides the best example of this strategy. Having tried to intervene in almost every regional dispute since the 1970s, its peace-keeping missions have helped it punch well above its weight in the Arab world. In 1977 UAE soldiers[33] were deployed overseas for the first time, when a contingent was sent to join the Joint Arab Deterrent Force in the Lebanon.[34] And in 1992 the UAE Armed Forces made its maiden intervention outside the Middle East by sending engineers and a peace-keeping force to assist US operations in Somalia.[35] During the mid-1990s more UAE troops arrived in Somalia in addition to Rwanda and Mozambique.[36] Significantly, in 1995 the UAE was the first Arab state to intervene in a modern European conflict when it airlifted wounded Muslims out of Bosnia. And by 1999 the UAE was again proactive in the Balkans, sending a force to help protect the embattled Kosovars[37] in tandem with its development assistance efforts to the region.

Probably the most important Gulf peace-keeping mission came to light in 2008, again involving the UAE. First revealed by the BBC, likely because the UAE authorities were initially cautious about publicising their anti-Taliban activities and explicit support for the US-led coalition, it was reported that about 250 UAE troops and a number of armoured cars had been deployed to Afghanistan since 2003 in order to maintain supply line security and deliver humanitarian aid. It was also reported by the BBC that the UAE contingent had had to fend off Taliban attacks, thus making it the only Arab force in Afghanistan that was actually engaging the enemy.[38] The commanding officer had stated 'if we have any types of personal attacks we react with fire. And after that we go to the elders in this area and say: "Why are you shooting us? We came here to help you." And we try to convince the people about the US, about British. They came to give peace'.[39]

More recently, the UAE's state-backed media has reported extensively on the contingent's activities, claiming UAE troops have been actively participating in the Afghan National Army's 'hearts and minds' campaign in Helmand province. According to one British observer attached to the troops, the presence of such Muslim troops in Afghanistan has been drawing crowds, with many Afghans 'willing to shake hands with these men from "Arabistan"… and with the Emiratis handing out copies of the Koran, notebooks, pens, and chocolate'. The observer went on to describe what he considered the UAE contingent's 'most effective weapon in the conflict in Afghanistan'—the offering of invitations from senior UAE soldiers to village elders to join them for midday prayers. He claimed this was '...a potent force at work—one the Taliban dared not challenge and one the [US-led] coalition cannot wield. The robust kindness offered by these Emirati troops is a simple but powerful weapon for change in Afghanistan'. The observer also connected the peace-keeping operation with the UAE's development assistance to Afghanistan, explaining that close to the UAE's base in the country 'Afghan men can drive their families along a UAE-funded tarmac road, visit a UAE-built clinic where their women and children can receive treatment from Emirati female doctors, while a UAE-funded radio station offers news and music programming in Pashtun'.[40]

Best reflecting the massive political benefits to the UAE's ruling families of the mission in Afghanistan was the widely reported screening of a documentary film at the crown prince of Abu Dhabi's *majlis* in August 2011. Attended by a vast number of UAE dignitaries, including most of the UAE's rulers, crown princes, and ministers, there were also delegations present from other Gulf monarchies, including Bahrain's minister for foreign affairs, along with about 400 other guests. Entitled 'Mission: Winds of Goodness', the documentary focused on 'honouring the brave individuals fulfilling important duties on behalf of their country' while also demonstrating 'how the UAE forces must rely on their courage, training, and most importantly each other, in order to carry out this important work in the most hostile and challenging of circumstances'. Significantly, the press release published by the UAE's official state news agency also described the 'UAE's policy to provide support to Afghanistan including healthcare and education projects, such as the construction of clinics and schools; and developing sufficient community infrastructure, such as mosques, roads, and schools' before concluding that '...the UAE's presence as part of an international coalition in Afghanistan has helped maintain security to ensure that humanitarian projects are not undermined by criminal forces that seek to disrupt the provision of aid'.[41]

As regards mediating conflicts and disputes, in recent years—and especially since the 1995 accession of its current ruler, Hamad bin Khalifa Al-Thani—Qatar has been by far the most prominent regional peace-broker, having hosted countless conferences and been intimately involved in several key peace deals, often in countries that have benefited from its development assistance. Moreover, as will be discussed later in this book, since the advent of the Arab Spring in 2011 Hamad's efforts have become even more prolific. Qatar's newfound role should perhaps come as no surprise, given that it is the smallest and, per capita, the wealthiest of the Gulf monarchies. The country would be a valuable prize for any foreign aggressor, and given these precarious geo-strategic circumstances Qatar's ruling family probably has the most to gain from positioning their state as the region's active neutral *par excellence* or, as other observers have described it 'the Switzerland of the Gulf'. An article in Qatar's current constitution even underlines its commitment to such a strategy, while also carefully stating that it would never involve itself in the domestic affairs of another state: '…the foreign policy of the State is based on the principle of strengthening international peace and security by means of encouraging peaceful resolution of international disputes; and shall support the right of peoples to self-determination; and shall not interfere in the domestic affairs of states; and shall cooperate with peace-loving nations'.[42]

Prior to 2011, Qatar's most notable success was its role in ending the standoff in Lebanon between Hezbollah and the broad, anti-Syrian 'March 14' alliance. Following nearly a year and a half of city centre protests that began in December 2006, Hezbollah-aligned militias finally occupied central Beirut in May 2008 and for more than a week brought the country to a standstill. Promptly inviting representatives from all factions to Doha, Qatar's ruler staged the Lebanese National Dialogue Conference which quickly resulted in the forming of a new national unity government and the appointing of a new Lebanese president.[43] Known as the 'Doha Agreement', Qatar's efforts in ending the deadlock were praised by the UN Security Council which stated that it 'welcomed and strongly supported the agreement reached by Lebanese leaders in Doha… which constituted an essential step towards the resolution of the current crisis'. In Lebanon firework displays and music concerts were held across the country, with several banners featuring the Qatari ruler being prominently displayed.

In 2007 Qatar then played a key role in brokering the extradition of six Bulgarian nurses from Libya. Having been accused of deliberately infecting over 400 children with HIV in 1998, they had been sentenced to death before having their sentences commuted to life imprisonment. Although France captured most of the headlines in facilitating their release, Nicolas Sarkozy conceded that '…some humanitarian mediation by the friendly government of Qatar was decisive in helping with the release of the medics'.[44] Perhaps most controversially, Qatar was heavily involved in brokering the 2010 ceasefire in the Sudan between the Khartoum government and the Darfur rebels. Having invited the Sudanese president—Omar Al-Bashar—to Doha, despite an International Criminal Court arrest warrant having been issued for his alleged war crimes and crimes against humanity, the Qatari ruler also invited the presidents of Chad and Eritrea.[45] A permanent truce was eventually signed in summer 2011, with Qatar's role again being fêted by both regional players and the international community. Significantly, the signing session took place in a Doha hotel, presided over by the ruler and in the presence of several African heads of state in addition to UN and African Union representatives. Emphasising Qatar's efforts, Hamad stated that '…the State of Qatar is keen to coordinate with its regional and international partners to see the people of Darfur and Sudan enjoy security and stability, as they are the two conditions for development and stability'.[46] Also in East Africa, Qatar's attempts to resolve the long-running border disputes between Eritrea and Djibouti have also received international attention, although success has not yet been forthcoming. In 2010 a high-ranking Qatari delegation arrived in Djibouti after previously visiting Eritrea. But without support from Ethiopia—which broke off relations with Qatar in 2008 on the grounds that 'Qatar's support for Eritrea had made it a major source of instability in the Horn of Africa'—an agreement was not reached.[47]

As a more established regional peace-broker, the UAE has also had a number of successful interventions, albeit more low profile than Qatar's efforts. The first example of such UAE mediation was in 1974 when Abu Dhabi's ruler solved a territorial dispute between Egypt and Libya.[48] More notably, in 1991 he then attempted to save Iraq from full scale invasion by meeting with the Saudi king and Egypt's Hosni Mubarak in an effort to forge an agreement between Saddam Hussein and the displaced ruler of Kuwait, Jabar Al-Ahmad Al-Sabah.[49] In early 2003 Abu Dhabi was again an active intermediary, proposing an emergency summit with the aim of diverting the US from attacking Iraq. A meeting was held in Sharm el-Sheikh and presided over by the Arab League Secretary-General.[50] Saddam Hussein and his family were reportedly offered sanctuary in Abu Dhabi if they complied with American demands to leave Iraq.[51] Since Khalifa bin Zayed Al-Nahyan's succession as ruler of Abu Dhabi in 2004, the UAE's has to some extent continued with these policies. In early 2007 the minister for foreign affairs flew to Iran to meet government representatives,[52] and later that year (and within the space of just one week) Khalifa separately hosted both Mahmoud Ahmadinejad and the US vice president Dick Cheney, seemingly in an effort to defuse the Iran-US nuclear standoff.[53] In 2008 the UAE was again active, inviting the US Secretary of State Condoleeza Rice, who was en-route to East Asia, to Abu Dhabi to debrief US envoy William Burns on his Iran negotiations and also to meet with the UAE minister for foreign affairs. Crucially, just one week before, Abu Dhabi's crown prince had received Ali Rida Sheikh Attar—an envoy of Mahmoud Ahmadinejad and under-secretary to the Iranian minister for foreign affairs.[54] Combined, these diplomatic actions earned the UAE praise during UN Security Council meetings in August 2008.[55]

Soft power in the West: strategic investments and development assistance

For many years the Gulf monarchies' soft power strategy in the West was primarily an offshoot of their sovereign wealth funds. In addition to these funds' investments in multinationals, blue-chip companies, and mature real estate; additional investments and associated sponsorships have been made in higher profile, headline-grabbing, ventures that may not necessarily turn a profit. The aim, it seems, has been to boost awareness of the Gulf monarchy in question with certain Western powers, at every level from government officials to members of the public. In almost all cases these brand-focused investments have been made in countries that either have a history of providing Gulf monarchies with protection or security guarantees, or can realistically be expected to provide assistance in a future emergency.

For the same reasons that it has emerged as the most energetic regional peace-broker, Qatar is unsurprisingly the most active proponent of the strategy. The ruling family-owned Qatar Holdings, for example, bought London's prestigious Harrods department store in 2010, after an earlier failed attempt to buy the British national grocery chain Sainsbury's. Having paid $2.3 billion for Harrods—believed to be an overly generous offer—Qatar Holdings' chairman (who is also Qatar's prime minister and a key member of the ruling family) announced that the purchase would not only 'add much value to its portfolio of investments' but that Harrods was also '…a historical place. I know it's important, not only for the British people, but it is important for tourism'. Similarly, the Qatar Holdings' vice-chairman described the purchase as a 'landmark transaction' for Qatar.[56] Meanwhile Qatar has been acquiring other iconic properties in London including the old Chelsea Barracks and the American Embassy building on Grosvenor Square. The building of Europe's tallest skyscraper—the London Shard—was also financed mostly by Qatar, namely the Central Bank of Qatar, which holds an 80 per cent share. The $3 billion, 310 metre tower houses two duplex apartments specifically for use by the Qatari ruling family, and its official opening ceremony in July 2012 was hosted by the Qatar Holdings' chairman.[57] When asked for comment, the Central Bank governor was clear about the rationale behind the investment, explaining that he was confident '…the Shard would become a symbol of the close ties between Qatar and the UK'. Likewise, the Qatari ambassador to the UK stated that '…the UK is a dear country to us… our investment is a long term investment, we don't need the cash now… we think the UK is the right place to put our investment. The UK is a strategic partner with our country'.[58]

Elsewhere in Europe Qatar has also been active, with the Qatar Foundation—chaired by the ruler's wife—signing a record $230 million sponsorship deal in 2011 with Spain's Barcelona Football Club,[59] one of the biggest brands in international soccer. Having previously shied away from shirt sponsorship and preferring to display the UNICEF children's charity logo, in 2010 an audit revealed that the club was nearly $500 million in debt. Although marketing experts were reported to have been working on finding a way of displaying both logos on the new shirts, it was admitted that if that proved impossible then the Qatar Foundation logo would take precedence.[60] This now appears to be the case, with the UNICEF logo having been relegated to the back. In France, it has been the turn of Qatar's largest sovereign wealth fund—the Qatar Investment Authority—which has also bought into soccer via a new, sports-focused investment vehicle, Qatar Sports Investments. In 2011 QSI took a controlling, 70 per cent stake in Paris St. Germain[61] and promptly appointed a Qatari national as the club's new president—the first non-French president in the club's history.

Although now out of the limelight, and a little less spendthrift since Dubai's 2009 crash and the subsequent Abu Dhabi bailout packages, the

UAE has also been a prominent brand-focused sovereign wealth investor in the West, and especially in Britain and the US. Dubai's various
investment vehicles have, for example, purchased the Carlton Tower and
Lowndes hotels in central London along with a fashionable art deco
hotel in Manhattan,[62] and more conspicuously, the London Eye and the
Madame Tussauds waxworks,[63] which were acquired in 2006 by Dubai
International Capital. In 2007 Dubai's Nakheel even purchased the
decommissioned iconic British cruise liner the QE2 for about $100 mil-
lion, planning to convert it into a floating hotel.[64] Most successful, in
terms of branding, has been Dubai's Emirates airline's $150 million fif-
teen year naming rights for London's Arsenal Football Club's new stadium, which was opened in 2006 in parallel with an eight year Emirates
shirt sponsorship deal for the club.[65] Now simply referred to as the 'Emirates Stadium', the Emirates logo is emblazoned on the side of the building and has become a key London landmark.

Abu Dhabi's iconic investments in the West are now also numerous,
with the Abu Dhabi Investment Company having paid a reported $800
million just before the beginning of the 2008 credit crunch for the famous
Chrysler Building in New York—a staple of Hollywood movie Manhattan panorama shots.[66] Equally conspicuous, in 2005 the crown prince's
Mubadala Development Company purchased a 5 per cent stake, worth
$130 million, in Italy's celebrated Ferrari car manufacturer.[67] Signifi-
cantly, this was followed up by Mubadala's sponsoring of the Ferrari Formula One team which involved the Mubadala logo appearing prominently
on the nosecones of Ferrari F1 cars.[68] Soccer, too, has been a priority for
Abu Dhabi, exemplified by the Abu Dhabi United Group for Development and Investment's purchase of Manchester City Football Club for
about $360 million in summer 2008.[69] Led by one of the crown prince's
younger brothers (and a deputy prime minister of the UAE), Mansour
bin Zayed Al-Nahyan, the group quickly installed one of the crown
prince's right hand men (who also serves as the chairman of Abu Dhabi's
Executive Affairs Authority) as the club's new chairman. Mirroring
Emirates' naming of the Arsenal stadium, Abu Dhabi's airline—Etihad
Airways—has now paid $642 million for naming rights for Manchester
City's stadium, which was originally built to host the Commonwealth
Games in 2002. The club's former chief executive officer[70] described it as
'one of the most important arrangements in the history of world foot-
ball'.[71] Today, Abu Dhabi's association with Manchester City is widely

reported and discussed in the British newspapers, with its chairman l
a frequent subject of articles in the sports supplements.

The other Gulf monarchies have also made high profile purchases in
the West, although due to greater caution or more limited resources they
have tended to capture less attention. Kuwait's Investment Dar, for
example, currently owns 51 per cent of Britain's Aston Martin luxury car
company[72]—a brand normally associated with James Bond and other
British action movies. Even Bahrain has been active, despite more modest sovereign wealth investment capabilities, with the state-backed
Mumtalakat Holding Company taking a 30 per cent stake in Britain's
McLaren Group in 2007—manufacturer of the McLaren supercar and
owner of the multiple F1 championship-winning McLaren Formula
One team.[73] In 2011 Mumtalakat increased its stake to 50 per cent, perhaps explaining McLaren's initial reluctance to boycott the 2011 Bahrain
Grand Prix following the first wave of protests in the kingdom, as discussed later in the book.

The Gulf monarchies' hosting of increasingly high profile international
sports events can also be considered a component of this strategy, as
although these are not directly connected to investments in Western
companies and are also intended to contribute to economic diversification (namely supporting nascent tourism industries) in the region, they
nonetheless make a strong contribution to the international sports industry and help boost awareness of the Gulf monarchies among primarily
western audiences. Alongside Bahrain, Abu Dhabi also hosts an annual
Formula One Grand Prix, while Dubai hosts an ATP tennis tournament
and European PGA golf tournament, among numerous other events.
Qatar's hosting of the 2022 FIFA World Cup is now by far the strongest example. Having defeated bids from several other countries, including the US and Japan, Qatar has committed to massive spending in order
to create the necessary infrastructure for the event, including at least
twelve brand new, world class stadiums. It has been estimated that the
total cost will be around $211 billion, with $163 billion being spent on
the stadiums and $47 billion being spent on transport infrastructure.
Thus a decade looms of lucrative contracts for construction companies
and sports-related industries, with Qatar likely to keep winning soccer-
related headlines in Western and other international newspapers for years
to come. Meanwhile Qatar is also intending to bid for both the 2017
World Athletics Championships and the 2020 Olympic Games.[74]

Offering further evidence of the Gulf monarchies' soft power strategy has been the increasing number of explicit gifts and donations to institutions and organisations in the West. In some senses, even though these involve wealth transfers from developing countries to developed countries, they can be viewed as a form of development assistance. Unsurprisingly, Qatar has been particularly active in this regard with its ambassador to the US visiting New Orleans in 2006 and pledging $100 million to help the victims of Hurricane Katrina. When asked to explain, the ambassador stated that this 'wasn't about improving Qatar's image in the US… or about public diplomacy'. Nevertheless, Qatar's gift was one of the largest foreign grants in the wake of Katrina, with one prominent Louisiana observer predicting that 'the [Qatari] ambassador would be met with lots of questions and praise for his country's benevolence when he comes to the region'.[75] But even more directly underlining the emirate's soft power strategy, when Qatar's prime minister was thanked by a US dignitary for the gift, he reportedly replied that 'We might have our own Katrina one day',[76] clearly hinting at Qatar's vulnerability and potential need for US protection. Another recent example of Qatari development assistance to the West is its setting up of a $50 million fund in 2011 to help young entrepreneurs in Paris' impoverished and predominantly immigrant North African suburbs or *banlieues*. Described as 'part of a broadening effort by the small country to expand its international presence through investment and diplomacy' the gift is likely to be well received by the French government, which has been accused of abandoning these restive, high unemployment, districts.[77]

The UAE has similarly been involved in urban regeneration projects, With Abu Dhabi having signed an agreement worth a reported $1.5 billion with Manchester City Council and regeneration body New East Manchester in 2011 to develop an 80 acre site close to the soccer stadium, thus tying in with Abu Dhabi's ownership of Manchester City Football Club. There are plans to build a cluster of new sporting facilities in addition to a swimming pool with the aim of 'using sport to inspire and transform the lives of children in an area with massive deprivation—and some of the lowest life expectancies in Britain'.[78] In September 2009, at the exact time when the UAE was waiting for the US Congress to ratify its civilian nuclear deal (which had been delayed due to allegations concerning the Abu Dhabi ruling family, as discussed later), a large donation was made to the Children's National Medical Center in Washington, DC. Amounting to $150 million—reportedly the largest ever grant given to paediatric surgery—the money has been channelled via the Abu Dhabi government-backed Sheikh Zayed Institute and, according to the Center's president, will '…allow us to serve the world for the next 100 years'.[79] Connecting the strategies of development assistance to the West and support for Islamic credentials, both the UAE and Saudi Arabia have also been building new mosques in Western Europe. Most recently, in late 2010 construction work was completed on Europe's largest mosque, in the Netherlands, financed by Dubai's Al-Maktoum Foundation—named after the emirate's ruling family. Located in Rotterdam, the mosque can accommodate 3,000 worshippers, boasts two fifty metre tall minarets, and also houses a centre for 'charity, mutual understanding, and forgiveness'. Strongly opposed by Dutch far-right movements, which have stated that 'this horrible thing doesn't belong here but in Saudi Arabia', the mosque is nevertheless likely to prove extremely popular with Rotterdam's substantial Muslim population.[80]

Elsewhere, however, opposition has been more robust, and the mosque financing strategy in Western Europe may prove increasingly awkward for the Gulf monarchies involved. In Norway, for example, attempts by Saudi Arabia's Tawfiiq Islamic Centre to spend tens of millions of dollars on building new mosques have been blocked by the government. Explaining in 2010 that '…it would be a paradox and unusual to accept funding from sources in a country where there is no religious freedom' and that '…the acceptance of such money would be a paradox since it is a punishable crime to establish the Christian faith in Saudi Arabia',[81] Norway's minister for foreign affairs has seemingly closed the door on further Saudi funding.

Soft power in the West: cultural institutions

In some ways an extension of the development assistance model, especially when the Western institutions involved have run into financial difficulties, and in others a more subtle example of the sponsorship and naming rights strategy, the Gulf monarchies have been increasingly active in supporting well known museums, art galleries, and other cultural institutions. The UAE has been financing a new art research centre in Paris and is providing $32 million to help the Louvre repair a wing of the Pavilion de Flore. When complete, the latter will host a new gallery of international art named after the former ruler of Abu Dhabi.[82] Moreover, Abu Dhabi has reportedly been paying for the $10 million restoration of Chateau Fontainebleau's Napoleon III theatre—controversially to be renamed after Khalifa bin Zayed Al-Nahyan, the current ruler. Following the signing of the deal in 2007 Abu Dhabi's representative stated that 'This is proof to the deep-rooted cultural and tourism relations between the UAE and France. We consider it as an additional pillar of our bilateral relations' before explaining that 'Sheikh Khalifa's initiative is part of a long history of cooperation between France and the UAE and is set to be followed by other cultural partnerships'. Despite allowing the renaming of a building that is part of a classified UNESCO World Heritage Site and was home to more than thirty French monarchs and emperors, the French minister for culture claimed that '…this current cultural cooperation is proof to the approach the two counties adopt in further boosting cooperation and peaceful rapprochement among the world's cultures and civilisations'.[83]

As part of the same strategy, although in reverse, some Gulf monarchies have imported the biggest western cultural institutions into the Gulf itself, often by providing massive financial inducements which have clearly been used to bolster the resources of the home institutions. Most astonishingly, at a total cost of over $27 billion, Abu Dhabi's Tourism and Development Investment Company is currently developing Saadiyat—'the island of happiness'. Intended to become the emirate's main cultural hub, it is being linked by ten bridges to the mainland and will host branches of the Louvre and Guggenheim in addition to a new Sheikh Zayed National Museum, a performing arts centre, a maritime museum, and a nineteen-pavilion cultural park. The Louvre Abu Dhabi will alone cost $110 million to build, and TDIC has agreed to pay a further $520 million for the Louvre brand name and the loan of various exhibitions and collections. Being built at similarly great expense, the Guggenheim Abu Dhabi will be the sixth international branch of the renowned New York museum. Designed by Frank Gehry, described by *Vanity Fair* as 'the most important architect of our age',[84] the new building will cover over 30,000 square metres and become one of the world's largest exhibition centres.[85] When the French president visited Abu Dhabi in 2009 to open a new French military base in the emirate—as discussed later—he went out of his way to state that '…relations between the two countries go beyond economic issues … there are rich cultural relations between the two countries in light of innovative, promising initiatives such as Louvre Abu Dhabi' before assuring that '…France is on your side in the event your security is at risk. France… is ready to shoulder its responsibilities to ensure the stability in the region. This region is strategic for the world balance'.[86]

Although the Sheikh Zayed National Museum is not a product of western branding, it is nonetheless being designed by Norman Foster's Foster and Partners of London, and the British Museum is being paid to be the project's primary consulting partner, advising on a range of issues from design, construction, and museography, to educational and curatorial programming as well as training. Upon completion, the British-designed museum will feature at least five different galleries dedicated to glorifying aspects of the former ruler's life, namely his 'interest in protecting the environment', his commitment to heritage and the 'traditional values close to his heart through his life', his 'role in the political and social unification of the Emirates', his role in 'establishing education for all of the UAE', and his 'humanitarianism… and support of Islamic values and religious tolerance'.[87]

As with building mosques in Europe and other development assistance to Western countries, the funding of such high profile cultural institutions by Gulf monarchies has also on occasion generated opposition. The various Saadiyat Island developments, which were originally scheduled to be completed in 2013 but which have now been delayed pending a government bailout of TDIC,[88] have recently been boycotted by 130 leading artists on the grounds that the expatriate workers involved in constructing the museums are being routinely exploited. Published in March 2011, the artists' pledge states that '[they will] refuse all co-operation with the project until the Guggenheim and its partners guarantee enforcement mechanisms to reimburse workers for any recruitment fees paid, and hire a reputable independent monitor that will make its findings about working conditions public'. Meanwhile a spokesperson for Human Rights Watch has stated that 'this leading group of artists is making it clear that they will not showcase their work in a museum built by abused workers, and that the steps taken to date by Guggenheim and TDIC are inadequate… if the Guggenheim and TDIC fail to address the artists' concerns, the museum may become better known for exhibiting labour violations than art'.[89]

Saudi Arabia's attempt to fund Book World Prague—one of the world's largest book fairs—also proved controversial. In 2011 Saudi

Arabia was listed as one of the fair's 'guests of honour' and reportedly a 'huge and lavish stand' was erected, taking a central position in the fair. This was '…in the form of a turreted (and carpeted) mock fortress, replete with scale models of Mecca and Medina, a children's play area, some blonde women in Saudi costumes, and plenty of individually plastic-wrapped dates for all. There were even a few books, presumably as a concession to this being a book fair'. There were, however, no Saudi authors present at the fair, most notably no Abdo Khal, despite his winning of the 2010 International Prize for Arabic Fiction for a book—*Spewing Sparks as Big as Castles*—that remains banned in Saudi Arabia. Saudi Arabia's involvement, therefore, was heavily criticised, being described as '…an oppressive regime hoping to buy itself some cultural legitimacy with its petrodollars' and '…the hijacking of literary culture for use as instant kudos by the distinctly anti-literary regime of the Kingdom of Saudi Arabia'.[90]

Soft power in the West: financing universities and manipulating research

All six Gulf monarchies have for years sponsored a number of leading Western universities and some of their professors, research centres, and research programmes. Of special interest have been those universities and departments which have historically focused on Middle Eastern Studies, Islamic Studies, and especially Persian Gulf studies. In the past, most of these donations—many of which amount to millions of dollars—tended to come directly from members of Gulf ruling families. While this still sometimes happens, it is now more frequent for the funding to be channelled through state-backed charities or 'foundations', as this seems to smooth the way for recipient institutions to perform due diligence on their foreign backers, helping them to create some distance from regimes or unpalatable individuals whom their staff and student bodies may object to. Nevertheless the various buildings, jobs, and programmes that have been sponsored in this manner invariably still are adorned with the names of Gulf rulers or their powerful relatives.

Most of these gifts have no strings attached per se, and there is generally no follow-up control after the gift is made. However, donors have usually been able to rely on a culture of self-censorship taking root in the recipient institutions. After all, if a university or institute receives a major grant from such a forthcoming source—as opposed to bidding for competitive research grants—it is likely that it will hope to get more from the same pot in the future. In these circumstances junior members of staff or postgraduate students tend to feel uncomfortable discussing either the source of the funding or pursuing sensitive topics relating to the donor country. It is almost inconceivable, for example, to imagine an academic with no alternative source of income researching and writing a serious critique of a regime that has either paid for his or her salary, scholarship, or the building that houses his or her office. In many leading universities this is now no longer a possible scenario, but instead a likely one.

In addition to promoting self-censorship, the donations also tend to encourage the steering of academic debate away from the Gulf monarchies themselves—and especially studies on their domestic politics or societies—by instead promoting research on 'safer topics' in the broader region or on Arabic language or Islamic Studies. Indeed, the latter two fields are particularly palatable as they provide further support for the monarchies' attempts to build up cultural and religious legitimacy resources. In Saudi Arabia's case the funding of leading Islamic Studies centres also seems to be part of an effort to make the Saudi state's highly controversial interpretation of Islam more 'mainstream' and acceptable, at least in scholarly and government circles. What all of this will soon lead to (and in some cases already has led to) is an academic discipline that carefully skirts around the key 'red line' subjects such as political reform, corruption, human rights, and the prospects of revolution—as these are usually perceived by university fundraisers and executives as likely to anger or antagonise their Gulf patrons. As such, this particular stream of funding is in some ways an even more powerful and sensitive soft power strategy for the Gulf monarchies, as it is not primarily aimed at influencing public or even government-level opinion in the West. Rather its more subtle objective is to sway academic opinion in the West, or at the very least foster a 'chilling atmosphere' of apologetic behaviour or avoidance when it comes to intellectual discussion of the Gulf monarchies.

The historic links between Britain and the region have meant that the Gulf monarchies have been particularly attracted to funding British universities, and these currently represent the best examples of the strategy. Indeed, it is now difficult to find any leading British institution focusing on the Middle East that has not received all of the varieties of gifts. Exeter University, home to Britain's only centre for Gulf Studies, presently lauds the ruler of Sharjah—Sultan bin Muhammad Al-Qasimi—as its most generous donor, having installed him as the founding member of its College of Benefactors in 2006. This is unsurprising as Sultan paid for the university's Al-Qasimi Building (which houses its Institute for Arabic and Islamic Studies),[91] and funds two endowed professorships—the Al-Qasimi Professor of Arabic Studies and Islamic Material Culture and the Sharjah Chair of Islamic Studies. In the past, there was also an Al-Qasimi Chair of Gulf Politics, but no longer. Similarly at Durham University, home to one of the Britain's largest clusters of academics working on Middle East studies, the ruler of Sharjah has paid for another Al-Qasimi Building (which originally housed Durham's Institute for Middle East and Islamic Studies and now houses its School of Government and International Affairs), and funds an endowed professorship—the Sharjah Chair in Islamic Law and Finance. Elsewhere in the UAE, the Abu Dhabi-funded Emirates Foundation for Philanthropy gave some $15 million to launch the London School of Economics' new Centre for Middle Eastern Studies, and a further $3 million to name the main lecture theatre in LSE's New Academic Building after Zayed bin Sultan Al-Nahyan.[92] It has also funded an endowed professorship—the Emirates Chair of the Contemporary Middle East—the holder of which does not focus on the Gulf states. On a smaller scale, before becoming Abu Dhabi's current ruler, Khalifa bin Zayed Al-Nahyan had already paid for the Khalifa Building at the University of Wales in Lampeter,[93] which now houses the university's Department of Theology, Religious Studies and Islamic Studies, along with a small mosque. Dubai has also been active, with members of its ruling family having funded the Al-Makoum College in Dundee, which is currently accredited by Aberdeen University and focuses on several niche fields including Muslim communities in Britain and 'Islamic Jerusalem' studies.

Kuwait has been a similarly generous donor to British academia, with the British Society for Middle East Studies' main annual book prize being named after and funded for many years by a member of the ruling family.[94] Since 2010 the prize has been administered by Cambridge University, with the ruling family member remaining as one of the five judges. More substantially, since 2007 the government-backed Kuwait Foundation for the Advancement of Sciences has been funding a substantial $15 million, ten year research programme at the LSE on 'development, governance, and globalisation in the Gulf states' and has funded an endowed professorship—the Kuwait Professorship of Economics and Political Sciences. Despite KFAS stating that the incumbent professor should '… take a first hand interest in key issues affecting the economic development of resource rich economies, particularly the Gulf States as well bringing recognition of Kuwait to prestigious academic and policy-making circles around the world', it appears that neither of the two post-holders since 2007 have actually focused on the Gulf states.[95] In May 2011 the prime minister of Kuwait—a key member of the ruling family—began sponsoring Durham University, funding an eponymously named $3.5 million research programme along with a similarly eponymous endowed professorship—the His Highness Sheikh Nasser bin Muhammad Al-Sabah Chair in International Relations, Regional Politics, and Security.[96] Only months later, as discussed later in this book, Nasser was ousted as prime minister following popular protests and allegations of corruption, but the university has opted to retain the gift.

There are now many examples of substantial donations from other Gulf monarchies in British universities—again mostly from government-backed entities or influential ruling family members. Qatar's ruler has paid Oxford University about $3.5 million to endow a new professorship named after himself—the His Highness Hamad Bin Khalifa Al-Thani Chair in Contemporary Islamic Studies[97] while Oman's ruler has paid for two endowed professorships at Cambridge University, which again seem to be safely distanced from any discussion of Gulf politics—the His Majesty Sultan Qaboos Bin Said Professor of Modern Arabic Studies and the His Majesty Sultan Qaboos Chair for Abrahamic Faiths and Common Values.[98] Not to be outdone, in 2008 Saudi Arabia's influential Al-Waleed bin Talal Al-Saud paid for a $13 million Centre for Islamic Studies, also at Cambridge,[99] and provided comparable funding for setting up the Prince Al-Waleed Bin Talal Centre of Islamic Studies at Edinburgh University. Most symbolic perhaps, is the Oxford Centre of Islamic Studies, which is a 'recognised independent centre of the University of Oxford'. Founded in 1985, it has a substantial new building nearing completion and many endowed fellowships. Although some of its funding has come from British and US entities and other parts of the Islamic world, the bulk of the funding is believed to originate in the Gulf monarchies. Saudi Arabia alone is believed to have already donated about $30 million to the centre.[100]

Although not a university as such, Britain's Sandhurst Academy—the elite training school for Britain's military and the *alma mater* for several current Gulf ruling family members—has also been receiving substantial donations. In 2009, for example, the UAE was reported to have financed the building of a new hall of residence at the academy to house a hundred cadets.[101] Tellingly, the following day it was announced by Britain's ambassador to the UAE that the Queen's Household Cavalry would perform at Abu Dhabi's International Hunting and Equestrian Exhibition later that year—the first overseas display ever performed by the squadron. He also went on to state that 'The fact is that there is no relationship the United Kingdom has with countries in the Middle East that is more important to us than that with United Arab Emirates' while a senior British military personality stated that 'I think that anything we can do to cement the relations between Abu Dhabi and the UK is a good thing'.[102]

Similar, although often smaller donations, have been made to universities in other parts of Western Europe and the Commonwealth. At the Australian National University, for example, there exists the Sheikh Hamdan bin Rashid Al-Maktoum Senior Lectureship at the Centre for Arab and Islamic Studies, funded by Dubai's deputy ruler. In Canada, at McMaster University, there exists the Sharjah Chair in Global Islam, funded by Sharjah's ruler. And in France, at Sciences-Po, a five year KFAS-funded Kuwait Programme has been running since 2007—much like the KFAS-LSE programme. Such funding has found its way into US universities, too, but the US has historically been a more troublesome recipient given the relative influence of its Israel lobby, which has on occasion sought to block such gifts. In 2000, for example, the Harvard University staff and student body signed a petition to reject an offer of an endowed professorship in Islamic studies from Abu Dhabi's ruler on the grounds that a think-tank linked to the ruling family—the Zayed Centre for Co-ordination and Follow-Up—was allegedly promoting anti-Semitism and that there were well-documented human rights abuses in the UAE. The original plan for the professorship, which would have been named after the ruler, was to have the usual broad focus, thus allowing the incumbent to circumvent discussion of the Gulf monarchies.[103] Similarly in 2007 the University of Connecticut pulled out of a relationship with Dubai for much the same reasons.[104] Nevertheless significant donations have still been made over the years, with funds from Saudi Arabia having been channelled to the University of Arkansas (which received $27 million for its Middle East Studies Center), and with

Cornell University, Rutgers University, Princeton University, and a number of others also receiving donations. The University of Southern California's Chair in Islamic Thought and Culture, for example, is named after the former Saudi king, Faisal bin Abdul-Aziz Al-Saud, while Georgetown University's renowned Centre for Muslim-Christian Understanding was renamed the Prince Al-Waleed Bin-Talal Center for Muslim-Christian Understanding following a $20 million gift from Al-Waleed in 2005. This prompted a congressman in 2008 to question whether the centre had ever been critical of the Saudi government.[105]

Most recently, in 2011 the College of William and Mary, one of the oldest higher education institutions in the US, accepted a gift from Oman's ruler to establish an endowed professorship—the Sultan Qaboos bin Said Academic Chair of Middle East Studies. Meanwhile Harvard University now appears to have accepted a $1 million donation from the Abu Dhabi Crown Prince's Court, despite its earlier rejection of Abu Dhabi ruling family funds. The gift, made out to Harvard's John F. Kennedy School of Government, has helped set up a graduate training scheme at Harvard for Abu Dhabi's top public officials, while also helping to 'advance the mission of the School's Middle East Initiative, a nexus for convening policymakers and scholars on the region'. Upon signing the agreement, the Abu Dhabi crown prince's court stated that 'this… echoes President His Highness Sheikh Khalifa Bin Zayed Al Nahyan's steadfast belief that the progress of nations is built on education, and Crown Prince His Highness General Sheikh Muhammad bin Zayed Al-Nahyan's unwavering commitment to education and the constant development of the future ranks of leaders'.[106]

In an almost mirror image of the funding of cultural institutions strategy, the Gulf monarchies' funding of Western universities and research programmes has now also been taking place in reverse, with several leading US and British higher education institutions having been invited to set up branch campuses in the region. It is important to differentiate, however, between those Western universities (usually mid-or low-ranking institutions) that have set up campuses in free zone operations—such as those in Dubai's Knowledge Village—which have sought commercial success and have usually not received financial inducements from the governments involved,[107] and those higher ranked institutions that have been building much larger, more lavish campuses—most notably in Abu Dhabi and Qatar. It is the latter category of universities which matter, as these are receiving massive funding from the governments in question and are now tied in to these monarchies' soft power strategies. After all, if a monarchy can claim to have a working and highly visible relationship with a big brand university from one of the world's most established democracies, one with a powerful military, then any reputational price that is being paid—no matter how high—is certainly deemed to be a wise investment. In Abu Dhabi both New York University and La Sorbonne have established operations, with one of Abu Dhabi government's key personalities now sitting on the former's board of trustees back in New York.[108] While in Qatar a whole host of universities are establishing themselves in 'Education City'—a giant complex funded by the Qatar Foundation, the aforementioned vehicle of the ruler's wife. Described as 'five star universities imported *profectus in totum* from abroad',[109] these currently include Georgetown University, Texas A&M University, Virginia Commonwealth University, the Weill Cornell Medical College, Carnegie Mellon University, Northwestern University, and University College London. In many cases, with generous salaries to offer, they have attracted leading academics in their given specialities. It is difficult to ascertain the real running costs of these campuses; however it is likely that Education City's total cost is about $33 billion dollars, with the individual campuses costing between $100 and $200 million each.[110] While there are very few UAE national students attending NYU[111] or La Sorbonne in Abu Dhabi,[112] there are at least a modest number of Qatari nationals attending the various Education City institutions.[113] However, most students are expatriates (either those from families resident in the Gulf states or the wider region or, in Abu Dhabi's case, those flown in on very generous scholarships),[114] and with the exception of Georgetown University[115] very little academic attention is currently being paid to the Gulf monarchies themselves—especially in the field of political science.

Soft power in the East: China and Japan

Although the Gulf monarchies have little shared modern economic history with the principal Pacific Asian powers[116]—notably China and Japan—their economies are now becoming increasingly intertwined. What began as a simple, mid-twentieth century marriage of convenience based on hydrocarbon imports and exports is rapidly evolving into a comprehensive, long-term mutual commitment that is not only continuing to capitalise on the Gulf's rich energy resources and Pacific Asia's massive energy needs, but is seeking also to develop strong non-hydrocarbon bilateral trade and is facilitating sizeable sovereign wealth investments. Although this increasingly extensive relationship does not yet encompass the Gulf monarchies' military security arrangements—which remain predominantly with the Western powers—and although few serious attempts have been made by either side to replace or balance these with new Pacific Asian alliances, there is nonetheless compelling evidence that the Gulf monarchies are seeking to strengthen their non-hydrocarbon economic ties and even non-economic ties with these states. Indeed, an abundance of state-level visits, often at much higher levels than with western powers, and a plethora of cooperative agreements, gifts, loans, and other incentives are also undoubtedly helping the Gulf monarchies build up a soft power base in the East as well as the West.

China and Japan now have the second and third greatest oil consumption needs in the world, behind only the US, while Japan still has the fifth greatest gas consumption needs in the world, ahead of Germany and Britain.[117] According to the Organisation of Petroleum Exporting Countries although Japan's demand for oil is likely to fall by 15 per cent by 2030, China, South Korea, and other Pacific Asian economies are likely to make up 80 per cent of net global oil demand growth over the same period.[118] Most of this increased Pacific Asian demand is already being met by the Gulf monarchies, with their total hydrocarbon trade now close to $200 billion per annum[119]—a figure likely to increase dramatically over the next decade. The Pacific Asian economies do little to disguise their dependency on hydrocarbon imports from the Persian Gulf, in contrast to many Western powers which are openly trying to reduce their dependency and diversify their sources. Although the non-hydrocarbon trade that takes place between the two regions is on a much smaller scale, there has nevertheless been an historical precedent for the importing of certain goods from Pacific Asia into the Gulf monarchies, especially textiles and electrical goods. And since the substantial rise in per capita wealth on the Arabian Peninsula following the first oil booms, the demand for such imports has increased correspondingly, along with new demands for cars, machinery, building materials, and many other products associated with the region's oil and construction industries. In total, the Gulf monarchies' imports from Japan, China, and South Korea could now be worth as much as $63 billion per year.[120] Moreover, there is no longer as much of an imbalance in non-hydrocarbon trade between the two regions as there used to be, as some of the Gulf monarchies' export-oriented industries—especially those producing metals, plastics, and petrochemicals—are now gearing their sales to Pacific Asian customers.

While the Gulf monarchies' sovereign wealth investments in the Eastern powers remain much more modest than in the West, this is also slowly changing as investments in Pacific Asia become regarded as realistic and more hospitable alternatives to the more mature western economies. Such an alternative was viewed as being particularly necessary following 9/11, after which many western governments and companies did little to disguise their distrust of Gulf sovereign wealth funds, with many commentators arguing that Gulf investments were not merely commercial and that power politics could be involved.[121] With regards to Japan, Saudi Aramco has, for example, been holding a 15 per cent stake since 2004 in its fifth largest oil company, Showa Shell Sekiyu.[122] In 2007 Dubai International Capital purchased a 'substantial stake' in the beleaguered Sony Corporation—the first ever major UAE investment in Japan.[123] And in summer 2009 the Japan External Trade Organisation named the UAE as one of its top three target countries for sourcing FDI.[124] Since JETRO's drive began, Abu Dhabi's International Petroleum Investment Company has taken a 21 per cent, $780 million, stake in Japan's Cosmo Oil Company[125] Although Kuwait's sovereign wealth investments in Japan are more modest, the Kuwait Investment Authority nonetheless recently stated that it intends to increase by threefold its investments in Japan.[126]

In 2005 China's Ministry for Commerce revealed that investments from the Gulf monarchies in China totalled $700 million,[127] most having come from Kuwait. Back in 1984 a subsidiary of the Kuwait Petroleum Company took a 15 per cent stake in China's Yacheng offshore gasfield, while the following year KPC set up a joint venture—the Sino Arab Chemical Fertiliser Company to invest in the Qilu petrochemicals facility in China's eastern Shandong province.[128] In the 1990s the Kuwait Investment Authority increased its portfolio share in Chinese investments from 10 to 20 per cent,[129] and it is now the largest foreign investor in the Industrial and Commercial Bank of China.[130] This has effectively made the Kuwaiti government the biggest investor in one of China's first major public offerings. The relationship between the two countries was also strengthened greatly following the setting up of a $9 billion joint venture between the Kuwait Petroleum Corporation and Sinopec in 2005. Since then, the two companies have been jointly financing the construction of a massive 300,000 barrels per day capacity oil refinery and ethylene plant in China's southern Guangdong province. When the project comes online in 2013 it will be China's largest ever successful joint project.[131] But the most innovative and symbolic aspect of the investments between the two countries has been the establishment of the Kuwait-China Investment Company. Set up in 2005 and 15 per cent owned by KIA, the KCIC now has a capital base of about $350 million, about half of which is held in cash in order to facilitate rapid responses to strategic opportunities. It has specialised in investments in Chinese agribusinesses, particularly those producing crops with a high export value such as rice, wheat, corn, and sorghum. Meanwhile Saudi Aramco now has more offices in China than in any other country, and has taken a 25 per cent stake in a major joint venture with Sinopec and the China National Petroleum Corporation's Petrochina subsidiary in 2001.[132] The venture, named the Fujian Refining and Petrochemical Company, has involved the two companies expanding an existing refinery in China's southeastern Fujian province along with building a brand new ethylene plant. Moreover, Aramco is now the largest shareholder in the Thalin refinery project in China, and in the near future it may embark on another joint venture with the two Chinese companies to build a refinery in the Chinese coastal city of Qingdao, again with Aramco taking the majority stake.[133] This could lead to the building of one of the largest oil-refining facilities in the world and may require as much as $6 billion to complete.

Similarly to Aramco, SABIC has already helped to initiate three petrochemicals projects in China as part of its 'China Plan', which aims to facilitate mutual investments between the two countries by supporting China's economic development and, as its premier supplier of petrochemicals, helping to satisfy its ever-increasing demand.[134] And in 2009 SABIC entered into an agreement to build a fourth petrochemical complex, costing $3 billion, in China's northeastern Tianjin province.[135] The Qatari Investment Authority is also becoming active in China, and has recently followed Kuwait's lead by signalling its intent to purchase $200 million worth of shares in subsequent public offerings from the Industrial and Commercial Bank of China.[136] It has also opened a permanent office in China with the intention of pursuing further sovereign wealth investment opportunities in the country, with QIA's CEO having explained that 'China and Asia are growth markets for Qatar—we are really serious about finding the right opportunities there'.[137] Most significantly perhaps, it was announced that Qatar Petroleum would enter into a joint venture with Petrochina worth $12 billion. This deal, if followed through, would eclipse even Kuwait's investments in China and would lead to the construction of a new petrochemicals plant in China's eastern Zhejiang province, along with an oil refinery, an ethylene plant, and a port for oil supertankers.[138]

Much like its neighbours, the UAE, and more specifically Dubai, is also investing in China, and has been since the late 1980s following the establishment of the Dubai Oriental Finance Company.[139] More recently Dubai Ports World has made significant investments in Chinese coastal cities, and now operates seven container terminals in the country, three of them in Hong Kong. Crucially DPW has faced none of the opposition it experienced in its 2006 bid to operate ports in the US, and its success has been attributed to its well developed partnership with China's Tianjin Port Group Company.[140] In the near future the joint venture will also open a terminal in China's northeastern Qingdao province and in 2009 it announced that it would also take an 80 per cent stake in a joint venture with both a Chinese company and Vietnam's state-owned Tan Thuan Industrial Promotion Company in order to build yet another Asian container port outside Ho Chi Minh City.[141] Abu Dhabi has thus far been more cautious than Dubai with regard to investing in China, but there are nonetheless some proxy examples: IPIC has a 65 per cent controlling stake in Borealis[142]—a plastics company based in Austria that has links with the Abu Dhabi Polymers Company—and in turn Borealis is investing in a polypropylene plant in China, to help boost the supply of plastics for its booming automobile industry,[143] which now comprises more than forty-five car manufacturers, including Beijing Automobile Works and Chery Automobile.[144]

With regards to building non-economic soft power ties, a part of the strategy seems to have been regular and high level diplomatic visits from the Gulf monarchies to Pacific Asia. While economic and trade matters are certainly discussed at these carefully staged events, the meetings are nonetheless also valuable opportunities for rulers and their ministers to convene with their Pacific Asian counterparts and consider a range of other matters. Often substantial gifts or interest free loans are granted during these meetings—especially to China, in an effort to build more sturdy political and cultural understandings, and undoubtedly to generate further goodwill. The frequency of these visits has greatly intensified, but more important has been the increasing seniority of the visitors, which now eclipses that of those dispatched to Western capitals.[145] A report published by the US-based Middle East Institute in 2009 also identified the trend, stating that there has been a 'steady, incremental process in the building of personal and institutional relations—the essential latticework of Gulf-Asia economic interdependence… [and the diplomatic visits] have been capped by a slew of ambitious cooperation programs and joint ventures'.[146]

In 2006 the Saudi king visited China to sign several new agreements that were intended to 'write a new chapter of friendly cooperation with China in the twenty-first century'. As a gesture of goodwill he also agreed to grant China a substantial loan in order to build infrastructure in the oil rich Xingjiang province.[147] This was his first international trip as the newly-installed king—before visiting any western states—and the Chinese president declared that the visit 'would begin a new phase in partnership between the two countries in the new century'.[148] Following the Abu Dhabi ruler's visit to China in 1990 the UAE has made many large donations to China, including grants to establish an Arabic and Islamic Studies Centre at Beijing Foreign Studies University and the financing of the expansion of a printing factory for the China Islam Association. Subsequent visits also led to China being granted permission to set up UAE branches of the Xinhua News Agency and the *People's Daily* newspaper.[149] And soon the UAE's Zayed University will establish a Confucius Institute as a result of an 'imaginative new partnership' that is being developed with China's Xinjiang University.[150] Meanwhile, Kuwait has been one of the most generous suppliers of low interest loans to China, with the Kuwait Fund for Arab Economic Development having provided China with over $600 million in such loans since the 1990s.[151] There have also been several large gifts, including a disaster relief package in 1998 following serious flooding in China.[152] The poorer Gulf monarchies have been less active in providing gifts and development assistance to China. Nevertheless, in 2001 Oman's ruler donated $200,000 to assist the Guangzhou Museum of Overseas History build a new Arab and Islamic exhibition room.[153]

4

MOUNTING INTERNAL PRESSURES

Despite the Gulf monarchies' internal and external survival strategies, many of which have contributed to their relative stability over the past few decades, there are nonetheless several weaknesses and pathologies that have been undermining their polities. These have often been under-reported or ignored, given the various rulers' ability to continue buying acquiescence from their people and cultivating legitimacy. Moreover, they have often been subtle problems, and have rarely led to violent protests or headline-grabbing incidents. But given that most of these weaknesses are deep-rooted, structural, and seemingly unsolvable, it can be argued that they cut to the very core of the Gulf monarchies' political and economic structures, often exposing the vulnerability and unsustainable nature of the current practices. As the later parts of this book demonstrate, the Gulf monarchies are not immune to the Arab Spring, which is undoubtedly serving as a catalyst for reform and revolution in the region, but it is perhaps these domestic, Gulf-specific problems which are most central to understanding the monarchies' looming challenges.

Affecting all six Gulf monarchies are their declining hydrocarbon reserves and rising patterns of domestic energy consumption, coupled with their rapidly increasing indigenous populations—most of which are now under the age of twenty-one. This is already placing great strain on these states' ability to keep fulfilling their citizens' economic expectations, while their welfare states and distributive systems are also feeling the strain, even in the wealthier Gulf monarchies, due to the costs of perpetually subsidising their populations. Connected to this has been the structural problem of 'voluntary unemployment': despite frequent labour nationalisation initiatives, most Gulf monarchies remain unable to motivate their citizens to gain meaningful employment and contribute to the national economy given their reliance on state welfare and expectation of automatically remaining members of a wealthy national elite, courtesy of their citizenship. Exacerbated by the lack of transparency in these monarchies, other pressures on their increasingly limited national resources include the ongoing financing of prestige projects, the squandering of government spending, and the accumulation of vast wealth by the ruling families and their closest allies.

Already apparent in the poorer Gulf monarchies has been the increase in poverty among citizens, with real unemployment increasing as states can offer no longer the same kind of economic opportunities as in the past. This is leading to stark wealth gaps emerging between the wealthiest and poorest families in some of the national populations, which in turn is undermining any sense of equality between them and thus jeopardising the tribal heritage and religious legitimacy resources that the rulers have previously enjoyed. Widespread, and in many ways state-sanctioned, discrimination against large sections of the Gulf monarchies' national populations is also on the increase—again undermining the ruling families' credentials—with hundreds of thousands of stateless persons now probably further away from being naturalised than ever before, and with substantial indigenous Shia populations—especially in Bahrain and Saudi Arabia—now firmly relegated to second class citizenship. Of equally great concern, and similarly weakening the ruling families' ability to uphold their social contracts and maintain legitimacy, has been the reliance on increasingly repressive forms of censorship—in some cases long before 2011. Affecting citizens and expatriates alike, this has choked off most remaining channels of expression and discontent, and is thus making it much harder for the Gulf monarchies to keep disguising the authoritarian nature of their polities.

Resources, populations, and subsidies

Although some Gulf monarchies still command substantial hydrocarbon resources, even these will face pressure to maintain the same level of subsidies for their populations in the coming years, especially as reserves rapidly deplete and meaningful diversification of their economic bases remains limited. Meanwhile, those monarchies that are already suffering from severely depleted reserves are now failing to maintain certain subsidies. Given the obvious political ramifications of declining benefits and any cutbacks to their welfare states, the Gulf monarchies have been understandably sensitive and often secretive with regards to their remaining resources. According to US diplomatic cables despatched between 2007 and 2009 it was claimed, for example, that Saudi Arabia may have been overstating its crude oil reserves by as much as 300 billion barrels—or 40 per cent. Quoting a senior geologist, the cables disagreed with Saudi Aramco's senior vice president for exploration, who claimed in 2007 that Aramco had 716 billion barrels of total reserves, of which 51 per cent were recoverable, and that in twenty years Aramco would have 900 billion barrels of reserves. Instead it was argued that Saudi Arabia will soon reach a plateau in total output that will last only fifteen years before beginning to decline.[1]

Importantly, cables from 2009 also noted that Saudi Arabia's ability to export oil (and thus keep financing the welfare state and providing subsidies) will decline as its domestic energy demands rapidly increase. The cables stated that '…demand [for electricity] is expected to grow 10 per cent a year over the next decade as a result of population and economic growth… as a result [Saudi Arabia] will need to double its generation capacity to 68,000MW in 2018', while also claiming that various major project delays and accidents in Saudi Arabia are 'evidence that Saudi Aramco is having to run harder to stay in place—to replace the decline in existing production'.[2]

In the weakest position has been Bahrain, where as early as 1965 half of its onshore oil reserves were already thought to have been depleted and in 1987 production from its offshore Abu Safah field (shared with Saudi Arabia) began to slow. Since then Bahrain has had to rely heavily on about 147,000 barrels per day (about 77 per cent of its total output) from Saudi Arabia,[3] as compensation for this loss. In 1993 Bahrain's remaining reserves were estimated at just 200 million barrels with total depletion expected in 2005.[4] Although this may have taken place, it has been somewhat disguised by Bahrain's oil-refining capacity, which now primarily refines Saudi oil. As with many other Gulf monarchies, Bahrain is now a prominent gas producer, but again it is estimated that an increasing proportion of its output will be required by the domestic sector.

Similarly Oman is believed to have shrinking oil output,[5] with recent discoveries having either proved commercially unviable or on a much smaller scale than in the past.[6] In total it is thought to have only 5.5 billion barrels of oil in known reserves—most of which are spread out over disparate fields. This means Oman will soon become a net hydrocarbon importer[7] as its domestic energy consumption has more than doubled over the past decade.[8] While Abu Dhabi still has a few decades of oil reserves remaining—with an estimated 98 billion barrels of oil left,[9] its gas production is hampered by high sulphur rates and is increasingly being earmarked for the domestic sector. Abu Dhabi is already importing Qatari gas via the Dolphin pipeline—a joint project with Qatar and Royal Dutch Shell originally conceived in 1999. But most problematic for Abu Dhabi is the increasing amount of energy it has to supply to the six other UAE emirates as their demands also increase. Although the poorest four emirates have never had significant hydrocarbon reserves, both Dubai and Sharjah were once oil and gas producers. Sharjah's production is now minimal, and in 1995 Dubai's daily oil output slowed to just 300,000 barrels.[10] Although the ruler of Dubai made an announcement in early 2010 that a new offshore oilfield had been discovered,[11] this seemed to be primarily a political move as the emirate was trying to restore investor confidence following the difficulties it faced in late 2009. Indeed, analysts quickly expressed doubts over the commercial viability of the field and described the find as 'a drop in [Dubai's] ocean of debt'.[12]

Kuwait is in a much stronger position, with official estimates of 100 billion barrels of oil remaining, most of which will come from the massive Burgan field—the second largest in the world. However, some analysts and Kuwaiti members of parliament have disputed this figure, claiming Kuwait has only about 48 billion barrels remaining, while several of its other onshore fields are now nearly seventy years old and maintaining existing levels of production will become increasingly difficult. Since 2008 Kuwait's consumption of gas has exceeded its production, requiring the emirate to import. This shortfall is likely to increase over the next few years, as domestic electricity demand is believed to be increasing by 8 per cent per year, having eliminated what was once a comfortable reserve margin.[13] In the best position of all is Qatar, which has a much smaller population and massive gas reserves which will likely allow it to keep exporting substantial quantities of gas for several more decades. As officials have claimed, Qatar could even '…meet all of the UK's gas needs for 250 years'.[14] Nonetheless the emirate will soon face pressures with regard to oil consumption, as it only has about 25 billion barrels of oil reserves—making it the second smallest OPEC oil producer. Since 2000 its domestic consumption of oil has tripled and is likely to rise by 5 per cent per year over the next decade due to its rapidly growing economy and in particular growing demand from its transport sector.[15]

In tandem with these declining reserves, and already placing pressure on the wealth distribution systems are the Gulf monarchies' rapidly increasing indigenous populations. Although often overlooked, given the large size of their urban expatriate communities, the number of nationals in these states has also risen substantially in recent years. This is due to indigenous communities not only living longer, due to vastly improved healthcare, but also because of some of the highest fertility rates in the world, mostly due to the various economic benefits still on offer. Saudi Arabia has always had the highest ratio of nationals to expatriates in its total population, with the former accounting for about 70 per cent of the total, or 19 million persons, according to the 2010 census.[16] Significantly, 47 per cent of Saudi nationals are now thought to be under the age of eighteen, with 80 per cent under the age of thirty, thus making the Saudi population one of the youngest in the world.[17] An exact fertility rate is hard to measure for Saudi nationals—and for all Gulf nationals—due to most statistics being based on total resident populations (and thus being artificially lowered by the inclusion of the much lower expatriate fertility rates).[18] Nonetheless it is likely that it is still much higher than in developed states, while life expectancies have become comparable with those in developed states. Similarly, the national populations of the other five Gulf monarchies also have very high growth rates, with modest or high fertility rates and greatly increased life expectancies. Although a recent UN report discussing the UAE claimed that the country's birth rate has halved over the past thirty years and is now the lowest in the region, it erred by combining the national and expatriate populations. With the UAE having the highest ratio of expatriates to nationals in the region, this has obscured the fast growth of the indigenous population, which is likely growing just as fast as those of the other Gulf monarchies.[19]

Symptomatic of the strain engendered by these declining reserves, increased domestic energy consumption, and rising populations have been the frequent failures of governments to maintain cheap utilities and keep delivering low cost fuel and foodstuffs. These have historically been three of the most basic types of subsidies in the Gulf monarchies and continue to be regarded as an indispensable birthright by most nationals, especially the younger generations who have no living memory of the pre-oil era and the region's earlier poverty. They largely expect indefinite subsidies and, unlike their grandparents, rarely view them as gifts from rulers that have led to their lives being transformed. For expatriates, there are fewer political implications, yet it is undeniable that the Gulf monarchies must remain comparatively attractive and competitive places in which to live and work. With regards Saudi Arabia, a recent Brookings Center report argued that the 'burgeoning youth population' is now 'straining the capacity of the Saudi welfare state… characteristics of other societies that have experienced political upheaval'.[20] And in early 2011 a more specific BBC report claimed that Saudi Arabia was grappling with food price inflation of over 9 per cent, with some items such as beef, chicken, and vegetables having doubled in price over just a few years, presumably as a result of increased production and transport costs.[21] In Kuwait, the most obvious problem has been the increasing frequency of rolling electricity blackouts during periods of peak demand, especially during the summer. This led the Energy Information Administration to conclude in 2011 that Kuwait is now in a 'perpetual state of electricity supply shortage'.[22]

The UAE offers even clearer examples, not least because it is usually perceived as a wealthy state. After several summers of blackouts in Sharjah, due to increased demand and its government's inability to meet electricity costs, the Sharjah Electricity and Water Authority announced in 2009 that electricity charges were to be increased by 50 per cent— including those levied on UAE nationals. This led to much complaint, mainly from nationals, who claimed that the authorities were unable to cope with an expanding population. Since then blackouts have continued in the emirate, often forcing businesses to close due to lack of air-conditioning.[23] The Dubai and Abu Dhabi governments have also begun to falter, especially with regards to subsidising state-backed retail petrol companies such as the Emirates National Oil Company and the Emirates Petroleum Products Company (both owned by Dubai) and Emarat (owned by Abu Dhabi). In 2010 these companies' roadside petrol stations began to experience fuel shortages—a situation that continued well into 2011. Initially the shortages were blamed on logistical problems, but it later transpired that deliveries were not being made due to the companies' inability to make payments. Although fuel price hikes have taken place in recent years, most of which proved extremely unpopular with UAE nationals, there appeared to be no alternative as the various emirate-level governments had begun to phase out fuel subsidies on the grounds that they were costing the country hundreds of millions of dollars per year.[24] Indeed, at a secret meeting with Ministry for Finance and Industry officials both ENOC and EPPCO recommended removing the cap on fuel prices completely, which would have led to an immediate tripling of petrol prices from nearly $2 per gallon to nearly $6 per gallon. In 2011, however, due to the perceived political backlash of further price hikes in the wake of the Arab Spring, and the rising popularity of various opposition groups in the UAE, the Abu Dhabi authorities performed a u-turn by providing Emarat with even more capital. Meanwhile the federal government cancelled the licences of both ENOC and EPPCO given the Dubai government's inability to provide a comparable bailout, with the Abu Dhabi National Oil Company eventually taking over the running of their petrol stations.[25] Moreover, ministry officials even suggested introducing a new $550 fuel allowance specifically for UAE national families in order to cover future increases.

Voluntary unemployment

Although the poorer Gulf monarchies—which have fewer resources to finance public sector jobs for nationals or to provide incentives for their private sector employment—tend to have a more balanced workforce, the wealthier monarchies are increasingly faced with high levels of voluntary unemployment among their young national populations. In many ways, although there are some exceptions, the described cultivation of a national elite over the past four decades by these states has led to citizenries that are now not only accustomed to material benefits and to no forms of extraction, but are also—with all the various sponsorship systems, soft loans, and public sector employment opportunities—being deprived of any motivation to gain meaningful qualifications or enter into a more competitive job market, or even any form of private sector job. In other words, there is an increasingly significant drawback to the political benefits derived from cosseting the national population, and in many ways this is already leading to nationals in the Gulf monarchies' largest cities becoming little more than bystanders on the sidelines of their countries' development. Furthermore, there is evidence that this may be leading to a generation of Gulf nationals that are frustrated, bored, restless, and on occasion even delinquent.

In the mid-1990s even the ruler of Abu Dhabi warned of the phenomenon—seemingly oblivious that it was a problem partly of his government's creation—by criticising the inactivity of young nationals who should be gainfully employed. He stated that he 'could not understand how physically fit young men can sit idle and accept the humiliation of depending on others for their livelihood'.[26] Similarly, in the late 1990s the crown prince of Dubai seemed unaware of the root causes of the problem when he complained of 'voluntary unemployment' in his emirate, stating that 'unemployment is a waste of natural resources and is wrong when the UAE is providing all its sons and daughters with opportunities that were unattainable a generation ago'.[27] Writing in his memoires at about the same time, one of Dubai's veteran merchants predicted that '…of Dubai's young nationals, probably only 20 per cent will be worthwhile, becoming academics and professionals, and businessmen. About 60 per cent can probably be written off, the consequences of the all-too-easy acceptance of the pleasures which will be handed out to them'.[28] Similarly realistic, when the former ruler of Qatar[29] fell ill in the mid-1990s he reportedly expressed more shock at the fact that his paramedic was actually a Qatari national than over the actual heart attack he had just suffered.[30]

Although a number of labour nationalisation strategies have been implemented in the more resource-rich monarchies—'Saudification', 'Emiratisation', 'Kuwaitification', and 'Qatarisation'—they have in many ways only compounded the problem. In most cases they have avoided addressing the structural problem of most citizens being dependent on a distributive economy, and have served only to keep pricing nationals out of the market, which in turn has made them even less attractive employees. In particular, labour laws guaranteeing access to special pension funds and limiting working hours have greatly increased the cost of hiring nationals.[31] Even more heavy handed have been the aforementioned quota systems and job protection schemes for nationals imposed on certain industries.[32] These have often made expatriate colleagues resentful of their Gulf national counterparts and have made employers increasingly wary. As one recent report observed '…across the Gulf, and especially in states where rapid growth is driven by oil and gas, locals rarely have hands-on jobs in health—or anywhere in the private sector. In an unspoken pact between rulers and ruled, Gulf citizens seem all too happy to fill plush government jobs, where the pay is high, the hours short, and the work sometimes nonexistent. In the private sector, job after job is filled by South Asians, non-Gulf Arabs and Westerners'.[33]

In the UAE's case, conservative estimates according to Tanmia are that nationals make up only 9 per cent of the total workforce[34] and just 1 per cent of the private sector workforce,[35] and that there are currently 17,000 unemployed UAE national adults.[36] Other estimates have put the figure as high as 35,000,[37] with many of these being degree holders.[38] The majority of these are likely to be in Abu Dhabi and probably fit into the category of voluntary unemployment. Indeed, latest official reports claim that the UAE has an unemployment rate of 23 per cent, with the government simply stating that the majority are 'jobless by choice'.[39] More broadly, it is thought that at least half of those nationals in receipt of generous social security benefits are able-bodied and capable of work.[40] Interviewed by Reuters in 2010, one young UAE national explained that he 'couldn't not see the obvious' and was willing to 'hold out for up to a year for a government post rather than take a job with a private firm'. He also claimed that 'I can work in a bank from at least 8am to 5pm, and get half the salary that I would get in a government job working 8pm to 2pm. Anyone would choose the better option'. Similarly, another national stated that 'I will move to the government sector, I see it as a duty to my country' before explaining that 'You tell me, who wouldn't wish to just sit there and get paid lots of money?'[41]

The same comprehensive Reuters report estimated the situation to be little better in other Gulf monarchies, with only 10 per cent of Saudi nationals and 5 per cent of Qatari nationals being employed in the private sector,[42] despite the Saudification programme aiming to replace 10 per cent of the expatriate workforce with unemployed nationals[43] and the Qatarisation programme aiming for 40 per cent labour nationalisation. Speaking in late 2010 the Saudi minister for the interior (and up until recently the crown prince)[44] made it clear that '…the government could not keep providing jobs for everyone' and, according to a *Financial Times* report, he 'signalled an impatience with businesses that hire only foreigners and urged the private sector to employ more Saudis'.[45] Speaking a few months later the chairman of the Council of Saudi Chambers of Commerce and Industry[46] agreed with the urgency of the situation, calling on the government to 'appoint an international consultancy firm to help implement the Saudification program more effectively' and arguing that 'the problem... is that while [the government] has been relatively successful in creating a very good education sector, they are still not delivering people that are capable of working in the private sector'.[47] As with the UAE, it seems that the problem will be very difficult to solve, with the average expatriate's earnings in Saudi Arabia's private sector being about $200 per month compared to over $800 for Saudi nationals.[48] Understandably, the *Financial Times'* report concluded pessimistically that 'many young Saudis fresh out of college [still] feel entitled to a managerial post by virtue of their nationality, and complain that foreign bosses order them around' and that 'the government is grappling with the challenge of creating highly paid jobs for a young population with a strong sense of entitlement, poor education and, often, a weak worth ethic'. Similarly negative, and further hinting at the deep-rooted, structural nature of the problem, have been the recent views of chief economists at Saudi-based banks who have explained that 'the government has to work on changing nationals' attitudes, which were pretty much cultivated during the first oil boom in the 1970s' and have questioned 'how can you create jobs for Saudis if they do not want to join the private sector, and the private sector does not want them?'[49]

In Kuwait, over 12,000 nationals are believed to be waiting for public sector positions, preferring to remain unemployed in the meantime rather than work in the private sector.[50] Bahrain and Oman have suffered much less, but in part this is due to the increase in real unemployment in these states, as discussed later in this chapter. Moreover, there have been some relatively novel labour nationalisation schemes in these countries which have had some success, albeit still quite limited. In 2009, for example, Bahrain increased the charge on visas for foreign workers in an effort to make Bahraini workers more attractive to employers. In the end, however, too many businesses lobbied to protect the status quo and the visa charge was only raised to $27—which was deemed merely a minor obstacle to hiring expatriates. In Oman, the government has required taxi drivers and hotel reception workers to be nationals since the 1980s. This gives visitors to the country the impression that Oman's labour force is far more nationalised than in the other Gulf monarchies. Nevertheless it is still a narrow example.

Apart from the long term economic consequences of having almost no nationals engaged in the public sector, with many remaining unemployed, and in receipt of (often generous) social security benefits, there are also growing symptoms of the social and political problems in store for the Gulf monarchies. In summer 2010, for example, several hundred frustrated Saudi national university graduates reportedly gathered outside the Ministry for Education carrying posters demanding government jobs and carrying posters with slogans such as 'Enough Injustice'.[51] The problem is also increasingly being linked to terrorism and security concerns, with some analysts remarking that '...the Saudi government believes that the question of unemployment is a major problem with huge implications on security... and the great majority of those recruited for terrorist activities are the unemployed'.[52] Crime rates among Gulf nationals have also soared over the past few decades—mostly connected to acts of delinquency such as joyriding and shoplifting. Although official statistics are unavailable, given the sensitivities prevalent in conservative societies, alcohol and drug abuse have risen dramatically among the indigenous populations, despite the harsh penalties associated with narcotics. Most Gulf monarchies now have extensive rehabilitation centres. In Dubai, for example, the emirate's Training and Rehabilitation Centre—available only to nationals—has been described by the *New York Times* as 'a lush facility complete with swimming, art classes and a gym, deep in the desert'. In Saudi Arabia there are now television programmes that openly discuss drug abuse, while in Bahrain and Kuwait clerics increasingly preach about the dangers of narcotics. As a representative of Mentor Arabia—an organisation that aims to help regional governments formulate anti-drug policies—has claimed 'the taboo around drug addiction is fading because the problem is becoming too scary' and that 'there are many indicators that suggest this is going to be a big problem... what shows it is that the governments are beginning to ask for help'. Meanwhile, a former UAE national drug user has explained that '...the drug problem here is really an invasion... there is money, the place is open, so it's bound to happen here'.[53]

Squandering wealth

Although a pathology resulting from the opacity of politics in the Gulf monarchies rather than a side effect of the distributive economy, the massive squandering of national resources—sometimes to benefit ruling family members—is arguably just as damaging for these countries. For many years the most visible example of the problem was the 'copycat spending' of competing monarchies, as each seemed to try to out-do the other by buying or constructing better versions of the same, often prestigious article or totemic building. In many cases this led to a noticeable duplication of high profile investments in the region, usually with little cooperation between neighbours and with minimal regard for long term planning. Nowhere is this more obvious than in the air, as in addition to having at least one international airport, each Gulf monarchy now also has at least one international airline, despite the relatively small populations of these countries. Jointly owned by the UAE (specifically Abu Dhabi), Bahrain, Qatar, and Oman, Gulf Air was originally intended to be the principal carrier for these countries, before Dubai established Emirates Airlines, Qatar established Qatar Airways, Oman established Oman Air, and—eventually—Abu Dhabi established Etihad Airways. Today, therefore, Gulf Air is effectively the national carrier only of Bahrain, with its aeronautical siblings competing with each other along with other established Gulf carriers such as Kuwait Airways and Saudi Arabia Airlines. There are countless other examples, most of which connected to soft power strategies or diversification efforts, including the monarchies competing to acquire European football clubs and scrambling to host the most spectacular Formula One Grand Prix. Both Bahrain and Abu Dhabi now stage such events, despite their very close proximity, and back in 1981 Dubai held an unofficial 'Dubai Grand Prix'—the posters for which displayed the face of the emirate's ruler[54] more prominently than any driver or car.

There has also been fierce competition between the Gulf monarchies to build taller skyscrapers than each other. Almost as soon as Dubai's 828 metre Burj Khalifa was completed in early 2010, Saudi Arabia's Al-Waleed bin Talal Al-Saud announced that he had signed a $1.2 billion contract to build a 1 kilometre tall tower outside Jeddah. Intended as the centrepiece for his new model town—Kingdom City—and due to be completed by 2016, Alwaleed claimed that '...building this tower in Jeddah sends a financial and economic message that should not be ignored... It has a political depth to it to tell the world that we Saudis invest in our country despite what is happening around us from events, turmoil and revolutions even'.[55]

Given the existence of seven ruling families in the UAE, the federation provides a particularly good micro-level case study of such duplicated investments and unnecessary projects. Even in the mid-1970s the UAE's minister for planning[56] was already complaining of the problem, explaining that '...economic necessity will require the eventual cessation of the costly duplications of projects that have occurred throughout the UAE since it was established'. He also claimed that 'officials recognise that this duplication of projects only wastes time and money that could be used more effectively elsewhere. The intense rivalry between the various emirates and the important status issue dictates that if one emirate acquires an airport or factory then a similar one has to be built in the other emirates'.[57] Writing in the mid-1980s, a Western observer also emphasised this lack of co-ordination and the resulting unnecessary duplications in the UAE, stating that 'Abu Dhabi, Dubai, Sharjah, and Ra's al-Khaimah all have airports that service both international and domestic flights. This overbuilding, prompted by inter-emirate rivalry, has left the latter two facilities under-utilised. Abu Dhabi, on the one hand, recently opened a new, large civilian airport to handle its traffic. Dubai, with the busiest airport in the Gulf, is upgrading its facilities...'[58]

Clearly, this under-utilisation of major airports was a direct result of so many facilities having been built in a relatively small country. This is a problem still very much in evidence today, with new international airports in Al-Ayn and Fujairah, and with foreign airlines having long since cut back their flights to Sharjah airport as a result of the continuing expansion of Dubai's airport only a few miles away. In fact, Dubai airport is closer and now far more accessible to most parts of Sharjah than the Sharjah airport, and with the completion of Dubai's new airport in Jebel Ali and the further expansion of Abu Dhabi's airport the competition will increase even further. With regards to the UAE's airlines there has been much the same problem, especially since Abu Dhabi's withdrawal from Gulf Air. The launch of Etihad Airways in 2003 was deemed by many analysts to be wholly unnecessary for the UAE, not least because Dubai's highly successful Emirates airline—set up by the former crown prince and current ruler—was headquartered only a few hundred miles away. Designated by an Abu Dhabi law as being the new 'national airline of the United Arab Emirates' and chaired by a key member of the Abu Dhabi ruling family,[59] the establishment of Etihad Airways must be viewed as a response to Dubai's highly successful operation, as much as anything else.

Another visible example of the squandering of national wealth has been the funding of expensive, prestige projects that have usually been on the whim of ruling family members or their affiliated development companies with direct access to resources, and thus have bypassed regular government channels or planning controls. Often referred to in the region as 'follies' or 'white elephants', these have frequently resulted in empty buildings, half-finished schemes, or other high cost misadventures. In some cases this has led to grumbling and discontent among nationals, with the most outspoken claiming that these projects are evidence of corruption and waste at the highest levels. In the late 1980s, for example, the ruler of Sharjah[60] was heavily criticised for his 'sanctioning of expensive and unnecessary prestige projects including… an unfinished television station and several empty museums'. Indeed, when his elder brother briefly ousted him during the 1987 coup, one of the reasons given was his high spending, despite the emirate's limited resources.[61] Over the past decade Dubai has provided an even better example, with the emirate now being littered with unfinished, often environmentally damaging projects. These include an incomplete $11 billion 'Arabian Canal' which was originally supposed to extend 75 kilometres all the way around downtown Dubai,[62] a third, unfinished 'Palm Island', which is currently just a pile of sand and rubble dumped out at sea, and the undeveloped 'Dubai World'—an archipelago of dozens of artificial islands shaped like the countries of the world, but with only one being currently occupied. The building of these various islands was condemned by many environmental groups, as they were thought to be destroying natural maritime habitats, including coral reefs.[63] Even the Burj Khalifa can be considered a white elephant, with more than two thirds of its commercial units reportedly being unoccupied more than two years after its official opening.[64] Although most of these Dubai projects were financed by real estate companies rather than the government or the ruling family, many were nonetheless personally sanctioned and encouraged by the ruler, and the companies involved can best be described as parastatals of the emirate's government. As such, their misadventures directly contributed to Dubai's 2009 crash and the emirate's continuing debt burden.

Elsewhere in the UAE, Abu Dhabi's rulers have also been facing criticism, with a slew of recent projects appearing to have little connection to official development plans. In early 2011, soon after it was revealed that Abu Dhabi was contemplating funding the construction of nine 'energy-generating solar pyramids' in the desert, including a central pyramid that would stand 50 metres tall,[65] it was also reported by the British press that many UAE nationals were puzzled as to the increasing density of clouds and the increasing frequency of rain and storms. Residents of the city most affected—Al-Ayn—were becoming concerned over the violence of some of these storms, which were often accompanied by lightning, gale force winds, and even hail. According to *The Sunday Times*, the storms were the result of a secret project funded by the ruler of Abu Dhabi since 2010, which had been launched without consulting any Al-Ayn residents. Involving a Swiss weather systems company, the controversial scheme had aimed to increase rainfall over the city in question by seeding clouds with various chemicals, and had apparently generated more than fifty man-made rainstorms over the year.[66] Although a website with limited information was later published, it has since been removed and the total cost of the project remains unknown. A little later in the year a similar project in Qatar was also reported by the British press, when it transpired that the emirate had been paying for technology to create artificial clouds to provide shade for its football stadiums in the event that its 2022 FIFA World Cup would have to be played in the extreme heat of the summer months. If the system is implemented, each cloud will reportedly cost about $500,000 to produce, and will be remotely controlled by solar powered engines.[67]

Of greater concern, perhaps, has been the accumulation of vast personal wealth by key members of the ruling families. This has been taking place since the mid-twentieth century and has been shrouded in near complete secrecy, often with the assistance of expatriate financial managers and 'personal bankers'. With many rulers and their relatives still 'owning' most of their country's land and natural resources, it remains very difficult to separate the wealth of ruling families from the state. Indeed, most of the original hydrocarbon concessions were signed between foreign oil companies and rulers, rather than with state officials. Although this is now no longer the case, it still appears that in some Gulf monarchies hydrocarbon revenues are first subjected to a share being taken by the ruling family, before the remainder is divided between the government and its various sovereign wealth funds. As with the various prestige projects, this is increasingly becoming the subject of criticism among national populations, with concern mounting over the complete unaccountability of the ruling elite and the impact this was likely to have on their welfare states and the continuing distribution of wealth. In 2011, this was described by one scholar as '...the king sometimes undertaking to redistribute the national wealth in favour of the underprivileged... but even this kind of social paternalism is limited by the predatory tendencies of the ruling clique, a close-knit network of families and clients, which ends up controlling a substantial part of the national resources'.[68]

Given the obvious secrecy surrounding the source of the wealth, it is now little more than a guessing game as to the exact size of the fortunes that have been built up by the Gulf's ruling families. It is likely that they are now the richest families in the world, with substantial assets placed overseas in the name of private shell companies rather than via official sovereign wealth funds. Occasionally there are glimpses and hints of the extent of the wealth, though these are usually the result of overseas scandals and investigations. In the early 1990s, for example, the extensive international investigation into the collapse of the Bank of Credit Commerce International—headquartered in Abu Dhabi, managed by expatriate Pakistani bankers, and part funded by the ruling family—temporarily lifted the lid on the 'web-like multi-layered structure of shell companies and private investments established on behalf of key family members'.[69] Similarly, a recently leaked US diplomatic cable, written in 1996, provided a detailed account of the mechanisms of wealth distribution (and the resulting waste) within Saudi Arabia's ruling family. In addition to reporting that 'corruption abounds largely unchecked' in Saudi Arabia, the cable concludes that '...getting a grip on royal family excesses is at the top of priorities' for the kingdom, and that '...many in the Kingdom feel that royal greed has gone beyond the bounds of reason'. In particular, the cable explains that the Ministry for Finance siphons off a portion of the country's hydrocarbon revenues. This is then distributed in varying portions to each ruling family member in the form of monthly stipends. Back in 1996 this was believed to be on a scale ranging from $800 per month for the thousands of lowly princes up to $270,000 for the few hundred top princes and their families. Moreover, it was reported that many princes could gain bonuses of about $3 million for getting married or building palaces, with further increases to their stipends for having more children. For about five or six princes it was thought that stipends equivalent to a million barrels of oil per day were being distributed. Today these figures are likely to be much higher with the number of recipient princes having greatly increased. Other, almost institutionalised benefits enjoyed by the ruling family were believed to be the 'royal rake-offs' resulting from confiscating land from non-ruling family members and then selling it on to the government, bank loans which were defaulted on, and princes acting as 'super sponsors' to hundred of expatriates under the aforementioned *kafala* system.[70]

The exact mechanisms of ruling family enrichment vary in the other Gulf monarchies, with some—such as those in Kuwait, where stipends are more modest—being more transparent than others. Nevertheless in all cases their wealth has continued to grow largely unchecked, regardless of economic downswings or recessions. In the most recent *Forbes* magazine royal rich list—published in 2009—Abu Dhabi's Khalifa bin Zayed Al-Nahyan is estimated to be worth $18 billion, while Saudi Arabia's Abdullah bin Abdulaziz Al-Saud is estimated to be $17 billion. Close behind is thought to be Dubai's Muhammad bin Rashid Al-Maktoum at $12 billion, while Qatar's Hamad bin Khalifa Al-Thani is estimated to be worth $2 billion, Oman's Sultan Qaboos bin Said Al-Said about $700 million, and Kuwait's Sabah Al-Ahmed Al-Jaber Al-Sabah about $400 million.[71] However, given that these estimates were produced soon after losses resulting from the credit crunch, the figures today are likely to be a little higher.

For many years the most noticeable manifestations of this wealth were overseas, with the various ruling families buying and building stately homes in Britain, Spain, Morocco, and other locations in addition to hundreds of other properties including game reserves, penthouse apartments, and farmsteads. This continues today, more or less unabated, with most Gulf monarchs and other powerful individuals seeking both solid foreign investments and safe overseas boltholes. A good recent example is the Abu Dhabi ruler's new palace in the Seychelles. Having personally spent $2 million on buying up land in the Seychelles, the UAE's presidential office has also spent $15 million on improving the country's water piping. Meanwhile the UAE's federal government has also pledged more than $130 million in aid to the island nation, has provided it with fast attack patrol boats, and has pumped in $30 million to help alleviate government debts.[72]

More recently, however, the relative discretion of overseas palace-building seems to have been abandoned, with dozens of new palaces now being built at home. In Oman, for example, despite his public image of modesty and the country's clearly limited resources, the aging Qaboos is understood to own at least eight palaces including the heavily guarded Royal Court at Seeb and an extensive waterfront palace in his hometown of Salalah. The palaces also have berthing facilities for super yachts, of which Qaboos is thought to own at least five, including the *Al-Behar*, which was the largest yacht built in Italy during the 1980s, and the 150 metre long *Al-Said*, which was constructed in Germany and houses a helipad, a swimming pool, and space for an orchestra. In Bahrain, the ruling family has been accused of building several new palaces and coastal resorts in recent years on land that was previously public. In early 2010 a group of opposition politicians united across sectarian lines to demand an investigation into such corruption. They collaborated on a report that accused the ruling family of having 'illegally appropriated one tenth of Bahrain's scarce public land'.[73]

Similarly in Abu Dhabi the ruling family has spent the past decade or so colonising almost all of the emirate's smaller outlying islands, often then building 'sea palaces' complete with outdoor swimming pools and extensive berthing facilities. These are now heavily defended, with most having armed patrols along their beachfronts and in some cases Patriot missile batteries discreetly installed. Some of the roads, sewerage facilities and lighting on these islands have been installed by the Abu Dhabi Municipality, despite the land now clearly being in the private hands of the ruling family. Just a few years ago most of these islands were public land, where nationals and expatriates alike could camp and hike. One particularly striking development has been on Futaisi Island, owned by a lesser member of the ruling family, Hamad bin Hamdan Al-Nahyan. Having already built a golf course and a fake fort on the island, in 2011 he began to carve his name 'Hamad' in giant letters into the surface of the island. Despite Futaisi being home to mangrove swamps and teeming with gazelles and other wildlife, each letter on the island is a kilometre long and deep enough to be filled with water to allow motor launches to navigate. With the whole name spanning three kilometres it is clearly visible on satellite mapping images. Even more ostentatiously, given that it will be located on the main Abu Dhabi island, is the new UAE Presidential Palace. Although being built by the UAE's Ministry for Presidential Affairs, it will de facto become the main seat of Abu Dhabi's ruler and crown prince, given their dominance over the federation. Spanning a secure 150 hectare site, the giant compound will contain several smaller ancillary palaces and be comparable in size to

Muammar Gaddafi's Bab al-Azizia government-cum-residential compound in Tripoli. The construction contract was awarded to a Greek company in 2007 with the value of the deal remaining secret due to a confidentiality agreement signed between the contractor and the Abu Dhabi government.[74] Nevertheless its total cost is believed to be at least $490 million.[75]

Poverty and real unemployment

Although perhaps less visible, a more immediate concern—especially for the poorer Gulf monarchies of Bahrain, Oman, and to some extent the more populous Saudi Arabia—is the now evident breakdown of their capacity to provide the most basic facilities and economic opportunities for their citizens. As well as suffering from a declining ability to keep offering subsidies and the structural problem of voluntary unemployment, these states are increasingly experiencing a widening wealth gap within their national populations, with rising involuntary or real unemployment, and in some cases even citizens living in conditions of poverty. As with the personal fortunes of the ruling families, the latter issue has been another highly sensitive, even taboo, topic of discussion in the region for many years. It has been dangerous for the Gulf monarchies to admit that there are now substantial numbers of indigent nationals in their countries after decades of hydrocarbon exports and sizeable government revenues.

In Bahrain's case, unemployment in 2005 was thought to be as high as 15 per cent,[76] although official figures have usually been lower. In early 2011 the official unemployment rate was still less than 4 per cent[77] while independent studies in mid-2011 claimed it was about 15 per cent. Similarly in Oman, recent independent studies have estimated the rate at 15 per cent.[78] Total unemployment in Saudi Arabia, most of which is probably now involuntary, is the subject of even more speculation, with estimates ranging from 10 to 20 per cent among adult males, especially among the youth. In 2009 official statistics were produced indicating that 27 per cent of men under the age of thirty were unemployed, while employment opportunities for young women remained extremely limited.[79] Indeed, it was even reported that some Saudi women were having to work as maids in Qatar.[80] In late 2010 the Saudi minister for labour stated that 500,000 Saudi nationals were unemployed, promising a gathering at the Riyadh Chamber of Commerce and Industry that 'We are going to have to solve this unemployment problem'. At about the same time, however, fresh official figures were released indicating that unemployment had risen to 10.5 per cent, with analysts claiming that Saudi Arabia's published aims of halving unemployment by 2014 are unrealistic and that unemployment is likely to remain high.[81]

Unsurprisingly, this is leading to increasing criticism of the government from unemployed Saudi youth or those having to take on menial jobs. At a protest held by unemployed teachers in 2010, their spokesman claimed they were '…surprised about the lack of opportunities despite the need for teachers but the ministry was not interested in this', while a recent Reuters report highlighted the case of those educated Saudi nationals who can now only find work as taxi drivers, private security guards or other low-paid jobs.[82] Increasingly, complaints are being directed at expatriates rather than the government, with a now popular—although seemingly inaccurate—belief among many Saudi nationals that foreigners are being paid more than citizens and are taking jobs that used to be reserved for them. According to a *Financial Times* report in late 2010 some Saudi newspaper columnists and social media users were lamenting publicly the '…money that they believed foreigners were skimming off Saudis, portraying expatriates as wallowing in luxury while the country struggles with unemployment'. In particular one columnist claimed 'We are not surprised. Foreigners control all retail business, grocery stores… they are given facilities and priority, killing all job prospects for Saudis… nine million foreigners are bleeding the country dry'.[83] Even in the smaller, wealthier Gulf monarchies there are signs that involuntary unemployment is rising, particularly in the UAE where there remains a great imbalance between the more developed emirates of Abu Dhabi and Dubai, and the poorer 'northern emirates'. In Fujairah, for example, official statistics from 2009 indicated that the emirate's unemployment rate was 20.6 per cent, well above the UAE's national average of 14 per cent.[84] More significant is that most of the unemployed in the more developed emirates are likely to be voluntarily unemployed, while most unemployed in the northern emirate are likely to be involuntarily unemployed.

With regards poverty and poor living conditions, there is increasing evidence in Saudi Arabia of large numbers of nationals struggling to make ends meet. In a recent *Financial Times* report it was claimed that

'…many young men cannot afford to marry or buy a home, raising concerns of social unrest and higher crime rates… many foreigners complain of bag-snatching or robbery at knifepoint by young Saudis, as unemployment stokes xenophobia'.[85] Meanwhile chief economists at Saudi-based banks have warned that '[although] the unemployment rate is not new it has become more of a political concern now. Prices are going up in very critical areas like food and housing. Purchasing power is being quickly eroded'.[86] In Bahrain the situation is believed to be much worse, with some 50,000 Bahraini nationals estimated to be on waiting lists to receive affordable housing.[87] In some cases Bahraini nationals have had to wait over twenty years before being properly housed. In a report published in 2011, for example, a fisherman's life was used to typify the poor social conditions endured by many Bahrainis. It was claimed that he had always '…shared the cramped, run-down family home in Sitra with his parents, four brothers and two sisters. The four adult brothers slept in one small room. One of his sisters is married with four children, who also live in the family home'. His income was believed to be only about $210 per month, which he complained was barely enough to cover a weekly food bill. Moreover, he had stated '…how much he wanted to get married and start a family, but he couldn't afford a house. Like many young Bahraini men, he couldn't start a family because he was too poor'.[88]

As well as their high unemployment rates, the UAE's northern emirates provide perhaps the most interesting example of poverty in the Gulf monarchies, given the increasingly visible divide between the country's richer and poorer emirates. According to statistics from 2008, Abu Dhabi's contribution to the UAE's overall GDP was nearly 56 per cent, while Dubai's contribution was about 32 per cent. As such, the five other emirates combined accounted only for 12 per cent of GDP. Even more alarming, perhaps, was that Abu Dhabi's contribution to the federal budget—from which most development assistance for the poorer emirates is funded—was only 3 per cent of its GDP, while Dubai's contribution was only half a per cent of its GDP.[89] It can be argued that since the UAE's independence in 1971 the relative GDP contributions of the northern emirates have actually declined.[90] The poor conditions have manifested themselves in different ways. Small protests have occurred, some of which have been bought off with promises of increased housing benefits, while others have been quashed by federal security forces.[91] In 2006 inhabitants from a village outside Ra's al-Khaimah blocked roads to stop trucks getting through. The authorities responded by sending in tanks and then followed up with substantial financial compensation for the villagers. More often, however, nationals of these emirates simply complain of a variety of problems ranging from a lack of basic utilities to housing shortages. But in all cases their remonstrations serve to dispel the myth that all UAE nationals are wealthy and content.

In Ra's al-Khaimah, for example, residents continue to complain about the water supply being cut, sometimes for several days at a time,[92] and 'major rodent infestations'.[93] Some national families also complain of small houses that they cannot afford to repair. Interviewed by a state-controlled newspaper, one UAE citizen claimed that she slept on the floor with her three children, and could only afford to treat the damp and mould by selling her marriage dowry gold. She further claimed that she wouldn't have been able to afford furniture unless her daughter—a policewoman—was able to help. Having waited since 2008 for a new house, she has visited the housing office daily asking why her name is not yet on the list and demanding that 'All I want is a house from the Government for my babies... I don't want a lot of money in the bank'.[94] A Reuters report from 2011 painted a similarly gloomy picture, describing the '...absence of digital billboards, shopping centres, and hotels that typify Dubai. Instead, desert roads are dotted with clusters of small apartment blocks, car repair workshops and discount retailers. Clotheslines are laden with laundry left to dry in the sun, and diesel generators are placed near commercial and residential buildings, to compensate for power shortages'.[95]

For years various rescue packages have been dispensed to the northern emirates, but these are understood to have either been too little, or have quickly been swallowed up by corrupt officials in the emirate-level governments. In 2008 a $4.3 billion grant was allocated by the federal government to oversee physical infrastructure projects in the northern emirates. But despite the size of the sum, the announcement of the package was greeted with scepticism by some of the recipient municipalities, with one anonymous spokesperson stating 'We often hear about these projects from Abu Dhabi, but we haven't seen them come into action'.[96] In 2011, shortly after the Tunisian and Egyptian revolutions, it was announced that the northern emirates would receive an additional $1.6 billion in aid. The federal government also claims that it has a twenty year plan in place that will address some of the 'gaps and other issues such as healthcare, education, housing, roads, and water'.[97] It also promised to build more than 100 kilometres of new rural roads,[98] and doubled the funding for a small business development programme that aims to increase job creation in the region.[99]

These planned improvements have prompted some analysts to argue that '...the federal government is capable of increasing spending in these smaller emirates to stave off any social unrest'.[100] It seems likely, however, that the UAE's wealth gap will keep on growing. A report from summer 2011 remarked of Ra's al-Khaimah that '[although] less than 300km from the UAE's capital territory of Abu Dhabi, its neighbourhoods of low cement buildings and dusty cars feel as if they are in a different country'.[101] Similarly, UAE nationals interviewed by reporters complained that '...the wealth disparity between the northern emirates and Dubai and Abu Dhabi remains the most challenging issue for the stability of the country as a whole'. They also agreed that developing utilities, health care and education were the most pressing needs and added that they rarely travelled to emirates outside Dubai and Abu Dhabi because they lacked adequate services.[102]

Usually considered immune from economic deprivation or other such problems due to the country's very high wealth per capita, even some Qatari nationals have recently begun to bemoan their circumstances. In 2007, a prominent Qatari cleric[103] began to highlight their cause, claiming that there is 'poverty in cash-rich Qatar and [there need to be] programmes to alleviate it by providing long-term interest-free housing loans and opportunities for self-employment to low-income citizens'.[104] In early 2011 a state-backed newspaper threw more light on the issue when it was reported that some Qatari nationals had been posting on internet fora about the need for greater assistance for 'low income families who are living off a meagre dole', the problem of 'salaries being high, but resources getting exhausted by the middle of the month since rents and food prices were skyrocketing', and the increasing need to cross the border to the nearby Saudi city of Hassa to 'buy household provisions every month... in order to make ends meet'.[105] And later in 2011, although a rather narrow example, the same newspaper claimed that a number of Qatari families were upset over the Qatar Tourism Authority's cancellation of the annual Doha Summer Festival. Explaining that these families were hard-pressed due to 'piling bank loans which make it more difficult for them to afford holidaying abroad' and had been 'looking forward to the summer festival... due to [their] financial problems',[106] the report again seemed to challenge the stereotype that all Qatari nationals enjoy substantial state-provided benefits. More recently, an extensive report by a Qatar-based consultancy firm argued that it was a 'myth that all Qataris were rich... this is not the case', and claimed that nearly three-quarters of Qatari national families were actually in debt, often to the tune of $65,000 or more.[107]

Discrimination, statelessness, and sectarianism

A similarly under-reported problem affecting the indigenous or de facto indigenous populations of many Gulf monarchies has been the ongoing discrimination—in some cases state-sanctioned—against various minorities. In particular, there has been a continuing failure to address the issue of statelessness, with large numbers—perhaps now hundreds of thousands—of *bidoon jinsiyya* or people 'without nationality', whose families have lived in the region for many generations, but who have, for a variety of reasons, failed to secure sufficient documentation to acquire full citizenship. There is also a worrying trend in some of the Gulf monarchies of bias and intolerance—including sectarian violence—from predominantly Sunni political and business elites against indigenous Shia populations. This has undoubtedly been exacerbated in recent years and, as later sections of this book will demonstrate, has now become a key flashpoint for opposition in the region in the wake of the 2011 Arab Spring. Both these phenomena are undermining the ruling families' legitimacy, especially as divisions within national populations have not been bridged, resentment has been allowed to build, and—more subtly—increasing stratification within supposedly equitable societies has either gone unchecked or even been encouraged.

With regard to statelessness, Kuwait is by far the worst offender—at least in proportion to its total population—with some 106,000 bidoon now living in the emirate.[108] The majority are classed by the government as 'illegal residents' and the issue is dealt with by the Ministry for Interior, indicating its treatment as a matter of security,[109] but in practice the bidoon are best viewed as second class citizens who are unable to access the benefits of the state. Many of Kuwait's bidoon claim they are indigenous, but missed out on full citizenship because their parents did not complete the necessary registration papers with the government after the country's independence in 1961. This was mostly due to illiteracy, or a lack of understanding of how significant citizenship papers were going to become. For most of the 1960s and 1970s the bidoon had access to the welfare state and its benefits in the same way as regular citizens, although they were not eligible to vote in Kuwait's parliamentary elections.[110] Causing much resentment during this period, however, a Saudi tribe[111] was granted full Kuwaiti citizenship—an attempt by a prominent member of the ruling family (and the present day chief of the National Guard) to boost his support base.[112] Following a period of instability in the 1980s—which led to increased xenophobia and a government-perpetuated belief that the bidoon were originally from neighbouring countries such as Iraq and had deliberately destroyed their documents in the hope of becoming Kuwaiti—their situation worsened considerably.[113]

In particular they have faced great difficulties in acquiring official documentation such as birth and marriage certificates, driving licences, and passports. As a result many have never been able to access free government schooling,[114] have failed to secure government housing, and are thus obliged to pay rent on property in much the same way as expatriates. Moreover, most also fail to secure public sector employment and thus have much lower salaries, on average, than the poorest 'full' Kuwaiti citizens. According to a recent BBC report many of the bidoon only earn a few hundred dollars per month.[115] A number do, however, seem to acquire employment in the police or the security services, likely because unswerving loyalty in these jobs is highly valued by the state and has been set up as one possible route to naturalisation.

In 2011, the plight of the Kuwaiti bidoon seemed little better, with a Human Rights Watch report arguing that 'For 50 years, Kuwait has dawdled in reviewing bidoon citizenship claims, while creating a straightjacket of regulations that leave them in poverty and extreme uncertainty'. Moreover, it claimed that 'Kuwait has every resource it needs to solve this problem, but chooses to stall instead'.[116] Similarly, prominent journalists in the region have recently concluded that the bidoon have '… been dehumanised and rendered invisible by government policies coupled with pervasive social stigmatisation'.[117] Notably, the government's new Central System for Resolving Illegal Residents' Status—known colloquially as the 'Bidoon Committee' seems to have made little progress. While it has recently issued ration cards to bidoon, allowing them to receive subsidised foodstuffs via government-run cooperatives, the committee more importantly continues to reject applications for birth, marriage, and death certificates, and thus continues to prevent the bidoon from establishing any form of legal relationships in Kuwait. Moreover, according to Human Rights Watch it still regularly claims to have evidence of the bidoon's 'true nationalities', although bidoon applicants have not been allowed to see this.[118] In late 2010 officials even publicly claimed that at least 42,000 bidoon in Kuwait were really Iraqi citizens and suggested that '[Kuwait] has possession of documents that prove their affiliation to other Arab countries, so diplomatic measures need to be taken'.[119]

In February and March 2011 over one thousand bidoon reportedly took to the streets to demand better rights. Although there has since been a more broad-based Kuwaiti movement which, as discussed later in this book, opposes the current government and members of the ruling family, the bidoon protests can nonetheless still be viewed as an early Arab Spring protest. A group representing the bidoon—the Kuwaiti Bidoon Gathering—was formed, with its representatives stating that '…the most important right that we are asking for, and this is non-negotiable, is the right for a Kuwaiti citizenship' and arguing that '…there are some basic human rights, like the right for healthcare, the right to work, the right to mobilise, the right to have identity papers, the right for education and travel'. Moreover, claiming that '…these are the normal and basic rights for any regular human being living anywhere' the group has stated that its first protests were the result of '…the events in the Middle East inspired the young bidoon to go out and ask for their rights—the rights that were taken away from them'.[120] Interestingly, at the rallies the protestors were sighted carrying flags with swastika symbols and slogans that complained of the fascist nature of the Bidoon Committee. With the security services responding to the protests with water cannon, teargas, smoke bombs, and concussion grenades, and with dozens reportedly injured and large numbers held in custody, the situation seems likely to deteriorate further.[121] Indeed, the Kuwait Bidoon Gathering has hinted that the situation in Kuwait is now a 'ticking time bomb' and that 'the bomb hasn't burst yet and these are only sparks before the big explosion'.[122]

Although having received far less attention than in Kuwait, the bidoon issue is becoming increasingly significant in the UAE, where there are believed to be between 10,000 and 100,000 stateless persons, with some even living in the wealthier emirates of Abu Dhabi and Dubai. Much like in Kuwait, they have been unable to obtain key documentation or access most benefits of the welfare state. In particular they lack the vital 'family card' or *khulsat al-qaid*, which is required to prove one's lineage. At best they have only been able to receive temporary passports—thus excluding them from employment in the public sector. Moreover, they are often publicly discriminated against and—to a great extent—stigmatised by the government. In April 2011, when—as described later—six pro-democracy activists were arrested, the UAE's state-backed news agency kept referring in all press releases to one of their number as being a 'person without valid documentation'. This gave the impression that he was somehow of dubious character in addition to not being a bona fide UAE national.

In an extensive report by the UAE-based *Arabian Business* magazine in 2009 a number of UAE bidoon were interviewed—a rare occurrence and a voice not usually heard in the country. One female interviewee claimed that she was just one of thousands living in difficult conditions, explaining that 'when you are a bidoon you cannot do so many things. You are not expatriate or a local; you are in-between'. Although she admitted that her family were originally from Iran, she explained that they had arrived in the country—then the Trucial States—back in 1953 and had received Sharjah passports. However, after the UAE's independence in 1971 they were only given temporary passports which were renewed every six months until 1982 when their application was denied. Many other UAE bidoon claim descent from local tribes and can trace their lineage back several generations. Indeed, the report claimed that 'according to anecdotal evidence, nearly 50 per cent of the [UAE] bidoon's fathers were born in the Gulf monarchies while around 30 per cent of their grandfathers were born in the region... [but] today they find themselves in no man's land'. Speaking of this diversity, a spokesperson for Refugees International explained that '[a UAE bidoon] could be someone who finds themselves in that situation for a number of reasons; their family may have lived historically in the country, but for some reason was not documented or chose not to be documented at the time; it could be someone who entered the country seeking asylum... there is no one stereotypical situation; it really is a diversified community of individuals'.[123] Recent research has also demonstrated that some of the UAE bidoon often move back and forth between being citizens or not, with temporary passports seemingly being dispensed and then revoked at whim.

Described as a 'liminal population' that is politically managed depending on the government's priorities of the day, these more fortunate bidoon are still left unable to plan for any kind of future.[124] Nevertheless, regardless of their precise backgrounds or their exact passport status, all of the UAE's current bidoon firmly claim to be Emirati, with most alluding to the fact that they, their parents, and their grandparents have never known life in another country. One interviewee simply stated '...my life is here; all of my close friends are Emiratis. I know more about the UAE than I know about Iran. It would be impossible for me to live anywhere else'.[125]

The issue seems to be being dealt with in more or less the same way as in Kuwait, with the government forming committees, but then being slow to act. In 2008, following the setting up of several bidoon registration centres, about 1300 bidoon were naturalised, but only because they were somehow able to prove their pre-1971 ancestry.[126] As reported by a state-backed newspaper, many of those queuing at the centres were in a highly emotional state, being conscious of the decades-long wait their families had suffered. As one hopeful bidoon described of the process: 'this will change everything for us and for our children... becoming Emirati will be like being born again'.[127] Another stated that 'I will carry the country's emblem on my head and my love for it in my heart'. Significantly, after this small number of naturalisations the minister for the interior was quick to underline the fact that citizenship in the UAE is a privilege and a reward for loyalty and political acquiescence, rather than a right. Specifically, he warned that 'loyalty is a condition of citizenship and new citizens are expected to embrace the values that have ensured social stability and security for all. The constitution allows for revoking citizenship from anyone who does not deserve it'. When a newly naturalised citizen was asked for his thoughts on this message, he stated simply that 'those who drink from a well would never throw dirt in it'.[128]

Since then, there have been no tangible improvements, with government officials and other pro-government spokespersons usually highlighting the potential disloyalty and reliability of bidoon given their uncertain pasts. The director of the immigration and naturalisation department in Abu Dhabi, for example, not only claimed that the main problem was that bidoon were registering under different names because they treated citizenship as a 'lottery', but also echoed the arguments of Kuwaiti officials, explaining in 2009 that '...the vast majority of those who claim to be bidoon are in fact illegal immigrants... who have destroyed documents from their home country in a bid to be granted UAE nationality... there are some who are real bidoon, but unfortunately they get mixed up with the vast majority who claim to be bidoon'. Similarly, a UAE national academic argued that '...many of these people came here in the 1980s and destroyed their documents to stay in the Emirates [because] they don't want to leave the country. They came to the country for political reasons and many came into the country illegally'.[129] Furthermore, the government remains committed to using the threat of revoking citizenship as a means to ensure acquiescence. As discussed later in this book, in December 2011 seven activists promoting an Islamist agenda were stripped of their passports and thus relegated to being bidoon.

Other significant stateless populations are believed to exist in Saudi Arabia, where there are an unknown number of bidoon. These also appear to be subjected to widespread discrimination, especially in legal cases, with frequent reports of government officials or other spokespersons claiming they have no rights. In December 2011, for example, six stateless persons who were sentenced to hand and foot amputations after having signed coerced confessions to a crime of armed robbery, were told by prison staff that as bidoon they had no rights.[130] In Bahrain there are thought to still be several thousand bidoon. Although the Bahraini government did naturalise a few thousand Iranian-origin bidoon in 2001, following on from the aforementioned national action charter, the state has, like the UAE, recently demonstrated its willingness to revoke citizenship and return residents to bidoon status if necessary. In 2010 a prominent cleric and former bidoon who has criticised the government was promptly stripped of his passport on the grounds that he and his family had 'not obtained citizenship via legal means' back in 2001.[131] This was a clear warning to other former bidoon.

Discrimination against Shia communities in the Gulf monarchies is now as commonplace as that against stateless persons. The worst example has always been in Bahrain, where historically the Shia have formed the majority of the indigenous population yet—in a dynamic not dissimilar from Saddam Hussein's Iraq—for much of the modern period they have been ruled by a Sunni minority, since the described ascendancy of the Bani Utub clan and eventually the Al-Khalifa family. Sporadic protests and insurgencies by the Shia in the early and mid-twentieth century—notably a 1920 petition to Britain that they were facing mistreatment from the ruling family and a 1956 general strike—were put down with force, often on the grounds that the Shia were in effect a fifth column of the Shah's Iran. Indeed, in 1957 Iran's parliament had passed a bill declaring Bahrain to be Iran's 14th province, although this claim was later dropped following a United Nations' administered opinion poll of Bahrain's residents in which the overwhelming majority voted to remain independent. But later in the twentieth century, especially following the 1979 Islamic Revolution in Iran and the Al-Khalifa's claims in 1981 that they had uncovered a pro-Iran plot,[132] the persecution of Bahrain's Shia increased. The resulting tensions, along with a widespread belief that Shia were being discriminated against in terms of employment opportunities and state benefits, eventually led to a full scale intifada in the 1990s which claimed the lives of over forty protestors and led to the jailing and exiling of several major opposition figures. Moreover, in 1996 the government claimed to have uncovered a fresh Shia plot, this time by an Iran-backed offshoot of Hezbollah in Bahrain.[133] By the end of the intifada and the launch of the aforementioned 2001 national action charter, approximately 70 to 75 per cent of Bahrain's national population were still believed to be Shia—mostly indigenous Shia Arabs[134] or ethnically Persian Arabs who had long been settled on the island.[135] Since then it is believed that the proportion of Sunni Bahraini citizens has increased, mostly due to government manipulations and 'demographic engineering'. In particular, the government is believed to have been offering citizenship to non-indigenous Sunni Arab and African families in an effort to boost the Sunni contingent of the national population and thus limit the influence of the Shia.

In 2006 details of the policy unexpectedly came into the public domain following the publication of a lengthy report by Salah Al-Bandar—a British citizen of Sudanese origin who had been working for Bahrain's Ministry for Cabinet Affairs. The report—now dubbed Bandargate—claimed to have uncovered a secret plot by a group within the government to 'deprive an essential part of the population [the Shia] of their rights'.[136] Moreover, it inferred that the group was trying to turn the Shia into a minority within just a few years and was busy working on ways to gerrymander electoral constituencies so as to reduce the clout of Shia members of parliament. Although Al-Bandar was promptly deported and the state-backed media was banned from reporting on the story, a protest was held demanding a thorough investigation.[137] In 2008, following the publication of official figures indicating that Bahrain's total population had increased by more than 40 per cent between 2002 and 2007, tensions increased further, as it was deemed unlikely that all of the increase was due to expatriates or the naturalisation of stateless persons. Analysts have claimed that the natural rate of growth for the national population would have only yielded an increase of 47,000 persons, thus more than 72,000 were probably granted citizenship during this period.[138] Indeed, in summer 2010 opposition groups in Bahrain estimated that between 65,000 and 100,000 Sunni nationals have been added to the country's voter rolls in the last decade. Most of the newcomers[139] seem to be housed in brand new villages in Bahrain's hinterland, suitably distanced from the older, predominantly Shia villagers. Many seem to work for the state security services, the police, or the royal court, likely due to their unswerving loyalty to the Sunni elites. Interviewed by the *New York Times* in summer 2010, a resident of one such village—a settlement specifically for Sunnis employed in the security sector—stated that he and his two brothers worked for the police and that '…if the Shia took control of the country, they would pop out one eye of every Sunni in the country'.[140]

Unsurprisingly, Shia-led protests, most of which have focused on their socio-economic discrimination or the jailing of their leaders, continued to gather pace following these revelations and the issue of sectarian manipulation is now very much at the core of the bloody revolution underway in Bahrain. However, even prior to 2011 these protests were being met with extreme force. In March 2009, for example, following the arrest of twenty-three Shia leaders, crowds had gathered to demand their release and carried placards with the slogans 'We are against sectarian discrimination' and 'No, no to oppressing freedoms'. The Bahraini police—mostly made up of Sunni Bahraini nationals or Sunni expatriates from Jordan, Pakistan, and elsewhere—shot teargas canisters into crowds and for several days fought pitched battles in several Shia villages. Interviewed by the *New York Times*, Shia protestors complained that they were all but banned from holding military and security positions, and that '…there are no jobs because of naturalisation of foreigners, because of the political prisoners, because of the abuse of the rights of the citizen'.[141]

In August 2010, shortly before parliamentary elections were due to be staged, four more Shia activists were arrested including the spokesperson for a Shia political group called the Haq Movement for Liberty and

Democracy,[142] the head of a Shia human rights group committed to help-ing those who have been tortured,[143] and others belonging to a group that had—according to the government—been 'created to undermine the security and stability of the country'.[144] Commenting on the arrests, the head of the Bahrain Centre for Human Rights claimed 'I don't think anyone in Bahrain believes those stories' and predicted they would fur-ther inflame sectarian tensions in the country.[145] By the end of the month it was thought that nearly 160 activists had been detained—initially high profile Shia political and human rights leaders, but later including 'many young men not known as activists'. The official view was again one of denial, with spokespersons claiming that the detainees were 'suspected of security and terrorism violations, and were not being held for express-ing dissident political views' and that '…the only thing the government did wrong was that it went too easy at first'. The government also stated that it would '…no longer tolerate unrest among the Shia' and that those convicted of '…compromising national security or slandering the nation can be deprived of health care and other state services'.[146]

Writing for *The Economist* in October 2010, one week before the elec-tions, one analyst tried to sum up the mood in Bahrain following these harsh government counter measures. In the short term, it was argued, the measures might work, as 'Opposition and human-rights people could be frightened into acquiescence'. However, it was pointed out that due to the '…government's mishandling of events in the past few weeks [it] has stirred a well of resentment that may, in the longer term, spell dan-ger for the Sunni ascendancy—and even for the ruling house'. Signifi-cantly, the article also claimed that the government was 'blatantly harassing the opposition parties, particularly the main Shia-dominated one' and that its leaders were being '…assailed in the pro-government press with accusations of encouraging terrorism and being in the pocket of "outside powers", meaning in essence Iran'.[147] Indeed, when a British member of the House of Lords[148] met with Bahraini Shia leaders in London, and when the British ambassador to Bahrain met Shia leaders in Manama, the Bahraini state-backed newspapers were full of allega-tions of British- or Iranian-engineered plots to overthrow the ruling fam-ily. A petition was even signed by prominent Bahraini Sunnis demanding the expulsion of the British ambassador on these grounds.

The Shia of Saudi Arabia have for many years also complained bit-terly of discrimination. Unlike their Bahraini counterparts, they form only a minority of Saudi nationals, albeit now a substantial minority of between 5 and 15 per cent, with most dwelling in the Eastern Province, close to Bahrain, and home to several of the kingdom's key oil fields. Over the years, most of their complaints have been over the province's relative underdevelopment compared to the rest of Saudi Arabia and the institutional discrimination they have faced, especially over public sector employment opportunities. There have been fewer protests than in Bahrain, nonetheless riots broke out in 1979—which were brutally suppressed—and in 2009 there were reports of attacks by Saudi security forces on Shia pilgrims.[149] On occasion there has also been organised opposition, with 450 Shia activists signing a petition in 2003 entitled 'Partners in One Nation' which demanded the equal treatment of Shia under Saudi Arabia's laws.[150]

As with Bahrain, Shia protests were taking place in Saudi Arabia immediately prior to 2011. In December 2010 for example, violent clashes erupted in the holy city Medina during the Ashoura commemorations—a key religious day for Shia. It transpired that hundreds of Sunni hardliners had attacked Shia worshippers, reportedly using poles and stones. Although security forces were eventually deployed, there was apparently a delay of more than two hours before the attackers were dispersed. Moreover, while several state-backed newspapers reported the attacks, they eschewed mention of the sectarian element, with one[151] even blaming 'young zealots wearing black clothes'—in a reference to Shia worshippers—for inciting the violence.[152]

The situation in Kuwait has generally been better, as although the Shia community is estimated to be a fairly substantial 15 per cent of the national population, it is much more closely integrated into the emirate's business elite. Nevertheless, there have been a growing number of incidents which indicate rising sectarian tension, especially with regard to allegations of strengthening links between Kuwait's Shia and Bahrain's Shia, and between Kuwait's Shia and Iran. In late 2010 for example, the state-backed *Al-Qabas* newspaper reported that there were Shia cells throughout the Gulf monarchies, including Kuwait, which were ready to strike in the event of any attack on Iran. Meanwhile two Kuwaiti Shia activists were stripped of their citizenship on the grounds that they were 'trying to stir up conflict amongst Muslims'. Most dramatically, four Kuwaiti Shia were also arrested at about the same time and charged, along with three Iranian expatriates, with spying for Iran in Kuwait and leaking confidential military information, a charge which the Iranian government has vehemently denied.[153] In early 2011, soon after the beginning of the Bahraini revolution the tension in Kuwait escalated further, with other state-backed newspapers publishing anti-Shia articles. Many described the Bahraini revolution through a sectarian lens, promoting evidence of connections to Iran, while *Al-Watan* newspaper carried an article specifically on one of the denaturalised Shia activists.[154] Although nothing compared to Bahrain's Al-Bandar scandal, the Kuwaiti government has also recently been criticised for compiling demographic statistics based on sect. In June 2011 a report began circulating widely on the internet which claimed that the government was trying to determine the exact number—rumoured to be 15.7 per cent—of the Kuwaiti Shia national population. This prompted a strong response from the Kuwaiti Ministry for the Interior which stated that 'There is no truth whatsoever in the allegations that the interior ministry has prepared statistics about the number of Kuwaiti nationals based on their Sunni or Shiite sects' and that '...the interior ministry does not have the prerogatives to issue such statistics'.[155]

Evidence of sectarian tension in the UAE, where there is believed to be a Shia minority making up about 5 per cent of the total national population, is currently more anecdotal. As in Kuwait, most of the Emirati Shia tend to be well integrated, especially in Dubai where they are a major force in the emirate's business community. In recent years, however, there has been a discernible shift in attitudes, with many Shia complaining of more limited employment opportunities and—on occasion—discrimination in the workplace. With the situation in Bahrain and Saudi Arabia, and with the rising tension between the UAE and Iran this is likely to get much worse in the near future. Already there are clear indications that the UAE authorities distrust Arab Shia expatriates in their country, including even those who have loyally worked in the UAE's public sector for decades. In 2009, for example, the UAE reportedly began deporting dozens of long-term Lebanese Shia expatriates, seemingly on the grounds that they had financial or other connections to Lebanon's Hezbollah. Since then many other Lebanese and other Arab Shia have been deported from the UAE, usually with no notice. Interestingly, a committee has now been formed in Lebanon to combat this sectarian discrimination, and has provided details of many of the Lebanese deportees, including one man who had worked as a journalist in Sharjah for twenty-two years and another who had lived in the UAE for thirty-five years, owned three companies and had $5 million worth of contracts in the UAE, and employed more than eighty Arab Sunni expatriates in the country. The former claims that he had no warning and was not even allowed to pack his bags, while the latter explained that he was held at the airport after returning from a vacation and denied entry into the UAE for 'security reasons'. Confirming the deportations, a senior Hezbollah representative has argued that the UAE has 'violated their rights and freedom' and has called on the UAE authorities to 'save the hundreds of Lebanese families who have contributed to the development of your country'.[156]

Censorship and limiting expression

Best viewed as an early response to the accumulating internal pressures in the Gulf monarchies, coupled with a lack of transparency associated with prevailing political structures, there has been a dramatic increase in censorship in the region. For decades there have been crude attempts to black out articles in foreign newspapers, ban certain books, fire journalists, and harass academics who spoke out of line. But with the advent of new communications—especially involving mobile telephones and the internet—the governments' responses have had to become far more sophisticated, often employing the latest technologies, methods, and new legal apparatus to cut off channels of free expression and remove or discredit those responsible. As the final chapter of this book demonstrates, this is becoming harder for governments to do, as media evolves and opponents manage to keep information and ideas flowing beyond governmental control.

Nevertheless, there have been notable examples of effective censorship in all of the Gulf monarchies in the past few years. This has not gone unnoticed, with all six states having slipped further down the World Press Freedom Index, as compiled by Reporters without Borders. As of early 2012, the highest ranked Gulf monarchy was Kuwait—in 78th position—with the UAE, Qatar, and Oman ranked firmly below dozens of African dictatorships—in 112th, 114th, and 117th positions respectively—and with Saudi Arabia and Bahrain ranking among the very worst countries in the world.[157] Although superficially successful in the short term in limiting opposition voices, the various censorship strategies employed have been leading to heightened fears and widespread criticism and condemnation of the regimes responsible, not only from the international community, but also from resident national and expatriate populations. In a summer 2011 YouGov poll commissioned by the BBC's Doha Debates, which collected the responses of 1000 participants from the region, it was revealed that more than half of the Gulf respondents were 'too afraid to speak out against their rulers'. This contrasted sharply with a similar poll amongst nationals of North African Arab Spring states, where respondents reportedly expressed optimism about their freedoms.[158]

Bahrain unsurprisingly provides some of the most extreme examples of censorship and attacks on free speech, with a large number of recent assaults and arrests involving opinion-makers and commentators. In August 2010, for example, it was reported by the Bahrain Centre for Human Rights that the editor in chief of Bahrain's *Alwatan* newspaper[159] was attacked by several masked men outside the newspaper's headquarters in the early hours of the morning. He claimed that they asked him if he worked for the newspaper, to which he said 'yes', and then they began to beat him and set fire to his car.[160] Although *Alwatan* is believed to be funded by a member of the ruling family, has close links to the regime, and has been accused of promoting sectarianism in Bahrain, its pro-government stance is thought to have wavered in recent years. The following month another disturbing incident happened when the founder of Bahrain's most popular internet forum[161]—Bahrainonline.org—was arrested by security services and his website blocked on the grounds that it was 'spreading false news'. Thought to be one of more than 200 bloggers and internet activists seized that summer, he was increasingly seen as a threat to the government as his forum allowed opposition voices to discuss matters freely with other Bahrainis. Visited by thousands every day, the forum was particularly well known for having helped break news of the Bandargate scandal, along with 'highlighting cases of sectarian discrimination, police brutality, state corruption, and political naturalisation'. According to one user, the forum was so active that '…if [she] heard a bang at night [she] would be able check on the internet [forum] and, sure enough, someone would have posted about it within minutes. Some users even posted photos of government security agents who show up at protests, prompting the agents to start covering their faces when appearing in public'. Hundreds of other websites have since been blocked, with all surviving websites in Bahrain now having to register their details with the Ministry for Information. Even Google Earth has been blocked, after activists began using satellite images from the software to demonstrate how vast and lavish the ruling family's palaces were in comparison to the poor suburbs that most Bahrainis have to live in.[162]

Other incidents in 2010 included the fining of journalists who had attempted to report on money-laundering scandals involving ministers, despite their cases having shifted from the mandate of the prosecution to the law courts and thus no longer being subjected to gag orders.[163] That year was notable also for a statement from the Ministry for information that BlackBerry mobile devices were no longer to be used for 'circulating any form of news'. This was a government reaction, much like that to the internet fora, based on a growing concern that BlackBerrys were being used by Bahrainis to pass on information about government corruption and abuses. The statement went on to explain that: '…mobile phones have been relaying news of incidents and topics in Bahrain. In view of the impact of such news in causing disarray and confusion to the public… those individuals and agencies were summoned by the Ministry, and legal and judicial procedures will be filed against violators of laws…' Although it is unclear how successful the ministry has been in controlling the use of BlackBerrys, it seems that the Blackberry World application feature has been blocked in Bahrain, thus preventing the installation of messenger and discussion applications.

The UAE has also seen a varied and forceful response to channels of free expression in recent years. Unlike Bahrain, where the government does little to disguise its practices, the UAE has been more cautious in its methods, not least because its non-oil economic sectors rely increasingly on a sound international reputation. Moreover, a deeper sense of irony pervades these debates in the UAE compared to Bahrain, as its rulers have on occasion tried to position themselves as champions of free speech and take credit for it. Notably, in 2004 the minister for higher education and scientific research[164] stated at a book fair held in Abu Dhabi that '…the UAE now lives in an age in which people should be supplied with all kinds of information… all people have the right to choose and select information and are wise enough to make that choice. No information should be withheld from the public in this day and age'.[165] Later that year the crown prince of Dubai—Muhammad bin Rashid Al-Maktoum—repeated an earlier freedom of speech statement he had first made during the opening of Dubai Media City in 2000,[166] by urging media representatives to 'maintain objectivity in their pursuance of truth… and by promising to iron out difficulties hindering them as they carry out their duties', before stating that 'all authorities must render all facilities and moral support to media corporations operating in Dubai… which must remain an oasis of responsible freedom and democracy of opinion and expression'.[167] In 2008 Abu Dhabi even set up a new English language newspaper—*The National*—with the aim of promoting transparency and hard-hitting coverage of both domestic and regional issues. Launched by a highly paid team of experienced western journalists and editors, the newspaper began with great fanfare, before the realities of being a state-backed newspaper set in and staff began to leave. In 2010 Muhammad bin Rashid was back to the subject, this time as ruler of Dubai, with a Ramadan speech to journalists and editors replete with clichés and truisms on the nature of free speech: '…my directives are clear and beyond any questioning, as we rely on candour and transparency. We strongly believe that media is the mirror of the nation. It has a noble message to disseminate and to enlighten the public, away from exaggeration, bias and distortion of facts. Media is the nation's voice. The sun cannot be blocked by a sieve'.[168]

After the onset of the 2008 credit crunch and the dramatic effect it had on the UAE's economy, especially Dubai's real estate sector, the UAE finally clarified its well-known restrictions on the media—most of which had previously relied on informal threats and self-censorship—by introducing new legislation. In particular, a draft law began to circulate that introduced massive new financial penalties for journalists who crossed red lines such as 'disparaging senior government officials or the royal family' or 'misleading the public and harming the economy'. While jail sentences were withdrawn, the huge fines were viewed by most critics as a highly effective way of stifling free speech, as newspaper editors would be unwilling to allow journalists to tackle risky topics. In a comprehensive report on the new law, Human Rights Watch concluded that '[it would] regulate the news media unlawfully by restricting free expression and would unduly interfere with the media's ability to report on sensitive subjects'. Furthermore, the report also observed that '…the pending law includes provisions that would grant the government virtually complete control in deciding who is allowed to work as a journalist and which media organisations are allowed to operate in the country'.[169] In April 2009 the law was finally passed, with a government official claiming that it was 'consistent with the UAE's pioneering regional role in promoting freedom of the press'.[170]

As with Bahrain, the internet has become a key battleground for the UAE, with the authorities paying great attention to the information viewed by its citizens and resident expatriates. In 2009 a report on internet filtering in the UAE was published by the OpenNet Initiative—a partnership of the University of Toronto, Harvard University, and the SecDev Group of Ottawa. It claimed that the UAE government 'pervasively filters websites that contain pornography or content relating to alcohol and drug use, gay and lesbian issues, or online dating or gambling' while concluding that the UAE '…continues to prevent its citizens from accessing a significant amount of internet content spanning a variety of topics…' Interestingly, the report also concluded that the filtering scheme is now being applied to Dubai's aforementioned free zones, including Dubai Media City, which previously enjoyed unfettered internet access. In 2010, another report claimed that the UAE was going even further than filtering, with its state-owned telecommunications company having been provided by the US-based firm CyberTrust since 2005 with the ability to fake secure connections,[171] despite it being an arm of an authoritarian state. This, it has been argued, allows it to position itself potentially as a 'man in the middle' during web transactions between users.[172]

In practice, a wide range of websites and internet activities are now blocked in the UAE, including all of the categories identified by the OpenNet Initiative and those listed in a leaked memorandum from the UAE's telecommunications regulatory authority.[173] In addition, every website in Arabic or English that contains criticism of the UAE's ruling families, or indeed other Gulf monarchies' ruling families, is also blocked, as are websites or sections of websites that focus on human rights, prison conditions, and civil liberties in the region. On occasion even the websites of leading international non-governmental organisations are barred if they feature negative headlines or articles relating to the UAE. Sometimes the websites of major international news organisations will also be temporarily inaccessible if they are carrying a specific headline. A more recent and popular strategy has been to block access to specific articles on the websites of foreign newspapers. In 2009, for example, a lengthy essay about Dubai appearing on *The Independent*'s website was blocked,[174] while in 2011 a similar article in *Vanity Fair* was also barred without explanation. In parallel to internet censorship, the UAE's National Media Council still sometimes requires shops and newsagents to either remove pages or blackout offending articles in the hardcopy versions of these publications. *Vanity Fair* was reportedly tampered with in this way,[175] while in late 2009 an entire edition of *The Sunday Times*[176] was removed from the UAE's shelves and pulped, given that it featured negative reporting on Dubai's economic problems and a cartoon depicting Dubai's ruler drowning in a sea of debt.

BlackBerrys have also been subjected to censorship in the UAE, with most attention being focused on its encrypted messenger system which was allowing users to communicate free from monitoring by state-controlled spyware. In 2009 the UAE's biggest state-owned telecommunications companies began offering a 'performance enhancing' patch to its BlackBerry subscribers which claimed that it 'provided the best Black-Berry service and ultimate experience'. Users reported that the patch slowed down their BlackBerrys and drained its batteries. Research in Motion—the Canadian manufacturer of BlackBerry—quickly released a counter-application to uninstall this patch, explaining that it was in fact a surveillance application designed to allow the UAE authorities to monitor BlackBerry users' messages and emails.[177] Exactly a year later, the UAE authorities' worst fears seemed to be realised when small protests began being organised with the help of BlackBerry messenger. In particular, many UAE nationals had been using the messenger to discuss leaked correspondence showing that some government members considered themselves above paying traffic fines,[178] while others were using the messenger to plan protests against the government over increased petrol prices. Although the protests were eventually called off and an eighteen year-old was arrested (because he had included his PIN in a BlackBerry message and thus revealed his identity) along with five other UAE nationals,[179] the prospect of further such protests prompted the UAE authorities to announce a total ban on BlackBerrys in just one month unless Research in Motion provided access codes for the encrypted messaging system. In July 2010 the government announced that 'BlackBerrys are operating beyond the jurisdiction of national legislation' because they are 'the only devices operating in the UAE that immediately export their data offshore'. Tellingly, the statement also claimed that '…certain Black-Berry applications allow people to misuse the service, causing serious social, judicial, and national security repercussions'.[180] Placed in a difficult position, given that it appeared that access had already been granted to governments in the US, Britain, China, and Russia, Research in Motion had apparently decided that the UAE authorities should not be granted access to BlackBerry services, presumably due to its track-record of—as described by Reporters without Borders—intimidating BlackBerry subscribers.[181] Although the ban was never imposed, with outspoken UAE lawyers[182] describing it as 'unconstitutional' and '…a blatant attack on freedom of expression' in newspaper interviews,[183] it remains unclear whether the UAE authorities' demands were actually met.

Censorship in Kuwait is also increasingly revolving around the internet and new communications technologies, with arrests of bloggers and social media users now occurring. The authorities still seem to rely on making scapegoat arrests of various Kuwaiti citizens, especially journalists that speak out against the government, or—more seriously—criticise the ruling family. In one remarkable case in 2008, the editor-in-chief of the *Al-Shahed* newspaper was sentenced to three years in prison and ordered to pay a fine for having 'insulted the ruler' despite the ruler having previously written to him 'forgiving him and wishing him success with the paper'. Although a member of the ruling family himself, the editor was believed to have allowed cartoons of the ruler and the crown prince to have appeared on the newspaper's entertainment page, with captions asking readers to spot the differences between the two cartoons.[184] Also involving members of the ruling family, in 2010 it was reported that three lesser members of the family had attacked a private television station which had recently aired a comedy show that was deemed offensive to that branch of the family. All parties involved were eventually released on bail, but not before the television station owner had been accused of trying to 'overthrow the government'.[185] More seriously, also in 2010 a Kuwaiti journalist was sentenced to one year in prison for supposedly 'undermining the status of the ruler' and slandering the unpopular prime minister who, as described, was a key member of the ruling family. Specifically, he was accused of saying in public that the prime minister was 'incapable of running the country'[186] and was also accused of inferring that Iranian intelligence agents were gaining access to Kuwaiti affairs via a prominent businessman who was an associate of the prime minister. Half way through his sentence the journalist was rushed to hospital with a heart condition, but even then he was reportedly still bound by his hands and feet to his bed.[187] Accusations of insulting or undermining the ruler have not been limited to Kuwaiti nationals, and on occasion expatriates have also been arrested. In 2009, for example, an Australian national of Iraqi origin was jailed for six months for supposedly criticising the ruler. She claimed to the international media that she was beaten, on occasion held in solitary confinement, and browbeaten into renouncing her Australian passport. She also claimed she was told to keep repeating that she was really an Iraqi.[188]

Shortly prior to the Arab Spring the Kuwaiti authorities had also begun cracking down on public gatherings, most notably in December 2010 when security forces attacked a group of opposition MPs and other Kuwaiti nationals that had convened a public meeting to discuss a 'government plot to amend the 1962 constitution in order to suppress public freedoms'. At least a dozen gatherers were injured and hospitalised, prompting a fifty-two person petition to be signed by Kuwaiti intellectuals and activists that 'expressed regret and condemned the excessive use of force against Kuwaiti citizens'. Opposition MPs also filed a motion requesting the questioning of the prime minister on the grounds that he was 'suppressing freedoms'. The petitioners and the MPs further claimed in their statements that the Kuwaiti government had an active policy of 'suppressing media coverage' and linked the crackdown to Kuwait's recent blocking of Qatar's Al-Jazeera news network in the emirate.[189]

Saudi Arabia's response to censorship more or less mirrors the UAE and Kuwait, but with a new, clearer set of internet regulations having been introduced in early 2011. Apparently to 'protect society from erroneous practices in electronic publishing,' the new regulations are wide-ranging but also ambiguous, covering all forms of "electronic journalism" from blogs to chat rooms and archives, in addition to 'any other form of electronic publishing that the Ministry may choose to add'. Seemingly recognising the difficulty of getting bloggers and other internet activists to register their sites with the Ministry in the same way that online newspapers and other more established fora have had to, the rules instead require their 'voluntary registration'. Crucially, under the new regulations the Ministry has the right to request details from website owners of their servers—even if outside the country—thus allowing government officials in theory to take offensive websites offline entirely if required.[190] Meanwhile, much like Kuwait, Saudi Arabia has continued to arrest countless activists and intellectuals who have spoken or written in a critical manner about the government or the ruling family. In later 2010 for example, a Saudi law professor[191] was seized after he published an online article that questioned the ruling family's legitimacy and speculated about divisions within the family and what they could mean for the future of the monarchy. He was reportedly taken from his family home by four men who did not have a court-issued arrest warrant and then held without charge.[192]

Of all the Gulf monarchies, Qatar has had the least to worry about with regard to censorship, given its economic circumstances and the general popularity enjoyed by its ruling family. Moreover, as the home of the Al-Jazeera network—which is widely regarded as enjoying relatively free speech—Qatar's credentials have been further strengthened. Nevertheless, as with its neighbours, the government has ensured that it has powerful mechanisms to monitor and control most forms of media, including electronic and internet communications. A few activists and bloggers have recently been arrested, which indicates the structural similarities between Qatar and the other Gulf monarchies. The biggest problem so far seems to have been the very public embarrassment over a high profile attempt by the ruling family to brand Qatar as a regional haven of free expression. Launched in 2008 by the ruler's wife—perhaps to allow the ruler to enjoy a little distance from the project, if need be[193]—the Doha Centre for Media Freedom appointed Robert Ménard, former director of the Paris-based Reporters Without Borders, as its founding director. The Centre then established two safe houses in Doha for journalists fleeing from neighbouring countries and positioned itself to pay the legal fees of such refugees.

But only months after the launch, Ménard sent an open letter to the ruler's wife claiming that visas to such journalists were being denied by Qatari officials and that '…some people close to you and others you have appointed to senior positions at the centre are obstructing its activities'. Furthermore, Ménard had fired a Qatari national at the Centre, allegedly for this reason, and he argued that Qatar's media was operating 'under orders'.[194] Unsurprisingly Ménard resigned from the Centre shortly afterwards, and was quoted in the international media as follows: 'How can we have any credibility if we keep quiet about problems in the country that is our host?'[195] He also explained that '…the Centre has been suffocated. We no longer have either the freedom or the resources to do our work' and argued that '…some Qatari officials never wanted an independent Centre, free to speak out without concern for politics or diplomacy, free to criticise even Qatar'. Finally, he turned attention to Qatar itself, complaining that 'Qatar has still not ratified the International Covenant on Civil and Political Rights, despite frequent promises… and the committee that was supposed to discuss a new law on the media—and on which I had been invited to sit—has still not held any meetings'.[196]

5

MOUNTING EXTERNAL PRESSURES

Although the external survival strategies employed by the Gulf monarchies have generally succeeded in securing their position in a volatile environment and boosting their status and influence in more powerful states, they remain prey to pressures and weaknesses that are either by-products of these relationships or that result from the mismanagement of external forces impacting on the region. Among the latter are efforts to diversify their economic bases away from hydrocarbons that have precipitated the development of new economic sectors geared towards foreign investors, tourists, or simply an increased number of expatriates. In many cases this has led to economy-driven, top-down changes and relaxations in the Gulf monarchies' societies, especially with regard to cultural and religious practices. Already these are leading to mounting frustration and resentment from some sections of the national populations, especially those who believe that their governments and ruling families are not doing enough to preserve their values and traditions. In turn this is eroding the monarchies' legitimacy resources, especially relating to traditional authority and Islam.

Also imposed on the broader population with seemingly little consultation have been the Gulf monarchies' efforts to deepen their security ties with the Western powers. This has led to the establishing of many Western military bases on their soil in recent years, including several discreet installations that most citizens remain unaware of. It has also led to increased spending on Western armaments, with many Gulf monarchies now assigning a huge proportion of their GDP to such expenditure in what now resembles a protection racket, rather than a legitimate attempt to build up indigenous defensive capabilities. Closely related to this expensive militarisation of the region, Gulf nationals are also becoming concerned over the now rampant hawkishness of many of their governments, especially with regards to Iran. Despite shared economic histories and the historic efforts of many ruling families to position themselves as active neutrals, it seems that a new generation of Gulf monarchs are now more willing than ever to publicly antagonise their powerful neighbour.

Notwithstanding the region's track record of boycotting and limiting contact with Israel in support of the Palestinian question, and despite having national populations which mostly continue to oppose recognition of Israel, many Gulf rulers seem willing, indeed keen, to strengthen economic and political relations with Israel as part of a dangerous, multipronged strategy to appease Western backers and further isolate Iran. The lack of any meaningful collective security or in some cases even basic co-operation between the Gulf monarchies is also a growing concern, not least due to these new, high stakes policies on Iran and Israel. More than thirty years after the founding of the Gulf Co-operation Council the six member states remain at loggerheads over many issues, including border disputes and other long running territorial arguments. In some cases grievances are so strong that diplomatic rifts develop, violence erupts, or one monarchy interferes in the domestic politics of another, sometimes even stirring or sponsoring coups in an attempt to re-arrange power within neighbours.

Welcoming foreigners and eroding legitimacy

In some Gulf monarchies, and especially those that have made the greatest efforts to attract foreign direct investment and tourists, or present an inviting visage to expatriates, there have been several noticeable relaxations in recent years,. While these measures have certainly been viewed as beneficial or necessary for economic development, it has often prompted strong criticism from more conservative elements of the national populations, many of whom have focused their anger on the apparent indifference of ruling families to their religious and cultural sensibilities. By far the strongest example is Dubai, where, as shown, a considerable attempt has been made to transform the emirate's economic base by building up free zones, tourism, a real estate industry, and a financial sector. In addition to requiring considerable economic liberalisation such as rulings that allow foreigners to purchase freehold property, the emirate's government has also striven to ensure that its massive expatriate population and legions of foreign investors and tourists feel as welcome and comfortable as possible. Given that many of Dubai's newcomers are now either non-Muslim or share very few of the historical and cultural linkages with Dubai that were enjoyed by the earlier immigrants from Persia, India, or other parts of the Arab world,[1] the relaxations have usually revolved around Islamic values and traditions. In Abu Dhabi, Bahrain, Qatar, and Oman the same phenomenon can also be observed, although to a lesser extent.

One of the most obvious relaxations in the region relates to alcohol consumption, as (apart from Saudi Arabia and Kuwait) up until recently alcohol could only be purchased in hotel bars and restaurants or in specific and very discreet stores if a resident could prove their non-Muslim status to the police and had been provided with a 'liquor consumption licence'. Now almost anybody can purchase alcohol, especially in Dubai and Bahrain, as licences are rarely checked and hotels are non-discriminatory. Moreover, in Dubai's case, and in violation of the original Trucial States alcohol regulations that date back to the mid-1950s,[2] over the past decade it has become possible to consume alcohol during Ramadan and on Islamic holidays. Many of its hotels serve alcohol after 6pm during Ramadan, and bars no longer close on the eve of major holidays or during mourning periods for deceased members of the ruling family. This also now applies in Abu Dhabi and other parts of the UAE. Nor is there any real prohibition on the daytime consumption of food during Ramadan in Dubai. It is now almost acceptable to walk down a busy street eating a takeaway meal, and indeed major fast food chains remain open for this purpose—in the recent past a policeman or offended national would have remonstrated at such a sacrilegious act, but now, with all year round tourism and an increasingly culturally insensitive expatriate population, such protests have become rare.

Remarkably, in early 2011 it was reported that the Gulf monarchies had some of the highest alcohol consumption growth rates in the world. Dubai's growth rate was believed to be between 26 and 28 per cent during the boom years of 2006–2008, while since then Abu Dhabi has taken the lead with an estimated growth rate of 28 per cent. Indeed, regional

distributors point to the emirate's rapidly expanding tourism and entertainment industry and expect the demand for alcohol to grow even faster.
At present, the region's beer industry is dominated by Dubai, with a joint
venture between the state-backed Emirates airline and Heineken International enjoying a two-thirds market share in the UAE and with its
products also being the market leaders in Oman, Bahrain, and Qatar.[3]
Meanwhile, the spirits industry is dominated by imports, with Scotch
whisky being the preferred liquor and described as the 'mainstay choice
of the region'. According to research conducted in 2010, Euromonitor
International concluded that the UAE is now the world's biggest consumer of Scotch, with its volume sales having grown by 9 per cent in
2010 to reach a total of 10.2 million litres, enough to push France into
second place. One of the main distributors also claimed that the 'increased
investment from global drinks giants [in the UAE] would lead to the
country retaining its importance in the future' and '[with] the persistently
lacklustre figures coming from developed core markets, the UAE should
stop raising eyebrows and become the focal point of rising [alcohol con-
sumption] expectations in the region'.[4] With regard to officially dry Gulf
monarchies such as Saudi Arabia and Kuwait, alcohol consumption
growth has also been very high, but has been harder to measure. Industry insiders believe that margins are getting higher, with the average black
market bottle of whisky now selling for about $150. Much of the smug-
gled liquor is believed to originate from alcohol stores that operate in the
UAE's poorer northern emirates. These undercut the licensed outlets in
Dubai and Abu Dhabi, and it is estimated that more than half of the
alcohol sold to traders in these emirates ends up being smuggled into
Saudi Arabia.[5]

Also seen as eroding the status of Islam, and in particular Islamic holidays, has been the shopping mall-backed rise of the commercial and secular Christmas. In the 1990s Christmas trees were rarely seen in public
places in the Gulf monarchies, but are now featured prominently in many
retail outlets, hotels, bars, and restaurants, especially in the UAE. While
in the past government-sponsored *Eid* and national day street lights and
decorations were always dismantled shortly before Christmas, so as to
avoid any confusion, they now often remain in place throughout the
Christmas period, especially if Ramadan is late and finishes in December. On occasion, the UAE's high spending on Christmas has caught out
the establishment. In late 2010, having spent approximately $10 million

assembling a giant 43 foot tall Christmas tree festooned with diamonds, Abu Dhabi's most prestigious hotel, the Emirates Palace, was forced to admit that it had 'taken the holiday spirit a bit too far' and removed the tree following a large number of complaints. In its defence, the hotel—which is regularly used for high level government conferences—explained that it was simply an effort to '...boost the holiday mood for its guests, based on the UAE's values of openness and tolerance'.[6] Further to the changing status of holidays, even the Muslim Sabbath day is now considered to be under threat, given that in late 2006 the UAE's official public sector weekend changed from Thursday and Friday—as it had been for thirty-five years—to Friday and Saturday. Ostensibly to bring the UAE more in line with other Middle Eastern states[7] (including Kuwait, which had already switched), the real reason was to provide government departments and state-backed companies in the UAE with an extra day of contact and trade with their internationally based counterparts and colleagues. There is now a fear among some UAE nationals that the country will soon fully follow the western weekend, especially given that many private sector employees are already following such a schedule.

While gambling remains a fragile taboo, with no lawful casinos in operation, some Gulf monarchies have nevertheless legitimised such thrills by allowing lottery-style tickets at horse-racing events and, in the UAE's case, by recently introducing prize-carrying 'national bonds' which offer savers the 'chance to win 41,750 rewards [per annum]'.[8] Perhaps most controversially, as part of the aforementioned overseas investments strategy, some of the Gulf monarchies have been investing in Western companies that focus on gambling. In 2007, for example, the state-backed Dubai Holdings acquired a $5 billion, 9.5 per cent stake in the Nevada-headquartered MGM Mirage Corporation—the world's second largest gaming group and the proprietor of the Monte Carlo, the Bellagio, Caesar's Palace, the Luxor, the Mirage, and several other extravagant casinos on the Las Vegas strip. At the same time it was also reported that Dubai Holdings had bought a 50 per cent stake in MGM Mirage's $7 billion residential and leisure CityCenter project.[9] And in 2008 it was reported that Abu Dhabi's Mubadala Development Company was setting up a joint venture with MGM Mirage.[10] This has resulted in the building of a $3 billion MGM resort in Abu Dhabi, including a 600 bedroom MGM Grand hotel.[11]

Prostitution is also on the rise in the Gulf monarchies, with Dubai and Bahrain having long stood out as major centres in the region's sex tourism industry, and with the authorities in Abu Dhabi and Qatar increasingly turning a blind eye to the activity. Almost all demands appear to be catered for, with many hotels in these cities—including luxury establishments—being awash with high class escorts in the evenings, while in Dubai there are also many streetwalkers in certain areas. Although there are occasional crackdowns, usually preceding Ramadan, in practice the police rarely intervene and soliciting and kerb crawling is usually left unchecked. Most prostitutes arrive in the Gulf monarchies on tourist visas, or are initially employed as hostesses or waitresses in hotels and restaurants. In many cases they are separated from their passports by their sponsors or employers, and often end up trapped in a debt cycle, where they have to find ways to pay off the cost of their visas and accommodation. While some originate from other parts of the Arab world and Iran, a large number come from much further afield, including Central Asia, East Asia, and Eastern Europe.

The exact routes into prostitution in the Gulf monarchies tend to differ, varying from country to country, but in general it is either a story of entrapment or human trafficking. Entire books have now been devoted to the subject, especially regarding the women who end up in Dubai.[12] In most cases it is a story of economic deprivation, misery, human rights abuses, and a disregard of the values and traditions that the indigenous populations of the Gulf monarchies are supposed to uphold. Commenting on the situation from the perspective of a major supplier country, an Iranian military officer has explained that '…notorious women used to identify young women and girls from [Iranian] families with financial difficulties, then under the pretext of happiness for these girls in Persian Gulf countries, they offered a ransom to the families and in a matter of three weeks they transferred these girls to Dubai. After arrival in Dubai, through their network, they introduced these girls to Arab businessmen. Each girl was sold for $5000 profit for their families and ten times the amount for the traffickers. The buyers used these girls for their sinister business'. Providing another example, he explained how men masquerading as taxi drivers would drive around Tehran identifying runaway girls, and then report them to traffickers who would then arrange for their visa and passport to go to the Gulf monarchies. The travel details were described as '…taking no more than a month, and were arranged under the pretext of tourism. While waiting for passport and visa, these girls were promised a better and prosperous life and marriage to Arab Sheikhs.

However, after entering UAE, the ring members handed these girls over to brothels and prostitution networks'.[13]

Criticism of these many problems and issues is, as would be expected, becoming increasingly loud. A few years ago, for example, a prominent UAE national claimed to a major US newspaper that the city he lives in—Dubai—is now unrecognisable and is not even Arab anymore. Moreover, he complained that when he visits one of the many malls, the vast majority of patrons are foreigners, and that he rarely hears Arabic. Most damningly the article recorded the man's concern that despite religious prohibitions '...drinking is unabashed, and [he fears] public wine-tasting parties are on the way, with the beaches of his youth having been taken over by hotels and their occasionally topless sunbathers and other westerners whose dress is deemed inappropriate... he grimaces at women jogging in the streets, sometimes with their dogs, considered unclean under Islamic law, and the celebration of Islamic holidays and the country's national day pale before the more commercialised commemoration of Christmas'. He concluded his interview by stating that he and his family felt they were in 'internal exile' and in an effort to maintain their Arab and Muslim identities they had had to move away from the central area of Dubai to an outlying suburb.[14] This is far from being an isolated case, with there being many other examples of UAE national families relocating from Dubai completely, or at least building a new family home in another emirate so that their children could still feel they were growing up in an Arab city. Most recently, in 2012 there has been an extensive, grass roots social media campaign to uphold modest dress codes. Launched by two women and now centred on a Twitter subject entitled #UAE-DressCode, the campaign has seen large numbers of UAE nationals criticise the inaction of their government to enforce basic standards.[15]

Famously outspoken, even Dubai's chief of police[16] has publicly discussed the situation, arguing that expatriates and tourists pose a serious threat to national identity and societal norms in the Gulf monarchies. Speaking on a popular call-in show on Qatar Television, he was debating 'Whether the rising numbers of foreign workers posed a serious threat to the Gulf's identity and culture, and if so, what steps the governments in the region could take to reduce the danger?' Among other statements, he argued that '...if the Gulf governments do not take bold steps to check the inflow of foreign workforce, a day could come when locals would be marginalised in their own countries and become like Red Indians [sic] in the US'.[17] Interestingly, since the credit crunch and the slowdown of Dubai's economy, there have been some small signs that the government has begun to take the matter more seriously—perhaps because it has been concerned that many UAE nationals were becoming increasingly frustrated with the authorities due to poor-performing investments or substantial losses. Notably, in 2009 fresh 'decency regulations' were introduced in Dubai, leading to posters appearing in shopping malls and other public places that instructed what women could and could not wear, and warned about public displays of affection. Moreover, in summer 2011 standalone bars and restaurants that were not connected to hotels were banned from displaying alcohol in full view, while bars inside hotels were ordered to tint the glass on display cases. To some extent these mirrored similar regulations introduced in neighbouring Sharjah in 2001.[18] Perhaps most dramatically, especially given their aforementioned attempts to build up a tourist industry and host international sporting events, in 2009 alcohol was completely banned in Bahrain's three star hotels, following criticism from pressure groups, and in early 2012 Qatar announced that alcohol would be banned on the Pearl—one of its major tourism and real estate developments.[19]

Most vulnerable to criticism with regard to these trends in the region has been Saudi Arabia, given the ruling family's closeness to the religious establishment and its greater reliance on religious legitimacy. While most nationals are aware of the quantities of alcohol, drugs, and prostitutes in their country, the authorities have nonetheless managed to keep these vices out of the immediate public gaze. Nevertheless several recent developments have sparked anger and outrage amongst Saudi nationals, especially the various construction projects in the two holy cities and the sense that the regime is trying to 'cash in' on the pilgrimage industry. In late 2010 it was reported by the *New York Times* that several new buildings were nearing completion in Mecca. Among these was the Royal Mecca Clock Tower, also known as the Abraj al-Bait Tower, which in 2011 became the second tallest building in the world.[20] Covered in neon lights and topped with a crescent-shaped spire, it has been described as a 'kitsch rendition of London's Big Ben' while being a 'cynical nod to Islam's architectural past'. In order to make way for it, the authorities had to demolish an eighteenth-century Ottoman castle—a practice which is usually justified on the grounds that buildings prior to the founding of the Saudi state were built during a 'corrupt era'. Unsurprisingly, many have been appalled by the clock tower and the slew of new luxury hotels and high rises that have sprung up in Mecca in recent years. One Saudi architect explained that it as 'the commercialisation of the house of God' and that 'the closer [one gets] to the Grand Mosque, the more expensive the apartments... in the most expensive towers, you can pay millions.... If you can see the mosque, you pay triple'. On this point, it has been claimed that the new buildings will effectively divide Mecca along 'highly visible class lines, with the rich sealed inside exclusive air-conditioned high-rises encircling the Grand Mosque and the poor pushed increasingly to the periphery... like the luxury boxes that encircle most sports stadiums, the apartments will allow the wealthy to peer directly down at the main event from the comfort of their suites without having to mix with the ordinary rabble below'. According to another Saudi critic '...The irony is that developers argue that the more towers you build the more views you have... but only rich people go inside these towers. They have the views... We don't want to bring New York to Mecca'.[21]

Western bases and armaments

Still viewed as a necessity by the governments of the Gulf monarchies—most of which remain fearful of foreign aggression or in some cases even each other—the Western security guarantees they have sought and maintained are nevertheless becoming increasingly problematic, not least because of the significant expansion of the physical Western military footprint in their territories, often described as 'boots on the ground'. Despite receiving encouragement from the ruling families that serve as their hosts, the existence of substantial non-Arab, non-Muslim bases on the Arabian Peninsula has always been controversial and potentially delegitimising for the Gulf monarchies. And as more details emerge of their size and scope it is likely the bases will draw further criticism, perhaps serving as another flashpoint for opposition movements while of course undermining the ability of these states to keep positioning themselves as peaceful neutrals.

Among the most entrenched Western bases in the Gulf monarchies is Qatar's Al-Udeid Airbase. In 1999 Qatar's ruler told the US that he would like to see 'up to 10,000 American servicemen permanently based in the emirate' and over the next few years the US duly began shifting personnel from a camp at Saudi Arabia's Prince Sultan Airbase.[22]

Although Al-Udeid has only ever housed a few thousand American servicemen at a time, it has nevertheless been used as a forward headquarters of the US Central Command—CENTCOM—along with housing a US Air Force expeditionary air wing, a CIA base, and an array of US Special Forces living in compounds. Similarly, nearby Bahrain continues to host a US Naval Support Activity Base that houses the US Naval Forces Central Command and the entire US Fifth Fleet. Although the American role in Kuwait has recently been downsized, there still exist at least four infantry bases, including Camp Patriot, which is believed to house about 3000 American soldiers, and two air bases: Camp Ali Salem and Camp Al-Jabar.

Although there are no US infantry bases in the UAE, the country's ports are heavily used by the US. Dubai's Jebel Ali is now the US Navy's most highly visited 'liberty port', with warships such as the *USS John Kennedy* regularly being refuelled or serviced in Dubai's dry docks,[23] which remains one of only two ship repair yards in the Persian Gulf.[24] It was recently estimated that around 4,000 American sailors come ashore at Jebel Ali each year, with many claiming in anonymous US Navy surveys that Dubai is their favourite stop-off location due to the availability of alcohol and nightclubs.[25] Moreover, Jebel Ali together with Port Rashid also serve as major transit hubs for US military goods, with most such freight being delivered by three inconspicuous European shipping companies.[26] Meanwhile Abu Dhabi's Port Zayed is the US Navy's second most used port in the Persian Gulf[27] and, on a lesser but still significant scale, Fujairah's deep water port is also used by the US Navy, with the emirate's major hotels having a longstanding arrangement to bloclet many of their rooms for Navy personnel. Similarly, following the 2003 invasion of Iraq some of Abu Dhabi's hotels began to billet US soldiers on leave from Iraq. In mid-2006 the US president stated that '...the UAE is a key partner for our navy in a critical region, and outside of our own country Dubai services more of our own ships than any other country in the world'. Moreover, commenting on the aforementioned Dubai Ports scandal in the US, a US rear admiral declared that '...in a sense Dubai Ports has already been responsible for American security because we dock here in Dubai, and from personal experience I can confirm they are wonderfully efficient'.[28]

The use of UAE air infrastructure has also proved to be a key area of co-operation with the US military, as after 9/11 Dubai International Airport's Terminal 2 became one of the busiest airports involved in invasion of Afghanistan. For some years since it was one of the few airports in the world that had regular flights to Baghdad and Kabul, with a high proportion of seats being reserved for American military personnel or for employees of big US contractors such as Halliburton. Also important have been the airport's military freight facilities, with many commercial companies using it to ship US military goods and even armoured vehicles. Shrouded in secrecy for many years Abu Dhabi has also been making available its airbase in Al-Dhafrah to the US Air Force and to the CIA, with RQ-4 Global Hawk unmanned reconnaissance aircraft being stationed there and with KC-10 tanker aircraft having used the base to support operations in Afghanistan. Most embarrassingly for the UAE authorities, in the summer of 2005 it was revealed that US drones and U2 aircraft were also being serviced in Al-Dhafrah, following the crash landing of an unmanned spy plane on its return to Abu Dhabi from a mission in Afghanistan. The incident prompted the US Air Force to confirm that its 380th Air Expeditionary Wing had been based there since 2002[29] and at the time it was thought that there were over 100 US military personnel stationed in Al-Dhafrah.[30] The UAE has also been secretly making available an airbase in Pakistan to the US military. Following a leaked US diplomatic cable and a Reuters report describing the base as a 'mystery wrapped in a riddle', it emerged that the Al-Shamsi base in Baluchistan had been leased by the Pakistani government to the UAE since 1992, but had then been sub-leased more recently by the UAE to the US, presumably to facilitate the latter's operations in both Afghanistan and Pakistan. According to the cable 'the UAE government desired to keep details of the UAE co-operation with the US military in Afghanistan and Pakistan confidential, because the government is concerned that public acknowledgement of this assistance could pose risks to the UAE security within the UAE and in Pakistan'.[31]

Despite pleas and offers of financial aid from certain Gulf rulers to keep British servicemen based in the region after their independence,[32] Britain's military role in the Gulf monarchies has been greatly reduced since 1971. Nonetheless the Royal Air Force continues to deploy an expeditionary air wing at Qatar's Al-Udeid base, and has its own desert air base at Thumrait in Oman.[33] Moreover, other Western powers have recently been establishing bases in the region—sometimes openly, and sometimes covertly. Most prominent has been the aforementioned French base in Abu Dhabi, opened at Dhafrah in 2009. Although Abu Dhabi's former ruler, Zayed bin Sultan Al-Nahyan, had long forbidden the overt presence of Western servicemen in Abu Dhabi, sensing the risk it would carry, it seems that his successors have been much less cautious. If anything, the French base—dubbed the 'Peace Camp'—was inaugurated with considerable fanfare, with even the French president being in attendance.[34] It was followed up by announcements that the French Navy would begin using facilities at Abu Dhabi's Port Zayed, and that UAE diplomats could begin using French embassies in countries where there was no UAE presence.[35] Moreover, writing in a high profile opinion editorial for one of the UAE's state-backed newspapers, the French president openly stated his case, claiming that 'We have been strategic partners for fifteen years, linked by the defence accord we signed in 1995. With this permanent base, our commitment alongside you becomes even stronger. This base proves that our country is prepared to commit itself fully, together with you, to the security of the region'. Later in his article he also claimed that the base '…proves that France is prepared to take every risk for its friends. The message is clear: we will stand by you under all circumstances, even the most difficult' before concluding that '…it is in adversity that one recognises one's friends. You should know that you can always count on us if the security of the region were ever to be threatened'.[36]

Canada has also been operating military bases in the Gulf monarchies, with a little-known military camp—dubbed 'Mirage'—located outside Dubai and used as a rest and supply station for Canadian and Australian troops fighting in Afghanistan. Following a dispute over air landing rights for UAE airlines in Canada in 2010—likely the combined result of Canadian protectionism for Air Canada[37] and the UAE's alleged lobbying against Canada's bid for a UN Security Council seat[38]—existence of the camp finally became public knowledge when it was closed down by the UAE authorities in an apparent tit-for-tat retaliation. When the dust settles, however, it is likely that the camp will quietly re-open and Canadian access resume.

The Western military presence in Gulf monarchies will accelerate following an announcement by the US CENTCOM commander[39] that at least four Gulf states were due to receive the latest US antimissile systems—new versions of the Patriot anti-missile batteries—presumably in an effort to assuage fears of Iranian missile attacks. Tellingly, the general was unable to reveal exactly which states had agreed to deploy the US weapons, with one media report explaining that 'many countries in the Gulf region are hesitant to be publicly identified as accepting American military aid and the troops that come with it. The names of countries where the antimissile systems are deployed are classified, but many of them are an open secret'. Nevertheless it is widely understood that the unnamed states are Kuwait, the UAE, Qatar, and Bahrain, and that the US will now also keep Aegis cruisers equipped with early warning radar on patrol in the Persian Gulf at all times.[40]

Equally, if not more, problematic than hosting so many foreign military bases, has been the Gulf monarchies' ever-rising spending on Western armaments. With most of the arms being sourced from the US, Britain, and France, it seems this has become another price that these states must pay for their external security guarantees. Indeed, even if the purchased equipment is never used, is inappropriate for defensive capabilities, or is seemingly superfluous to the requirements of the Gulf monarchies' described peacekeeping operations, it has long been regarded as a necessary part of the overall cost of their protection, much like the aforementioned sovereign wealth investments and the soft power strategies employed in the West. In recent years there have been many signs that this spending has been getting out of hand, with the Gulf monarchies now being by far the biggest arms purchasers in the world—at least as a proportion of their GDP. This even includes the poorer Gulf monarchies, which, as discussed, are now grappling with declining resources and serious socio-economic pressures. With more and more information on their purchases appearing in the public domain, it will become much harder for governments and ruling families to justify these massive and usually opaque transactions to increasingly beleaguered national populations.

According to World Bank and Stockholm International Peace Research Institute data on total military spending, Saudi Arabia devoted somewhere between 10 and 11 per cent of GDP in 2010 to its military. This was the highest such proportion in the world and more than double the military spending of major military powers such as the US and Russia, and nearly five times greater than that of Britain, France, and China. Incredibly, the comparatively indigent state of Oman is the second biggest spender as a proportion of its GDP, with close to 10 per cent having been devoted to its military in 2009. The UAE is in third place among the Gulf monarchies, spending somewhere between 5 and 6 per cent of GDP on its military in recent years—still higher than the US and Russia.

Meanwhile the other Gulf monarchies have all been spending between 3 and 5 per cent on their militaries—a significantly higher proportion than other parts of the developing world.[41]

Most of the purchases have been valued at several billion dollars at a time, and have ranged from tanks and warplanes to naval vessels and missile systems. The Saudi and UAE procurements have tended to win the highest profile headlines given their commensurately higher GDPs than other Gulf monarchies and correspondingly greater ability to buy the very latest equipment. In 2009 alone it was reported that the UAE had purchased nearly $8 billion of US military equipment, making it the US' biggest arms customer that year, while Saudi Arabia had purchased about $3.3 billion of American hardware.[42] And in late 2010, after having invited fifty US-based arms manufactures to the country to 'see the opportunities for growth first hand',[43] it was reported that the UAE had spent close to $70 billion on arms in recent years and had accounted for nearly 60 per cent of the Gulf states' total purchases of tanks and rockets between 2005 and 2009. In addition to American arms, these imports are thought to have also been sourced from France, Russia, and Italy, and have included corvettes, frigates, and air defence systems.[44] Moreover, with Abu Dhabi hosting the annual International Defence Exhibition (IDEX) and with Dubai hosting the biannual Dubai Air Show, the UAE has cemented its role as the region's premier arms bazaar, with scores of major international weapons suppliers using these events to showcase their latest products to representatives from all of the Gulf monarchies and other nearby states.

In the aftermath of the Arab Spring and increased conflict in the broader region it is likely that all six states are increasing their military spending further. In December 2011 the US government announced it had finalised a $30 billion sale of Boeing-manufactured F15 fighter jets to the Saudi Royal Air Force.[45] With regards the UAE, following 2011's IDEX it was announced that Boeing would be delivering new military transport aircraft, while France's Nexter Corporation would provide support for the UAE's LeClerc battle tanks and the US' Goodrich Corporation would provide spare parts for its air force. Most controversially, it was also reported that a partnership was planned between a UAE-based company and the US-based General Atomics Aeronautical Systems with the aim of selling Predator drones to the UAE. If successful, this would be the first time that US drone technology has been sold to a foreign buyer.[46]

Unsurprisingly, in addition to stiff criticism from domestic opponents, most of whom argue that the purchases are a colossal waste of precious national resources and send the wrong signals about the intentions of the Gulf monarchies, the recent sales have also generated opposition in the West. In the US, for example, the pro-Israel lobby repeatedly argues that the sale of such high grade equipment to the Gulf monarchies will erode Israel's 'qualitative edge' in the region. Moreover, given the protests and other opposition movements that are stirring the Gulf—as discussed later—some Western governments have sought to stem the supply of equipment to states that are likely to use it to repress their own people. In early 2012 for example several American congressmen sought to block proposed arms sales to Bahrain worth over $50 million, given the pitched battles raging on Bahrain's streets between protestors and security forces at the time.[47] Although sales were resumed in May 2012, items such as teargas canisters and 'crowd control' weapons were withheld from trade.[48] Other Western governments have baulked at the procedures associated with selling arms to the Gulf monarchies, with increasing opposition developing against what are perceived as corrupt practices. The British government's long-running investigation into allegations of bribery surrounding the massive $86 billion Al-Yamanah arms deal to Saudi Arabia is well known, even though it was eventually called off. But more recently the German government has been forced to investigate alleged bribes and kickbacks connected to the sale of 200 German Leopard tanks to Saudi Arabia. Moreover, critics have argued that the sale '...contravened Germany's strict rules on arms exports, which ban the sale of weapons to countries in crisis zones, those engaged in armed conflicts, and those with questionable human rights records'.[49]

Antagonising Iran

The increasing belligerence demonstrated towards Iran in recent years by some Gulf monarchies is symptomatic of the latter's reliance on Western security guarantees and the presence of Western military bases on their soil; thus they have little choice but to align themselves with Western policies regarding Iran, and if that involves helping to enforce sanctions or otherwise limit Iran's influence in the region then in practice there is little room for them to manoeuvre. Moreover, given the associated requirement of purchasing massive quantities of armaments from their principal guarantors, it can also be argued that it is in the interests of the governments and military-industrial establishments of the vendor countries to pit the Gulf monarchies against their most powerful neighbour. Ideally, in terms of arms sales, this should develop into a tense and bitter cold war situation where both sides view each other as a posing a military threat, thus encouraging the further militarisation of the region and further expensive procurements. In this light, the Gulf monarchies' present stance against Iran can be explained in the context of a dependent, core-periphery relationship:[50] even if the centre of gravity of the Gulf monarchies' economic relations may be steadily shifting eastwards, the Western powers are nevertheless still recognised as their principal security providers and can thus dragoon them into hawkish positions.

There are increasing signs that the posturing against Iran—no matter how dangerous—is also being viewed by certain Gulf monarchies as a convenient mechanism with which to contain domestic opposition. In addition to the routine creation of a nearby bogeyman state with which to frighten their national populations and thus help distract from some of the various socio-economic pathologies and pressures that are building, the branding of Iran as a dangerous and unpredictable Shia-dominated enemy intent on acquiring nuclear weapons also helps to justify the sectarian manipulation that is taking place in several Gulf monarchies. It also serves to delegitimise any revolutionary actors and tarnish protestors on the grounds that they are agents of Iran. Indeed—as will be shown in the following chapter—since the beginning of the Arab Spring the Gulf monarchies' governments have gone to great lengths to highlight the presence of any Shia in opposition movements, and to some extent this has allowed them to brand their opponents and critics as being fifth columnists rather than as pro-reform activists. Thus far, the strategy has enjoyed some limited success, with large sections of the national Sunni populations being quick to accuse Shia activists of being traitors, and with many Western opinion-makers continuing to lend support to the Gulf monarchies on the grounds that the alternative would be Iran-style theocratic, revolutionary and anti-Western governments. Such opinions have helped fuel what some writers have described as the 'geopolitical fantasy' of a 'Shia crescent' that would extend all the way from Afghanistan to the Lebanon, including the Gulf states, which would be headquartered in Tehran.[51]

The risks of such rabid elite-level anti-Iranianism in the Gulf monarchies are undoubtedly serious, and possibly existential. Self-evidently these states are allowing themselves to be considered legitimate targets, or the 'front line', of any fresh conflict in the Persian Gulf. In this sense, their external survival strategies—in particular relating to the distribution of development aid in the region and the long-running efforts to position themselves as benign, active neutrals and peace-brokers—are being badly undermined by the current generation of Gulf rulers. It is unlikely that their fathers would have allowed such an escalation to have taken place, no matter how much they distrusted Iran. Most previous confrontations—including even the 1971 seizure of three UAE islands by the Shah's Iran—were usually sidelined in favour of shared economic interests or the substantial Iranian-origin expatriate populations resident in many Gulf monarchies.

At the forefront of the antagonism are Saudi Arabia, Bahrain, and the UAE—or more specifically sections of the Abu Dhabi ruling family. According to a recently leaked US diplomatic cable, in 2008 the Saudi king had 'repeatedly exhorted the US to cut off the head of the snake' in reference to Iran, its perceived military capabilities, and the nuclear weapon-building programme that Iranian officials continue to deny exists.[52] The former Saudi intelligence chief has gone on the record stating that Saudi Arabia should 'consider acquiring nuclear weapons to counter Iran…',[53] and in another leaked cable from 2008 the veteran Saudi minister for foreign affairs[54] suggested a US or NATO-backed offensive in southern Lebanon to end the Iranian-backed Hezbollah's grip on power. Warning US officials that a Hezbollah victory in Lebanese elections would likely lead to an 'Iranian takeover' of the state, he claimed that the situation in Beirut was 'entirely military… and the solution must be military as well'. He also argued that of all the regional fronts on which Iran was advancing, Lebanon would be the 'easiest battle to win' for the 'anti-Iranian allies'.[55] Similarly, in a cable despatched in 2009 the Bahraini king had urged US military officials to 'forcefully take action to terminate Iran's nuclear programme, by whatever means necessary'. Moreover, he argued that '…the danger of letting it go on is greater than the danger of stopping it'.[56] Closely connected to the sectarian policies in Bahrain and in particular the discrimination against its Shia population, the kingdom took maximum advantage of the region's anti-Iranian sentiments in early 2011 by announcing that it would deport all those Shia 'with links to Hezbollah and Iran's Revolutionary Guard'. In practice, this meant expelling hundreds of long-serving Lebanese expatriates, much as the UAE had been doing since 2009, suspending all flights between Manama and Beirut, and warning Bahraini nationals not to travel to Lebanon due to 'threats and interference by terrorists'.[57]

The reaction from Abu Dhabi appears originally to have been more hesitant—perhaps because the more moderate policies of its former ruler still prevailed. In a leaked cable from 2006 the American Embassy in Abu Dhabi claimed that the UAE believed 'the threat from al-Qaeda would be minor compared to if Iran had nukes... but that it was reluctant to take any action that might provoke its neighbour'. The cable also explained that UAE officials had asked US officials to '...only seek their help as a very last resort' and had stated that 'if you can solve something without involving the UAE, please do so'.[58] Nevertheless, as Abu Dhabi's forceful crown prince, Muhammad bin Zayed Al-Nahyan, and his five full brothers gained control over most aspects of foreign policy and the security establishment, the emirate's views quickly began to fall into line with those of Saudi Arabia and Bahrain. Since 2007 Western embassy officials have been repeatedly encouraged by the crown prince's circle to get more troops on the ground in an effort to counter Iranian hegemony. And in summer 2009, as recorded in another leaked US diplomatic cable, the crown prince had warned the US of appeasing Iran and had stated that 'Ahmedinejad is Hitler'.[59] A few months later, the Qatar-based commander of US CENTCOM appeared to express his agreement with the UAE's new stance, stating on the record at a major security conference in Bahrain that 'the Emirati Air Force itself could take out the entire Iranian Air Force, I believe, given that it's got... somewhere around 70 Block 60 F-16 fighters, which are better than the US' F-16 fighters'.[60] Even more belligerently, in a summer 2010 interview with the American magazine *The Atlantic*, the UAE's ambassador to the US (an Abu Dhabi national)[61] openly stated his country's preference for war. When asked 'Do you want the US to stop the Iranian nuclear program by force?' he replied on the record with 'Absolutely, absolutely. I think we are at risk of an Iranian nuclear program far more than you [the US] are at risk... I am suggesting that I think out of every country in the region, the UAE is most vulnerable to Iran. Our military, who has existed for the past forty years, wake up, dream, breathe, eat, sleep the Iranian threat. It's the only conventional military threat our military plans for, trains for, equips for, that's it, there's no other threat, there's no country in the region that is a threat to the UAE, it's only Iran'.[62]

More broadly, the apparent nuclearisation of the UAE and other Gulf monarchies can also be interpreted as part of the strengthening anti-Iran front. This began in late 2009 with Abu Dhabi's awarding of a $20 billion contract to a South Korea-led consortium[63] to build four nuclear plants by 2020,[64] and has since gathered pace with Kuwait[65] and Saudi Arabia[66] also in discussion with foreign nuclear companies. Although the UAE programme is strictly civilian and rational in terms of diversifying its energy supplies, given declining hydrocarbon reserves and rising domestic energy consumption, the manner in which the programme was initiated was nonetheless also intended to signal a warning to Iran. There was a keenness to seek approval for the programme not only from the International Atomic Energy Agency, but also from the world's major nuclear powers. The UAE did not move ahead with its contract until it received approval from the US Congress, even though its intention was likely never to award it to the bidding US-Japan consortium.[67] This is in sharp contrast to Iran's efforts to press ahead with an indigenous programme that has not sought approval from the US or other nuclear powers.

Qatar, although much more careful with its public statements on Iran since its emergence as the region's most energetic peace-broker, has also been caught out by leaked cables. Notably, in one from 2009 the Qatari prime minister characterised the emirate's relationship with Iran as being one in which 'they lie to us and we lie to them'.[68] Nevertheless, Qatar seems to have avoided falling into the front line role now occupied by Saudi Arabia, Bahrain, and the UAE. This is likely due to its particularly precarious situation: hosting major US military facilities while at the same time having to share its largest gas resource—the offshore North Field—with Iran. Similarly Oman has been more cautious in opposing Iran despite the presence of western bases on its soil and its very high spending on western armaments. Speaking in 2008 in a private conversation with a senior US Navy official, Oman's Sultan came across as more pragmatic than his neighbouring rulers, while his public statements have been similarly realistic. This is unsurprising given that he is by far the longest serving ruler in the region and has had considerable experience of dealing with pre- and post-revolutionary Iran. Moreover, with Oman's Musandam Peninsula stretching into the strategic Strait of Hormuz, his is the Gulf monarchy closest to Iran, and—perhaps most importantly—as with Qatar, Oman shares a major offshore gas field with the Islamic

Republic. Indeed, 80 per cent of the Henjam field lies in Iranian waters, and the National Iranian Oil Company has earmarked $800 million for the field's development[69]—an investment Oman is unlikely to be able to match. Tellingly, in his 2008 conversation Qaboos bin Said Al-Said commented to the US official that the 'Iranians are not fools' and claimed that 'Tehran realised there are certain lines it cannot cross [i.e. direct confrontation with the US]'. Most significantly, on the subject of the Gulf monarchies and Iran he stated 'Iran is a big country with muscles and we must deal with it' but that 'as long as the US is on the horizon, we have nothing to fear'.[70]

Another interesting stance on Iran, although now having little bearing on the region's security situation, is that of the Sharjah and Dubai ruling families. As one of the Persian Gulf's most established ports Sharjah has long been home to a substantial Iranian-origin community and, despite having lost one of its outlying islands to Iran in 1971, relations have remained fairly warm. The Sharjah-based Crescent Petroleum has always maintained an office in Tehran and in 2001 the company signed a $1 billion 25 year agreement with the National Iranian Oil Company to pipe some 500 million cubic feet per day of Iranian natural gas to the emirate.[71] Similarly, as the region's biggest port, with a long history of laissez-faire policies, Dubai has been home to substantial Iranian-origin communities for over a century, and has a well documented track record of supporting, or at least remaining neutral with regards to Iran. Even when Abu Dhabi and most other Gulf monarchies openly backed Iraq during the Iran-Iraq War of the 1980s, Dubai's ruler remained famously impartial, with the city's port facilities remaining open to Iranian vessels and its radio station continuing to broadcast the Iranian version of the news. As the relevance of Dubai's foreign policies have declined following the integration of its armed forces into the Abu Dhabi-led UAE Armed Forces in the 1990s and—as many have speculated—following the bailouts of its economy by Abu Dhabi in recent years, it had been assumed that the emirate's stance on Iran would eventually fall into line with that of Abu Dhabi. To some extent this has been true, with Dubai's ruling family having had little choice but to accede to Abu Dhabi's desire to make the UAE conform to US-led sanctions on Iranian trade. Since about 2008 it has become much harder for Iranian businessmen to transfer money in and out of Dubai, or in some cases even to open bank accounts. Nevertheless such restrictions are viewed as harmful to Dubai's livelihood, and the emirate's ruler has publicly stepped out of line on Iran, arguing in a December 2011 CNN interview that Iran is not trying to acquire nuclear weapons 'despite Western suspicions that it is trying to develop them' and asking, rhetorically, 'What can Iran do with a nuclear weapon?'[72]

Israel: the unholy alliance

Perhaps even more controversial and risky than hawkishness towards Iran has been the discreet strengthening of political and economic relations between some of the Gulf monarchies and Israel. Seemingly a function of reinforcing relations with their Western security guarantors and hardening the anti-Iran front, but also a consequence of building lucrative trade links with one of the region's most advanced economies, some Gulf rulers appear willing to co-operate and collaborate secretly with Israel. This is an especially dangerous policy, given the Gulf monarchies' long history of boycotting Israel, their public alignment with the Arab 'Refusal Front',[73] and—as discussed—their provision of substantial development aid to Palestine. Moreover, their national populations are for the most part anti-Israeli and pro-Palestinian, with the topics of Israel and Zionism often stirring strong emotions. Certainly, many Gulf nationals grew up watching the Palestinian Intifada on television[74] and the liberation of Palestine definitely remains a shared ideal among the region's youth. It is likely too that most of the expatriate populations in the Gulf monarchies share similar views. And there are of course substantial, long-serving communities of Palestinians in every Gulf monarchy. In some cases there are even naturalised Palestinian-origin Gulf nationals who were born in refugee camps serving as senior advisors to rulers' courts and occupying other powerful positions.

Since their independence and the drafting of constitutions or, in Saudi Arabia's case, the promulgation of its Basic Law, there have been legal articles and clauses in the Gulf monarchies which have required government personnel, businesses, and even individual residents to boycott all connections with Israel. In the UAE's case for example there has always been an Israel Boycott Office squirreled away somewhere in the federal government, and since 1971 federal law number 15 has stipulated that '...any natural or legal person shall be prohibited from directly or indirectly concluding an agreement with organisations or persons either resident in Israel, connected therewith by virtue of their nationality or working on its behalf'.[75] For many years, however, the boycott office's work has extended far beyond a straightforward embargo on trade between UAE-based companies and Israel. Notably, telephone calls to Israel have been barred, websites with an Israeli suffix have been blocked by the state-owned telecommunications company,[76] and Israeli nationals have not been permitted to enter the UAE, nor—in theory—have any visitors been allowed to enter the UAE that possessed Israeli visa stamps in their passports.[77]

Up until 2003 Abu Dhabi's Zayed Centre for Coordination and Follow-up was frequently publishing anti-Semitic material and hosting internationally condemned anti-Semitic speakers.[78] According to the US Bureau for Democracy, Human Rights, and Labor, the UAE authorities also reportedly fail to prevent anti-Semitic cartoons from being published in the two bestselling state-backed Arabic newspapers—*Al-Ittihad* and *Al-Bayan*.[79] The cartoons often depict Israeli leaders being compared to Hitler, and Jews being portrayed as demons. In January 2009, at the height of the Gaza conflict, the UAE's bestselling English language newspaper, *Gulf News*, not only featured such a cartoon (featuring an Israeli soldier with a forked red tongue),[80] but also published a Holocaust revisionist piece which claimed '…it is evident that the Holocaust was a conspiracy hatched by the Zionists and the Nazis, and many innocent people gave their lives as a result of this inhuman plot… the Holocaust was a major crime in history and the Israeli culprit is at it again today'.[81]

After joining the World Trade Organisation in 1996, the UAE authorities were clearly under pressure to drop or at least relax their boycott of Israel. When Dubai agreed to host the 2003 annual general meeting of the WTO, delegations from all member states had to be invited, and there was no way to prevent the arrival of an Israeli delegation and the flying of an Israeli flag on top of the Dubai World Trade Centre tower.[82] The UAE's newfound leadership role in renewable energies has had similar results: after winning the bid to host the headquarters of the International Renewable Energy Agency, in early 2010 the Abu Dhabi immigration services had little choice but to allow an Israeli delegation—including a minister—to arrive in the emirate for IRENA meetings. Explaining that '…although Israel and the UAE have no diplomatic ties' an IRENA spokesperson confirmed that 'Israel was accommodated in accordance with specific UAE agreements'.[83] In addition to international organisations, there has also been increasing pressure directly from the US, with the US Department of Commerce's Office of Anti-boycott Compliance dutifully recording all examples of the UAE's boycott requests. These are normally clauses inserted into contracts issued by UAE companies, most often with the following wording: 'the seller shall not supply goods or materials which have been manufactured or processed in Israel nor shall the services of any Israeli organisation be used in handling or transporting the goods or materials'.[84]

Meanwhile, it was reported in late 2009 by the Toronto-Harvard OpenNet Initiative that—as something of an exception to the country's massive increase in internet censorship—the UAE had quietly unblocked internet access to web sites based in Israel with the '.IL' suffix. All such sites were suddenly found to be 'consistently accessible via the country's two ISPs' and it was stated that '…it is not clear why the UAE authorities have decided to remove the ban on .IL Web sites and whether this unblocking will continue'.[90] Even more curiously, in late 2010 it was reported by a Kuwaiti newspaper that a female member of the Abu Dhabi ruling family had been flown to Israel to undergo 'complex heart surgery'. The entry procedures were reportedly facilitated by a member of the Knesset, after the sheikha's doctor had recommended a specific hospital in Haifa. Interestingly, the sheikha's picture was featured in a report on Israel's Channel Two which emphasised the way in which 'medicine does not differentiate between patients and should be a means of rapprochement between the peoples of the region'.[91] And in February 2011 Amnesty International highlighted the disappearance of a UAE national teacher who had previously been detained in late 2008 for 'demonstrating in solidarity with the people of the Gaza Strip, then under Israeli military attack'.[92] In years past it is likely that a Gulf national taking such a stance would have had the tacit approval of the authorities, rather than face any difficulties.

In some ways Bahrain has gone even further than the UAE in improving its relations with Israel, at least on an official level. For the past few years government personnel have been instructed not to refer to Israel as the 'Zionist Entity' or 'The Enemy' and in 2005 the kingdom closed down its equivalent boycott office.[93] Moreover, according to leaked US diplomatic cables from the same year, the king confided to US diplomats that 'He [the king] already has contacts with Israel at the intelligence/

security level (i.e. with Mossad) and indicated that Bahrain will be willing to move forward in other areas'. When pressed on trade ties with Israel, however, the king did admit that it was 'too early, and that the matter would have to wait until after a Palestinian state'.[94] Indeed there are signs in Bahrain, as with the other Gulf monarchies, that revelations of any formal ties with Israel would be met with strong condemnation from the national population. In summer 2010, for example, large demonstrations were staged in Bahrain's principal mosques—both Sunni and Shia—to denounce the Israeli attacks on the Gaza Flotilla. Worryingly for a king nurturing security and trade links with Israel, the crowd's main slogan described the US president as being a liar for 'not exposing Israel as being a terrorist state'.[95]

There is some evidence that the governments of both Qatar and Saudi Arabia have also been relaxing their stance on Israel. Up until 2009 there was an Israeli 'commercial interest section' based in Doha,[96] and in 2010 it was reported that the Qatar Investment Authority and the Saudi Olayan Group had partnered with Credit Suisse and Israel's IDB Holdings in order to form a new fund to 'opportunistically pursue credit investments in emerging markets'. With each partner putting in $250 million, the $1 billion fund is one of the largest new funds created since the 2008 credit crunch. Although the resulting media coverage noted that Qatar and Saudi Arabia were still technically part of an Israel boycott group, analysts were quoted as stating that 'the Arab boycott is mainly on paper' and that 'there is a flow of Israeli know-how and products to the Arab world'.[97] Interestingly, it appears that Qatar's relaxations on Israel have now also extended to education. According to documents leaked to *Al-Arab* newspaper in summer 2011, documents and course material supplied to trainee Arabic teachers in the emirate were written in both Arabic and Hebrew and seemingly sourced from the Israeli Ministry for Education. When questioned on this matter, the distributors simply argued that 'there had been a mistake'.[98]

With regards to security ties, as with Bahrain an open channel of communication now exists between Qatar and the Israeli security services. In late 2010 a large delegation of senior Israeli policemen was in the emirate, ostensibly taking part in an Interpol assembly, with the head of the Israeli police's investigations and intelligence branch being among them. Remarkably, it was reported by Agence France Presse that the Israeli delegation also met with Dubai's chief of police 'by chance' and that 'there was no apparent tension... despite the dispute between their countries'.[99] Thus far there is little firm evidence of growing security ties between Saudi Arabia and Israel, or at least there have been no blatant admissions as with Bahrain and Qatar. Nevertheless, for the past few years there have been frequent and powerful rumours circulating that the two powers are co-operating, mostly as a result of Saudi Arabia's stance on Iran and the existence of a mutual enemy.[100]

Division and disunity

Despite a range of current shared threats, perceived or otherwise, and despite the invasion of Kuwait remaining fresh in the minds of many Gulf nationals, the Gulf monarchies nevertheless seem further away than ever before from enjoying basic co-operation and collective security. Although, as discussed in the following chapter, there have been a number of recent actions that have been branded as 'collective action' in the wake of the Arab Spring, in practise these have been effectively unilateral or bilateral efforts on the part of Saudi Arabia and the UAE to head off regime collapse in their most precarious neighbours. Indeed, while formal councils and various mechanisms now exist on paper, there is still no effective body to bind together these largely similar states into a meaningful alliance. In the short term this means the Gulf monarchies remain highly vulnerable to foreign aggression and petty disputes between themselves, and in the long term means that their dependency on external security guarantees and the resulting exposure to its associated pathologies will remain high.

The Co-operation Council for the Arab States of the Gulf, better known as the 'Gulf Co-operation Council' is the organisation many had expected to present a 'united front' for the Gulf monarchies. Founded in 1981 in Abu Dhabi, the Council's creation was spurred by the Iran-Iraq War and, in particular, Kuwaiti concerns of collateral damage or attack from its warring neighbours. On an economic level the Council was supposed to foster joint ventures between the monarchies, remove barriers to trade, and establish a common GCC currency by 2010. While there has been some limited success in establishing a GCC customs union, more serious economic integration has remained elusive, as a number of disputes have prevented stronger ties. In particular, Oman announced in 2006 that it would be unable to meet the requirements of the common currency, while in 2009 the UAE announced its complete withdrawal from the project, seemingly as retaliation to the GCC's announcement that its central bank would be located in Riyadh, not Abu Dhabi. Within days of the UAE's secession thousands of its truck drivers were left stranded at the border with Saudi Arabia. Described in a leaked US diplomatic cable as a 'humanitarian crisis' the problem was publicly blamed on a new, unexpected Saudi fingerprinting system,[101] but most analysts agreed that it was a tit-for-tat response to the UAE's currency stance. Moreover, although a GCC common market was launched in 2008, some Gulf monarchies have continued to sign bilateral free trade agreements with other states. Bahrain, which has developed an extensive FTA with the US, has been viewed by Saudi Arabia and other GCC members as having bypassed the GCC's common market.

On a military level, the GCC was intended to provide collective security for all members via its Peninsula Shield Force. Founded in 1984, the force was supposed to comprise 10,000 soldiers representing all six monarchies. However, even after the liberation of Kuwait in 1991 the force only had 5,000 servicemen, and because it had played no active role in the conflict it was temporarily disbanded, with participating units being returned to their respective national armies.[102] In recent years there have been claims that the force has grown to 40,000,[103] but it is unclear how many how many soldiers are actually based at its headquarters in Saudi Arabia's King Khalid Military City, while its command and control structure remains ambiguous. The force's existence has also been continually undermined by security disputes and even clashes between the Gulf monarchies. Even in the twenty-first century there is much evidence that nineteenth- and twentieth-century border problems and other grievances remain unresolved. Between Saudi Arabia and Abu Dhabi, for example, there continues to exist a bitter dispute over their frontiers. Dating back to the earliest Wahhabi attacks on Abu Dhabi's territory, a 1950s standoff over the Buraimi Oasis, and a contested border settlement in the 1970s, the subject remains highly controversial. Several institutions in Abu Dhabi today continue to produce maps that show the emirate's territory still including land that was ceded to Saudi Arabia years ago, and in March 2010 it was widely reported that a naval clash took place in disputed waters. According to *The Daily Telegraph*'s UAE-based reporter, a UAE vessel had opened fire on a Saudi vessel that had allegedly strayed into UAE territory. The Saudi vessel surrendered, but its sailors were taken to Abu Dhabi and held in custody for over a week before being deported. Although a spokesperson for the UAE's Ministry for Defence confirmed that the incident took place he was unable to provide any details. However, a Gulf-based diplomat stated that '…it looks as though attempts were made to keep this quiet, which is predictable given the important relationship between the two countries…But it does remind us of the simmering rows that there are in this part of the Gulf'.[104]

The ongoing disputes between Oman and the UAE have also undermined any sense of GCC collective security. For many years territorial issues were at stake, but over the past decade the situation has become much tenser. In 2003 the UAE began constructing a giant wall stretching across the desert border between the two states. Completed in 2008, it has effectively sealed off the UAE, closing the previously open border between the Abu Dhabi-controlled city of Al-Ayn and the adjoining Omani-controlled city of Buraimi. Greatly resented by residents of both cities and local agricultural businesses, who now have to use checkpoints to cross the border, the wall is seen as damaging centuries-old trade and familial ties between the two communities.[105] More seriously, especially at an inter-governmental level, was the widely reported cracking of a UAE spy ring in Oman. In late 2010 Omani bloggers began claiming that arrests of 'UAE agents' had taken place, and in early 2011 the Omani authorities confirmed these suspicions. Although the UAE authorities initially denied the existence of the spies, stating that 'The UAE expresses its full willingness to co-operate with…Oman in any investigations that it carries out in full transparency to uncover those who try to mar relations between the two countries',[106] the problem was only resolved following Kuwait-brokered personal visits to Oman by the Abu Dhabi crown prince and the ruler of Dubai.

Connected to the Gulf monarchies' divisions over relations with Iran, it also transpired that the UAE spy ring may have been seeking information on Oman's possible security links with Iran. As a prominent analyst at a Dubai-based think tank described '…one possibility is that the UAE wants to know more about Iran-Oman relations because of Tehran and Muscat's long ties in security and military co-operation'.[107] Indeed, shortly before the Omani authorities' revelation, it was reported in Iran's state-backed media that their minister for the interior[108] had recently visited Muscat. Upon meeting with Oman's ruler the minister reportedly described Oman as 'an old friend of Iran which has always been seeking to develop ties with Tehran' and praised Oman for 'sending the *Zinat Al-Bihar* vessel to Iran's southern waters with a message of peace and friendship' and releasing 101 Iranian prisoners that had been held in Omani jails. Meanwhile Oman's ruler had reportedly '…called for expansion of bilateral ties, especially in economic areas, and said Iran can serve as a route for transition of goods from Oman to Central Asia' before concluding that 'Iran and Oman stand beside each other like two brothers and nothing can make a split between them'.[109]

Such spying and bilateral regional security deals with other regional powers—whether real or fictional—understandably attenuate any sense of trust in the GCC and its capabilities. Certainly, there is little doubt that all six of the Gulf monarchies' governments continue to view separate, international security guarantees as their only effective safety net. Some of the Western powers have seized the opportunities presented by these weaknesses and have now begun to explore the possibility of widening their individual alliances and agreements to form sub-groups of Gulf monarchies. In other words, if two or three Gulf monarchies can be brought together under the umbrella of one Western power, then a sense of collective security can be created for those countries even if it is sponsored by a foreign power and involves bypassing the GCC and its Peninsula Shield Force. Following the founding of the French military base in Abu Dhabi in 2009, the French president's opinion-editorial in Abu Dhabi's state-backed English language newspaper hinted at such a possibility. Explaining that '…with this first French military base in the Middle East, our country also shows that it intends to be fully engaged in the security and stability of this region' he then went on to state that 'France has many allies in the region; our presence in Abu Dhabi will enable us to reinforce our strategic partnership with them' and that 'we [France] hope that solid multilateral defence co-operation will develop among our allies in the region'. He concluded that 'For this reason, we want to fully involve Qatar in the recent French-Emirates "Gulf Shield" military exercise. In a region as troubled as yours, it is essential that the countries defending the same values work together to reinforce their common security'.[110]

Interference and coups d'état

The bitter quarrels and differences between the Gulf monarchies have sometimes even led to attempts to alter the course of dynastic succession in each other. When opportunities have arisen in one Gulf monarchy—perhaps following the death of a ruler or a petty internal dispute—it is now commonplace for the other Gulf monarchies to interfere, either by discreetly backing a preferred candidate or, in more extreme cases, even sponsoring a coup d'état. Moreover, with the six monarchies failing to present a united front and often being divided over their choice of candidate in these 'succession contests', the resulting vacuums have often allowed foreign, non-regional powers to get involved. In some ways this is nothing new, as during Britain's period of influence in the Persian Gulf there were frequent cases of the political resident stepping in to shape the future of certain monarchies. As described, the colonial representative eased the transfer of power in Abu Dhabi in 1966 from one brother to another, while in 1970 Britain ensured that control of Oman passed from father to son. In most of these situations Britain was playing the role of facilitator rather than meddler, usually consulting members of the ruling family in question and helping the dynasty install its preferred successor at the expense of unpopular or overly cautious incumbents. The squabbles and coups of the late twentieth and early twenty-first century have, however, been quite different, as when neighbouring monarchies or foreign powers have been involved there has rarely been any effort to identify the most suitable or popular candidate, with most of the focus being on installing a ruler that will be the most amenable to their interests.

In the late 1980s, for example, the coup in the UAE's Sharjah—where one brother[111] ousted another[112] on the grounds of economic mismanagement and squandering—was only reversed following interference by neighbouring Dubai, which had provided accommodation for the ousted ruler and published newspaper stories supporting him.[113] Similarly in 1995 Abu Dhabi and Saudi Arabia tried to re-install the ousted ruler of Qatar[114] who, as discussed, was removed from power by his more popular, pro-reform, son.[115] Although the counter-coup was unsuccessful, fears of a repeat attempt continued to dog Qatar for several more years. Indeed, the following year some 6000 tribesmen were disenfranchised and several ruling family members were arrested after being linked to a Saudi-backed coup plot.[116] And in 2009 it was reported by Stratfor that a major coup in the emirate had been attempted, involving members of the Qatari military and the ruling family. Most of the subsequent press coverage hinted that the coup had Saudi Arabia's support.[117] Similarly, in February 2011 the Jordan and UAE-based *Al-Bawaba* news agency reported that another coup had been attempted in Qatar, with thirty military personnel being arrested. This had supposedly coincided with a statement signed by sixty-six opposition figures including sixteen members of the ruling family who were backing the ruler's exiled brother in France[118] and which claimed that the ruler and his wife were involved in 'cases of corruption and social injustice'.[119] Gaining traction, this time the story was even covered in bulletins issued to various UN agencies. Whether true or not, the foreign-sourced report proved damaging for the ruler and has kept the spectre of future coup attempts in the minds of most Qataris and resident expatriates. Indeed, in April 2012 Iran's Fars News Agency and Saudi Arabia's *Al-Arabiya* reported that yet another attempt had taken place, with high-ranking military officers being rounded up and placed under house arrest after clashes between Royal Guard troops and regular military personnel outside one of the ruler's palaces. Perhaps works of fiction, the reports claimed that the ruler and his wife were transported by American helicopters to a safe location.[120]

By far the best example of a modern-day coup and resulting foreign interference has been in the UAE's northernmost emirate of Ra's al-Khaimah. In 2003, after having allegedly burned an American flag at the head of an anti-Iraq war demonstration, the emirate's long-serving crown prince[121] was replaced by one of his younger brothers.[122] A decree was signed by their very elderly father in support of this change, but at the time many analysts questioned the ruler's decision-making abilities given his advanced age and poor state of health. The new crown prince had the apparent backing of Abu Dhabi, as tanks belonging to the federal UAE Armed Forces were moved from Abu Dhabi to Ra's al-Khaimah and positioned on street corners. The ousted crown prince's supporters demonstrated, chanting his name and holding flags, and thus indicating he still enjoyed popular support—but they were fired on by water cannon and dispersed. He was duly exiled, first crossing the border to Oman, and then living in the US and Britain.

However, with the emirate's Dubai-like development programme beginning to flounder in 2008, the new crown prince was becoming increasingly vulnerable to criticism. There were also widespread allegations of corruption in his administration, specifically relating to kickbacks in the construction industry. Still in exile, the deposed crown prince enlisted a US public relations company and a British solicitor to conduct an international media campaign with the dual aims of persuading Abu Dhabi and then the international community that the incumbent crown prince was a liability. In particular the campaign claimed that the 2003 decree was never authenticated, and that a later 2004 decree had in fact been signed by the aging ruler, which overturned the 2003 decision. In an effort to appeal to Abu Dhabi's stance on Iran, the campaign also focused on the new crown prince's apparent connections to Tehran, claiming that his effective deputy—a Shia Lebanese businessman—had major commercial interests, including factories, in the Islamic Republic. In 2009 the campaign even claimed that Ra's al-Khaimah's port was being visited by Iranian customs officers and that the emirate was being used as a conduit for nuclear materials destined for Iran. Connections were also highlighted in the media between Ra's al-Khaimah and al-Qaeda, with claims being made that recent terror plots in the UAE, including a 2009 attempt to blow up Dubai's then incomplete Burj Khalifa skyscraper, had originated in Ra's al-Khaimah.[123] And at one point it seemed that the campaign team had even tried to enlist the support of Israel, with it being reported that the exiled crown prince had met Israel's ambassador to Britain and, according to documents seen by *The Guardian*, that the ambassador had promised that he was '...working with certain people from his side' and 'promised that the matter will be solved in his [the former crown prince's] favour'.[124]

In 2010 there were signs that the campaign may have been gaining traction, as Abu Dhabi's ruling family seemingly allowed the former crown prince to return from exile in order to visit his father, who was being treated in a hospital in Abu Dhabi. He was reportedly also allowed to stay in his wife's palace in Kalba—a town controlled by Sharjah. Given Abu Dhabi's increasingly hawkish position on Iran, some observers believed that Abu Dhabi was unwilling to allow Ra's al-Khaimah to retain links to Tehran. However, when the ruler finally died in October 2010 several hours of confusion ensued. The former crown prince had re-entered Ra's al-Khaimah and installed himself in his pre-2003 palace with approximately 150 heavily armed guards and a larger number of loyal tribesmen. He believed he had Abu Dhabi's blessing to attend his father's funeral and had concluded that he would be installed as ruler later that day. By early evening, however, a brief announcement was made by the UAE's Ministry for Presidential Affairs in Abu Dhabi that his younger brother was after all going to be the new ruler of Ra's al-Khaimah.

Tanks were again deployed on the outskirts of Ra's al-Khaimah and all of the former crown prince's retainers—including two of his cousins, several Omani citizens, and a Canadian military advisor—were arrested and detained for questioning.[125] Two months later the emirate's new ruler was invited to a banquet in Abu Dhabi held in his honour, where the ruler of Abu Dhabi congratulated him and his new crown prince—one of his sons—on their successes. The new ruler was then described as '… expressing happiness over meeting the president [the ruler of Abu Dhabi] and assuring that he would work with dedication and honesty in the shade of the directives of the president and his wise leadership'.[126]

The immediate future is likely to be marked by more such coup attempts in the region, as a number of the Gulf monarchies now have very aged rulers and—given the ever increasing size of the ruling families—powerful factions have coalesced around rival candidates. In each of these cases it is likely that internecine contests will develop and, given the high stakes involved, the discreet involvement of foreign powers is all but inevitable. In Oman, for example, the seventy-one year-old Qaboos bin Said Al-Said has no children or other natural heirs and has always shied away from appointing a crown prince. Moreover, given the exclusion of most ruling family members from senior government positions, no real candidate has emerged as a potential successor, as nobody has been able to accumulate the necessary administrative or military experience and expertise normally expected of an heir apparent in a Gulf monarchy. At present, much seems to hang on a clause in Oman's constitution[127] that permits the non-appointment of a crown prince, thereby allowing a 'ruling family council' to meet after the ruler's death to decide upon the succession process. Indeed, Qaboos has stated his intention that such a council should meet after his death, but that if the council fails to reach a consensus then it should open a sealed envelope containing his two recommended candidates, in descending order. Two copies of these recommendations are believed to have been made, and are kept in safekeeping in two different places. Their contents are the subject of much speculation, with most Omanis believing them to name at least one of the sons of a popular uncle of Qaboos who died in 1980.[128] The obvious concern in Oman—and currently the subject of great speculation—is that should the family council be divided over its decision and then pursue one of Qaboos' posthumous recommendations, then the newly installed ruler would have little personal legitimacy and thus be vulnerable to rivals.

The situation in Abu Dhabi—and thus the UAE presidency—is also worthy of attention. In late 2010 the sixty-four year-old ruler, Khalifa bin Zayed Al-Nahyan, returned to the country after a lengthy period of medical treatment in Switzerland, having failed to return in time for the Eid Al-Fitr festival—the attendance of which is customary for a Gulf ruler. Moreover, he appeared to have suffered considerable weight loss, and the state-backed media published little or no information about his condition. Having been unable to appoint one of his own sons as crown prince, his heir apparent is instead one of his younger half brothers, Muhammad bin Zayed Al-Nahyan. Now fifty-one, and crown prince since 2004, Muhammad enjoys considerable clout in the emirate and is in de facto control of the UAE's military in addition to the aforementioned Mubadala Development Company and several other state-backed entities. Moreover, Muhammad has the advantage of having five full brothers and a still influential mother[129] who was always considered the favourite of the late ruler's many wives and is now officially referred to as 'Mother of the Nation'.[130] Among them, these brothers control several further key portfolios in the Abu Dhabi and federal governments, and Muhammad's eldest son is now seemingly in control of internal security. When Khalifa dies, however, all may not be smooth for Muhammad and his full brothers, as despite their strong influence they do not yet control all of the strings in Abu Dhabi. Notably the all-important Supreme Petroleum Council, the massive Abu Dhabi Investment Authority, and several other key institutions still remain beyond their collective reach. Furthermore, although Muhammad and his brothers undoubtedly enjoy popularity within some circles in Abu Dhabi, it seems that in other emirates as many UAE nationals fear him as love him. Certainly, with the described hawkish stance on Iran, the relations with Israel, and—as discussed later in this book—a recent crackdown on opponents by the UAE's security services—the fear factor is likely to keep building. Although critics and potential rivals within the extended ruling family have kept a low profile, they nevertheless exist, and there are some individuals who enjoy discreet support and—courtesy of their maternal ancestry and marriage links—are believed to be favourably viewed by some of the UAE's largest and most influential tribes.

The most recent bout of speculation centres on succession in Saudi Arabia, as the main players are all very elderly and in some cases are perceived as having differing viewpoints on key issues such as relations with the US, the influence of the religious establishment, and women's rights. A spate of deaths at the top of the establishment, which already seems to have begun, could see an unpopular king being installed and will likely expose deep divisions within the ruling family. In turn, this could easily force a stalemate or prompt a coup d'état in the kingdom. The current king, Abdullah bin Abdul-Aziz Al-Saud, is fairly well liked. However, he is now believed to be about eighty-eight, having outlived a number of his younger brothers and relatives. Notably, his crown prince since 2005, Sultan bin Abdul-Aziz Al-Saud, died in 2011 aged eighty-three. Seemingly with little choice, Abdullah then appointed another of his younger brothers, Nayef bin Abdul-Aziz Al-Saud as his crown prince and successor.

Having served as Saudi Arabia's minister for the interior since 1975, Nayef was believed by many to be responsible for a large number of human rights abuses and incidents of torture. Further illustrating the precariousness of Saudi succession prospects, Nayef was known to be one of the most conservative members of the ruling family and was thought to have cultivated many opponents. According to a 2003 *New York Times* article, Nayef's alleged promotion of extremist elements in the kingdom was sufficiently extensive to prompt a US Senator[131] to write a letter to the Saudi Ambassador to the US asking that Nayef be removed from office due to his 'well-documented history of suborning terrorist financing and ignoring the evidence when it comes to investigating terrorist attacks on Americans'.[132]

More recent criticism focused on Nayef's apparent stance on conservative values and women, with one diplomat remarking that 'He [Nayef] is a conservative who will give more rope to the religious establishment than any of his brothers would' while others have speculated that recent reforms that have made it easier for women to work and have aimed to curb extremism in the education system would have been abandoned if he had succeeded. Certainly there was evidence that Nayef had obstructed some economic reforms in his earlier role as minister for the interior and, a month after Abdullah's announced appointment of the first female deputy minister, Nayef was reported to have publicly stated that he saw no need for female members of the Consultative Council.[133] Indeed, a leaked US diplomatic cable from 2009 claimed that 'Nayef is widely seen as a hard-line conservative who at best is lukewarm to King Abdullah's reform initiatives' and at a gathering for foreign journalists held in late 2011 at his house in Riyadh he was reported to have '...answered a question about whether Saudi Arabia would improve its relations with the Muslim Brotherhood, which was surely coming to prominence in Egypt... by lambasting the questioning journalist, excoriating him as a terrorist sympathiser and raging on until 4am about the many plots targeting the House of Saud'.[134]

With Nayef's death in June 2012, the immediate succession crisis seems to have passed, as Abdullah has now been able to appoint his seventy-six year-old brother Salman bin Adul-Aziz Al-Saud as crown prince. As the kingdom's long serving governor of Riyadh and with a reputation as a good diplomat and peacemaker,[135] Salman seems to have to have managed his relationship with the religious establishment more carefully than Nayef. And more recently, as minister of defence since 2011, he appears to have enjoyed much better relations with the Western powers than his predecessor. Overall, he is expected to continue with many of Abdullah's policies and reforms.[136] Nevertheless, given that the combined age of the Saudi king and crown prince is now 164, the prospect of several further rapid successions in the next few years or months is all but certain. With a very large number of contenders and competing factions within the higher echelons of the Al-Saud dynasty, the likelihood of destabilising disputes or unsuitable and unpopular office-holders is very high. In particular, at some point in the very near future there will need to be a generational shift from the sons to the grandsons of the former patriarch Abdul-Aziz bin Saud. With several 'branches' having formed around Abdul-Aziz's forty-five sons, many of which have forged relationships with other Gulf states and foreign powers, such a struggle could easily tear the monarchy apart. Both Nayef and Salman, for example, were part of a powerful seven member bloc of full brothers—the Sudairi Seven.[137] Now there are only five left, but their number includes the new minister for the interior[138] and they can serve as one of many counterweights to the king's power. Already there have been key defections from Abdullah's aforementioned 'Allegiance Commission', which was set up in 2005 to help choose successors in an orderly manner and avoid such problems. Notably, in late 2011 Talal bin Abdul-Aziz Al-Saud resigned his membership, having earlier criticised what he referred to as a 'monopoly on Saudi power by an unnamed faction within the royal family'.[139]

6

THE COMING COLLAPSE

The Gulf monarchies have faced down different opposition movements over the years, but these have not been broad-based and represented only narrow sections of the indigenous populations. Moreover, the Gulf monarchies have generally been strong and confident enough to placate or sideline any opposition before it has gained too much traction. The Gulf monarchies have also been very effective in demonising opponents, either branding them as foreign-backed fifth columnists, as religious fundamentalists, or even as terrorists. In turn this has allowed rulers and their governments to portray themselves to the majority of citizens and most international observers as being safe, reliable upholders of the status quo, and thus far preferable to any dangerous and unpredictable alternatives. When reformist forces have affected their populations—often improving communications between citizens or their access to education—the Gulf monarchies have been effective at co-option, often bringing such forces under the umbrella of the state or members of ruling families, and thus continuing to apply the mosaic model of traditional loyalties alongside modernisation even in the first few years of the twenty-first century.

More recently, however, powerful opposition movements have emerged that have proved less easy to contain, not least because they are making the most of potent new modernising forces that have been less easy for governments to co-opt. As a result an increasing number of regular Gulf nationals have become emboldened enough to protest against and, often for the first time, openly question their rulers. In 2011, spurred on by developments elsewhere in the region, these opponents and critics have presented the most serious challenges yet to the ruling families. In something of a perfect storm for the incumbent regimes, the Arab Spring revolutions in Tunisia, Egypt, Libya, Yemen, and Syria have not only given hope for those Gulf nationals and Gulf-based movements committed to serious political reform and to unseating the current autocracies, but they have also made it harder for the Gulf monarchies to depict their new enemies as anything other than pro-democracy activists or disillusioned citizens who have recognised the inevitable collapse of the political and economic structures underpinning their rulers. Furthermore, the 2011 revolutions—or at least the first few waves of protest in Tunisia and Egypt—have also helped expose the Gulf monarchies' strong preference for supporting other authoritarian states in the region and their fear of having democratic, representative governments take shape in neighbouring states. The initial responses of most of the Gulf monarchies were markedly anti-Arab Spring, even if they later tried to change tack. This had a massive delegitimising effect on the ruling families and governments involved, as in the eyes of many of their citizens they positioned themselves as part of a distinct and anachronistic counter-revolutionary bloc.

Unsurprisingly the new, post-2011 opposition in the Gulf monarchies has manifested itself in different ways depending on the circumstances and pressures in each state. This has ranged from full-blown street riots complete with killings and martyrs in the poorer Gulf monarchies to more subtle intellectual and even internet-led 'cyber opposition' in the wealthier Gulf monarchies. But in all cases the regimes have responded with more repression than ever before, thus further exposing the ruling families. In some instances brutal police crackdowns have taken place and foreign mercenaries have been deployed while in others political prisoners have been held, judicial systems manipulated, and civil society further stymied. Thus far only Qatar has avoided such heavy-handedness, mostly due to its more favourable circumstances and its rather different stance on the Arab Spring. Nevertheless even its ruling family is not without critics, and there are already indications that opposition is building and greater repression may follow.

Evolving opposition

Much of the early opposition in the Gulf monarchies focused on the economic grievances and frustration of merchant or worker communities in the post-pearling industry era, and—especially in the 1960s and early 1970s—the ruling families' perceived connections to non-Arab, non-Muslim powers and the need to bring these states closer into line with the region's Arab nationalist republics. Particular hotbeds were in Dubai, Bahrain, and Kuwait, although there were also some protests in Qatar from indigenous oil workers concerned with the excesses of their ruling family.[1] Several national fronts were established, but only one of these—the Dhofar Liberation Front, later the Popular Front for the Liberation of the Occupied Arabian Gulf—ever led to an armed insurrection. In many ways the Gulf monarchies were well placed to counter these threats, as Israel's victories over the main Arab military powers in 1967 and 1973 had taken much of the gloss off Arab nationalism. Moreover, with increasing oil exports and expanding state treasuries this was also the period when many of the region's wealth distribution practices were inaugurated. Not only were most Gulf nationals enjoying better lifestyles than hitherto, but many were kept busy with the new activities and opportunities resulting from the first major oil booms. In Dubai's case, many of the families that had been involved in national front activity and opposition to the ruling family in the 1960s became massively enriched in the 1970s, mostly due to being granted exclusive import licenses for the various products demanded by the emirate's fast growing economy. And today their descendants, now regarded as key allies of the ruling family, are at the helm of some of the region's biggest trade and retail empires.[2]

Subsequent opposition movements have been more difficult to contain, as most have focused on the illegitimacy of the Gulf monarchies and in particular their manipulation of Islam. Given that they have often been based on religious platforms, or led by disillusioned or discriminated against sections of the populations, these movements have not been entirely placated with material benefits. In Saudi Arabia, for example, the most serious opposition to the ruling family in the 1990s came from a diffuse movement of young religious dissidents and conservative university students. Critical of the official religious establishment's seemingly hypocritical support for American bases on Saudi territory following the 1990 invasion of Kuwait, this *Sahwa* or awakening movement was only dealt with by granting more control over social institutions and the education sector to religious conservatives. Confirming a long held view in the ruling family that their main opposition would eventually come from religious circles rather than liberal reformers, this was deemed a necessary if unpleasant manoeuvre in order to head off further criticism.[3] Similarly in the UAE and Kuwait, where Muslim Brotherhood organisations or 'reform associations' have existed for many years, there was a tacit understanding in place that these groups would be tolerated and given some influence over the religious and educational establishments. In the UAE this led to the Brotherhood's de facto control over the Ministries for Education and Social Affairs, with its members presiding over curriculum committees and—for many years—dominating the UAE's principal university.[4] Up until 2003 senior members of the Abu Dhabi ruling family were even holding meetings with Brotherhood representatives, trying to establish a set of compromises.[5]

Following 9/11, the subsequent US-led War on Terror, the CIA's capture of a major al-Qaeda figure in the UAE in 2002,[6] and a violent campaign launched against the Saudi oil industry and western expatriates in 2003 by 'Al-Qaeda on the Arabian Peninsula', the Gulf monarchies have made a volte-face on such Islamist opposition movements. Partly this has been out of fear, with unpublished polls in Saudi Arabia after 2001 indicating that most young Saudi men sympathised with Osama bin Laden and opposed any form of Saudi co-operation with the US over the Iraq War.[7] But it has also been due to the increasing ease they have experienced in simply branding opponents as 'terrorists' or alleging their connections to ill-defined al-Qaeda plots. Indeed, in recent years the Gulf monarchies' security services have usually been able to arrest activists and repress any Islamist organisations in their territories without fearing any international scrutiny. In many cases these crackdowns won praise from Western powers, being described as part of the Gulf monarchies' 'commitment to battling terrorism'.[8]

In the UAE, for example, the previous concessions granted to the Muslim Brotherhood were soon reversed, with hundreds of teachers, academics, and ministry employees being fired in 2006 from their jobs on the grounds of Islamist affiliations. Some have since been accused of 'dual loyalties' or threatening 'violent acts in the occupied Arab emirates',[9] and in 2008 a large number of activists were imprisoned and accused of being part of an 'underground movement in the UAE trying to promote their own strict view of Islam'.[10] Meanwhile in Saudi Arabia new anti-terror legislation has been repeatedly used to imprison men who have been described by international human rights organisations as being political activists. In late 2010 Canada's *Global Post* reported on sixteen Saudi nationals—including businessmen, university professors, and a judge—who were charged in a secret court with 'supporting terrorism and plotting to overthrow the government'. Having been held in custody for more than four years, they were believed to be 'widely known for peacefully demanding political reforms'. Their case was not reported in the Saudi press, although some Saudi nationals commented on the matter, claiming that the accused were only '…seeking reform and to open people's minds' and that they were '…extremely anti-Al Qaeda'. Moreover, fellow activists complained that such terrorism charges are now widespread in the kingdom as they are '…one of the most convenient charges [because] no one will defend you and you will become hopeless'.[11] There are now countless other such examples in Saudi Arabia and elsewhere in the region, with a Saudi surgeon having been held in custody and accused of 'backing and funding terrorism' since appearing on Al-Jazeera television and criticising the government.[12] Similarly in Bahrain a trial was held in late 2010 for a group of twenty-five dissidents who were accused of 'financing terrorism' and 'inciting hatred of the ruling family'. Reportedly beaten, tortured, and with the Bahraini media barred from covering their case, the men included prominent bloggers, journalists, and even a member of a human rights group.[13]

Overall, the branding of such opposition movements and the positioning of the Gulf monarchies as a better, safer alternative to Islamist-dominated governments or other such scenarios has been highly effective. Indeed, as described in a recent book on the Arab Spring, these '…rulers became well versed in their routine of no alternative argumentation: towards the West, they posed as the only ones able to deter an Islamist takeover'.[14] Moreover, it was argued that there is a now a '…sad irony that the powers in place have ended up believing their own fantasises about the Islamist threat; they not only displayed that card for external consumption, but they also fed their own masses with gory stories about the inevitability of… ruin'.[15] And that the Gulf monarchies—and their now fallen Arab autocrat neighbours—have been responsible for '…rushing to enrol in the global War on Terror, provided that their domestic opposition would fall under the extensive category of al-Qaeda supporters'. The anti-terrorism legislation and emergency laws that have been used to neutralise opponents have since been heavily criticised for being an 'oxymoron to describe the suspension of the rule of law and the absolute vulnerability of the citizen'.[16]

In much the same way as the Islamist groups, some opposition movements in the region, especially in Bahrain and Saudi Arabia—where there are substantial Shia populations—are now being branded both as terrorists and as part of some greater plot to further Iran's interests in the Gulf monarchies. Linked to growing hawkishness towards Iran, this has been another relatively straightforward and convenient mechanism in these states with which to portray opponents—no matter how peaceful—as being dangerous fifth column movements serving a foreign power or entity. Again this has allowed the monarchies to discredit opponents in the eyes of other citizens, while also allowing them to demonstrate their willingness to support Western policies on Iran. Frequently in Bahrain, for example, the government has claimed that the opposition is either being funded by Iran or is receiving weapons or other logistical support. In May 2011 military officials claimed that the opposition was made up of 'traitors and saboteurs' who were drawing '...guidance lines from Iran that drew the acts of sabotage and barbarism in the kingdom'.[17] And even following the publication of an independent report into Bahrain's crackdown in November 2011—as discussed below—which concluded that the 'Iranians are [merely] propagandists and that they can't be expected not to take advantage of the situation' and that '...to say they were funding, agitating... we found no evidence of this', Bahraini government officials still claimed that there was a link, stating that they had 'evidence you cannot touch or see physically, but we know it is there'.[18]

Modernising forces

Since the beginning of the oil era and the rapid socio-economic transformation of the Gulf monarchies, many of the modernising forces impacting on the region were, as described, expected to lead to significant political openings or, at least, more conscious and demanding national populations. In many ways what happened instead was the careful control or in some cases even harnessing of these forces by the regimes. Despite massively improved access and a large number of schools and universities being established, educational curricula have usually been tightly monitored or even shaped to support directly the state or the ruling family in question. This has usually led to skewed or inaccurate history being taught in the region, the absence of some fields of political science and law from university faculties, and a reliance on self-censoring, often expatriate, staff in these institutions. Similarly, with regards to communications, the Gulf monarchies have invested considerable resources and efforts in finding ways to censor interactions between their citizens and between their citizens and other parties. As such, each new communications technology that has become available in the region has either been sponsored by the state (for example the state-backed newspapers, radio stations, and television stations), or—if that proved difficult—has been blocked (such as unpalatable foreign newspapers, unwanted foreign radio and television signals, satellite broadcasts, and foreign books).

A case can even be made that the internet itself—predicted by many to lead to sweeping changes in such tightly controlled societies—was also successfully co-opted by the Gulf monarchies, at least in the early days. The blocking of offensive websites, including blogs critical of the regimes, has occurred, while many other basic internet communications methods such as email or messenger software can either be blocked or—more usefully—monitored by the state so as to provide information and details on opponents and opposition movements.[19] Moreover, some Gulf monarchies have actively exploited internet communications, and arguably done so much better than most governments in developed states, with an array of 'E-Government' website services having been launched—most of which allow citizens to feel more closely connected to government departments and thus help echo the earlier era of direct, personal relations between the rulers and ruled.[20] Meanwhile, as demonstrated, the rulers themselves have often established presences on the internet, and their self-glorifying websites usually also feature discussion fora to facilitate interaction between themselves (or rather their employees) and the general public. Many other lesser ruling family members, ministers, police chiefs, and other establishment figures in the region have also set up interactive Twitter feeds and Facebook fan sites for the same purposes, and some of these are now 'followed' by thousands of citizens and other well-wishers. The ruler of Dubai's Twitter feed, for example, exceeded one million subscribers in July 2012. Tweeting on this success, he emphasised the participatory nature of the software: 'Together we came up with many social, humanitarian and cultural initiatives and I have personally benefited from your constructive thoughts. Thank you all, and I hope that we take our communication and interaction to the next level soon, for the good of our communities'.[21]

More recently a wave of new internet technologies—often loosely bundled under the banner of 'Web 2.0' applications—seems to be finally having the kind of impact on the region's access to education and communications that would have been predicted or desired by the earlier modernisation theorists. Popularly defined as 'facilitating participatory information sharing, interoperability, and user-centred design' these applications allow users to connect to each other using 'social media' based on content created by themselves in co-operation with other users, rather than simply retrieving information from the internet in the format that is presented to them. Among the best examples of such applications are the more recent incarnations of Facebook, which is now no longer just focused on personal pages and fan sites but has become home to thousands of active discussion groups; the more recent versions of Twitter, which is now host to thousands of third party applications that aid users in finding and following the most appropriate content and personalities based on their interests; and YouTube, which allows regular users to upload, share, and comment on videos from their mobile phones, or even create their own television channels. While these and other Web 2.0 applications can still be blocked in their entirety by cautious regimes, this is now unlikely to happen in the Gulf monarchies as the inevitable outcry from the large numbers of users would be difficult or perhaps impossible to appease.

Inevitably these applications are being increasingly used to host discussions, videos, pictures, cartoons, and newsfeeds that criticise ruling families, highlight corruption in governments, and emphasise the need for significant political reform or even revolution in the Persian Gulf. Leading opposition figures are now attracting as many followers on these applications (often anonymous Gulf nationals) as members of ruling families. While there have been some attempts by regimes to counterattack against this cyber opposition, often by deploying fake social media profiles so as to threaten genuine users, or by establishing 'honey pot' websites to lure in activists and help reveal their identity, for the most part the applications are effectively bypassing censorship controls and the mechanisms used to control earlier modernising forces. As such they are facilitating an unprecedented set of horizontal connections forming between Gulf nationals and between Gulf nationals and outside parties—connections which are crucially now beyond the jurisdiction or interference of the ruling families and their security services.

The exact role played by Web 2.0 applications, social media, and other such modernising forces in the 2011 Arab Spring revolutions is still not clear, as at present it is unknown what proportion of the populations of North Africa, Yemen, and Syria actually had access to the internet or were using it for revolutionary purposes. Indeed, some have argued that Web 2.0 applications did not lead to 'Revolutions 2.0' as not everybody was internet-savvy in these countries and that the *abtal al-keyboard* or 'keyboard heroes' of the Arab world may have posted many angry messages online but did not necessarily take part in street protests.[22] Nevertheless, many observers do hold the view that the very recent internet-led expansion of the Arab youth's public sphere has been of enormous consequence and was certainly an 'important instrument added to the protest toolbox'.[23] In January 2011, for example, the newly installed Tunisian minister for Youth and Sports claimed that '…in reality we have been ready, we people of the internet, for a revolution to start anywhere in the Arab World'. Stressing the interconnectedness made possible by the Web 2.0 applications, he stated that 'we've been supporting each other and trying hard since a long time, and you know how important the internet was for the revolution'.[24] Indeed, in both Tunisia and Egypt human rights defenders and activists were believed to be using social media and proxy websites, often hosted in other countries, to keep track of the repression taking place and to keep countering inaccuracies reported by the state-backed media.

In many ways claims of a direct link between opposition activity and Web 2.0 applications in the Gulf monarchies appear much stronger than in North Africa, as the considerably higher internet and smart phone penetration and usage rates in these relatively more developed states indicate that most Gulf nationals—and the overwhelming majority of the younger generation—not only have the necessary access to such technologies, but are also well acquainted with their capabilities. As regards internet-enabled phones, for example, four of the Gulf monarchies now have the highest per capita penetration rates in the world, with 1030 for every 1000 persons in Bahrain, 1000 per 1000 in the UAE, 939 per 1000 in Kuwait, and 882 per 1000 in Qatar. This compares with an OECD average of only 785 per 1000.[25] In 2011 it was also reported that high speed broadband internet subscriptions had risen massively in the region, with 50,000 new subscribers over the first half of the year in the UAE alone, taking the country's total number of internet-enabled households to about 1.3 million. Over the next few years the penetration rate will continue to increase, as will the quality of access, with many of the Gulf monarchies having invested heavily in fibre optic networks. Interviewed in summer 2011, the chairman[26] of the UAE's largest state-backed telecommunications provider[27] even claimed that the UAE was going to be 'one of the top five connected countries in the world' following government investments of more than $15 billion in such networks.[28]

Web 2.0 and social media usage in the region is a little harder to measure, nevertheless most indications are that it is increasingly rapidly. An April 2011 report published by the Governance and Innovation Program at the Dubai School of Government claimed that the total number of Arab Facebook users had increased by 30 per cent in the first quarter of that year, bringing the total to over 27 million.[29] Only a year later, in May 2012, Facebook's operating company announced that it had reached 45 million users in the region, with a penetration rate of about 67 per cent, and had decided to open a regional office in Dubai.[30] Significantly, the 2011 report claimed that over 70 per cent of Arab users were in the age bracket of fifteen to twenty-nine years of age. It also estimated that there were over 1 million active Twitter users in the Arab world, who had collectively posted over 22 million tweets during the first quarter of 2011. Significantly the report claimed that the UAE, Qatar, Bahrain, and Kuwait, together with the Lebanon were the five leading countries in the region in terms of the proportion of their population using social media, with over 400,000 Twitter users in Saudi Arabia and 200,000 Twitter users in the UAE. It was also estimated that there were about 4 million Facebook users in Saudi Arabia, and that over 50 per cent of the UAE's population was using Facebook, while 36 per cent and 30 per cent of Qatar and Bahrains' populations were using Facebook. Claims were also made in the 2011 that there had been a 'substantial shift in the use of social media from social purposes towards civic and political action' in the region, with social media usage being perceived by many of the report's interviewees as being 'mainly for organising people, disseminating information and raising awareness about… social movements'. Interestingly, the majority of Tunisian and Egyptian interviewees also argued that their ousted regimes' attempts to block social media access '...actually provided a boost to the [opposition] movements, spurring protesters to more decisive and creative action'.[31]

Countering the Arab Spring: the wrong side of history

During the first Arab Spring revolutions in Tunisia and Egypt most of the Gulf monarchies quickly and instinctively positioned themselves on the side of the region's remaining autocracies. Perhaps assuming that the revolutions would fail, or that American and other Western interests in the area would ultimately deny the opposition movement's sufficient international support, a number of the Gulf monarchies' governments and advisors seemingly misunderstood or underestimated the scale of these uprisings. Consequently they chose to portray their states as being bastions of authoritarianism and—collectively—as something of a counter-revolutionary bloc. Although the full impact of this stance is not yet clear, it is likely that the new post-revolutionary electorates and governments in the Arab world will not view the Gulf monarchies favourably, even if they remain open to Gulf investments and development assistance. Moreover, and arguably more significantly, it is likely that many of the younger and more idealistic Gulf nationals will also view their governments and ruling families with distrust or as being 'on the wrong side of history', especially as more and more of these nationals study the Arab Spring and correspond and interact with fellow Arabs from post-revolutionary states. In early February 2011, for example, at the height of the Egyptian revolution, a new region-wide group of Gulf nationals including academics, journalists, and human rights activists gathered to 'urge the conservative monarchies which have ruled the region for centuries to embrace democracy and freedom of expression'. Referring to itself as the Gulf Civil Society Forum, the group issued a statement calling for '...the ruling families in the Gulf to realise the importance of democratic transformation to which our people aspire', and warned the Gulf monarchies not to crack down on activists planning to stage peaceful protests. Significantly, the statement also called for the ruling families to 'understand that it is time to free all political detainees and prisoners of conscience and issue constitutions that meet modern day demands' and claimed that 'the Gulf peoples look forward for their countries to be among nations supporting freedom, the rule of law, and civil and democratic rule which have become a part of peoples' basic rights'.[32]

At the same time as these statements were being issued, however, Saudi Arabia's leading religious authority and Grand Mufti, the aforementioned Abdul-Aziz bin Abdullah Al-Sheikh—a septuagenarian cleric who had earlier claimed that 'reconciliation between religions was impossible'[33]—was publicly criticising the Tunisian and Egyptian revolutions. After claiming that '…these chaotic acts have come from the enemies of Islam and those who serve them', he then went on to say that '…inciting unrest between people and their leaders in these protests is aimed at hitting the nation [the Muslim world] at its core and tearing it apart'. Having already provided the ousted Tunisian president with asylum in a Jeddah palace, and with the king having earlier telephoned the embattled Egyptian president, Hosni Mubarak, to offer his support and to 'slam those tampering with Egypt's security and stability'[34] it was abundantly clear that the Saudi ruling family both feared and opposed the Arab Spring. Moreover, soon after Mubarak's ousting members of Egypt's Supreme Council of the Armed Forces went on record to claim that they had '…received information that certain Gulf countries had offered to provide assistance to Egypt in exchange for not bringing Mubarak to justice'.[35] Thought to refer to Saudi Arabia, this again seemed to indicate the kingdom's position on the revolution and perhaps how its government hoped to use development aid to limit or influence the actions of any new Egyptian government. On a foreign policy level Saudi Arabia also made it quite clear that the new Egyptian and other post-revolutionary Arab governments posed a risk to the region's security, not least undermining the Gulf monarchies' aforementioned stance on Iran. After the post-Mubarak administration granted permission for Iran to sail two warships through the Suez Canal in February 2011[36] and then announced it would restore diplomatic relations with Tehran, Gulf-based analysts quickly remarked that 'Gulf policymakers are concerned about Iran making inroads into Egypt', that '…there's no doubt the Saudis are very concerned about Egypt's new foreign policy orientation', and that 'Saudi Arabia is seeking to regain its heavyweight position in the region and doing so in a very assertive manner. It does not want to see Egypt erase any Saudi gains'.[37]

The UAE's official position on the Arab Spring, at least in the early days, also appeared in line with Saudi Arabia's. An attempted rally to 'silently and peacefully protest against Mubarak' by Egyptian activists outside their country's consulate in Dubai was swiftly broken up by police.[38] And a UAE national[39] who had apparently tried to express support for Tunisian and Egyptian demonstrators in a mosque was later seized from his home in Sharjah on the grounds that he was 'disturbing public security'. For several days his location was unknown, with Amnesty International filing a request that the UAE authorities confirm his legal status and whereabouts.[40] Two weeks after protests began in Egypt, the UAE's minister for foreign affairs[41] became the first—and only Arab—international diplomat to meet with Mubarak during the revolution. Described by another Arab diplomat as 'showing extraordinary political support for Egypt', the UAE visit was treated with great suspicion by many Egyptian protestors, not least because the crown prince of Abu Dhabi[42] had stated earlier in the week that '...the UAE rejects all foreign attempts to interfere in the internal affairs of Egypt'.[43] Moreover, soon after Mubarak's fall one of the crown prince's aides was reported by Reuters to have '...vented his frustration over the downfall of a major ally who Gulf Arab rulers once thought was as entrenched in power as they are', and to have questioned 'how could someone do this to him [Mubarak]?' before explaining that 'he was the spiritual father of the Middle East. He was a wise man who always led the region... We didn't want to see him out this way...'[44] Meanwhile, in Dubai's most read state-backed newspaper, *Gulf News*, a leading member of the emirate's merchant community argued that 'there is a very real danger that mob rule is destroying Egypt's reputation, stability and economy while Mubarak was the symbol of stability, economic prosperity and peace'.[45]

As with Saudi Arabia and some of the other Gulf monarchies, the UAE was also reportedly alarmed that Mubarak would have to face the indignity of a trial. As claimed by Egypt's *Al-Masry Al-Youm* newspaper '...certain princes offered to pay the hospital bill of deposed President Hosni Mubarak, when they heard that the Egyptian government would not meet the costs of his [private] medical treatment'.[46] More recently, even after the success of the Muslim Brotherhood's Muhammad Morsi in Egypt's May 2012 elections, senior UAE officials have gone on record with inflammatory statements. Dubai's veteran chief of police,[47] for example, claimed in July 2012 that members of the Brotherhood had 'been meeting people from the Gulf and discussing toppling Gulf regimes' and warned the Egypt-based group that 'they would lose a lot if they challenged the Gulf states'.[48] Beyond Egypt, the UAE's diplomatic stance has been much the same on other Arab Spring revolutions, or at least when they began. In April 2011, nearly two months after the beginning of the Bahrain revolution and a month after the deployment of UAE and Saudi troops in the kingdom—as discussed below—the crown prince of Abu Dhabi received a delegation from the Bahraini government which had come to 'express its gratitude… for the supportive stance that had contributed to establishing security and stability in the kingdom'. Despite the crown prince having no formal foreign policy role in the UAE's federal government, he reportedly welcomed the delegates by 'stressing the deep fraternal bond between the UAE and Bahrain as well as all other Gulf countries' and stated that 'these relations are based on strong historical ties, shared interests, and mutual destiny'. Despite the brutal crackdown that was taking place in Bahrain that very week, the crown prince also expressed his 'support for Bahrain and its people as well as the measures adopted by Bahrain's wise leadership for establishing peace and security'. He also 'hailed the efforts of the king and the crown prince [of Bahrain] for reforms and development as well as for protecting the values of national unity, tolerance, and peaceful coexistence among sects'.[49]

On a broader level, there are indications that the Gulf monarchies are now working harder than ever to portray themselves collectively as being inherently different from the Arab authoritarian republics. A concerted effort has been made to convince both their own populations and the international community that there are somehow enough structural differences between their style of authoritarianism and that of their neighbours such as to exempt them from Arab Spring-type revolutions. Most notably, there have been recent attempts to broaden the Gulf Co-operation Council to include the fellow Arab monarchies of Jordan and Morocco. Despite these states being geographically separated from the Gulf monarchies and having few economic or social commonalities it has nonetheless been reasoned that their survival now matters to the Gulf monarchies. Jordan and Morocco have faced serious protests since early 2011, but the regimes remain in place for the time being, and thus provide some temporary evidence for the 'monarchy is different' theory. In May 2011 a GCC consultative summit was held during which it was decided to offer both Jordan and Morocco GCC membership. The summit's main topic of discussion was likely to have been the Arab Spring and how the Gulf monarchies could best find ways of delivering financial aid to the region's two other monarchies. Moreover, given that the usefulness of foreign mercenaries has become increasingly apparent since the beginning of the Arab Spring, it is likely that Jordan and Morocco—both of which are manpower rich—were viewed as possible suppliers in the event that the Gulf monarchies have to rapidly expand their security services.

Shortly after the summit the Moroccan minister for foreign affairs[50] visited Abu Dhabi to convey the '…gratitude of King Muhammad to the UAE under the leadership of Sheikh Khalifa for the sincere and fraternal call stated in the final statement of the recent GCC consultative summit for the accession of Morocco to the GCC'. Adding that 'such a move would further strengthen bilateral ties', the minister also referred to the '…fraternal coordination and co-operation that bind us with these countries since a long time at all levels', despite Morocco having never had any previous formal engagements with the GCC.[51] Unsurprisingly, within a few months of this and similar meetings between Jordanian officials and GCC representatives, an announcement was made in September 2011 that the GCC would be funding a five year development programme in Jordan and Morocco. Finalised in December 2011 with $2.5 billion being allocated to each state, the deal was viewed by some analysts as being a '…consolidation of monarchies that are solidly Sunni' and with the '…attraction [for the Gulf monarchies] being assistance… from [Jordan's] well-trained military'.[52] Similarly Reuters reported that the deal reflected the Gulf monarchies' need for '…closer ties with Arab kingdoms outside the Gulf as part of efforts to contain the pro-democracy unrest that is buffeting autocratic ruling elites throughout the Arab world'.[53]

Bahrain: rage and revolution

Bahrain, unsurprisingly, has been the biggest flashpoint in the Persian Gulf since the onset of the Arab Spring. As one of the poorest of the monarchies and, beset by a long history of sectarianism, its ruling family has had to contend with almost all of the mounting pressures discussed in this book. On the back of the Egyptian revolution, the Bahraini protests saw an estimated 150,000 nationals streaming onto the streets of Manama following an initial 'day of rage', on 14 February 2011.[54] Organised by various youth groups, rather than established political societies, the size and strength of this movement took many by surprise. Although the majority of the protestors were Shia—understandable given the long-running discrimination they have faced and their reduced economic opportunities—there were also many Sunni participants,[55] with slogans of 'No Sunni, No Shia, Just Bahraini' being chanted.[56] Calling for the fulfilment of the 2001 National Action Charter, these early demonstrations were not specifically aiming to topple the ruling Al-Khalifa family, but were more modestly focused on getting the government to deliver on earlier promises of political reform and the release of political prisoners. With surprising vigour, however, the Bahraini security services clamped down heavily on the protests, deploying teargas, water cannons, and even live ammunition. The Pearl Roundabout monument—a focal point for the first wave of protests—was even bulldozed in March 2011, despite it representing a key period of Bahrain's history. Clearly fearing a revolutionary landmark such as Cairo's Tahrir Square, the rubble around the roundabout was cordoned off, and at least thirty well-established Shia mosques and other religious structures in the kingdom were similarly destroyed—officially on the grounds that they were operating without licences.[57]

At about this time the protests had begun to reach Manama's financial district and were being predicted to soon reach palaces and government buildings. The Bahrain Formula One Grand Prix—a central pillar in Bahrain's economic strategy—even had to be called off,[58] much to the consternation of the ruling family. Clearly concerned that the king was due to be ousted in the same manner as the Tunisian and Egyptian regimes, the Bahraini security forces unleashed a massive series of reprisals on the suburbs and villages believed to be home to most of the protestors. Moreover, in order to bolster the defences of their key government and security installations a deployment of about 1500 Saudi soldiers and over 500 UAE security personnel were invited to cross the King Fahd Causeway that links Bahrain to mainland Saudi Arabia. An unprecedented move for these Gulf monarchies,[59] the deployment was justified on the grounds that it was an official response of the GCC's aforementioned Peninsula Shield Force, despite there being no threat of foreign invasion and despite there being no significant contingents from the other Gulf monarchies.[60] Although the Bahraini authorities communicated to their citizens that '…the foreign [Saudi and UAE] troops have started arriving to Bahrain in light of the regretful situation the king-

206

dom is currently witnessing' and called upon '…all citizens and residents to co-operate fully with the GCC forces and welcome them warmly'[61] within days there were reports that Saudi and UAE forces had been engaging with protestors and taking part in arrest squads.[62]

Unable to quell the protests, several hundred more political prisoners were taken, including academics, journalists, human rights activists, and even doctors and nurses—the latter groups having witnessed the injuries and deaths sustained by the protestors. Further delegitimising the regime, reports also began to circulate that the Bahraini government was trying to bolster its security services with fresh mercenaries from Pakistan and elsewhere. Having always had a substantial contingent of Pakistani nationals serving in its security sector, along with many Jordanian and Yemeni soldiers, it was believed that the authorities were trying rapidly to increase rapidly the number of non-Arabs in their employment, presumably on the grounds that such foreigners would be more willing to open fire on Bahraini nationals. A Pakistani conglomerate with close links to the Pakistani military was understood to have been recruiting and airlifting thousands of soldiers to Bahrain, while adverts for the 'Urgent Need of the Bahraini National Guard' had begun to appear in Pakistani newspapers soon after the first protests in Bahrain.[63] Later in 2011 reports also began circulating that Bahrain was trying to recruit from Indonesia and Malaysia, with a noted Saudi scholar claiming that the 'Bahraini monarchy was at the end of its rope' and that 'they [the monarchy] do not trust even the loyalists in Bahrain so they need to seek mercenaries from elsewhere—and these mercenaries will one day be captured and tried in public'.[64]

Unsurprisingly, the protestors' key demands soon evolved from simple demands for political reform to full blown regime change, with chants of 'Down with Hamad'—referring to the king[65]—becoming commonplace. Moreover, Bahrain's aforementioned long-serving prime minister[66]—a member of the ruling family and an uncle of the king—was being publicly accused of leading the crackdown and inviting the Saudi, UAE, and other foreign troops into the kingdom. Over the summer of 2011 the protests continued unabated with frequent reports of killings, arson, and the seizing of activists. Many of these crackdowns were recorded by onlookers on their smart phones and uploaded onto YouTube or other video-sharing websites. These have been viewed by thousands of other Gulf nationals and heavily discussed on social media platforms. Facing criticism that Al-Jazeera was not covering the various Arab Spring revolutions in a uniform manner, the Qatar-based network even produced a documentary on the Bahraini protests. Entitled *Shouting in the Dark* it was watched by more than 200,000 YouTube users in the first week that it was broadcast. Depicting police brutality and various other human rights violations, it led to a diplomatic rift between Qatar and Bahrain, with the latter's minister for foreign affairs[67] tweeting 'It's clear that in Qatar there are those who don't want anything good for Bahrain. And this film on Al-Jazeera English is the best example of this inexplicable hostility'.[68]

Since then the government has hastily tried to create more public sector jobs and raise salaries—following a $10 billion emergency package from the GCC—and has sought to convene a 'National Consensus Dialogue' with the various opposition groups and political parties in order to 're-launch the political reform processes' and 'write a new chapter in the country's history'.[69] But the leading Shia political society—Al-Wefaq National Islamic Society—boycotted the discussions and in many ways the other societies involved in the dialogue now no longer really represent the substantial popular protests on Bahrain's streets. The king also initiated the Bahrain Independent Commission of Inquiry to investigate and report on the crackdown. By appointing several world renowned human rights lawyers above reproach, including former UN lawyer Cherif Bassiouni, the king's intention was likely to buy some breathing space when dealing with the international community. Indeed, the commission was described by some Bahraini opposition members as being the 'king's perfect defence shield' as it allowed him to continue suppressing protests for several months while appeasing concerned western diplomats and other observers by convincing them that something was being done.

Although the commission's findings, published in November 2011 and broadcast to the nation, were suitably damning, describing how prisoners were tortured to death, threatened with rape, and often hooded, whipped, beaten, and subjected to electric-shock treatment,[70] little significant action has since been taken by the authorities. Most individuals and departments blamed by the commission have not been punished, with only ten junior police officers having stood trial,[71] and only a few of the hundreds of political prisoners have been released. Moreover, crackdowns on protests have continued and appear to be no less brutal than before with reports of deaths and torture remaining frequent. These accelerated after the lengthy hunger strike of a key opposition figure[72] and the reinstatement of the Bahrain Formula One Grand Prix in March 2012—deemed by *The Independent* newspaper to be the 'most controversial race' in F1 history.[73] With F1's governing body seemingly oblivious to the situation, over 100,000 protestors reportedly took to the streets, with security forces firing teargas and stun grenades into the crowds.[74] One demonstrator was even found 'peppered with birdshot... after having been beaten and partially burned'.[75] Opposition sources now claim that over eighty Bahrainis have died since the uprisings began,[76] with nearly 5000 Shia having been fired from their jobs,[77] with hundreds of homes having recently been raided, and with over $10 million having been looted by security personnel from Shia communities.[78]

Oman: protests and promises

As another relatively poor Gulf monarchy, Oman also faced serious protests and riots in 2011. Much like in Bahrain, the protestors were not initially calling for the overthrow of the regime, but were rather expressing their grievances over poor economic opportunities, the lack of political reform, and widespread corruption in the government. Unsurprisingly the most serious protests occurred in Oman's more indigent areas, notably the northern city of Sohar where a number of protestors—most of whom had congregated around the Globe Roundabout as part of the 'Green March'—died in clashes with the police in February 2011. But several hundred protestors were also reported to have rallied in the capital city of Muscat where they had translated their banner slogans into English and French for the benefit of the international media. Following swift promises of increased subsidies, pay rises for the public sector, social security benefits for the unemployed, and other benefits estimated to have cost the government $2.6 billion,[79] Oman's ruler[80] went on to dismiss twelve ministers in a further effort to appease the opposition.[81] But in early April 2011 Omani newspapers ran headlines that makeshift weapons had been discovered in the houses of protestors, including members of a group called 'Gang of the Dragon'. Photographs were displayed indicating that knives and swords were being manufactured.[82] And by the end of the month fresh protests had erupted elsewhere in the country, with hundreds spilling onto the streets of Oman's southern city of

Salalah and with smaller protests taking place in Haima, a key oil-producing region, and in Ibri. The demands again focused on economic concerns and greater government accountability, but this time the authorities found it harder to disperse the protestors, many of whom remained encamped in Salalah's central square for weeks.[83]

Although several hundred protestors were imprisoned during this period, only a small handful was kept in custody.[84] Nevertheless, with fresh demonstrations in May 2011 there were reports of much greater heavy-handedness from the security forces—including armoured vehicles being deployed to evict protestors from their tents and dismantle roadblocks, and with shots being fired into the air. Hundreds more prisoners were taken and two protestors were reported to have been shot. Protestors in Salalah claimed that the government was 'trying to crush [their] movement'[85] and dozens of activists were given one year prison sentences for 'damaging public property' and 'attacking public employees'.[86] Seven were even sentenced to five years' imprisonment, having been charged with 'shutting down work at a government organisation'.[87] In turn the wave of arrests led to further protests in summer 2011 when demonstrators in Sohar called for the release of these prisoners in addition to the meeting of their other, earlier demands. Although the 'young protesters' were reported to have decided to end their demonstration and return home so as to 'avoid confrontation with security forces that could have bad consequences', security forces were nonetheless described as having been 'present in big numbers' and teargas and baton charges were used to disperse the remaining crowds.[88]

In parallel to the security clampdown, the Omani authorities also began encouraging loyalist rallies, which often involved motorcades of several hundred cars driving around Muscat. Although the state-backed media claimed these were spontaneous displays of affection for the ruler, opposition activists claim that the state-owned telecommunications company[89] had been sending out multiple SMS messages during the nights preceding the rallies, urging Omani nationals to join in. Since the beginning of the protests the authorities have also sought to limit further the actions of existing civil society organisations, especially those relating to human rights. As with most of the other Gulf monarchies a state-backed human rights organisation was set up, and although it did offer support and advice to protestors and political prisoners, its lack of independence and neutrality has been criticised by many observers. Moreover, in 2011 there was a noticeable rise in media censorship, with journalists and bloggers having been arrested. Most significantly, in August 2011 one of Oman's few independent newspapers—*Al-Zaman*—was threatened with closure following the publication of an article alleging corruption in the Ministry for Interior. The newspaper's editor-in-chief was interrogated while the article's author[90]—a prominent Omani journalist and filmmaker, and a participant in some of the protests—was arrested and brought in for questioning. Without access to a lawyer he was charged with 'insulting the minister for justice and his deputy', 'attempting to create a division in society', 'abusing the judiciary in Oman', 'violating the publications and publishing law', and 'practising a profession without a permit from the Ministry for Information'. Representatives for the Committee to Project Journalists explained the writer's subsequent trial was due to 'the Omani authorities engaging in retaliatory tactics against [the accused] for his critical writing' and that 'the steps taken by the Omani judiciary suggest that this is a political vendetta rather than an effort to apply justice'. Similarly a group of Omani intellectuals, journalists, and activists issued a statement condemning the closure of *Al-Zaman*, stating that it would '… take us back to a world of repression and restriction of freedoms'.[91]

By autumn 2011 the situation in Oman appeared to have stabilised, following scheduled elections in October for its Consultative Council and promises from the ruler that the Council would be granted more legislative power and that 50,000 new jobs would be created, mostly in the public sector. On this latter promise it became clear that Oman had sought assistance from Saudi Arabia and the other Gulf monarchies, as a GCC rescue package of about $10 billion—to be spread out over ten years—had earlier been allocated to Oman,[92] in much the same way as Bahrain's abovementioned financial assistance. But over the course of 2012 there have been several further arrests, with a round-up of several bloggers and internet activists in May 2012. Including a well-known Omani photographer and a female student who writes under the pen name 'Rose of Dhofar', they were accused of defaming the ruler and given prison sentences of between twelve and eighteen months.[93]

Saudi Arabia: the cracks appearing

Having intervened militarily in Bahrain and having now positioned itself as the de facto bank-roller of the Bahraini and Omani ruling families in order to help them stave off riots and revolution, any political instability in Saudi Arabia itself will have major ramifications for all of the Gulf monarchies. Indeed, while it can be argued that a revolution or civil war within one of the smaller Gulf monarchies could be contained by its neighbours, any significant strife in Saudi Arabia would quickly spread across its borders. Although still in command of substantial resources, the kingdom is nevertheless under increasing strain, with several of the mounting pressures discussed in this book—including high youth unemployment, poverty, and a growing sectarian divide between its Sunni and Shia populations—reducing its ruling family's room for manoeuvre. As with Bahrain and Oman there have been protests and numerous killings in the wake of the Arab Spring, but given the kingdom's much more repressive police apparatus, its even stronger controls over the media, and its generally inhospitable atmosphere for foreign journalists and international non-government organisations, these have not yet received the attention they deserve.

Described as 'Arabia's silent protests' and later as 'the Middle East's most under-reported conflict',[94] the Saudi protests began at about the same time as those in Bahrain and not long after crowds began congregating in Cairo's Tahrir Square. In a direct rebuttal of the Grand Mufti's position on the Arab Spring, in early February 2011 several senior Saudi scholars and religious leaders openly called on Mubarak to step down in order to 'prevent further bloodshed' and to respect 'the thousands protesting for social and political reforms'.[95] The same week a Facebook group was set up by Saudi activists focusing on their own country's plight. Entitled 'The People Want to Reform the Regime' the group soon attracted several thousand followers, most of whom seemed to be Saudi nationals. In addition to demanding 'the equal distribution of wealth' and 'seriously addressing the problem of unemployment', the group also called for an independent judicial system, anti-corruption measures, and 'respect for human and women's rights'. More formally, after Mubarak's ousting several petitions began circulating in Saudi Arabia. Signed by thousands of prominent Islamists and liberal figures 'from across the political spectrum',[96] the documents included a 'Declaration of National Reform' and one entitled 'Towards the State of Rights and Institutions'. As with the Facebook group the documents focused on the need for further political and social liberties and improved management of the economy.[97] In mid-February a political party was even launched by opposition figures, despite such organisations remaining illegal in the kingdom. Described as 'an act of protest', the new 'Islamic Umma Party' was made up of not only Islamists, but also many secular academics, human rights activists, and lawyers. In a letter sent to the king and posted on their website, the party wrote to the king that 'You know well what big political developments and improvements of freedom and human rights are currently happening in the Islamic world' and bluntly stated that '… it's time to bring this development to the kingdom'. Meanwhile in an unprecedented public attack on the monarchy a party member and prominent Saudi lawyer[98] told Reuters that 'You cannot just have the royal party governing the country. We want to raise this issue with government officials and persuade them'.[99]

In parallel to these gestures of defiance a number of street protests have also taken place. Although these initially suffered from low turnouts, seemingly due to fear of reprisals by security forces, by April 2011 they had gathered pace and increasingly resembled those in Bahrain and Oman. Unsurprisingly, the largest protests were taking place in the kingdom's Eastern Province. In some instances several hundred protestors were convening, especially in the Shia-dominated town of Qatif, with most calling for improved human rights and greater political reforms. A protest of more than 200 Saudi nationals also took place in the town of Awwamiya, despite a fatwa having been announced the day before by the government-backed Council of Senior Religious Scholars which stated that demonstrations were against *Sharia* law. Significantly, the Awwamiya protestors turned out to condemn the Saudi military's role in Bahrain and in particular the alleged Saudi involvement in the destruction of Shia mosques there.[100]

The regime's response to these challenges has thus far been multipronged, much like the responses in Bahrain and Oman, with a mixture of threats, violence, appeasement, and increased government largesse. Having had to imprison some 160 political prisoners in the first two months of the protests,[101] the king moved quickly to announce the establishment of a new anti-corruption commission while at the same time promising thousands of new public sector jobs. However, the majority of these jobs were viewed as strengthening the kingdom's security sector as 60,000 were earmarked for the Ministry for Interior—already one of Saudi Arabia's biggest employers.[102] In a massive ramping up of the wealth distribution strategy, a raft of new subsidies and public sector salary increases was also announced. Estimated to have cost over $130 billion, which included some $14 billion worth of bonuses paid out to civil servants and a new $530 per month unemployment benefit, the package was clearly intended to provide the majority of Saudi nationals with a temporary panacea in order to insulate them from any further impact from the Arab Spring. To some extent this seemed to work, as by May 2011 a 58 per cent year-on-year increase in consumer spending was reported, as many Saudis began to enjoy their windfalls.[103]

As 2011 progressed and protests continued unabated, especially in Eastern Province, it became evident that these measures would be insufficient to quell all unrest in the kingdom. As with Bahrain, there were reports that the Saudi authorities were seeking foreign mercenaries to join their security forces. In June 2011 a noted Saudi scholar claimed that 'the Saudis are doing the same [as Bahrain], trying to invite Indonesia and Malaysia to send military troops to protect the monarchy, and we see that from Jordan as well'.[104] Similarly it was reported by Al-Jazeera that the chairman of the Saudi National Security Council[105] had made 'two quiet trips to Pakistan to seek their support in case protests erupted at home'. With the Pakistani media claiming that the Pakistani prime minister[106] had told the Saudi visitor that '...his country supported the Saudi stance in the Gulf and the Middle East and would stand by Riyadh for regional peace', one observer remarked that 'the potential need for foreign troops in case protests spiral out of control has forced the Saudis to work with the current Pakistani civilian government for whom they have nothing but utter contempt'.[107]

By this time a number of hastily introduced new laws had also come into effect, most of which aimed to limit the kingdom's increasingly vocal opponents' use of the media and especially the internet. A decree was issued in late April 2011 that amended the kingdom's existing press and publications law so as to prohibit all expression, including online comments, that 'contradicted the rulings of Sharia law' along with 'anything that called for disturbing the country's security, or its public order, or serves foreign interests that contradict national interests'. Moreover, seemingly fearing a backlash against the controversial fatwa, the new law also consolidated the position of the religious establishment by announcing a prohibition on 'violating the reputation, dignity, or the slander of the Grand Mufti... and members of the Council of Senior Religious Scholars'. By also prohibiting the defamation of 'any other government official or government institution', and preventing the 'publishing without consent of proceedings from any investigations or court trials', the law effectively elevated senior members of the ruling family above criticism and legitimised the already rampant practice of secret court proceedings. Described by Human Rights Watch as 'eviscerating any gains in freedom of expression under [the king's] reign', the law was accused of 'effectively throwing the kingdom back to a time when dissent of any sort resulted in arrest'.[108]

Although the financial penalties for infringing the law are very high—now approximately \$130,000[109]—a number of bloggers and journalists covering the 'red line' topics have also been imprisoned since its introduction. These include a writer[110] who documented the various arrests that had taken place in the Eastern Province and the peaceful nature of a candle-lit march by female protestors in Qatif; and two young men[111] who were seized after they blogged about the early protests in February and March 2011. Considered by Human Rights Watch as 'having brought the climate for reform in Saudi Arabia to freezing point' the arrests have also been viewed as clear evidence that 'the Saudi ruling family shows no signs that it might ease its iron grip on the right to express political opinions'.[112] Most dramatically, in early 2012 it became apparent that a young Saudi journalist[113] who had been arrested in Malaysia, to where he had fled, was likely to face the death penalty upon his extradition to the kingdom. Having posted tweets that were deemed blasphemous by the Council of Senior Religious Scholars on the grounds that they revealed his uncertainties about the Prophet Muhammad's teachings, he had also posted controversial tweets in defence of women's rights in the country, including one that stated 'No Saudi women will go to hell, because it's impossible to go there twice'.[114]

Moves have also been made to strengthen Saudi Arabia's anti-terror legislation even further in an effort to legitimise the arrests of opposition figures and other activists. Indeed, in July 2011 Amnesty International claimed that a secret new anti-terror decree was being drawn up by the Saudi authorities in order to 'strangle peaceful protest' and 'pave the way for even the smallest acts of peaceful dissent to be branded terrorism'. Having seen a classified copy of the draft law, the BBC confirmed that the proposed changes would allow for even more lengthy detention of suspects without trial (for over 120 days at a time), would further restrict their legal access, and would likely increase the use of the death penalty. Moreover, any questioning of the integrity of Saudi Arabia's ruling family would become an offence automatically punishable by a minimum of ten years in prison. This has led Muhammad Fahad Al-Qahtani,[115] the co-founder of Saudi Arabia's Civil and Political Rights Association to claim that '[the law] will give an open hand for the minister of the interior to do whatever he wants to do. Basically he will be controlling the judiciary, controlling the public prosecutor, he's in charge already of the prison system, and there is no way to get a fair trial'.[116]

Kuwait: 'The People's Spring'

As a wealthier Gulf monarchy with a relatively small population and a government that can continue distributing wealth to most of its citizens, Kuwait has mostly avoided violent demonstrations in the wake of the Arab Spring and, thus far, there have been few calls for outright regime change. Moreover, with a slightly more robust parliament than its neighbours the emirate has enjoyed something of a safety valve, as some degree of free expression has been tolerated. Nonetheless there were still intense periods of street protests in 2011 along with strong and very public opposition of the government and the ruling family—most especially the unelected prime minister, Nasser bin Muhammad Al-Sabah. And, as with the other Gulf monarchies, there has been a noticeable crackdown on dissenting intellectuals, journalists, and other activists. Most of the criticism has been centred on government corruption, the squandering of national resources, and the lack of meaningful political and economic reforms, which many Kuwaitis believe are long overdue.

In December 2010, only a week before the beginning of the Tunisian revolution, an outdoor rally was staged in a suburb of Kuwait City by a group of opposition members, including MPs and academics. Accusing the government of trying to amend the emirate's 1962 constitution and thus limit the powers of Kuwait's parliament, and protesting that fifteen of the Kuwaiti cabinet's sixteen ministers remained unelected, the men were only dispersed following a baton charge by Kuwaiti special forces. Dozens of participants were reportedly beaten, with five Kuwaiti nationals being taken to hospital for treatment of their wounds and fractures.[117] A month later, in January 2011, the opposition began making further claims, namely that the government was buying off MPs to ensure their loyalty in parliamentary votes. Calling themselves the 'Anything but the

Constitution' bloc, the fairly broad-based group then met to discuss and plan their agenda to 'protect the constitution, basic freedoms, and national unity' while also condemning the government for 'putting pressure on media outlets that comment negatively on the government'. In particular, the government's closures of *Al-Mustaqbal* daily newspaper and of the Mubasher satellite television channel earlier that month were strongly criticised. Warning the government that it was violating freedoms by suppressing the constitution, one member argued that the authorities '…should investigate the sources that fund corrupt media instead of targeting the brave youth of Twitter, who are honest and loyal to Kuwait'. Meanwhile several other members called for the outright removal of the prime minister on the basis that attempts by opposition MPs to pass non-co-operation motions against him should have pushed him to resign his post.[118] In early February 2011, with the Egyptian revolution in full flow, the formal opposition's demands were bolstered by the emergence of an informal coalition of younger Kuwaiti activists, most of whom were made up of students, young professionals, and other social media users. Calling themselves the 'Fifth Fence', the group began using Twitter to urge Kuwaiti nationals to stage a mass rally outside the parliamentary buildings in order to protest the government's 'undemocratic practices' and 'to press for the legitimate right of holding sessions and to declare our rejection of the continuity of this government'.[119]

As with Saudi Arabia, the Kuwaiti government's instinctive response to this mounting opposition was massively to increase public spending. An announcement was made that free food coupons would be issued to all Kuwait nationals for a period of 14 months, and that each citizen—including newborn babies—would receive a one-off payment of about $3500. As such those Kuwaiti families with several children received lump sums of $15,000 or more. Although carefully timed to coincide with the emirate's celebration of fifty years of independence, the spending package—which was estimated to have cost over $4 billion[120]—was widely viewed as a quick remedy to keep poorer Kuwaiti nationals off the streets. In parallel to the increased spending the government also began using defamation suits and other legal mechanisms to pursue the more vocal members of the opposition movements. In June 2011, for example, two Kuwaiti nationals were arrested and put on trial for using Twitter to 'harm the state's interests' and allegedly insult the Kuwaiti ruling family along with the ruling families of Saudi Arabia and Bahrain.[121]

Similarly, a young female Kuwaiti national of half-British descent was believed to have been arrested for tweeting that 'Sheikh Sabah should give us our money and don't bother coming back' in reference to the Kuwaiti ruler's[122] absence in London receiving health care. Most worryingly, a Kuwaiti journalist working for a daily newspaper was subjected to a gun attack in a northern suburb of Kuwait City. After confirming that there were bullet holes in his car the matter was reported to the Kuwait Journalists' Association which stated that 'we hope to have [some information] about the identity of the person who fired the bullet and the motives' and that 'we are not used to using firearms in Kuwait to express our views. We have always opted for dialogue to communicate, regardless of our differences'.[123]

As with its neighbours, the mixture of largesse and increased repression was not enough to curtail protests in Kuwait, and the latter part of 2011 saw major developments as opposition movements continued to gather strength. Despite the military intervention in Bahrain having taken place under the guise of the GCC, a large number of sympathetic Kuwaiti nationals were believed to have funded the Bahraini opposition, with some having even visited Bahrain to take part in the protests. Indeed, the Bahraini authorities stated that 'we have full knowledge about their support [for the opposition], for them this was an ideological support, and there were figures who visited, including businessmen and those of influence' and explained that this was 'the reason behind our calls through official channels to prevent them from entering Bahrain and they are not welcomed and added to the blacklist'.[124] More worryingly for the Kuwaiti ruling family, by summer 2011 further protests were held in an effort to force the prime minister's resignation and investigate his alleged corruption. In June, for example, around 5,000 Kuwaiti nationals, including a delegation from the Kuwaiti Lawyers' Society, rallied outside the parliamentary building under the banner of 'For the sake of Kuwait'. Shouting 'Leave, leave Nasser, we don't want to see you tomorrow' and 'Leave, Kuwait deserves something better than you', they demanded the removal of the prime minister, his deputy, and several of the ministers. Addressing the gathering, one activist accused some MPs of being 'government mercenaries' while a former MP claimed that the prime minister was trying to 'empty the constitution of its contents'. Most damningly, other protestors claimed that the prime minister's reign was 'full of corruption and that citizens were being killed at police stations under interrogation' and that parliament had been 'abducted during his premierships... with honest MPs being prosecuted for saying the truth'.[125]

With the prime minister refusing to acknowledge the protestors' demands, more extensive rallies were held in September 2011 following what was dubbed 'People's Day' when banners were unfurled calling for an elected prime minister with no connection to the ruling family. Chanting 'the people want to topple the prime minister', and claiming that more than $350 million of public funds had been used to buy off MPs, protestors argued that Kuwait needed to be transferred urgently from being 'a family state into a state of the people'. In particular they proposed that Kuwait became a constitutional monarchy, with the ruling family stepping out of government and only retaining the ceremonial posts of emir and crown prince.[126] Most dramatically, in mid-November dozens of activists broke into the parliamentary building where they began singing the national anthem, while thousands reportedly marched on the prime minister's house.[127] With a government spokesmen having describing the protestors as 'traitors who aim at toppling the regime'[128] and with the ruler having publicly stated that he would not dismiss the prime minister or dissolve the parliament, it appeared that the emirate had reached an impasse. Indeed, amid a crackdown on those who took part in the marches and the arrests of dozens of activists, the ruler told the opposition that 'you held demonstrations and insulted people, using expressions that are alien to the Kuwaiti society' and stated that 'what happened was a crime against Kuwait and the law will be fully applied against those who stormed the parliament. We will not forgive'.[129]

Yet by the end of November and just days after the ruler's condemnation the prime minister finally resigned, following the largest protests ever seen in a Gulf monarchy—since dubbed the 'Kuwaiti Spring'. Claiming that he wanted 'to comply with the national interest' and was responding to 'the danger the situation had reached',[130] the prime minister had clearly become an unacceptable liability for the ruling family and the wider power elite in Kuwait. Given the public humiliation incurred by the ruler in having so speedily to make a u-turn, the episode has greatly tarnished the legitimacy of the ruling family. Moreover, even though the new prime minister[131] is also a member of the ruling family and is similarly unelected, having been the former minister for defence, a fresh parliamentary election held in February 2012 saw opposition blocs making significant gains and winning the majority of seats.[132] This led to renewed investigations of corruption and further calls for an elected prime minister and a constitutional monarchy. An attempt was also made to block the government's proposed $111 billion four year spending plan, on the grounds that it was 'unrealistic'.[133]

United Arab Emirates: opposition emerges

As another small, wealthy state the UAE has yet to face street protests, however its seven ruling families are now finally being challenged directly by citizens, some of whom are publicly calling for regime change. This is because the UAE currently suffers from some of the heaviest restrictions on free speech and the media in the region, and there has been mounting frustration among the more educated sections of the population, especially with regards to corruption, lack of transparency, human rights abuses, and some of the government's more questionable policies. Moreover, as discussed, there is a widening wealth gap in the UAE and not all of its national population are being provided with adequate economic opportunities. This is leading to many of its less educated citizens—especially in the northern emirates—also beginning to voice their discontent. Thus, even though the UAE embarked on a massive Saudi-style spending splurge in the wake of the Arab Spring in order to appease the national population, this has not always been enough, with 2011 and 2012 witnessing the unprecedented detaining of dozens political prisoners along with a marked tightening of civil society.

The roots of the UAE's most serious Arab Spring challenges and the current opposition movement date back to summer 2009 when a number of activists, including university students and bloggers, launched a discussion website entitled www.uaehewar.net. Soon visited by thousands of UAE-based internet users, and featuring hundreds of posts—almost all in Arabic, and almost all by bona fide UAE nationals—the site quickly gained a reputation as being the best place to put forward grievances, challenge the authorities, and discuss the country's future. Within weeks, very lively debates were taking place on many issues including the growing personal wealth of the ruling families and the sustainability of some of the UAE's overseas investments and prestige projects. By January 2010 the website's most controversial debate was gathering pace, with thousands of users reading posts about the acquittal of an Abu Dhabi ruling family member who had been accused of torture and sodomy.[134] Most of the posts stated the concerns of UAE nationals over the application of the rule of law to the ruling families and the broader impact of the verdict on the UAE's international reputation. Within days UAE-based visitors to the site were no longer able to gain access it, being greeted with a peculiar 'server problem' message appearing when they tried. Moreover, one of the state-backed telecommunications companies[135] asked website owners to identify themselves to help solve 'technical issues'.

Unable to block the website outside the UAE, www.uaehewar.net survived well into 2011, with mirror sites being used to allow UAE-based users to keep accessing its contents. Discussions included the Tunisian and Egyptian revolutions, the lack of a proper UAE parliament, and the shortcomings of the UAE's rulers. The website's most accessed thread was entitled 'The Paradoxes of Muhammad bin Zayed's Policies', referring to the Abu Dhabi crown prince.[136] Emboldened by Mubarak's fall and the Bahrain demonstrations, in March 2011 the website's founders along with many other activists began circulating petitions which were eventually forwarded to the ruler of Abu Dhabi.[137] One of these, signed by 130 intellectuals, demanded a fully elected parliament and universal suffrage, and asked that the UAE worked towards becoming a constitutional monarchy that was committed to human rights and other basic principles. One signatory, Nasser bin Ghayth—a prominent UAE academic and an adjunct lecturer at the Sorbonne's Abu Dhabi campus— had also blogged about the Gulf monarchies' stance on the Arab Spring, and the strategy of distributing wealth in order to achieve political acquiescence. He stated that 'they [the Gulf monarchies] have announced benefits and handouts assuming their citizens are not like other Arabs or other human beings, who see freedom as a need no less significant than other physical needs', before moving on to explain '…they use the carrot, offering abundance. But this only delays change and reform, which will still come sooner or later…. No amount of security—or rather intimidation by security forces—or wealth, handouts, or foreign support is capable of ensuring the stability of an unjust ruler'.[138]

Signing the petitions as institutional actors, four of the UAE's civil society organisations—the associations for jurists, teachers, national heritage professionals, and university faculty—added their weight to the demands and soon after published their own joint statement. In this they argued that 'civil society in the UAE considers that the time has come to ensure the right of political participation of every citizen, with direct elections for a council with full federal oversight and legislative powers' and lamented 'the lack of involvement of citizens to choose their representatives, decades after the establishment of the state'.[139] In parallel to these developments, there were also examples in early 2011 of growing informal opposition activity, with an extensive Reuters report revealing that students planned to upload videos onto YouTube and Facebook regarding the need for political reform, and to meet in secret to discuss democracy and how the country's oil wealth should be spent. Referring to the economic benefits received courtesy of her nationality, but explaining how this was no longer sufficient, one student interviewee stated 'I'm well off. I don't need a revolution because I'm hungry. I want my freedoms, my dignity'. Having provided the journalist with an alias, she explained this was because of her 'fear of pursuit by security forces'. Meanwhile, other students complained of their rulers, stating that 'times have changed, they need to change their mentality… they act like we're kids. We're conscious, educated people', while others focused on economic mismanagement, arguing that 'young people can't get jobs. We have bad hospitals … and this is a wealthy country'. Some also referred to the inevitability of the Arab Spring impacting on the UAE, explaining that '… it's like wave. If the whole world is changing and this wave is coming and taking everyone with it, well, it's somehow going to cross this place as well'.[140]

The authorities' reaction to the petition and the civil society organisations' demands took many UAE nationals by surprise, as most had not expected a heavy-handed response. In early April 2011 five men—later referred to collectively as the 'UAE Five'—were taken from their homes, seemingly as a random sample from among the signatories. Bin Ghayth was one of these, along with Ahmed Mansour Al-Shehhi, a founder of www.uaehewar.net. The latter claimed he had been offered a well-paid position in Pakistan by his state-backed employer only a week before. Having refused to leave the UAE, stating that '…if they think I'm going to back off, they're mistaken. As long as I have the ability, I will continue my efforts',[141] Al-Shehhi was then reportedly arrested by ten officers— only two of whom were in uniform—and his passport and computer seized. In his final tweets that evening he had predicted his arrest, suspecting the police would plant something in his car, and then detailed their attempts to call him down to the street from his apartment.[142] Held in custody without explanation, the authorities appeared unsure how to explain the UAE Five's disappearance to the broader population. Early indications were that they would be charged with some sort of illegal possession, with reports circulating in the state-backed media that bottles of whiskey had been discovered in Al-Shehhi's apartment.[143]

As a further response to the petition the authorities also moved to weaken the civil society organisations involved by dismissing their elected board members and replacing them with government-appointed individuals. A group of loyalist lawyers then began preparing a counter petition and a 'statement of allegiance' to demonstrate the profession's supposed commitment to the regime, with their spokesperson stating that 'we, the lawyers, call upon all citizens to deny activists' allegations denouncing our government. We ourselves are united in refuting these false claims, and remain fully loyal to His Highness President Shaikh Khalifa bin Zayed Al Nahyan… and all other crown princes and rulers'. Moreover, their statement also claimed that '…activists who try to incite others against the government are therefore creating unnecessary civil unrest and attempting to destabilise the country'.[144] Although the lawyers were careful not to refer specifically to the political prisoners, stating that 'this is not directed at the detained people, as the independent judiciary in the UAE classifies everyone innocent until proven guilty' there was nonetheless little doubt that the government attempted to manipulate the trial of the UAE Five. In particular, loyalist rallies outside the court buildings were staged while relatives of the accused were harassed upon entering and leaving the buildings. Most interestingly, the authorities also attempted to influence public opinion by encouraging a number of tribal leaders to denounce the men and even file law suits on behalf of tribes that felt the activism had 'offended the state and nation'. The state-backed media, however, provided details of only one such tribal meeting and resulting denouncement[145]—an Abu Dhabi-based tribe which includes one of the ruler's key advisors among its senior members and which for historic reasons has been extremely loyal to the ruling family.[146] Interestingly, a senior member of Al-Shehhi's tribe—the Shihuh—was reluctant to condemn him, being quoted as saying 'we still do not know the nature of the accusations directed against Ahmad Al-Shehhi as of yet, nor if he has been officially charged… thus, how are we expected to denounce him before any official accusation takes place?'[147]

With the UAE Five in prison and with www.uaehewar.net eventually going offline after the website's owners were unable to renew its subscription from their prison cells, the government shifted its focus to top-down reforms and distributing largesse to the national population. In addition to an expansion of the electorate for the September 2011 Federal National Council elections, massive salary increases were also announced for public sector employees, in some cases of up to 100 per cent, while welfare benefits were increased by up to 20 per cent and a $2.7 billion package to assist poorer nationals with outstanding loans was set up. Interviewed by a state-backed newspaper, ministerial employees benefiting from the salary increases stated 'this is not the first time the President has surprised us with his generosity... it is not about the financial benefit, but about how the people of the country are taken care of' and 'it was a big surprise that makes everyone happy, it is like a prize for all'. Similarly, other interviewees stated they planned to use the increases to buy new cars, indulge their wives and children, and upgrade rooms in their houses.[148] A seemingly minor perk, highly symbolic free parking permits for UAE nationals in Dubai, was also announced.[149]

In parallel to this spending programme, it was exposed in May 2011 that the UAE had been hiring a private army of foreign soldiers. Much like the focus on mercenaries in Bahrain and Saudi Arabia, it seemed that the UAE authorities were similarly unwilling to take any chances on uncontrollable street protests in the wake of the Arab Spring. Revealed by the *New York Times* in an extensive report, the crown prince of Abu Dhabi had been employing the founder of Blackwater, a private military company, to create a secret 800-strong force made up of Columbian and South African fighters. At a cost of over $500 million, a base had been constructed in Abu Dhabi's interior and the men brought into the UAE posing as construction workers. According to documents associated with the project, the force's *raison d'être* was to conduct special operations missions inside and outside the country, defend oil pipelines and skyscrapers from terrorist attacks, and—crucially—'put down internal revolts'. Further to this latter objective, the report also stated that the Blackwater founder was under strict instructions to hire no Muslim mercenaries as 'Muslim soldiers... could not be counted on to kill fellow Muslims', while another document associated with the project described 'crowd-control operations where the crowd is not armed with firearms but does pose a risk using improvised weapons such as clubs and stones'.[150]

Within days of a November 2011 report by the UN Working Group on Arbitrary Detention, which concluded that the imprisonment of the

UAE Five was arbitrary and that the UAE government should release the men and pay them reparations,[151] they were freed in time for the UAE's national day celebrations on 2 December. Although the men were convicted of 'publicly insulting the UAE's leaders', sentenced to three years imprisonment, and then pardoned within 24 hours—seemingly in an effort to portray Abu Dhabi's ruler as being magnanimous—their names were not cleared of the supposed crime. Nonetheless, soon after their release UAE Five immediately resumed their online activities, appearing stronger than before. They renewed most of their demands and were quickly followed by thousands of UAE nationals on various social media platforms. By the end of the year the opposition seemed to have broadened, with the government facing further criticism for stripping seven Islamist critics, including a judge, of their citizenship. Referred to as the 'UAE Seven', they claimed they were 'unjustly targeted for their political views' after having earlier signed a petition on behalf of an indigenous Islamist organisation entitled the Reform and Social Guidance Association[152] which was calling for an end to 'all oppressive measures against advocates of reform in the country'.[153]

Over the course of 2012 the situation has greatly deteriorated. In March a young UAE national[154] was arrested for tweeting about the Arab Spring. He was accused of 'damaging national security and social peace' and handed over to a state security court,[155] before being re-arrested at a mosque in April. In May a prominent stateless person[156]—one of the original UAE Five and well known for running a website detailing the plight of the UAE's bidoon—was arrested, stripped of his residency papers, and deported to Thailand—a country he had never visited before.[157] By the end of July dozens more activists had been arrested, bringing the total number of political prisoners to fifty-four. These included academics, human rights activists, Islamists, and even a ruling family member.[158] The former of director of Abu Dhabi's educational zone[159] and former president of the Jurists' Association[160] were arrested along with a number of lawyers,[161] some of whom were detained when they tried to represent arrested activists.[162] In some cases the sons of these have men were imprisoned[163] and lawyers from Kuwait and Qatar trying to travel to the UAE to defend the detainees were denied entry. Interestingly, the fifty-four prisoners represent all seven emirates, almost all had active Twitter accounts prior to their arrests, and they represent more or less the full spectrum of opposition in the country. Most are being held without charge and several have reported incidents of torture, with some having been beaten or followed by plain clothes security prior to their detainments. One prisoner, originally detained for being a member of a terrorist organisation, was then accused of Muslim Brotherhood membership, before finally being officially accused of embezzlement at his workplace.[164]

Qatar: champion or charlatan?

As the smallest of the Gulf monarchies, with a tiny national population and one of the world's highest GDP per capita, the Qatari ruling family and its government have largely escaped the past year unscathed, with few serious opponents emerging and with no significant calls for political reform. Indeed, the November 2011 announcement that elections would be held in 2013 for Qatar's Advisory Council was less a concession to popular demands and more a case of being a top-down, pre-emptive strike by a forward-thinking ruler. Moreover, with 2011 and 2012 witnessing Qatar's public and diplomatic support for various Arab Spring movements elsewhere in the region—as an extension of its described role as peace-broker and mediator—the emirate has been careful to distance itself from its neighbouring Gulf monarchies and their predominantly anti-Arab Spring, counter-revolutionary stances. This strategy, although high risk, has allowed Qatar's ruler[165] to avoid losing legitimacy in the manner of his peers, and in many respects has allowed him to capitalise on the Arab Spring despite being one of the region's most autocratic rulers.

Most notably, after Qatar's Al-Jazeera news network seemed to have played a pivotal role in galvanising support for the Tunisian and Egyptian protestors in early 2011 by relentlessly broadcasting the events that led to their dictators' respective downfalls, Qatar then took a leading role in efforts to solve the Libyan crisis, ultimately backing the Benghazi-based rebel government in its campaign to oust Muammar Gaddafi's regime. In April 2011 Qatar became the first country in the world to offer diplomatic recognition to the Libyan National Transitional Council, and Doha hosted a meeting of the Libya Contact Group—a collection of entities committed to finding a 'new political direction' for the war-torn country.[166] Remarkably, Qatar then despatched six of its fighter jets to contribute to the NATO-led no fly zone over Libya,[167] and in the latter days of the conflict was believed to have provided weapons and even small detachments of special forces to facilitate the rebels' storming of Tripoli. Since then Qatar has been similarly supportive of the Syrian opposition, having formally recognised the Free Syrian Army and the coalition of rebel movements working towards Bashar Al-Assad's ouster. Most dramatically, in January 2012 the Qatari ruler made a public call for Arab troops to intervene in Syria, stating in a high profile interview on CBS News that the rest of the Arab world had a duty to 'stop the killing'.[168] Since then, there have been very frequent reports that Qatar is among a handful of countries actively arming the Syrian rebels.[169]

Qatar's Arab Spring policy has not been without its obstacles, however. Despite the official line, as summed up by a prominent member of the ruling family, being that 'we believe in democracy, freedom, dialogue, and we believe in that for the entire region' and despite the aim seeming to be '[hoping] that the people of the Middle East will see us as a model, and they can follow us if they think it is useful',[170] the Qatari ruling family is still treated with suspicion by revolutionary forces in the region. A number of Gulf nationals and even Qatari nationals have voiced their suspicions, seemingly believing that the emirate's maverick foreign policy and public support for democratic movements is simply another aspect of the monarchy's wily survival strategy. The most obvious discrepancy has been the Qatari position on the Bahraini revolution, as although Qatari forces did not contribute to the Saudi-led military intervention, and although Al-Jazeera did eventually broadcast the 'Shouting in the Dark' documentary, this seemed to be an inconsistent response when compared with Qatar's vociferous and high profile support for Tunisian, Egyptian, Libyan, and Syrian protestors. Notably, Qatar did not publicly condemn the brutal crackdowns in Bahrain, and the Arabic version of Al-Jazeera has been heavily criticised for shying away from covering the events in Manama. Moreover, when a live discussion programme on Al-Jazeera English was scheduled following a repeat broadcast of 'Shouting in the Dark', the producers removed a prominent Bahraini human rights activist from the three person line-up at the last minute, permitting only a member of the Bahraini government and the author to put forward their views.[171]

Following senior resignations at Al-Jazeera Arabic in 2011, seemingly as a result of the network's inability to offer fair coverage of the Arab

Spring, suspicions over Qatar's intentions continued to mount. These were further exacerbated following the widespread dissemination in 2011 of a leaked US cable, originally dating from 2009, which described the Qatari regime's apparent manipulation of the network to suit its policy objectives. Referring to several memoranda, the cables claimed that Al-Jazeera was being built up by the Qatari ruling family as a 'bargaining tool to repair relationships with other countries', and cited the example of Qatar's improved relations with Saudi Arabia being based on the network's 'toning down of criticism of the Saudi royal family'. Before concluding that Al-Jazeera was 'proving itself a useful tool for the station's political masters', the cable also damningly claimed that the Qatari prime minister[172] had told a prominent US senator[173] that Qatar had proposed a bargain with Hosni Mubarak which involved 'stopping [Al-Jazeera] broadcasts in Egypt for one year in exchange for a change in Cairo's position on Israel-Palestinian negotiations'.[174]

Meanwhile, on a domestic level there continues to be criticism that the Qatari authorities promote self-censorship of the media, with local newspapers and television stations being unable to cover a number of delicate issues in the emirate. Indeed, further to the difficulties faced by the Doha Centre for Media Freedom, the leaked cable also commented that the US embassy had 'assessed a steady lack of overall media freedom in Qatar' and believed that 'although overt and official censorship is not present, self and discreet official censorship continues to render Qatar's domestic media tame and ineffective'.[175] There has also been criticism that the Qatari authorities—in much the same way as the other Gulf monarchies—are quite prepared to repress their own citizens, if necessary. In March 2011, for example, Amnesty International reported that a Qatari blogger and human rights activist[176]—the founder of an organisation that monitors cases of arbitrary detention in the emirate—was himself seized. He was reportedly arrested by eight members of Qatar's security services and his home, car, and computer were searched without warrant.[177]

CONCLUSION

The state formation processes of the smaller Gulf monarchies, and in particular their historic relationships with Britain and other foreign powers, are crucial to understanding the political institutions that developed—especially those that fit with the neo-patriarchy and liberalised autocracy arguments. Equally, in Saudi Arabia knowledge of the state that formed around the long-running alliance between the ruling family and the religious establishment remains central to any contemporary analysis. Important too have been the various components of the ruling bargains or social contracts that have been constructed by these polities. As per the rentier state model, the distribution of wealth along with the creation of a national identity and the formation of an indigenous rentier elite class that sits above all expatriates have been paramount. But other, non-economic legitimacy resources also clearly matter. As expected by revised modernisation theory approaches, Michael Hudson's mosaic model, and observers of these regimes' re-orientalisation strategies, these bargains have included cults of personality, the co-option of religion, tribal heritage, and other traditional sources of power and authority.

The survival explanations can now be pressed even further, appreciating how the Gulf monarchies have applied aspects of their domestic strategies to both the wider region and even the international community. Notably, the distribution of rentier wealth has by no means been limited to national populations; it is increasingly used to buy influence and goodwill elsewhere, especially in other Arab and Muslim countries. Similarly, extensive and often costly peacekeeping missions are despatched to nearby conflict zones, which have again positioned the Gulf monarchies as benevolent, wealthy neighbours. More subtly these states have attempted to buy influence and support in Western and Eastern superpowers, with headline-grabbing sovereign wealth investments, selective development assistance, and with the generous sponsorship of projects run by prestigious universities, museums, and other respected cultural and opinion-making centres of excellence. In this manner the Gulf monarchies have become quintessential brokers of Joseph Nye's 'soft power' approach[1]— as the various ruling families and their governments have not only sought to use their resources to provide payments to key external actors, but have also tried to position themselves as attractive, well-meaning, and responsible members of the international community.

Internal pressures and weaknesses are nonetheless already manifest, or soon to be so, in all of the Gulf monarchies. Affecting the six regimes' ability to keep distributing wealth and meeting the expectations of citizens, the region's declining natural resources and looming 'youth bulge' now really matter, as do the mounting challenges of unsustainable subsidies, labour nationalisation, and 'voluntary unemployment'. In many ways, these are the by-products of rentier state structures—in particular the cradle-to-grave welfare systems that continue to underpin political acquiescence. Corruption and the squandering of national resources by the ruling families and their neo-patriarchal governments is also a growing concern. These polities—which do not have legal-rational authority—are now playing host to unaccountable elites and decision-makers. These have been allowed to squander national resources by financing prestige projects, making duplicate investments, and accumulating vast personal wealth. Further interconnected internal pressures are also evident, including increasing poverty among Gulf nationals, even in the wealthiest of the monarchies, along with rising real unemployment, and a widening wealth gap between the richest and poorest citizens. Discrimination against certain sections of society is equally noticeable, especially relating to the hundreds of thousands of stateless persons living in the Gulf monarchies and the rights of Shia citizens and other religious sects that have lived there for centuries. The more extensive use of censorship is similarly worrying, as although the regimes have largely been effective in choking off channels of free expression, they are now required to deploy the latest and most sophisticated technologies. In this manner, and as predicted by Michael Ross,[2] the Gulf's rentier wealth is not always being used to distribute wealth to citizens, but is instead being used to finance powerful, expensive, and highly sophisticated police state apparatuses.

External pressures are having a similarly negative impact on the Gulf monarchies' ruling bargains or socio-economic contracts. The dangers of rapid economic liberalisation in many of these states—and most particularly those that have opened up to foreign direct investment and tourism—are already apparent. Various relaxations have taken place, often without the consent of citizens, as governments have tried to make their countries more appealing to foreign investors, residents, and visitors, despite necessarily eroding religious and tribal heritage legitimacy resources. The monarchies' close military relationships with the Western and other non-Muslim powers are becoming another major source of concern for citizens as there are a growing number of foreign military bases being established on their soil and there has been accelerating spending on imported armaments. Also disquieting is the hawkish and seemingly dangerous stance being taken on Iran, and the monarchies' discreet efforts to improve relations with Israel, despite official boycotts being in place and again regardless of public opinion, Meanwhile the lack of collective security and basic unity between the six monarchies, in particular their inability to settle long-running disputes and strengthen the existing Gulf Co-operation Council, and the frequent coup attempts in the region, all continue to expose these states to malicious neighbours and other foreign interests.

Most of the earlier opposition groups that challenged the Gulf monarchies were successfully contained, as the various regimes were able to co-opt most of the modernising forces impacting on the region and keep the number of dissidents small. But the post-2011 opposition has been markedly different, with new pro-reform and pro-democracy figures and movements emerging in the region that can no longer be placed into the old categories. In particular, the impact of new, 'greater' modernising forces on the Gulf monarchies is becoming vitally important, especially relating to improved education and more advanced communication technologies. These include satellite television, and crucially social media and other peer-to-peer networking. Despite their best efforts the regimes seem unable to co-opt these effectively. Connecting back to the modernisation theory debate, these new forces may soon validate earlier lines of thinking, in addition to more recent writings such as Ronald Inglehart's co-authored 2005 book *Modernization, Cultural Change, and Democracy*,[3] as an increasing number of Gulf nationals are now able to share information freely amongst themselves in an educated manner, and can communicate more easily with activists in revolutionary Arab states and with the rest of the international community. Added to this, the Arab Spring revolutions elsewhere in the Middle East seem to be serving as catalysts for the beginning of the new movements in the Gulf, or at the very least have emboldened hitherto frightened opposition voices. Further eroding their stability, many of the Gulf monarchies have erred in their foreign policy since the onset of the Arab Spring, having openly positioned themselves on the side of other Arab authoritarian regimes and thus presented themselves as 'status quo powers'—essentially trying to counter the pro-reform momentum that has been building in the region.

Of the six monarchies, Bahrain's has by far the bleakest future, with little hope that the ruling family can restore sufficient legitimacy to ever govern again without resorting to martial law and extensive repression. It is currently being kept afloat by its regional allies—namely Saudi Arabia and the UAE—which will have to continue committing troops and supplying the kingdom with financial assistance. Although—unlike the other regimes that have faced Arab Spring revolutions—the Bahraini ruling family is not yet facing significant pressure from the international community, this will change within the next year or so, as the weight of evidence against the authorities grows. But for the time being the US and other Western powers are still willing to treat the revolution as an exceptional case, mainly due to the presence of the US Navy base in Bahrain and its potential front line role in any regional conflict with Iran. As described, the temporary block on the US arms trade to Bahrain has been lifted, and senior British and American police advisors have now been appointed by the king.[4] Dozens of ill-researched opinion pieces have also been appearing in Western newspapers highlighting the supposed connection between Bahrain's opposition and Iran. As a good example of the kingdom's latest soft power strategy, these fear-mongering pieces have usually been written by Western academics, former diplomats, and other distinguished personalities who have been approached and paid by public relations companies employed by the Bahraini government. In most cases they have presented a skewed and inaccurate picture of the Bahraini opposition and have made unsubstantiated claims about Iran's intentions in the Gulf monarchies. References to the Bassiouni report's findings on the lack of Iranian connections are never discussed, and explanations are rarely made that most Bahraini Shia do not subscribe to the

Iranian doctrine of *wilayet-e-faqih* or rule by clerics, and instead look to Iraqi Shia clerics,[5] rather than Iranians, for direction.[6]

Although the Omani ruling family's outlook is less precarious than Bahrain's, with the state not suffering from the same levels of sectarian strife or discrimination, nor having had to invite troops from neighbouring countries to assist in suppressing protests, there are nonetheless serious concerns about political stability. As with Bahrain, Oman only has limited resources and cannot rely indefinitely on creating public sector opportunities for its citizens in order to appease protests and demands. Indeed, Oman's stability already rests on external assistance, mostly from Saudi Arabia, and over the next year or two this will serve to delegitimise the aging, heirless ruler and his government. Moreover, when fresh protests erupt—either as a result of continuing government corruption or the state's likely failure to deliver on its economic promises—these will undoubtedly be met with an even heavier response than the 2011 riots, as the ruler's new backers will be unwilling to tolerate fresh challenges to another monarchy on its doorstep.

In many ways the kingpin of the Gulf monarchies, Saudi Arabia's ruling family may appear more stable than its Bahraini and Omani neighbours given that its government still has the ability to keep distributing wealth in order to appease citizens; but in reality the Saudi system is equally unsustainable and probably prone to implosion within the next couple of years. With ongoing demonstrations regardless of the new subsidies and job creation schemes, and with increasingly repressive tactics being used to suppress freedom of expression, the kingdom is now looking very brittle. If, as is likely, conditions in Bahrain deteriorate further, then more serious protests and even revolutionary activity will occur, especially in Saudi's Shia-dominated Eastern Province. And if unemployment, the wealth gap, and other socio-economic problems remain unchecked it is probable that insurgency will spread further across Sunni communities, thus helping the reform movement gain much broader support beyond the Shia population.

The most recent Saudi protests and demands have already been quite varied, occurring all over the country. They have ranged from men[7] being arrested for filming and then uploading onto YouTube a video about widespread poverty among Saudi nationals in Riyadh—a video which has now been watched by more than 1 million,[8] to women in Jeddah, Riyadh, and the Eastern Province filming themselves driving on motorways—a flagrant act of civil disobedience given the prevailing ban on women driving. The women involved tweeted that they were carrying their belongings as they were 'ready to go to prison without fear' while others told the international media that 'this is a right for women that no law or religion bans… [we] went out to get our rights, so that it would be up to us to drive or not'.[9] As expected, Facebook and Twitter are also playing a key role, with leading activists claiming that 'they can now speak to thousands across the world… without the strict censorship they live under in the off-line world' and that 'we're so thirsty for freedom of expression and a forum for expression that you see [we] are far more involved [in social media] than our neighbours'. Certainly, as the aforementioned Muhammad Fahad Al-Qahtani has claimed, 'the government has underestimated the power of social media in Saudi Arabia and now it's too widespread to censor'.[10]

Meanwhile there are now frequent *samood* or 'resistance salons' being held in the villas and apartments of known activists, despite some having already been threatened with the death penalty. Writing in the *Washington Post* in April 2012 one of these embattled figures, Waleed Abu Alkhair, related that such events are giving him 'the pleasing epiphany that religious hard-liners have begun to lose control of a young generation that is hungry for freedom'. He gave the recent example of a 'brave young man who responded passionately to clerics [also] invited to participate in the salon and who had threatened him for supporting freedom of expression and belief'. According to Alkhair, the young man replied to the clerics by asking 'Who are you? Who are you to inflict your religious guardianship upon us?' and then stating 'We are free, free to say what we like. You are just like us, not better. The era of religious guardianship is over'.[11] Similarly, other Saudi activists have been congregating in 'safe houses', claiming that their country is little more than a 'prison', and arguing that 'we are not far away from the uprisings that are happening in other countries'.[12] Indeed, fresh protests outside ministries by unemployed graduates have been staged in Jeddah and Riyadh. At these events participants lamented that '…after seven years of unemployment we have no other choice' and '[we] plan to stay here until we find a solution', while—rather worryingly for the government—others stated that 'we expect to hear promises to calm us down and disperse us but we will be back. We will be back until they find a solution'.[13] And more seriously, in January 2012 following the killing of a young Shia man[14] by police due to their 'indiscriminate use of force' a reported crowd of thousands or even tens of thousands took to the streets of Awwamiya to commemorate his death. Together with several other dead activists he is now being described as a martyr in the Eastern Province, and the opposition movement is increasingly being referred to as the 'Intifada of Dignity'.[15] A total of ten protestors are believed to have been killed since the beginning of the uprising with regular firefights now taking place,[16] and in July 2012 one of the regime's strongest critics was badly wounded by security forces.[17]

In Kuwait's case, with the ruler choosing to dissolve parliament in June 2012 rather than allow calls for anti-corruption investigations to continue, and asserting that the election result was 'illegal', he has undoubtedly made his position even weaker. With opposition MPs claiming that his self-described 'final and unchallengeable decision' amounts to being a 'coup against the constitution',[18] it is likely that the government will find it much harder to keep control over future protests. Indeed, most of the recent examples of dissent have been dealt with in a very heavy handed manner. In April 2012 a young Kuwaiti Twitter user was jailed for posting blasphemous tweets about Prophet Muhammad,[19] while in July 2012 even a member of the ruling family[20] was arrested following his tweets that he wanted to stand in the next parliamentary elections and 'expose corruption among top officials'.[21] Thus, while Kuwait may not yet have witnessed the violent confrontations that have occurred in Bahrain, Oman, and Saudi Arabia, the outlook for its ruling family is perhaps just as bleak, with the monarchy's traditional authority being gradually eroded by a more confident and demanding citizenry that has already proven that it can embarrass and contain the ruler and his appointed prime ministers.

The UAE's ruling families appear to be in a stronger position, as most citizens currently seem content with the state's ability to keep distributing wealth. But as with the Saudi and Kuwaiti spending programmes, it is questionable how long such generosity can be sustained. Indeed, a decree was circulated in Abu Dhabi government departments in March 2012 stating that a number of the promised big salary increases could not, after all, be delivered.[22] Moreover, it is unlikely that the situation in the poorer northern emirates can be contained or remedied in the near future, and street protests or other manifestations of opposition will probably soon emerge, most probably in Ra's al-Khaimah. Most importantly, the UAE monarchies have faced a serious and likely permanent loss of legitimacy over the past year, largely because of the alacrity with which they resorted to repression. Although the bulk of the population has certainly been scared by the large number of arrests, especially as they have included prominent and educated UAE nationals, the strategy seems to have backfired as total acquiescence has not been achieved and the UAE's international reputation—which is very important given its described economic model and emphasis on soft power strategies, especially in the West—is undoubtedly going to become tarnished.

Reminiscent of 2011's collapsing North African regimes, a number of the recent UAE arrests have been accompanied by official government press releases claiming that there is an 'international plot' and that the opposition has connections to 'foreign organisations and outside agendas'.[23] Meanwhile, the ruler of Ra's al-Khaimah delivered a speech in May 2012, also reported by the official state news agency, warning 'those who poked their noses into the UAE's [internal] affairs to mind their own business'. He went on to explain 'We hear today... that there are some who are trying to tamper with the stability of the UAE. I would like to say to them: the people of the UAE don't need lessons from anyone. They are confident in themselves and in the solidarity that they share. They don't change'. Referring to the aforementioned citizenship-stripping practice, he also explained that 'He who does not like this should leave for another place. Any treachery is a shame for him, and for his country', before concluding that 'the UAE is sheltered by the heritage of Sheikh Zayed and by the achievements of the president, His Highness Sheikh Khalifa, and of the rulers and Supreme Council members, and is safeguarded by its people, who are loyal to the nation, the country and its leadership. We don't care about the raising of trivial things and arguments that have already been defeated'.[24] Most recently, even the ruler of Sharjah—as described, a key benefactor to several Western universities—joined the chorus, explaining that '...these people were held at airports, or at border crossings with Oman or Qatar... they were running away to establish an outside organisation'. Most worryingly, in a sort of twisted paternalism he claimed that the arrests were part of a measure to 'help those who deviated' and that the state's measures were 'to protect its sons' and to provide 'treatment, not punishment'.[25] These ruling family backlashes—likely to become anti-Western—will most probably intensify, as a London-based, Syrian-style observatory for human rights—

the Emirates Centre for Human Rights—has now been established. Detailing the various human rights abuses in the UAE and recording the status of all political prisoners, it has begun to lobby against the UAE regime in the international community.[26]

As the only outlier, the Qatari ruling family's future is a little rosier than that of the other Gulf monarchies: the state can actually sustain high spending and wealth distribution to its national population. As one recent study put it, 'It seems at first glance Qatar has bought itself out of the possible ill effects of modernity'.[27] Furthermore, it lacks a poor hinterland, is relatively calm, and has fewer issues of sectarianism or discrimination, and it is generally perceived as having played a positive role in the Arab Spring. The ruler also seems to be more sympathetic than his regional counterparts towards his citizenry's cultural and religious practices, and it's possible he may follow a route towards constitutional monarchy in the next few years. Nonetheless there are a number of areas of concern, and if mismanaged these could still derail the ruler's liberal autocratic ambitions. In particular, if a more organised opposition does emerge, the authorities might still be tempted to resort to heavy handedness, which could delegitimise the ruler and expose his limitations to his own people and the rest of the Arab world. Various websites and Facebook groups have already been set up, including a 'Revolution in Qatar' forum which features cartoons of the ruler dressed as an Orthodox Jew or depicted naked, with a US flag draped around his body and horns protruding from his head. It also features photographs of the ruler meeting with Israeli officials. Although these groups are not yet very active—at least compared to similar groups focusing on other Gulf monarchies—and although they still seem to focus mostly on Qatar's foreign policy, they could be used to discuss future arrests or crackdowns against activists in the emirate itself, or could facilitate discussions about the ruling family, corruption, or other red line issues. Already, for example, the groups contain much criticism of the ruler's wife's dress code which is deemed 'too open and public for the wife of a ruler',[28] along with calls for genuine democracy. Indeed, as reported by the *New Statesman*, the audience of a recent *Doha Debates* forum voted overwhelmingly in favour of democratisation over economic liberalisation which—although perhaps not yet representative of the nation—indicated that the increasingly well-educated Qatari youth are likely to push soon for a new environment where legitimate democratic discussion can take place.[29]

POSTSCRIPT

The original, British edition of this book went to press in summer 2012. At that time there was little, if any, mainstream discussion outside the region of the prospect of serious political unrest or regime failure in the Gulf monarchies. Academia and the policy community, at least among the monarchies' Western allies, had for the most part 'ring-fenced' these states as exceptional and somehow aloof from the Arab Spring movements sweeping the broader Middle East. With extensive trade and military ties to the West, coupled with the described accumulation of 'soft power' influence, this position was both predictable and understandable. With a mixture of carrots and sticks the poorer Gulf monarchies had, after all, managed to contain most of the protests that had spilled onto their streets in the immediate aftermath of the revolutions in North Africa. Meanwhile, the wealthier monarchies seemingly remained in command of largely apolitical, well-heeled societies with little, if anything, in common with those dwelling in the angry tenements of Tunis, Cairo, or Tripoli.

Since then, however, much has changed. By the winter of 2012 most leading Western broadsheets were carrying articles and predictions of either monarchical collapse or at least some serious impending turbulence. Veteran foreign affairs correspondents filing reports on protests, trials, growing poverty, and cyberspace activism in the Gulf states became commonplace, with even leading US think tanks publishing on the prospects of 'Revolution in Riyadh.' With a growing awareness of the rising discontent among increasingly large swathes of Gulf nationals, and being better plugged into regional grassroots campaigns and emerging opposition groups, the international commentariat seemed to have finally woken up to the struggle that had already begun to take place between the people of the region and their increasingly authoritarian and reactionary elites.

This current, unprecedented international interest in Gulf politics and the possibility of a 'Gulf Spring' is in many ways due to the hundreds of headline-grabbing incidents regarding political activism, human rights, and corruption that have taken place in the region over the past six months. Almost without exception, these have provided further, compelling evidence in support of the central thesis of this book. Namely that traditional monarchy as a legitimate regime type in the region is soon going to reach the end of its lifespan, especially as most of the Gulf states are now caught in a pincer movement of pressures between unsustainable wealth distribution mechanisms and increasingly powerful 'super modernising forces' that can no longer be controlled or co-opted by political elites. The former continue to manifest themselves in widening wealth gaps and increasing real unemployment, despite ramped-up public spending programmes and urgent public sector job creation schemes. These counter-revolutionary 'rentier outlays' are likely to keep spiralling, with the International Monetary Fund and other bodies having already predicted that even the wealthiest of the monarchies will be in budget deficit within a few years. Meanwhile, in the poorer states, where this strategy is now increasingly inapplicable, street protests keep growing and regimes have had little option but to openly crack down on dissidents, with ever larger numbers of political prisoners being taken.

As for 'super modernisation,' and especially improved communications in the form of social media, in recent months a veritable battle in cyberspace has now begun. New legislation has been introduced, or is about to be introduced, in all six monarchies, with the aim of tightly policing online dissent and meting out heavy punishments to all would-be critics. As unsustainable as the spiralling public spending, the strategy also seems likely to fail, with several of these states now having the highest social media usage rates in the world, and with massive, often well-organised, online political discussions having made Twitter, Facebook, and YouTube the region's de facto new parliament. Detailed, substantiated criticism of governments has thus become commonplace, with exposés of ruling family corruption and public insults directed at hitherto unchallengeable elites being broadcasted and digested by millions each day. As with the clamping down on street protests, this new form of repression is already damaging—probably irreparably—the described social contracts and legitimacy resources of these monarchies. Certainly, such disparagement of rulers was almost unimaginable prior to 2011, but now it is almost fashionable for young Gulf nationals to question their autocrats.

With regards to Bahrain—still the vanguard of the region's revolt – the past few months have witnessed only further tragedy and despair. Unsurprisingly, despite fresh promises of dialogue and some minor political concessions—including promotions for supposed moderates – the ruling family and its allies in Riyadh and Abu Dhabi have firmly held the line. By refusing any significant reforms and keeping hundreds of activists behind bars, the island's elites seem more distanced than ever from the majority of the population. The extensive public relations campaign to depict the long-running uprising, both to the Arab world and Western allies, as primarily a sectarian conflict or part of an Iran-Arab struggle, has continued unabated, albeit with declining plausibility. With a resurgence in mass protests in February 2013—marking the second anniversary of 2011's 'Pearl Revolution'—and with further deaths and clashes between security services and demonstrators, it seems increasingly unlikely that the Bahraini monarchy can regain a baseline position of legitimacy. As such, the Al-Khalifa family will effectively become the first of the Gulf dynasties to have been publicly rejected by the majority of its subjects.

Across the causeway in Saudi Arabia's Eastern Province, the protests have also continued to gather pace. While modest in size for much of 2012, not least due to continuing announcements from senior clerics and government officials that protests are 'un-Islamic' and illegal, by the end of the year they had become much larger. Notably, following the death of a young man at the hands of security services in December 2012—thought to be the twelfth such killing of the year—it was estimated that tens of thousands of protestors took to the streets, many chanting slogans opposing the ruling family. In some ways even more problematic for the Al-Saud have been the protests that have begun to break out in other, predominantly Sunni provinces of the kingdom. Much harder to frame as a sectarian clash, these have mainly been campaigns for the release of political prisoners, with large numbers of women and children in the northern Al-Qassim province taking to the streets. In some cases burning pictures of key ruling family members and resisting arrest, their movement is being widely discussed across the region, mostly on Twitter. Meanwhile, several other 'trigger incidents' have been taking place in

Saudi Arabia which continue to underline how brittle the state is becoming despite its enormous and unprecedented public spending programme. These include the jailing of leading human rights activists, including some of those discussed in this book, outrage over the apparent unaccountability of various ministers, the disappearance of activists from other Arab monarchies in Saudi territory, and the seizing of numerous social media users. 2012 also witnessed the highest rate of executions in the kingdom so far, many of which were widely debated and criticised as they included beheadings and crucifixions for crimes such as blasphemy and 'sorcery'.

Similarly in Kuwait, the alacrity with which the authorities—concerned over seemingly uncontrollable discussion of their government's shortcomings—have been arresting online activists has alarmed many over the past few months. The crackdown has continued offline too, with key critics—including leading former parliamentarians and members of powerful tribes – having been imprisoned after what have been described as 'show trials'. As with Bahrain and Saudi Arabia's rulers, the Al-Sabah's increasingly repressive tactics seem to be losing them support from significant constituencies, with continuing street protests undermining the ruler's legitimacy and with parliamentary elections in December 2012 being largely boycotted—thus denting the Kuwaiti elite's ability to keep employing 'liberal autocracy' strategies. Perhaps most worryingly for the monarchy, the previously fragmented opposition groups—ranging from youth movements, to Islamists and disaffected tribes—seem to be slowly coalescing, with a broad-based opposition coalition having been formed in March 2013. Pushing for a multi-party system with 'democratic rotation of power,' it is likely to become the first properly organised Gulf group to press successfully for significant political reform, with constitutional monarchy as its minimum demand.

The United Arab Emirates' rulers, or more specifically the tight-knit group of brothers surrounding the crown prince of Abu Dhabi, also seem more resolute than before to tackle their opposition head on, effectively side-lining their late father's well-honed social contract in favour of police state strategies. The dozens of political prisoners seized over the course of 2012 swelled to nearly one hundred by the beginning of 2013, with another 'national security trial'—reminiscent of 2011's 'UAE Five' trial—beginning in March 2013. Accused of trying to 'seize power', and at one point even accused of setting up a 'military wing', the detainees are likely to face heavy sentences. All foreign media have been banned, and foreign observers from non-governmental organisations and law firms were barred entry to the country. Despite comprising academics, lawyers, students, judges, and even a ruling family member, most of whom identify with a well-established and peaceful indigenous Islamist organisation that has been gently pushing for parliamentary elections, the authorities seem determined to forge a link between them and outside powers. Given the fairly homogenous, predominantly Sunni, makeup of the UAE's national population, it has proven harder to present opposition groups through the sectarian, Iran-Arab lens, with the detainees instead being regularly portrayed in the local, state-affiliated media as in league with the Egyptian Muslim Brotherhood. Disturbingly for the authorities, the detainees appear to be enjoying growing support across the country, with widespread online discussion taking place, often in their favour, and with their extended families campaigning for their release. The past few months have also witnessed the UAE playing an increasingly active role in the collective securitisation of the Gulf monarchies, having joined Saudi Arabia in providing significant financial assistance to Bahrain and Oman, and having denied entry into the country to academics, journalists, and lawyers who have expressed support for the opposition in Bahrain.

While Oman has not yet seen further protests, the mood in early 2013 is perhaps best understood as being in a 'holding pattern'. The various promises made by the government, especially regarding public sector employment, have not yet been fulfilled, and there is growing discussion about the sustainability of a system that has to rely on substantial Saudi and UAE grants. Youth groups appear more restive than ever, not least given the arrests and trial of several online activists accused of insulting the aging ruler, while intellectuals now openly talk of the vacuum that will develop in the wake of his death, and what political reforms will be needed to move the country forward. With billions of their dollars now invested in Oman's survival, much will rest on the Riyadh-Abu Dhabi axis' willingness to permit some kind of political opening at that stage without encouraging the same sort of repression that is being used in Bahrain or on their own populations.

To the surprise and disappointment of many, the past few months have weakened Qatar's credentials as the only significant outlier, and as such its status as the region's last remaining liberal autocracy. The detention and trial of a well-known poet who had expressed solidarity with Arab Spring movements elsewhere in the Middle East and had implicitly criticised the Gulf monarchies was followed closely, not least by the substantial expatriate population in Qatar's branch campus foreign universities and Al-Jazeera's journalistic community. Given Qatar's media, financial, and even military support for the Arab revolutions of 2011 and 2012, most had expected a full pardon for the prisoner, probably in the form of a magnanimous gesture from the ruler. But to widespread dismay, he was sentenced to life imprisonment for insulting the ruler, later commuted to a fifteen year sentence. Unable to report properly on one of Qatar's most important news stories, Al-Jazeera's coverage of the incident was initially non-existent, then poor, reflecting the reality of having to operate within the confines of a traditional Gulf monarchy still committed to regime survival. Since then a number of other Qatari activists have been arrested and detained. With most citizens continuing to enjoy an extremely high standard of living due to gas-rich Qatar's still rising gross domestic product per capita, the possibility of protests or large rafts of political prisoners is undoubtedly still very low. However, recent events have led to discernible tension, provoking more outspoken comments from intellectuals and sections of the elite, while youth activists seem to be following the regional trend: taking their dissent online and participating in mass, often critical discussions of ruling elites.

NOTES

INTRODUCTION

1. According to International Monetary Fund data from 2010, the six Gulf monarchies had a combined GDP of $993 billion. This was more than half of the $1903 billion total GDP for all twenty-two Arab League member states at the time. Most dramatically, Saudi Arabia and the UAE together accounted for 35 per cent of the Arab League total. International Monetary Fund 2010; author calculations.

2. For discussions of this activity see, for example, Davidson, Christopher M., 'Arab Nationalism and British Opposition in Dubai, 1920–1966', *Middle Eastern Studies*, Vol. 43, No. 6, 2007; Fuccaro, Nelida, *Histories of City and State in the Persian Gulf: Manama since 1800* (Cambridge: Cambridge University Press, 2009); Crystal, Jill, *Oil and Politics in the Gulf: Rulers and Merchants in Kuwait and Qatar* (Cambridge: Cambridge University Press, 1995).

3. For a full discussion see Kerr, Malcolm, *The Arab Cold War, 1958–1970* (Oxford: Oxford University Press, 1971).

4. Saudi Arabia, already an independent state, was able to join the Arab League upon its inception in 1945. Kuwait joined in 1961, and was followed by the other Gulf monarchies in 1971.

5. Saudi Arabia and Kuwait joined OPEC upon its inception in 1960. Qatar joined in 1961, and the UAE's principal oil-exporting emirate of Abu Dhabi joined in 1967. Bahrain, Oman, and the UAE's other constituent members eschewed OPEC.

6. See Calabrese, John, 'From Flyswatters to Silkworms: The Evolution of China's Role in West Asia', *Asian Survey*, No. 30, 1990. Referring to Said bin Taimur Al-Said.

7. The National Liberation Front.

8. For a good overview see Ismael, Tareq Y., *The Communist Movement in the Arab World* (London: Routledge, 2005).

9. Ladwig, Walter C., 'Supporting Allies in Counterinsurgency: Britain and the Dhofar Rebellion', *Small Wars and Insurgencies*, Vol. 19, No. 1, 2008, p. 73. Britain's

actions in Oman during this period were fictionalised by Ranulph Fiennes in his 1991 novel. See Fiennes, Ranulph, *The Feather Men* (London: Bloomsbury, 1991).

10. See Halliday, Fred, *Arabia without Sultans* (London: Saqi, 1974); Halliday, Fred, 'Arabia Without Sultans Revisited', *Middle East Report*, Vol. 27, No. 204, 1997.

11. Lerner, Daniel, *The Passing of Traditional Society: Modernizing the Middle East* (New York: The Free Press, 1958); Sigelman, Lee, 'Lerner's Model of Modernization: A Reanalysis', *Journal of Developing Areas*, Vol. 8, July 1974, p. 525.

12. Lipset, Seymour Martin, 'Some Social Requisites of Democracy: Economic Development and Political Legitimacy', *The American Political Science Review*, Vol. 53, No. 1, 1959; Lipset, Seymour Martin, *Political Man: The Social Bases of Politics* (Baltimore: Johns Hopkins University Press, 1960).

13. Deutsch, Karl, 'Social Mobilization and Political Development', *American Political Science Review*, Vol. 55, No. 3, 1961.

14. Huntington, Samuel P., *Political Order in Changing Societies* (New Haven: Yale University Press, 1968), pp. 140–142.

15. Ibid., p. 169.

16. Pollin, Robert, 'Resurrection of the Rentier', *New Left Review*, Vol. 46, July–August 2007, pp. 140–153.

17. Ross, Michael, 'Does Oil Hinder Democracy', *World Politics*, Vol. 53, No. 3, 2001, p. 329.

18. Mahdavy, Hussein, 'The Patterns and Problems of Economic Development in Rentier States: The Case of Iran' in Cook, M. A. (ed.), *Studies in Economic History of the Middle East* (London: Oxford University Press, 1970), p. 428.

19. Beblawi, Hazem, 'The Rentier State in the Arab World' in Beblawi, Hazem, and Luciani, Giacomo (eds.), *The Rentier State* (New York: Croom Helm, 1987), p. 51.

20. Lucas, Russell E., 'Monarchical Authoritarianism: Survival and Political Liberalization in a Middle Eastern Regime Type', *International Journal of Middle East Studies*, Vol. 36, No. 4, 2004. As Lucas explains, small population size was previously used as a possible explanation for explaining demise of other monarchies.

21. Hertog, Steffen, *Princes, Brokers, and Bureaucrats: Oil and State in Saudi Arabia* (Ithaca: Cornell University Press, 2010).

22. Ross, p. 331.

23. Ibid., p. 332.

24. Ibid., p. 333.

25. For a full discussion see Davidson, Christopher M., *The United Arab Emirates: A Study in Survival* (Boulder: Lynne Rienner, 2005), chapter 4.

26. With reference to the Bahrain system see Kinninmont, Jane, 'Bahrain' in Davidson, Christopher M. (ed.), *Power and Politics in the Persian Gulf Monarchies* (London: Hurst, 2011). With reference to the Omani system see Valeri, Marc, 'Oman' in Davidson (2011).

27. With reference to the UAE system see Davidson (2005), chapter 4.

28. See Gray, Matthew, 'A Theory of Late Rentierism in the Arab States of the Gulf',

Georgetown University Center for International and Regional Studies Occasional Papers, No. 7, 2011, pp. 23–36.

29. See Hudson, Michael, *Arab Politics: The Search for Legitimacy* (New Haven: Yale University Press, 1977).

30. Fromherz, Allen J., *Qatar: A Modern History* (London: IB Tauris, 2012), p. 5.

31. Sharabi, Hisham, *Neopatriarchy: A Theory of Distorted Change in Arab Society* (Oxford: Oxford University Press, 1992).

32. Weber, Max, 'Politics as a Vocation (*Politik als Beruf*)' (Munich: 1919). An essay originating from a lecture delivered to the Free Students Union of Munich University in January 1919.

33. Brumberg, Daniel, 'The Trap of Liberalized Autocracy', *Journal of Democracy*, Vol. 13, No. 4, 2002, p. 56.

34. Ibid., p. 57.

35. See Hobbes, Thomas, *The Leviathan* (1660); Locke, John, *Two Treatises of Government* (1689); Rousseau, Jean-Jacques. *The Social Contract, or Principles of Political Right* (1762).

36. Kamrava, Mehran, *The Modern Middle East: A Political History since the First World War* (Los Angeles: University of California Press, 2005).

37. For discussions of the Dubai and Abu Dhabi ruling bargains see Davidson, Christopher M., *Dubai: The Vulnerability of Success* (London: Hurst, 2008), chapter 5; Davidson, Christopher M., *Abu Dhabi: Oil and Beyond* (London: Hurst, 2009), chapter 6.

38. See for example Spooner, Lysander. 'No Treason: The Constitution of No Authority' (1867). In this essay Spooner argues that a genuine social contract cannot include government actions such as taxation because the collection of tax would require the government to initiate force against anyone unwilling to pay.

39. For discussions of expatriates in Dubai and Abu Dhabi see Davidson (2008), chapter 5; Davidson (2009), chapter 6.

40. Herb, Michael, *All in the Family: Absolutism, Revolution, and Democracy in the Middle Eastern Monarchies* (New York: State University of New York Press, 1999), p. 3. Herb claims in his comparative study of ruling families in the Middle East that the dominance of one large and cohesive family over the state, rather than oil wealth, education, military support, external political support, representative institutions, selective marriages, charismatic rulers, or any other factors is the key to survival.

41. Muhammad Idris Al-Mahdi Al-Senussi.

42. See Herb (1999).

43. Qaboos bin Said Al-Said.

44. See Valeri (2011).

45. For a fuller discussion see Lucas (2004).

46. For further discussion see Filiu, Jean-Pierre, *The Arab Revolution: Ten Lessons from the Democratic Uprising* (London: Hurst, 2011), p. 3.

47. Muhammad bin Rashid Al-Maktoum.

48. Reuters, 24 June 2010.

49. *Gulf News*, 29 December 2011.

50. Filiu (2011), p. 58.

51. Muhammad bin Zayed Al-Nahyan.

52. Wikileaks, US Embassy Abu Dhabi, 29 April 2006.

53. Abdullah Al-Ghaddami.

54. Ahmed Mansour Al-Shehhi.

55. Reuters, 24 June 2010.

56. Valbjørn, Morten, and Bank, André, 'Examining the Post in Post-Democratization: The Future of Middle Eastern Political Rule through Lenses of the Past', *Middle East Critique*, Vol. 19, No. 3, 2010, pp. 185–186.

1. STATE FORMATION AND ECONOMIC DEVELOPMENT

1. Peck, Malcolm, *The United Arab Emirates: A Venture in Unity* (Boulder: Westview, 1986), pp. 29–30.

2. Hawley, Donald, *The Trucial States* (London: George Allen and Unwin, 1970), pp. 96–97.

3. Belgrave, Charles, *The Pirate Coast* (London: G. Bell and Sons, 1966), p. 25.

4. The defeat took place in 1818.

5. For a full discussion of the Saudi-Wahhabi alliance see Commins, David, *The Wahhabi Mission and Saudi Arabia* (London: IB Tauris, 2009).

6. Bin Ali had initiated the 1916 Arab Revolt against the Ottoman Empire. See Teitelbaum, Joshua, *The Rise and Fall of the Hashemite Kingdom of Arabia* (London: Hurst, 2001), p. 243.

7. Roberts, David, 'Kuwait' in Davidson, Christopher M. (ed.), *Power and Politics in the Persian Gulf Monarchies* (London: Hurst, 2011), p. 89.

8. Muhammad Al-Sabah.

9. For a full discussion see Crystal, Jill, *Oil and Politics in the Gulf: Rulers and Merchants in Kuwait and Qatar* (New York: Cambridge University Press, 1995), chapter 1.

10. Roberts (2011), p. 90.

11. This took place in 1921.

12. Signed in 1921, the Uqair agreement required Kuwait to give up much of its territory to the Al-Saud, while also defining its borders with the British-mandated territory of Iraq. See Lauterpacht, E., Greenwood, C. J., Weller, Marc, 'The Determination of Boundaries between Iraq, Kuwait and Saudi Arabia (Najd)' in *The Kuwait Crisis: Basic Documents* (Cambridge: Cambridge University Press, 1991), pp. 45–49.

13. See for example Davies, Charles E., *The Blood Red Arab Flag: An Investigation into Qasimi Piracy, 1797–1820* (Exeter: Exeter University Press, 1997); Al-

Qasimi, Sultan bin Muhammad, *The Myth of Arab Piracy in the Gulf* (London: Croom Helm, 1986).

14. Nasser Al-Makhdur. The Al-Makhdur family also ruled over Bushire, on the Persian coastline. See Hopwood, Derek, *The Arabian Peninsula* (London: George Allen and Unwin, 1972), p. 40.

15. The rulers of Trucial States were all given gun salutes by the cannons of visiting British warships. The number of cannon blasts corresponded with Britain's perception of a ruler's relative power and influence in the region.

16. During this period Dubai was governed by Muhammad bin Hazza Al-Nahyan and his uncle Zayed bin Saif Al-Nahyan.

17. Davidson, Christopher M., *Dubai: The Vulnerability of Success* (London: Hurst, 2008), pp. 12–14.

18. See Valeri, Marc, 'Oman' in Davidson (2011).

19. See Davidson, Christopher M., *The United Arab Emirates: A Study in Survival* (Boulder: Lynne Rienner, 2005), pp. 30–31; Gause, Gregory F. *Oil Monarchies: Domestic and Security Challenges in the Arab Gulf States* (New York: Council on Foreign Relations Press, 1994), p. 22.

20. Lord George Curzon.

21. Al-Sagri, Saleh Hamad, 'Britain and the Arab Emirates, 1820–1956' (PhD thesis. University of Kent at Canterbury, 1988), p. 70.

22. Most notably the fratricides among the sons of Abu Dhabi's Zayed bin Khalifa Al-Nahyan.

23. Al-Sagri, p. 97.

24. Ibid., p. 92.

25. Ibid., p. 51.

26. Lorimer, John G., *Gazetteer of the Persian Gulf, Oman, and Central Arabia* (London: Gregg International Publishers, 1970), pp. 1450–1451.

27. Al-Sagri, p. 64.

28. Locational rent being a form of economic rent which is created by spatial variation or the location of a resource. The concept was put forward in the 1820s by Johann Heinrich von Thünen. See Von Thünen, Johann Heinrich, *The Isolated State* (1826). In this case, the sheikhdoms' location en route to India and the suspected oil reserves in their territories.

29. Buxani, Ram, *Taking the High Road* (Dubai: Motivate, 2003), p. 84.

30. India Office R/515/4; Abdullah, Muhammad Morsy, *The United Arab Emirates: A Modern History* (London: Croom Helm, 1978), p. 56.

31. Wilson, Graeme, *Rashid's Legacy: The Genesis of the Maktoum Family and the History of Dubai* (Dubai: Media Prima, 2006), p. 72. In the latter case Imperial Airways was allowed to land flying boats in between buoys on the Dubai creek.

32. Most notably American Standard Oil of New Jersey. Foreign Office 371/19975.

33. The Iraqi Petroleum Company was 51 per cent owned by the British Government. Foreign Office 371/19975.

34. Petroleum Concessions Ltd. was dominated by British Petroleum. See Hawley, Donald, *The Emirates: Witness to a Metamorphosis* (Norwich: Michael Russell, 2007), p. 67; Heard-Bey, Frauke, *From Trucial States to United Arab Emirates* (London: Longman, 1996), p. 295; and, (*in Arabic*) Al-Otaibi, Manna Said, *Petroleum and the Economy of the United Arab Emirates* (Kuwait: Al-Qabas Press, 1977), p. 45.

35. Al-Otaibi (1977), p. 155.

36. The first oil discoveries in Dubai were made in 1966 at the Fateh offshore field. See Butt, Gerald, 'Oil and Gas' in Al-Abed, Ibrahim and Hellyer, Peter (eds.), *The United Arab Emirates: A New Perspective* (London: Trident, 2001).

37. India Office l/P/S/18/B/458; Abdullah (1978), p. 70; Wilson (2006), p. 68.

38. India Office S/18/B/469.

39. India Office S/18/B/414.

40. The base was at Manama in Ajman. Hawley (2007), p. 278.

41. Muhammad bin Hamad Al-Sharqi.

42. Examples of these can still be viewed in the Fujairah museum.

43. Heard-Bey (1996), pp. 75–76; Hawley (2007). p. 113; Rush, Alan (ed.), *Ruling Families of Arabia: The United Arab Emirates* (Slough: Archive Editions, 1991), pp. 457–465.

44. Hawley (2007), p. 182.

45. The United Nations recognized Saudi Arabia in 1945.

46. Faisal bin Abdul-Aziz Al-Saud was assassinated by a nephew, Faisal bin Musaid Al-Saud. Faisal bin Musaid was declared insane by medical doctors, but was nonetheless beheaded later that year. BBC News, 25 March 1975.

47. Fahd bin Abdul-Aziz Al-Saud suffered a stroke in 1996 and handed over most duties to his crown prince and younger brother, Abdullah.

48. Obaid, Nawaf E., 'The Power of Saudi Arabia's Islamic Leaders', *Middle East Quarterly*, Vol. 6, No. 3, 1999, pp. 51–58.

49. Hassner, Ron Eduard, *War on Sacred Grounds* (New York: Cornell University Press, 2009), p. 143.

50. Coates Ulrichsen, Kristian, 'Saudi Arabia' in Davidson (2011), p. 70.

51. Referring to the 1990 invasion of Kuwait by Iraq and the subsequent liberation of Kuwait by a US-led international coalition.

52. Nolan, Leigh, 'Managing Reform? Saudi Arabia and the King's Dilemma', Brookings Doha Center Policy Briefing, May 2011.

53. Coates Ulrichsen, 'Saudi Arabia' in Davidson (2011), pp. 68–69.

54. See Herb, Michael, *All in the Family: Absolutism, Revolution, and Democracy in the Middle Eastern Monarchies* (New York: State University of New York Press, 1999).

55. Ibid., p. 70.

56. See Nolan, May 2011.

57. Coates Ulrichsen, 'Saudi Arabia' in Davidson (2011), p. 72.

58. *Associated Press*, 22 March 2011.
59. See Nolan, May 2011.
60. Coates Ulrichsen, 'Saudi Arabia' in Davidson (2011), p. 71.
61. See Nolan, May 2011.
62. US Department of State, 'Background Note: Kuwait' 2011.
63. Roberts (2011), p. 91.
64. Ibid., p. 93.
65. Ibid., pp. 93–94.
66. These 'primaries' were staged by a number of tribes between 1975 and 1998, when they were criminalised. See Salih, Kamal Eldin Osman, 'Kuwait Primary (Tribal) Elections 1975–2008: An Evaluative Study', *British Journal of Middle East Studies*, Vol. 38, No. 2, 2011, p. 142.
67. Roberts, p. 94.
68. Ibid., p. 94.
69. Ibid., p. 95.
70. On 16 May 2009 the voter turnout was 50 per cent. Kuwait Politics Database, Georgia State University 2011.
71. For a full discussion of the 2006 reforms see Salih, pp. 159–164.
72. The unpopular older brother being Shakhbut bin Sultan Al-Nahyan. See Davidson, Christopher M., *Abu Dhabi: Oil and Beyond* (London: Hurst, 2009), chapters 2–3.
73. Ibid., p. 99.
74. Davidson (2008), pp. 252–253.
75. Ibid., pp. 259–262.
76. Davidson (2005), chapter 1. The offer was rejected by the British government on the grounds that British armed forces could never be deployed as a mercenary force.
77. For a full discussion see Davidson (2009), chapter 3. Qatar also seemed to have hoped that the capital of the federation would be Doha. See Fromherz, Allen J., *Qatar: A Modern History* (London: IB Tauris, 2012), p. 18.
78. Comprising Abu Dhabi, Dubai, Sharjah, Ajman, Umm al-Qawain, and Fujairah.
79. Davidson (2009), pp. 56–61
80. Kinninmont, Jane. 'Bahrain' in Davidson, Christopher M. (ed.), *Power and Politics in the Persian Gulf Monarchies* (London: Hurst, 2011), pp. 37–38.
81. Ibid., p. 46. The *mataams* being the mourning houses for Imam Hussein bin Ali, a key Shia martyr and member of the Prophet Muhammad's household.
82. Ibid., p. 43.
83. Ibid., p. 40.
84. Ibid., pp. 41–42.
85. Wright, Steven, 'Qatar' in Davidson, Christopher M. (ed.), *Power and Politics in the Persian Gulf Monarchies* (London: Hurst, 2011), p. 118.
86. Ibid., pp. 119–120.

87. Ibid., p. 120.

88. Ibid., p. 119.

89. Kamrava, Mehran, 'Royal Factionalism and Political Liberalization in Qatar', *Middle East Journal*, Vol. 63, No. 3, 2009, p. 416.

90. Ibid., p. 416.

91. Ibid., p. 417.

92. *The Guardian*, 1 November 2011.

93. For a full discussion see Davidson (2009). pp. 61–69.

94. See Al-Nabeh, Najat Abdullah, 'United Arab Emirates: Regional and Global Dimensions' (PhD thesis. Claremont Graduate School, 1984).

95. Article 49. See Al-Gurg, Easa Saleh, *The Wells of Memory* (London: John Murray, 1998), p. 140; Kéchichian, Joseph A., *Power and Succession in Arab Monarchies: A Reference Guide* (Boulder: Lynne Rienner, 2008), p. 284.

96. Kéchichian (2008), p. 206.

97. Hadef Jawan Al-Dhaheri.

98. Sultan bin Said Al-Mansuri.

99. Muhammad bin Dhaen Al-Hamili.

100. Kéchichian (2008), p. 285. As per article 72 of the constitution.

101. Rizvi, S., 'From Tents to High Rise: Economic Development of the United Arab Emirates', *Middle Eastern Studies*, Vol. 29, No. 4, 1993, p. 665.

102. These have normally been over concerns that were already shared by the Council of Ministers, such as the need for tightening anti-drug legislation and the need for further modifying the UAE's property laws. Al-Nahyan, Shamma bint Muhammad, *Political and Social Security in the United Arab Emirates* (Dubai: 2000), pp. 122–123.

103. Especially in cases where the FNC's views were likely to diverge from the relevant minister's outlook, such as over the price of petrol or the cultural content of terrestrial television. Ibid., p. 121.

104. There have been examples of the FNC's letters to ministers having remained unanswered for several months, and occasions when the FNC has been unable to persuade ministers to attend their sessions and answer basic questions on their policies. Ibid., pp. 178–179,188.

105. Reuters, 24 September 2011.

106. *WAM*, 21 June 2011.

107. Reuters, 24 September 2011.

108. Davidson (2009), p. 125.

109. Valeri (2011), p. 140.

110. Valeri, (2011), p. 139; Katz, Mark, 'Assessing the Political Stability of Oman', *Middle East Review of International Affairs*, Vol. 8, No. 3, 2004.

111. Valeri (2011), p. 139.

112. Ibid., pp. 143–144.

113. Ibid., p. 144.

114. Article 6.
115. Valeri (2011), p. 139. Quoting articles 2, 3, 5, 9 and 41 of the 1996 Basic Law of Oman.
116. Davidson (2005), pp. 94–95.
117. Davidson (2009), chapter 4.
118. Dubai's share is now only 4 per cent, with the remainder being made up of minimal exports from Sharjah, Ra's al-Khaimah, and Fujairah. Ajman and Umm al-Qawain do not have commercially exploitable oil reserves. Davidson (2009), chapter 4.
119. *CIA World Factbook* 2009, Economics overviews on Saudi Arabia, the UAE, Kuwait, Qatar, Oman, and Bahrain, 2007 and 2008 estimates. Author calculations for totals.
120. Ibid.
121. Ibid.
122. British Petroleum Statistical Review, June 2008.
123. US Energy Information Administration (EIA). Qatar profile, 2009.
124. *CIA World Factbook*. People and economics overviews of Japan, China, South Korea, Saudi Arabia, the UAE, Kuwait, Qatar, Oman, and Bahrain. Statistics from 2007–2008, with 2009 population estimates. Supplementary data from the International Monetary Fund, World Bank, and OECD country overviews, 2009.
125. *Kuwait News Agency*, 15 January 2012. Combined assets are expected to reach $1.9 trillion in 2012.
126. *Euromoney*, 1 April 2006.
127. Davidson (2009), chapter 4.
128. Davidson, Christopher M. *The Persian Gulf and Pacific Asia: From Indifference to Interdependence* (London: Hurst, 2011), chapter 5.
129. Van der Meulen, Hendrik, 'The Role of Tribal and Kinship Ties in the Politics of the United Arab Emirates' (PhD thesis. The Fletcher School of Law and Diplomacy, 1997), p. 93.
130. Davidson (2009), chapter 4.
131. *The Economist*, 17 January 2008; Seznec, Jean-François. 'The Gulf Sovereign Wealth Funds: Myths and Reality', *Middle East Policy*, Vol. 15, No. 2, 2008, pp. 97,101. ADIA was believed to have had $875 billion in assets according to Deutsche Bank. However, Seznec believes the figure to be much lower. But he may have placed insufficient weight on ADIA's history of investments in emerging markets.
132. *CIA World Factbook*. People and economics overviews of Japan, China, South Korea, Saudi Arabia, the UAE, Kuwait, Qatar, Oman, and Bahrain. Statistics from 2007–2008, with 2009 population estimates. Supplementary data from the International Monetary Fund, World Bank, and OECD country overviews, 2009.

133. Officially the Investment Corporation of Dubai holds $19.6 billion in assets. 2012 figures.

134. According to Mumtalakat Holdings' official financial report for December 2011 its total holdings were just over $11 billion. Oman's State General Reserve Fund is thought to have just over $8 billion in assets.

135. Mansour bin Zayed Al-Nahyan.

136. Quoting official figures for total holdings supplied in 2011 by the Qatar Investment Authority, the Mubadala Development Company, and the International Petroleum Investment Company.

137. *Arab News*, 5 October 2009.

138. *Khaleej Times*, 20 December 2009.

139. Coates Ulrichsen, 'Saudi Arabia' in Davidson (2011), p. 78.

140. Roberts (2011). p. 102.

141. US Department of State. 'Background Note: Kuwait' 2011.

142. *New York Times*, 28 December 2008.

143. *Oxford Business Group*, 'Abu Dhabi: The Report 2007'. p. 202.

144. Also known as Borouge. *Oxford Business Group*, 'United Arab Emirates: The Report 2000'. pp. 94–95.

145. *Oxford Business Group*, 'Abu Dhabi: The Report 2007'. p. 212.

146. The latter being built at Ruwais in co-operation with Rio Tinto. *The National*, 24 July 2008; Seznec (2008), p. 101.

147. Borealis press release, 19 March 2008.

148. *Gulf News*, 1 March 2012.

149. Also known as the Higher Corporation for Economic Zones.

150. Davidson (2009), chapter 4.

151. *Gulf News*, 1 March 2012.

152. Davidson (2008), chapter 4.

153. Dubai Department for Tourism and Commerce Marketing, press release, 28 February 2011.

154. Abu Dhabi Tourism Authority, press release, 31 January 2011.

155. Davidson (2008), chapter 4.

156. *Emirates* 24/7, 13 September 2011.

157. *Bloomberg*, 12 January 2012.

158. *Wall Street Journal*, 5 April 2012.

159. The freehold legislation resulted from an Omani royal decree in February 2006.

160. *CIA World Factbook 2011*, country overview of Bahrain.

161. *Gulf News*, 30 May 2010.

162. *CIA World Factbook 2011*, country overview of Saudi Arabia; *Gulf News*, 30 May 2010.

163. *CIA World Factbook 2011*, country overviews of Qatar and Kuwait.

164. *CIA World Factbook 2011*, country overview of Kuwait.

165. *Saudi Gazette*, 24 November 2010.

2. EXPLAINING SURVIVAL—DOMESTIC MATTERS

1. See Huntington, Samuel P., *Political Order in Changing Societies* (New Haven: Yale University Press, 1968).

2. Eudemonic legitimacy was originally coined by Stephen White. See White, Stephen, 'Economic Performance and Communist Legitimacy', *World Politics*, Vol. 38, No. 3, 1986, p. 463.

3. E.g. in Qatar nationals do not pay for utilities or landline telephones. See Kamrava, Mehran, 'Royal Factionalism and Political Liberalization in Qatar', *Middle East Journal*, Vol. 63, No. 3, 2009, p. 406. In the UAE, the same also used to be true.

4. AME Info, 15 June 2008.

5. *Gulf News*, 23 January 2008.

6. *Gulf News*, 10 January 2011.

7. *Gulf News*, 5 January 2011.

8. Heard-Bey, Frauke, *From Trucial States to United Arab Emirates* (London: Longman, 1996), p. 397; Davidson, Christopher M., *Abu Dhabi: Oil and Beyond* (London: Hurst, 2009), see chapter 6.

9. Kamrava, 'Royal Factionalism' (2009), p. 406.

10. In 2009 the figure was $2800. See Davidson (2009), chapter 6.

11. AME Info, 31 January 2008.

12. Hertog, Steffen, *Princes, Brokers, and Bureaucrats: Oil and State in Saudi Arabia* (Ithaca: Cornell University Press, 2010), p. 3.

13. *Economist Intelligence Unit*, May 2005.

14. *The National*, 21 December 2009.

15. *Oxford Business Group*, 'Abu Dhabi: The Report 2007'. p. 16.

16. Nelson, Caren, 'UAE National women at work in the private sector: conditions and constraints', Tanmia Labour Market Study, No. 20, 2004, p. 30.

17. See Davidson, Christopher M., 'Dubai Foreclosure of a Dream', *Middle East Report*, No. 251, 2009.

18. *The National*, 24 December 2009.

19. Abdullah H. Al-Nameh.

20. Kamrava, 'Royal Factionalism' (2009), p. 408.

21. *The National*, 4 August 2008.

22. *Emirates 24/7*, 31 March 2011.

23. *Zawya*, 21 November 2011.

24. Hertog (2010), p. 3.

25. For a full discussion see Lucas, Russell E., 'Monarchical Authoritarianism: Survival and Political Liberalization in a Middle Eastern Regime Type', *International Journal of Middle East Studies*, Vol. 36, No. 4, 2004.

26. E.g. The UAE Federal Commercial Companies Law of 1984, article 22.

27. Agence France Presse, 30 November 2011.

28. *Egypt News*, 27 July 2009.
29. *WAM*, 21 October 2002.
30. *Emirates 24/7*, 27 December 2011.
31. Kamrava, 'Royal Factionalism' (2009), p. 406.
32. In the case of Abu Dhabi see Davidson (2009), chapter 6.
33. Fromherz, Allen J., *Qatar: A Modern History* (London: IB Tauris, 2012), p. 14.
34. US Department of State, 'Background Note: Saudi Arabia' 2011.
35. US Department of State, 'Background Note: Oman' 2011.
36. *Gulf Daily News*, 7 February 2011. Based on official population figures.
37. US Department of State, 'Background Note: Kuwait' 2011.
38. US Department of State, 'Background Note: United Arab Emirates' 2011.
39. Referring to official UAE Census (Tedad) April 2010 results.
40. US Department of State, 'Background Note: Qatar' 2011.
41. The Palestinian Liberation Organisation nominally backed Iraq during the Kuwait crisis.
42. *Voice of America*, 11 October 2009.
43. There has been one notable exception, when in 2008 groups of Bangladeshi leftist 'Naxalites' were reportedly stirring hatred against the Gulf monarchies in Kuwait worker camps. The Kuwait Ministry for the Interior claimed that the Naxalites viewed the Gulf monarchies as their 'Number 2 enemy after India' on the grounds of their capitalist exploitation of South Asian labour. *Outlook India*, 5 June 2008.
44. *Migrant Rights*, 23 May 2010.
45. *Migrant Rights*, 27 May 2010.
46. *The National*, 4 January 2011.
47. *Construction Week*, 27 January 2011.
48. *The News Pakistan*, 1 January 2011.
49. Adopt-a-Camp was established in summer 2010 by a Sharjah-based Pakistani activist. *The National*, 10 September 2010.
50. *Voice of America*, 11 October 2010.
51. See Lucas (2004). Lucas describes this situation as '…monarchs can stand above tribal, religious, ethnic, and regional divisions by acting as the linchpin of the political system. These potentially conflicting identities can then be subsumed under the monarch's benevolent patronage. The monarchy becomes the unifying symbol of the (newly created) nation'.
52. See Lucas (2004). Lucas argues that 'if a sultanistic regime attempts to mobilise society, it is only for the glorification of the ruler's ego or his personality cult'.
53. See www.sheikhmohammed.co.ae
54. For examples, see the crown prince's official website: www.fazza.ae
55. *Business Insider*, 25 July 2011.
56. Sayyid Fahd bin Mahmoud Al-Said.
57. Sayyid Haitham bin Tariq Al-Said.

58. Fromherz (2011), p. 29.
59. E.g. The ruler of Sharjah awards a biannual prize of $250,000 to reward an Arab citizen and a citizen from a non-Arab country whose intellectual or artistic works have contributed to the development, enrichment, and dissemination of Arabic culture throughout the world.
60. The sword was unveiled in Fujairah in 2011, and the *youla* (with 285 participants) was held in 2010, also in Fujairah. *Gulf News*, 26 December 2011.
61. See Khalaf, Sulayman, 'Poetics and Politics of Newly Invented Traditions in the Gulf: Camel Racing in the United Arab Emirates', *Ethnology*, Vol. 39, No. 3, 2000.
62. See Khalaf, Sulayman, 'Gulf Societies and the Image of Unlimited Good', *Dialectical Anthropology*, Vol. 17, No. 1, 1992.
63. Fromherz (2011), p. 2.
64. *Foreign Policy*, 21 September 2010.
65. Brumberg, Daniel, 'The Trap of Liberalized Autocracy', *Journal of Democracy*, Vol. 13. No. 4, 2002, p. 58.
66. Fahd bin Abdul-Aziz Al-Saud was the first Saudi king to change to this title.
67. Koranic verse 4/59.
68. Koranic verse 4/58.
69. Al-Azhar Statement in Support for the Arab Revolutions, released on 31 October 2011.
70. *Wikileaks*, US Embassy Abu Dhabi, 29 April 2006.
71. *Fanar* referring to 'Light house' as the mosque was founded to provide a guiding light for Qatari and expatriate Muslims living in Doha.
72. *WAM*, 18 August 2011.
73. *Catholic News Agency*, 16 December 2010.
74. *New York Times*, 5 April 2009. The Bahraini ambassador to the US was Houda Ezra Ebrahim Nonoo.
75. According to data supplied by the US Department of Energy's Carbon Dioxide Information Analysis Center.
76. *The National*, 9 July 2010.
77. World Bank Data 2011 referring to 'Motor Vehicles per 1000 people'.
78. For a full discussion see Luomi, Mari, *The Gulf Monarchies and Climate Change: Abu Dhabi and Qatar in an Era of Natural Unsustainability* (London: Hurst, 2012).
79. As stated on the Qatar Foundation official website.
80. See Kalra, Nidhi, *Recommended Research Priorities for the Qatar Foundation's Environment and Energy Research Institute* (Los Angeles: RAND Corporation, 2011).
81. *Gulf News*, 14 August 2008.
82. The prize fund was increased to $4 million in 2012.
83. See http://www.zayedfutureenergyprize.com/en/
84. *The National*, 23 July 2008.

85. *The National*, 22 July 2008.
86. *AMEInfo*, 23 September 2008.
87. Masdar City press release, July 2008.

3. EXPLAINING SURVIVAL—EXTERNAL MATTERS

1. For the most comprehensive analysis of this 'Al-Qaeda on the Arabian Peninsula' campaign see Hegghammer, Thomas, *Jihad in Saudi Arabia: Violence and Pan-Islamism Since 1979* (Cambridge: Cambridge University Press, 2010).
2. Wheatcroft, Andrew, *With United Strength: Sheikh Zayed bin Sultan Al-Nahyan, the Leader and the Nation* (Abu Dhabi: Emirates Centre for Strategic Studies and Research, 2005), p. 185.
3. *The National*, 11 July 2008.
4. *The Daily Telegraph*, 26 March 2006.
5. Stockholm International Peace Research Institute, Military Expenditure Database. In 2010 Saudi Arabia was at 11.2 per cent, UAE 7.3 per cent, and Kuwait 4.4 per cent.
6. *CNN*, 22 February 2006.
7. (*in Arabic*) Mutawwa, Khalid, *The Arabic Falcon* (Sharjah, 2005), pp. 214–215.
8. *The National*, 27 July 2008.
9. *Associated Press*, 12 July 2011. Senator Gary Ackerman of New York, a Democrat on the House Foreign Affairs subcommittee on the Middle East and South Asia, stated that 'As a matter of both law and basic decency, we will never do business with or provide aid to a government controlled by or reporting to terrorists'.
10. (*in Arabic*) Hamza, Kamal, *Zayed: A Mark on the Forehead of History* (Abu Dhabi, 2005), p. 166.
11. *The National*, 18 July 2008.
12. US Department of State, 'Background Note: United Arab Emirates' 2011.
13. *Voice of America*, 25 July 2006.
14. *Der Spiegel*, 13 March 2007.
15. Mutawwa (2005), p. 99.
16. *Islamic Republic News Agency*, 16 January 2004.
17. Davidson, Christopher M., *Abu Dhabi: Oil and Beyond* (London: Hurst, 2009), chapter 6.
18. Ibid.
19. *World Food Programme*, press release, 2 May 2006.
20. *The Peninsula*, 3 June 2011.
21. *New York Times*, 20 November 2005.
22. *Arab News*, 30 August 2010.
23. BBC News, 12 October 2005.
24. *The National*, 5 August 2008.

25. *The National*, 23 June 2008.
26. BBC News, 7 January 2005.
27. Kamrava, Mehran, 'Royal Factionalism and Political Liberalization in Qatar' in *Middle East Journal*, Vol. 63, No. 3, 2009, pp. 407–408.
28. *WAM*, 12 July 2011.
29. Saudi Arabia Ministry for Foreign Affairs, press release, 31 October 1999.
30. BBC News, 24 April 1999.
31. Wilson, Graeme, *Rashid's Legacy: The Genesis of the Maktoum Family and the History of Dubai* (Dubai: Media Prima, 2006), p. 516.
32. *The National*, 14 May 2009.
33. The UAE's federal armed forces were then called the Union Defence Force.
34. (*in Arabic*) Obaid, Nawaf E., *The Foreign Policy of the United Arab Emirates* (Beirut: Majd, 2004), p. 155.
35. Heard-Bey, Frauke, *From Trucial States to United Arab Emirates* (London: Longman, 1996), pp. 511–513; Davidson, Christopher M., *Dubai: The Vulnerability of Success* (London: Hurst, 2008), chapter 5.
36. Hawley, Donald, *The Emirates: Witness to a Metamorphosis* (Norwich: Michael Russell, 2007), p. 30.
37. *Jane's Defense Weekly*, 7 February 2007.
38. *The National*, 14 May 2009; BBC News, 28 March 2008.
39. BBC News, 28 March 2008.
40. *The National*, 22 July 2011.
41. *WAM*, 22 August 2011.
42. Article 7 of the 2005 constitution, as cited by Wright, Steven, 'Qatar' in Davidson, Christopher M. (ed.), *Power and Politics in the Persian Gulf Monarchies* (London: Hurst, 2011).
43. The Doha Agreement was reached on May 21 2008.
44. Broadcast on *Al-Jazeera*, 6 August 2007.
45. BBC News, 4 March 2009; *CNN*, 23 February 2010.
46. *Capital Eritrea*, 14 July 2011.
47. *Somaliland Press*, 7 June 2010.
48. Anthony, John Duke, *Arab States of the Lower Gulf: People, Politics, Petroleum* (Washington DC: Middle East Institute, 1975), p. 152.
49. Heard-Bey (1996), pp. 388–391.
50. Amr Moussa.
51. *The National*, 28 July 2008; Mutawwa (2005), p. 99.
52. *Oxford Business Group*, 'Abu Dhabi: The Report 2007', p. 25.
53. Reuters, 11 May 2007; BBC News, 13 May 2007.
54. *Gulf News*, 18 July 2008.
55. *The National*, 8 August 2008.
56. BBC News, 8 May 2010.
57. *Daily Mail*, 4 July 2012.

58. *The Guardian*, 30 December 2011.
59. *Associated Press*, 25 September 2011.
60. BBC Sport, 10 December 2010.
61. *ESPN*, 31 May 2011.
62. The Essex Hotel.
63. The latter of which was acquired in 2006 for $800 million.
64. *Daily Mail*, 16 March 2010.
65. *BBC Sport*, 5 October 2004.
66. Agence France Presse, 9 July 2008.
67. *The National*, 22 July 2008.
68. *Emirates 24/7*, 17 March 2008.
69. *International Herald Tribune*, 2 September 2008.
70. Garry Cook.
71. As cited by Dorsey, James, *Mideastposts*, 7 October 2011.
72. *The Guardian*, 27 September 2009.
73. *The Daily Telegraph*, 10 January 2011.
74. *The Daily Telegraph*, 8 November 2011.
75. *National Public Radio*, 7 May 2006.
76. *Foreign Policy*, 12 April 2011.
77. *Foreign Policy*, 5 January 2012.
78. *Manchester Evening News*, 3 March 2011.
79. *The National*, 15 June 2011.
80. Agence France Presse, 18 December 2010.
81. *VG Nett*, 19 October 2010.
82. *New York Times*, 7 March 2008; *Financial Times*, 17 December 2008.
83. Abu Dhabi Tourism Authority press release, 30 April 2007.
84. *Vanity Fair*, 22 July 2010.
85. *The Guardian*, 10 August 2006.
86. *WAM*, 24 May 2009.
87. AME Info, 11 June 2007; Tourism Development Investment Company press release, 25 July 2009.
88. *The Daily Telegraph*, 31 October 2011.
89. Human Rights Watch, 17 March 2011.
90. *The Guardian*, 16 May 2011.
91. The Al-Qasimi Building was built in 2000.
92. London School of Economics press release 19 December 2006.
93. The Khalifa Building was built in 1997.
94. Mubarak Al-Abdullah Al Sabah.
95. According to the official KFAS website.
96. *The Spectator*, 1 April 2011.
97. *Oxford University Gazette*, No. 4857, Vol. 139, 16 October 2008.
98. *Khaleej Times*, 26 February 2011.
99. *The Daily Telegraph*, 6 January 2008.

100. *National Observer*, No. 81, December 2009.

101. *The National*, 14 May 2009.

102. *Gulf News*, 15 May 2009.

103. According to a Harvard Divinity School press release from 15 September 2000 the appointee was to focus on 'broad teachings on the history, tenets, and practice of the Islamic faith and their implications for local and global societies' and provide 'leadership and direction for the wider, interdisciplinary program of Islamic Studies'.

104. The University of Connecticut had planned to open a branch campus in Dubai, but pulled out on the grounds of alleged anti-Semitism. *Gulf News*, 7 May 2007.

105. *Washington Post*, 15 February 2008.

106. Harvard University press release, 29 September 2010.

107. For example Michigan State University which closed down its campus in Dubai in 2008 after serious financial losses. *New York Times*, 27 March 2012.

108. Khaldun Khalifa Al-Mubarak, the chairman of Abu Dhabi's Executive Affairs Authority and in some respects the crown prince's right hand man.

109. Fromherz, Allen J., *Qatar: A Modern History* (London: IB Tauris, 2012), p. 2.

110. As reported by the Qatar-based management consultancy firm Almaras.

111. In the 2011 academic year only ten of the 161 NYU Abu Dhabi students were UAE nationals. *Khaleej Times*, 20 September 2011.

112. La Sorbonne claims to have 33 per cent of its student body being UAE nationals. *New York Times*, 27 March 2012.

113. Northwestern, for example, claims to have 36 per cent of its student body being Qatar nationals. *New York Times*, 27 March 2012.

114. NYU Abu Dhabi students, if accepted, are offered full fees, accommodation, flights, and a $2000 allowance. *Bloomberg*, 15 September 2010.

115. Georgetown Qatar's Center for International and Regional Studies has convened a number of international workshops in recent years which have focused on the Gulf monarchies. These have discussed the region's political economy, the nuclear question, international relations, and migrant labour. It is notable, however, that discussions on political reform, human rights, or democracy in the Gulf monarchies have not been held.

116. Davidson, Christopher M., *The Persian Gulf and Pacific Asia: From Indifference to Interdependence* (London: Hurst, 2011), chapter 1.

117. *CIA World Factbook 2009*. Economics overviews on Japan, China, and South Korea, 2006–2008 estimates. Author calculations for totals.

118. *The National*, 5th August 2009, citing OPEC data.

119. Davidson (2010), chapter 3.

120. Ibid., chapter 4.

121. *Arab News*, 7th May 2009. Quoting Nicholas Janardhan.

122. Japanese Ministry for Foreign Affairs. Overview file on Saudi Arabia from 2009.

123. *Arabian Business*, 26 November 2007.

124. Along with Russia and Brazil.

125. Reuters, 4 November 2009.

126. Calabrese, John, 'The Consolidation of Gulf-Asia Relations: Washington Tuned in or Out of Touch?', policy brief published by the Middle East Institute, Washington DC, June 2009, p. 5.

127. Ghafour, Mahmoud, 'China's Policy in the Persian Gulf', *Middle East Policy*, Vol. 16, No. 2, 2009, p. 87.

128. See Calabrese, John, 'China and the Persian Gulf: Energy and Security', *Middle East Journal*, Vol. 52, No. 3, 1998; Bin Huwaidin, Muhammed, *China's Relations with Arabia and the Gulf, 1949–1999* (London: Routledge, 2002), p. 194.

129. Calabrese (2009). p. 5.

130. *Washington Post*, 9 April 2007.

131. *Associated Press*, 26th June 2009.

132. Lee, Henry, and Shalmon, Dan, 'Searching for Oil: China's Oil Initiatives in the Middle East' discussion paper published by the Environment and Natural Resources Program, Belfer Center for Science and International Affairs Discussion Paper, Harvard University, January 2007, pp. 4–5.

133. *Saudi Gazette*, 21 November 2009.

134. Yetiv, Steve A. and Lu, Chunlong, 'China, Global Energy, and the Middle East' in *Middle East Journal*, Vol. 61, No. 2, 2007, pp. 207–208.

135. *The National*, 2 December 2009.

136. Ghafour, p. 87.

137. *Financial Times*, 2 November 2009.

138. *Gulf Times*, 6 August 2009.

139. Ehteshami, Anoushiravan, 'The Rise and Convergence of the "Middle" in the World Economy: The Case of the NICs and the Gulf States' in Davies, Charles E. (ed.), *Global Interests in the Arab Gulf* (Exeter: University of Exeter Press, 1992), p. 151.

140. Calabrese (2009), p. 4.

141. *The National*, 21 July 2009. Referring to the Saigon Premier Container Terminal.

142. *The National*, 5 August 2008.

143. Calabrese (2009), p. 5.

144. Davidson (2010), chapter 5.

145. Ibid., chapter 7.

146. Calabrese (2009), p. 2.

147. Ghafour (2009), pp. 87–88.

148. Yetiv and Lu (2007), p. 205.

149. Chinese Ministry for Foreign Affairs. Overview file on the UAE 2009.

150. Sourced from Zayed University's 'Destined to Lead' brochure, 2009.

151. Bin Huwaidin (2002), pp. 200–201.

152. Ghafour (2002), pp. 87,89. Chinese Ministry for Foreign Affairs. Overview file on Kuwait 2009.

153. Chinese Ministry for Foreign Affairs. Overview files on Qatar and Oman 2009.

4. MOUNTING INTERNAL PRESSURES

1. Wikileaks, US Embassy Riyadh, 10 December 2007.

2. Wikileaks, US Embassy Riyadh, 23 November 2009.

3. Kinninmont, Jane, *Bahrain: Beyond the Impasse* (London: Chatham House, 2012), p. 2.

4. See Metz, Helen (ed.), *Persian Gulf States: A Country Study* (Washington: GPO for the Library of Congress, 1993).

5. AME Info, 7 February 2008.

6. See Metz (1993).

7. CIA World Factbook, 2011, country overview on Oman.

8. US Energy Information Administration 2011. Country overview on Oman.

9. US Energy Information Administration 2011. Country overview on the UAE.

10. By 1995 production had dropped to around 300,000 barrels per day.

11. *The Daily Telegraph*, 4 February 2010.

12. Agence France Presse, 9 February 2010.

13. US Energy Information Administration 2011. Country overview on Kuwait.

14. Taken from the Qatargas official website, section entitled 'Amazing Facts About Qatargas 2'.

15. US Energy Information Administration 2011. Country overview on Qatar.

16. *Saudi Gazette*, 24 November 2010.

17. See Nolan, Leigh, 'Managing Reform? Saudi Arabia and the King's Dilemma' Brookings Doha Center Policy Briefing, May 2011.

18. A large proportion of expatriates working in the region are either single or have left their families in their home country.

19. *Emirates 24/7*, 5 October 2010. Quoting 'The World's Women 2010 report'.

20. See Nolan, May 2011.

21. BBC News, 6 February 2011.

22. US Energy Information Administration 2011. Country overview on Kuwait.

23. *Gulf News*, 1 October 2009.

24. *The National*, 7 June 2011.

25. *Gulf News*, 5 July 2011.

26. Wilson, Graeme, *Rashid's Legacy: The Genesis of the Maktoum Family and the History of Dubai* (Dubai: Media Prima, 2006), p. 528.

27. Ibid., p. 529.

28. Al-Gurg, Easa Saleh, *The Wells of Memory* (London: John Murray, 1998), p. 219.

29. Khalifa bin Hamad Al-Thani.

30. Reuters, 21 October 2010.

31. A labour law was introduced in 2002 in an effort to regulate the employment of nationals in the private sector. As part of the law, nationals were to benefit from a special pensions fund and were to be 'guaranteed better rights as employees' including a maximum number of working hours per week and a guaranteed finishing time of four o'clock in the afternoon for women with children of school age.

32. Notably banking and insurance companies. *Gulf News*, 23 September 2004; *Gulf News*, 8 December 2006.

33. Reuters, 21 October 2010.

34. *Oxford Business Group*, 'Abu Dhabi: The Report 2007'. p. 51.

35. Reuters, 21 October 2010.

36. *The National*, 27 July 2008.

37. *Gulf News*, 8 December 2006.

38. *Gulf News*, 28 July 2008.

39. Reuters, 21 October 2010.

40. *Oxford Analytica*, February 2007.

41. Reuters, 21 October 2010.

42. Ibid.

43. *Arabian Business*, 30 December 2010.

44. Nayef bin Abdul-Aziz Al-Saud.

45. *Financial Times*, 7 September 2010.

46. Saleh Kamel.

47. *Arabian Business*, 30 December 2010.

48. *Financial Times*, 7 September 2010.

49. *Financial Times*, 7 September 2010. Quoting Jarmo Kotilaine, an economist at NCB Capital (a Saudi investment bank) and John Sfakianakis, chief economist at Banque Saudi Fransi.

50. Reuters, 21 October 2010.

51. Reuters, 29 August 2010.

52. Ibid.

53. *New York Times*, 5 May 2006.

54. Rashid bin Said Al-Maktoum.

55. *MSNBC*, 2 August 2011.

56. Said Ahmad Ghubash.

57. Overton, J. L., 'Stability and Change: Inter-Arab Politics in the Arabian Peninsula and the Gulf' (unpublished PhD thesis. University of Maryland, 1983), p. 184. Taken from Overton's interview with Said Ahmad Ghubash in Abu Dhabi in 1976.

58. Peck, Malcolm, *The United Arab Emirates: A Venture in Unity* (Boulder: Westview, 1986), p. 100.

59. The chairman is Ahmad bin Saif Al-Nahyan. For details of the 5 November 2003 decree see Davidson, Christopher M., *The United Arab Emirates: A Study in Survival* (Boulder: Lynne Rienner, 2005), chapter 3.

60. Sultan bin Muhammad Al-Qasimi.

61. Brown, Gavin, *OPEC and the World Energy Market* (London: Longman, 1998), p. 359. It was believed that by 1987 Sultan had amassed debts of nearly $920 million following several ambitious construction projects.

62. Limitless press release, 10 October 2007.

63. See for example Purkis, S., and Riegl, B., 'Spatial and Temporal Dynamics of Arabian Gulf Coral Assemblages Quantified from Remote-Sensing and in situ Monitoring Data (Jebel Ali, Dubai, UAE)', *Marine Ecology Progress Series*, No. 287, 2005, pp. 99–113.

64. BBC News, 22 July 2012.

65. *The National*, 6 February 2011.

66. *The Sunday Times*, 2 January 2011.

67. *The Guardian*, 24 March 2011.

68. Filiu, Jean-Pierre, *The Arab Revolution: Ten Lesson from the Democratic Uprising* (London: Hurst, 2011), p. 35.

69. Davidson (2005), chapter 4.

70. Wikileaks, US Embassy Riyadh, 1 November 1996.

71. *Forbes*, 17 June 2009.

72. *Wall Street Journal*, 9 September 2010.

73. *New York Times*, 26 August 2010.

74. *Construction Weekly*, 3 August 2010.

75. *Business Insider*, 13 April 2011.

76. *CIA World Factbook 2011*. Country overview on Bahrain.

77. *Bloomberg*, 21 February 2011.

78. Al-Masah Capital Special Report 2011, 'MENA: The Great Job Rush'.

79. See Nolan, May 2011.

80. Fromherz, Allen J., *Qatar: A Modern History* (London: IB Tauris, 2012), p. 12.

81. *Arabian Business*, 30 December 2010.

82. Reuters, 29 August 2010.

83. *Financial Times*, 7 September 2010.

84. Reuters, 6 July 2011.

85. *Financial Times* 7 September 2010.

86. *Financial Times* 7 September 2010. Quoting Jarmo Kotilaine, an economist at NCB Capital.

87. Kinninmont (2012), p. 18.

88. *Global Research* Special Report on Bahrain, 10 April 2010.

89. *The National*, 27 June 2010.

90. Davidson (2005), chapter 3.

91. Reuters, 6 July 2011.

92. Reuters, 6 July 2011.

93. *Emirates 24/7*, 10 July 2011.

94. *The National*, 21 April 2011.

95. Reuters, 6 July 2011.
96. *The National*, 28 July 2008.
97. Reuters, 6 July 2011.
98. *The National*, 25 December 2010.
99. *Financial Times*, 27 June 2011.
100. Reuters, 6 July 2011.
101. *Financial Times*, 27 June 2011.
102. Reuters, 6 July 2011.
103. Ahmed Muhammad Al-Bunain.
104. *The Peninsula*, 16 January 2007.
105. *The Peninsula*, 18 January 2011.
106. *The Peninsula*, 14 April 2011.
107. As reported by the Qatar-based management consultancy firm Almaras.
108. Human Rights Watch, 13 June 2011.
109. BBC News, 18 July 2011.
110. Human Rights Watch, 13 June 2011.
111. The *Al-Ajmi*.
112. Personal correspondence, January 2012. The man being Salem Al-Ali Al-Sabah, the oldest member of the Al-Sabah family.
113. Human Rights Watch, 13 June 2011.
114. Ibid.
115. BBC News, 18 July 2011.
116. Human Rights Watch, 13 June 2011.
117. *Jadaliyya*, 26 March 2011. Article by Mona Kareem.
118. Human Rights Watch, 13 June 2011.
119. *Khaleej Times*, 7 November 2010.
120. BBC News, 18 July 2011.
121. *Jadaliyya*, 26 March 2011. Article by Mona Kareem.
122. BBC News, 18 July 2011.
123. *Arabian Business*, 13 July 2009.
124. Presentation by Noora Lori at the Middle East Studies Association annual conference, 4 December 2011. 'The Political Management of Rentier Transformations, Naturalization Policy, and Liminal Populations in the UAE'.
125. *Arabian Business*, 13 July 2009.
126. *The National*, 26 September 2008.
127. *The National*, 7 September 2008.
128. *The National*, 26 September 2008.
129. *Arabian Business*, 13 July 2009.
130. Human Rights Watch, 16 December 2011.
131. *Al-Jazeera English*, 22 September 2010. Referring to Ayatollah Hussein Mirza Najati.
132. In 1981 the government arrested seventy-three people accused of plotting a

coup on behalf of a pro-Iran organisation—the Islamic Front for the Liberation of Bahrain led by an Iraqi cleric, Hadi Modaressi. See Kinninmont, Jane. 'Bahrain' in Davidson, Christopher M. (ed.), *Power and Politics in the Persian Gulf Monarchies* (London: Hurst, 2011).

133. See Kinninmont (2011).
134. The Baharna.
135. The Ajam.
136. *International Herald Tribune*, 2 October 2006.
137. *International Herald Tribune*, 17 November 2006.
138. See Kinninmont (2011).
139. Many Bahrainis have observed an influx of new citizens from Pakistan, Yemen, and Baluchistan. See Kinninmont (2012), p. 18.
140. *New York Times*, 26 August 2010.
141. *New York Times* 27 March 2009.
142. Abduljalil Al-Singace.
143. Abdulghani Al-Kanjar.
144. Referring to Muhammed Al-Muqdad and Said Al-Nouri.
145. *The National*, 17 August 2010.
146. *New York Times*, 26 August 2010.
147. *The Economist*, 14 October 2010.
148. Lord Eric Avebury.
149. See Nolan, May 2011. The 1979 riots were in Qatif and Al-Hasa.
150. See Nolan, May 2011.
151. *Al-Riyadh*.
152. *Associated Press*, 18 December 2010.
153. *Al-Jazeera English*, 22 September 2010.
154. *Jadaliyya*, 26 March 2011.
155. *Gulf News*, 5 July 2011.
156. Agence France Presse, 1 October 2009.
157. Reporters without Borders January 2012. Citing the 'World Press Freedom Index 2012'.
158. Doha Debates press release, 25 June 2011.
159. Muhannad Abu Zeitoun.
160. Bahrain Center for Human Rights press release, 27 August 2010.
161. Ali Abdulemam.
162. *Foreign Policy*, 21 October 2010.
163. *Gulf News*, 29 December 2010.
164. Nahyan bin Mubarak Al-Nahyan.
165. The author's personal account.
166. The author's personal account.
167. *Gulf News*, 21 October 2004.
168. *Emirates 24/7*, 15 August 2010.

169. Human Rights Watch, 13 April 2009.

170. *WAM*, 28 April 2009.

171. *Electronic Frontier Foundation*, 13 August 2010; *New York Times*, 13 August 2010.

172. *Slate Magazine*, 27 August 2010.

173. UAE Telecommunications Regulatory Authority, 24 September 2006. The document was entitled 'Internet Content Filtering Policy and Procedure'.

174. *The Independent*, 7 April 2009. The article was entitled 'The Dark Side of Dubai'.

175. *7 Days*, 10 April 2009.

176. *The Sunday Times*, 29 November 2009.

177. *ITP Net*, 14 July 2009.

178. *Foreign Policy*, 10 August 2010. 'As the UAE was consumed along with the rest of the world by the World Cup fever in June, a leaked document surfaced and was distributed amongst Emiratis on BlackBerry Messenger. The document appeared to be an official request from the secretary general of the UAE's parliament… requesting that the Dubai Traffic Department waive the traffic fines of the parliament speaker…'

179. Reporters without Borders press release, 29 July 2010.

180. *The National*, 25 July 2010.

181. Reporters without Borders press release, 29 July 2010.

182. E.g. Abdul Hamid Al-Kumaiti.

183. *Asharq Al-Awsat*, 4 August 2010.

184. *Arab Times*, 14 December 2009.

185. *Gulf News*, 20 October 2010.

186. *Kipp Report*, 7 April 2010.

187. Agence France Presse, 7 December 2010.

188. Agence France Presse, 3 July 2009.

189. Agence France Press, 19 December 2010.

190. *The Guardian*, 2 January 2011. Referencing Brian Whittaker's blog.

191. Muhammad Al-Abdulkarim.

192. Agence France Presse, 6 December 2010.

193. As Fromherz describes '[the ruler] can support initiatives such as press freedom through [his wife] while distancing himself somewhat from the risks associated with such ventures'. See Fromherz, Allen J., *Qatar: A Modern History* (London: IB Tauris, 2012), p. 27.

194. *The Economist*, 14 May 2009.

195. *Financial Times*, 24 June 2009.

196. Doha Centre for Media Freedom press release, 23 June 2009. Since taken offline.

5. MOUNTING EXTERNAL PRESSURES

1. Davidson, Christopher M., *Dubai: The Vulnerability of Success* (London: Hurst, 2008), chapter 2.

2. Foreign Office 370/109814.

3. *Financial Times*, 3 January 2011.

4. *Arabian Business*, 19 January 2011.

5. *Financial Times*, 3 January 2011.

6. *The Guardian*, 19 December 2010.

7. *Gulf News*, 1 September 2006.

8. E.g. the 'Dirham Savings Scheme' offered by the UAE's National Bonds Corporation.

9. *Financial Times*, 27 August 2007.

10. AME Info, 14 April 2008.

11. *Construction Week*, 4 March 2010; *The National*, 6 June 2011. The Abu Dhabi MGM resort will, however, be a non-gambling resort.

12. See for example Mahdavi, Parvis, *Gridlock: Labor, Migration, and Human Trafficking in Dubai* (Palo Alto: Stanford University Press, 2011).

13. SINA News Agency press release, May 2004, translated by the Women's Forum Against Fundamentalism in Iran.

14. *Washington Post*, 30 April 2006.

15. BBC News, 5 July 2012. The authorities seem unwilling to take action, likely concerned that any enforcement of dress code will be viewed as a concession to Islamist groups in the country.

16. Dahi Khalfan Al-Tamim.

17. *Gulf News*, 26 December 2010.

18. *Gulf News*, 26 September 2001.

19. *Arabian Business*, 15 January 2012.

20. Council on Tall Buildings and Urban Habitat press release, February 2012.

21. *New York Times*, 29 December 2010.

22. Globalsecurity.org Special report on Al-Udeid Air Base, Qatar.

23. Davidson, Christopher M., *The Persian Gulf and Pacific Asia: From Indifference to Interdependence* (London: Hurst, 2010), chapter 7.

24. The other dry docks being in Bahrain.

25. Davidson (2010), chapter 7.

26. One company being British, one Danish, and the other Norwegian.

27. *Workers World*, 17 May 2007.

28. Davidson (2008), chapter 8.

29. *International Herald Tribune*, 22 June 2005.

30. *Jane's Defence Weekly*, 7 February 2007.

31. *Express Tribune Pakistan*, 4 July 2011.

32. For a full discussion see Davidson, Christopher M., *The United Arab Emirates: A Study in Survival* (Boulder: Lynne Rienner, 2005), chapter 1.

33. Davidson (2010), chapter 7.

34. *Washington Post*, 27 May 2009.

35. *The National*, 25 May 2009.

36. *The National*, 25 May 2009.
37. Reuters, 10 October 2010.
38. *CBC News*, 14 October 2010.
39. General David Petraeus.
40. *New York Times*, 31 January 2010.
41. World Bank 2011 data derived from Stockholm International Peace Research Institute, Military Expenditure Database.
42. *The National*, 2 January 2010.
43. *Foreign Policy in Focus*, 10 June 2011.
44. *Al-Arabiya*, 26 December 2010.
45. *New York Times*, 29 December 2011.
46. *Foreign Policy in Focus*, 10 June 2011.
47. *Al-Jazeera English*, 2 February 2012.
48. Reuters, 11 May 2012.
49. *The Independent*, 8 July 2011.
50. For dependency theory in the context of the Arab world see for example Amin, Samir, *Unequal Development: An Essay on the Social Formations of Peripheral Capitalism* (New York: Monthly Review Press, 1976).
51. Filiu, Jean-Pierre, *The Arab Revolution: Ten Lessons from the Democratic Uprising* (London: Hurst, 2011), p. 145.
52. Reuters, 29 November 2010.
53. Reuters, 7 December 2011.
54. Saud bin Faisal Al-Saud.
55. *The Guardian*, 7 December 2010.
56. Reuters, 29 November 2010.
57. Agence France Presse, 24 March 2011.
58. Reuters, 29 November 2010.
59. *New York Times*, 28 November 2010.
60. *Foreign Policy*, 17 December 2009.
61. Yousef Al-Otaiba.
62. *The Atlantic*, 6 July 2010.
63. The consortium comprising the Korea Electric Power Company (KEPCO), Samsung, Hyundai, Doosan, and Westinghouse.
64. *The National*, 29 December 2010.
65. *Associated Press*, 21 June 2009.
66. Agence France Presse, 30 July 2011.
67. The consortium comprising General Electrics and Hitachi.
68. *The Guardian*, 28 November 2010.
69. *Arabian Oil and Gas Magazine*, 2 January 2012.
70. Wikileaks, US Embassy Muscat, 1 March 2008.
71. *Dow Jones Newswire*, 14 July 2011.
72. Reuters, 7 December 2011.

73. Roy, Olivier, *The Politics of Chaos in the Middle East* (London: Hurst, 2008), p. 96.
74. Filiu, p. 133.
75. See Hall, Marjorie J., *Business Laws of the United Arab Emirates* (London: Jacobs, 1987).
76. The suffix: .IL.
77. In practice it is possible to enter the UAE with Israeli passport stamps, but no effort has been made to clarify the situation.
78. Davidson (2008). pp. 199–200. Until its closure in 2003 the ZCCF hosted a number of anti-Semitic speakers including members of the International Progress Organisation.
79. US Bureau for Democracy, Human Rights, and Labor 2007 report on the United Arab Emirates.
80. *Gulf News*, 11 January 2009. Article entitled 'Israel's War of Deceit, Lies, and Propaganda'.
81. *Gulf News*, 4 January 2009. Article entitled 'Zionists are the New Nazis'.
82. Davidson (2008), p. 200.
83. Reuters, 18 January 2010.
84. Davidson, Christopher M., *Abu Dhabi: Oil and Beyond* (London: Hurst, 2009), chapter 6.
85. *New York Review of Books*, 19 August 2010.
86. *Associated Press*, 25 October 2006.
87. *Wall Street Journal*, 18 February 2009.
88. The Hamdan bin Muhammed bin Rashid Sports Complex.
89. *Arutz Sheva*, 15 December 2010.
90. OpenNet Initiative press release, 20 November 2009.
91. *Al-Watan*, 22 November 2010.
92. Amnesty International press release, 11 February 2011.
93. *Gulf News*, 2 November 2007.
94. *Haaretz*, 8 April 2011.
95. *Al-Hayat*, 5 June 2011.
96. Fromherz, Allen J., *Qatar: A Modern History* (London: IB Tauris, 2012), p. 23.
97. *Gulf News*, 13 August 2010.
98. *Al-Arab*, 12 June 2011.
99. Agence France Press, 15 November 2010.
100. In summer 2010, for example, Iran's semi-official Fars News Agency reported that Israeli military aircraft had landed at a Saudi airbase close to the city of Tabuk in the northwest of the kingdom. Moreover, it was claimed in the Israeli press that Israel was investigating the usefulness of Tabuk as a possible base for striking Iran, and that a senior member of the Saudi ruling family was co-ordinating the operation. A commercial passenger travelling through the airport was even quoted as saying that all air traffic was closed down without explana-

tion during the alleged Israeli landings, but that all stranded passengers were compensated financially and housed in luxury hotels.

101. Wikileaks, US Embassy Abu Dhabi, 16 June 2009.

102. Cordesman, Anthony H. and Obaid, Nawaf, *National Security in Saudi Arabia: Threats, Responses, and Challenges* (Westport: Praeger Security International, 2005), p. 138.

103. *Asharq Al-Awsat*, 29 March 2011.

104. *The Daily Telegraph*, 26 March 2010.

105. *The National* 20 July 2008.

106. BBC News, 31 January 2011.

107. Ibid.

108. Mostafa Mohammad-Najjar.

109. *Tehran Times Political Desk*, 21 January 2011.

110. *The National*, 25 May 2009.

111. Abdul-Aziz bin Muhammad Al-Qasimi.

112. Sultan bin Muhammad Al-Qasimi.

113. For a full discussion of the 1987 Sharjah coup see Davidson (2008), chapter 7.

114. Khalifa bin Hamad Al-Thani.

115. Hamad bin Khalifa Al-Thani.

116. Kamrava, Mehran. 'Royal Factionalism and Political Liberalization in Qatar', *Middle East Journal*, Vol. 63, No. 3, 2009, p 415.

117. As referred to in Fromherz (2012).

118. Abdul-Aziz bin Khalifa Al-Thani.

119. *Al-Bawaba*, 28 February 2011.

120. *Fars News Agency*, 12 April 2012.

121. Khalid bin Saqr Al-Qasimi.

122. Saud bin Saqr Al-Qasimi.

123. Oxford Analytica briefing paper on Ra's Al-Khaimah, 28 October 2010. Written by the author.

124. *The Guardian*, 28 July 2010.

125. Oxford Analytica briefing paper on Ra's Al-Khaimah, 28 October 2010. Written by the author; *Financial Times*, 28 October 2010.

126. *WAM*, 20 December 2010.

127. Article 6 of the Omani constitution.

128. Tariq bin Taimur Al-Said.

129. Fatima bint Mubarak Al-Kitbi.

130. See www.motherofnation.ae

131. Charles E. Schumer.

132. *New York Times*, 1 August 2003.

133. *Press TV*, 26 December 2010.

134. *New York Times*, 23 October 2010.

135. *Al-Akhbar*, 3 November 2011.

136. Reuters, 18 June 2012.

137. The Sudairi Seven are named after their mother, Hassa bint Ahmed Al-Sudairi, who hailed from a powerful tribe from the interior.

138. Ahmed bin Abdul-Aziz Al-Saud.

139. *Associated Press*, 16 November 2011. Talal's criticism was first voiced in 2007.

6. THE COMING COLLAPSE

1. Fromherz, Allen J., *Qatar: A Modern History* (London: IB Tauris, 2012), p. 7.

2. For a full discussion of the Dubai opposition see Davidson, Christopher M., 'Arab Nationalism and British Opposition in Dubai, 1920–1966', *Middle Eastern Studies*, Vol. 43, No. 6, 2007.

3. Nolan, Leigh. 'Managing Reform? Saudi Arabia and the King's Dilemma', Brookings Doha Center Policy Briefing, May 2011.

4. University of the United Arab Emirates, in Al-Ayn.

5. According to a study of the Muslim Brotherhood in the UAE published by *Dar Al-Hayat* newspaper in Saudi Arabia. *Dar Al-Hayat*, 12 September 2010.

6. Abd Al-Rahim Al-Nashiri was captured in the UAE in November 2002.

7. Nolan, May 2011.

8. *Wall Street Journal*, 30 August 2010. With reference to the crackdowns in Saudi Arabia.

9. *Dar Al-Hayat*, 12 September 2010.

10. *The National*, 6 April 2010.

11. *Global Post*, 22 December 2010.

12. Agence France Presse, 30 December 2010.

13. *Los Angeles Times*, 23 December 2010.

14. Filiu, Jean-Pierre, *The Arab Revolution: Ten Lesson from the Democratic Uprising* (London: Hurst, 2011), p. 76.

15. Ibid., p. 74.

16. Ibid., p. 75.

17. Bahrain News Agency press release, 2 May 2011.

18. *Washington Times*, 23 November 2011.

19. Regimes have also used 'deep packet inspection' to censor private emails. See Filiu (2011), p. 46.

20. E.g. the case of Abu Dhabi's burgeoning E-Government. See Davidson, Christopher M., *Abu Dhabi: Oil and Beyond* (London: Hurst, 2009), chapter 6.

21. *Gulf News*, 30 July 2012.

22. *Foreign Policy*, 21 September 2010.

23. Filiu (2011), p. 46.

24. Ibid., p. xiii.

25. Ibid., p. 44.

26. Muhammad Omran.

27. Referring to Etisalat.
28. *Arabian Business*, 2 July 2011.
29. *Kipp Report*, 8 June 2011. Citing the second Arab Social Media Report published by the Governance and Innovation Program at the Dubai School of Government.
30. *Gulf News*, 31 May 2012.
31. *Kipp Report*, 8 June 2011; *Time Magazine*, 12 July 2012.
32. Agence France Presse, 9 February 2011.
33. This was Al-Sheikh's initial reaction to Pope Benedict XVI's Regensburg Lecture on 12 September 2006.
34. *Asharq Al-Awsat*, 5 February 2011.
35. *Al-Masry Al-Youm*, 10 April 2011.
36. BBC News, 22 February 2011.
37. Reuters, 27 April 2011. Quoting Shadi Hamid, an analyst at the Brookings Center in Qatar and Theodore Karasik, a defence analyst based in Dubai.
38. *Gulf News*, 28 January 2011.
39. Hassan Muhammad Hassan Al-Hammadi.
40. Amnesty International press release, 9 February 2011.
41. Abdullah bin Zayed Al-Nahyan.
42. Muhammad bin Zayed Al-Nahyan.
43. *The National*, 9 February 2011.
44. Reuters, 27 April 2011.
45. *Ahram*, 30 April 2011. Quoting Khalaf Al-Habtoor.
46. *Al-Masry Al-Youm*, 23 May 2011.
47. Dahi Khalfan Al-Tamim.
48. BBC News, 31 July 2012.
49. *WAM*, 11 April 2011.
50. Al-Tayeb Al-Fassi Fihri.
51. *WAM*, 16 May 2011.
52. *The National*, 13 September 2011; Reuters, 20 December 2011.
53. Reuters, 20 December 2011.
54. Kinninmont, Jane, *Bahrain: Beyond the Impasse* (London: Chatham House, 2012), p. 3.
55. *New York Times*, 15 February 2011.
56. Kinninmont (2012), p. 9.
57. Ibid. p. 10.
58. BBC Sport, 21 February 2011.
59. There are, however, many eyewitness reports that Saudi troops entered Bahrain during the various uprisings in the 1990s. See Kinninmont (2012), p. 3.
60. The exception being a reported Kuwaiti naval patrol.
61. *Los Angeles Times*, 15 March 2011.
62. Global Research special report on Bahrain, 10 April 2011.
63. *Al-Jazeera English*, 30 July 2011; *Express Tribune Pakistan*, 11 March 2011.

64. *Jakarta Globe*, 19 June 2011.
65. Hamad bin Isa Al-Khalifa.
66. Khalifa bin Salman Al-Khalifa.
67. Khalid bin Ahmad Al-Khalifa.
68. *Al-Jazeera English*, 5 August 2011.
69. BBC News, 2 July 2011.
70. *The Economist*, 26 November 2011.
71. Kinninmont (2012), p. 11.
72. Abdulhadi Al-Khawaja.
73. *The Independent*, 21 April 2012.
74. BBC News, 20 April 2012.
75. Kinninmont (2012), p. 12.
76. Reuters, 31 July 2012.
77. Kinninmont (2012), p. 3.
78. Al-Wefaq Society press release, 30 July 2012. Quoting the 'Gangs of Darkness' awareness campaign.
79. Reuters, 29 June 2011.
80. Qaboos bin Said Al-Said.
81. BBC News, 27 February 2011; Reuters, 9 April 2011.
82. *Gulf News*, 9 April 2011; *Oman Daily*, 8 April 2011.
83. *Voice of America*, 22 April 2011.
84. *Gulf News*, 8 May 2011.
85. *Al-Arabiya*, 14 May 2011.
86. *Gulf News*, 20 June 2011.
87. Reuters, 29 June 2011.
88. *Gulf News*, 22 July 2011.
89. Referring to Omantel.
90. Youssef Al-Haj.
91. *Al-Quds Al-Arabi*, 12 August 2011.
92. *The National*, 11 March 2011.
93. *Gulf News*, 17 July 2012.
94. *The Guardian*, 23 January 2012.
95. *Al-Basheer News*, 6 February 2011.
96. *Washington Post*, 20 April 2012. Quoting Waleed Abu Alkhair.
97. Nolan, May 2011.
98. Abdul-Aziz Al-Wahhabi.
99. Reuters, 10 February 2011.
100. Reuters, 22 April 2011.
101. Reuters, 22 April 2011.
102. Nolan, May 2011.
103. *Arabian Business*, 25 May 2011.
104. *Jakarta Globe*, 19 June 2011. Quoting Ali Al-Ahmad.

105. Bandar bin Sultan Al-Saud.
106. Yousaf Raza Gillani.
107. *Al-Jazeera English*, 30 July 2011.
108. Human Rights Watch, 3 May 2011.
109. *Al-Watan*, 5 June 2011.
110. Fadhil Makki Al-Manasif.
111. Mustafa Al-Badr Al-Mubarak and Husain Kazhim Al-Hashim.
112. Human Rights Watch, 3 May 2011.
113. Hamza Kashgari.
114. *The Independent*, 13 February 2012.
115. Not to be confused with Muhammad Al-Qahtani, the alleged twentieth 9/11 hijacker, who is currently in detention in Guantanamo Bay.
116. BBC News, 22 July 2011.
117. Agence France Press, 8 December 2010.
118. *Arab Times*, 5 January 2011.
119. Agence France Presse, 6 February 2011.
120. *The Peninsula*, 18 January 2011.
121. *Al-Arabiya*, 28 June 2011.
122. Sabah Al-Ahmad Al-Jabar Al-Sabah.
123. *Gulf News*, 14 April 2011.
124. Bahrain News Agency press release, 2 May 2011.
125. *Kuwait Times*, 5 June 2011.
126. Agence France Presse, 17 September 2011.
127. BBC News, 16 November 2011.
128. Agence France Presse, 17 September 2011.
129. *Gulf News*, 21 November 2011.
130. BBC News, 28 November 2011.
131. Jabar Al-Mubarak Al-Hamad Al-Sabah.
132. BBC News, 3 February 2011.
133. *Bloomberg*, 26 April 2012.
134. *The Guardian*, 10 January 2010.
135. Referring to Etisalat.
136. See Davidson, Christopher M., 'The Strange Case of the UAE's WWW.UAE-HEWAR.NET', Current Intelligence blog, 15 November 2010.
137. Khalifa bin Zayed Al-Nahyan.
138. *Foreign Policy*, 14 April 2011.
139. Sourced from the blog of Ahmad Mansour Al-Shehhi, 6 April 2011.
140. Reuters, 11 May 2011.
141. Reuters, 8 April 2011.
142. *Foreign Policy*, 14 April 2011.
143. *CNN*, 13 April 2011.
144. *Gulf News*, 29 May 2011.

145. *Gulf News*, 29 April 2011

146. In 1968 over half of the Zaab (Al-Zaabi) tribe, most of whom resided on the Jazirah al-Hamra near to Ra's al-Khaimah decamped *en masse* and moved to Abu Dhabi island, where the ruler had promised them prime plots of land. Davidson (2009), chapter 3.

147. *Gulf News*, 29 April 2011.

148. *The National*, 1 December 2011.

149. *Arabian Business*, 17 April 2011.

150. *New York Times*, 14 May 2011.

151. The Arabic Human Rights Network press release, 14 February 2012.

152. The UAE reform movement—sometimes referred to as 'Al-Islah'—is indigenous, founded in 1974, and is not affiliated to the Muslim Brotherhood.

153. *Associated Press*, 22 December 2011.

154. Salah Al-Dhafairi.

155. *Associated Press*, 12 March 2012.

156. Ahmed Abd Al-Khaleq.

157. *Al-Jazeera News*, 16 July 2012.

158. Sultan bin Kayed Al-Qasimi, a member of the Ra's al-Khaimah ruling family. He was held under house arrest at the ruler's palace.

159. Issa Khalifa Al-Suwaidi.

160. Muhammad Al-Mansoori.

161. Most notably Salim Hamdoon Al-Shehhi, Abdulsalam Darwish,and Muhammad Al-Roken.

162. Human Rights Watch, 1 August 2012; Emirates Centre for Human Rights, 31 July 2012.

163. For example Rashid bin Muhammad Al-Roken.

164. Muhammad Rashid Al-Kalbani, an Omani passport holder.

165. Hamad bin Khalifa Al-Thani.

166. *Foreign Policy*, 12 April 2011.

167. *New York Times*, 4 April 2011.

168. *Voice of America*, 14 January 2012.

169. Most reports highlight assistance from Qatar, Saudi Arabia, and Turkey. Turkish assistance can be viewed through the lens of border security while Saudi assistance can be viewed through the lens of countering Iran's presence in the region. Qatar's assistance, however, is best viewed through a moral lens. For a full discussion see Stephens, Michael, 'What Does Qatar Want in Syria?' *Open-Democracy*, 6 August 2012.

170. *New York Times*, 4 April 2011. Quoting Jabar bin Yusef bin Jassim Al-Thani.

171. *Al-Jazeera English*, 12 August 2011. The show was entitled *Inside Story: Bahrain*. The Bahraini government representative was Jamal Fakhro and the Bahraini human rights activist was Maryam Al-Khawaja, head of the Foreign Relations Office for the Bahrain Center for Human Rights.

172. Hamad bin Jassim Al-Thani.
173. John Kerry.
174. *The Guardian*, 6 December 2010.
175. *The Guardian*, 6 December 2010.
176. Sultan Al-Khalaifi.
177. Amnesty International press release, 3 March 2011.

CONCLUSION

1. Nye, Joseph, *Soft Power: The Means to Success in World Politics* (New York: Public Affairs, 2004). Now widely referred to by international statesmen and diplomats.
2. Ross, p. 335.
3. Inglehart, Ronald, and Welzel, Christian, *Modernization, Cultural Change, and Democracy* (Cambridge: Cambridge University Press, 2005).
4. Kinninmont, Jane, *Bahrain: Beyond the Impasse* (London: Chatham House, 2012), p. 12.
5. Most notably Ali Al-Sistani and his predecessor Abu Al-Qasem Al-Khoie.
6. Kinninmont (2012), p. 2.
7. Feras Bughnah and Hosam Al-Deraiwish.
8. This took place in late October 2011.
9. Agence France Presse, 17 June 2011.
10. *Time Magazine*, 12 July 2012.
11. *Washington Post*, 20 April 2012.
12. *Time Magazine*, 12 July 2012.
13. Reuters, 4 October 2011.
14. Issam Muhammad Abu Abdallah.
15. *The Guardian*, 23 January 2012. Quoting Toby Matthiesen.
16. BBC News, 4 August 2012. On 4 August 2012, for example, both a policeman and a protestor were killed in a firefight, as a security patrol was attacked by rioters on motorbikes.
17. *The Economist*, 14 July 2012. Referring to Nimr Al-Nimr, who had earlier called for the Eastern Province to secede from Saudi Arabia if Saudi Shia could not live with dignity.
18. BBC News, 12 June 2012.
19. Hamad Al-Naqi, who was later stabbed while in prison. See *Arab Times*, 19 April 2012.
20. Meshaal Al-Malek Al-Sabah.
21. *Gulf Today*, 20 July 2012.
22. Personal interviews, Beirut, March 2012.
23. *WAM*, 15 July 2012.
24. *WAM*, 7 May 2012.
25. *Gulf News*, 2 August 2012.

26. See www.echr.org.uk
27. Fromherz, Allen J., *Qatar: A Modern History* (London: IB Tauris, 2012), p. 8.
28. Ibid., p. 30.
29. *New Statesman*, 25 February 2011.

BIBLIOGRAPHY

Al-Abed, Ibrahim, and Hellyer, Peter (eds.), *The United Arab Emirates: A New Perspective* (London: Trident, 2001).

Abdullah, Muhammad Morsy, *The United Arab Emirates: A Modern History* (London: Croom Helm, 1978).

Allen, Calvin and Rigsbee, W. Lynn, *Oman Under Qaboos: From Coup to Constitution, 1970–1996* (London: Routledge, 2002).

Amin, Samir, *Unequal Development: An Essay on the Social Formations of Peripheral Capitalism* (New York: Monthly Review Press, 1976).

Anthony, John Duke, *Arab States of the Lower Gulf: People, Politics, Petroleum* (Washington DC: Middle East Institute, 1975).

Beblawi, Hazem, 'The Rentier State in the Arab World' in Beblawi, Hazem and Luciani, Giacomo (eds.), *The Rentier State* (New York: Croom Helm, 1987).

Belgrave, Charles, *The Pirate Coast* (London: G.Bell and Sons, 1966).

Brown, Gavin, *OPEC and the World Energy Market* (London: Longman, 1998).

Brumberg, Daniel, 'The Trap of Liberalized Autocracy' in *Journal of Democracy*, Vol. 13. No. 4, 2002.

Butt, Gerald, 'Oil and Gas' in Al-Abed, Ibrahim, and Hellyer, Peter (eds.), *The United Arab Emirates: A New Perspective* (London: Trident, 2001).

Buxani, Ram, *Taking the High Road* (Dubai: Motivate, 2003).

Calabrese, John, 'From Flyswatters to Silkworms: The Evolution of China's Role in West Asia', *Asian Survey*, No. 30, 1990.

———, 'China and the Persian Gulf: Energy and Security', *Middle East Journal*, Vol. 52, No. 3, 1998.

———, 'The Consolidation of Gulf-Asia Relations: Washington Tuned in or Out of Touch?', policy brief published by the Middle East Institute, Washington DC, June 2009.

Chaudhry, Kiren Aziz, *The Price of Wealth: Economies and Institutions in the Middle East* (Ithaca: Cornell University Press, 1997).

Coates Ulrichsen, Kristian, *Insecure Gulf: The of Certainty and the Transition to the Post-Oil Era* (London: Hurst, 2011).

Commins, David, *The Wahhabi Mission and Saudi Arabia* (London: IB Tauris, 2009).

———, *The Gulf States: A Modern History* (London: IB Tauris, 2012).

Cordesman, Anthony H. and Obaid, Nawaf, *National security in Saudi Arabia: threats, responses, and challenges* (Westport: Praeger Security International, 2005).

Craze, Joshua and Huband, Mark (eds.), *The Kingdom: Saudi Arabia and the Challenge of the 21ˢᵗ Century* (London: Hurst, 2009).

Crystal, Jill, *Oil and Politics in the Gulf: Rulers and Merchants in Kuwait and Qatar* (Cambridge: Cambridge University Press, 1995).

Davidson, Christopher M., *The United Arab Emirates: A Study in Survival* (Boulder: Lynne Rienner, 2005).

———, 'Arab Nationalism and British Opposition in Dubai, 1920–1966', *Middle Eastern Studies*, Vol. 43, No. 6, 2007.

———, *Dubai: The Vulnerability of Success* (London: Hurst, 2008).

———, *Abu Dhabi: Oil and Beyond* (London: Hurst, 2009).

———, 'Dubai, Foreclosure of a Dream', *Middle East Report*, No. 251, 2009.

———, *The Persian Gulf and Pacific Asia: From Indifference to Interdependence* (London: Hurst, 2010).

——— (ed.), *Power and Politics in the Persian Gulf Monarchies* (London: Hurst, 2011).

Davies, Charles E. (ed.), *Global Interests in the Arab Gulf* (Exeter: University of Exeter Press, 1992).

———, *The Blood Red Arab Flag: An Investigation into Qasimi Piracy, 1797–1820* (Exeter: Exeter University Press, 1997).

Deutsch, Karl, 'Social Mobilization and Political Development', *American Political Science Review*, Vol. 55, No. 3, 1961.

Ehteshami, Anoushivaran, 'The Rise and Convergence of the "Middle" in the World Economy: The Case of the NICs and the Gulf States' in Davies, Charles E. (ed.), *Global Interests in the Arab Gulf* (Exeter: University of Exeter Press, 1992).

Fandy, Mamoun, *Saudi Arabia and the Politics of Dissent* (London: Macmillan, 2009).

Fiennes, Ranulph, *The Feather Men* (London: Bloomsbury, 1991).

Filiu, Jean-Pierre, *The Arab Revolution: Ten Lesson from the Democratic Uprising* (London: Hurst, 2011).

Foley, Sean, *The Arab Gulf States: Beyond Oil and Islam* (Boulder: Lynne Rienner, 2010).

Fromherz, Allen J., *Qatar: A Modern History* (London: IB Tauris, 2012).

Fuccaro, Nelida, *Histories of City and State in the Persian Gulf: Manama since 1800* (Cambridge: Cambridge University Press, 2009).

Gause, Gregory F., *Oil Monarchies: Domestic and Security Challenges in the Arab Gulf States* (New York: Council on Foreign Relations Press, 1994).

———, *The International Relations of the Persian Gulf* (Cambridge: Cambridge University Press, 2009).

Ghafour, Mahmoud, 'China's Policy in the Persian Gulf', *Middle East Policy*, Vol. 16, No. 2, 2009.

Gray, Matthew, 'A Theory of Late Rentierism in the Arab States of the Gulf', *Georgetown University Center for International and Regional Studies Occasional Papers*, No. 7, 2011.

Al-Gurg, Easa Saleh, *The Wells of Memory* (London: John Murray, 1998).

Hall, Marjorie J., *Business Laws of the United Arab Emirates* (London: Jacobs, 1987).

Halliday, Fred, *Arabia without Sultans* (London: Saqi, 1974).

———, 'Arabia Without Sultans Revisited', *Middle East Report*, Vol. 27, No. 204, 1997.

Hamza, Kamal, *Zayed: A Mark on the Forehead of History* (Abu Dhabi, 2005) (*in Arabic*).

Hassner, Ron Eduard, *War on sacred grounds* (New York: Cornell University Press, 2009).

Hawley, Donald, *The Trucial States* (London: George Allen and Unwin, 1970).

———, *The Emirates: Witness to a Metamorphosis* (Norwich: Michael Russell, 2007).

Heard-Bey, Frauke, *From Trucial States to United Arab Emirates* (London: Longman, 1996).

Hegghammer, Thomas, *Jihad in Saudi Arabia: Violence and Pan-Islamism Since 1979* (Cambridge: Cambridge University Press, 2010).

Herb, Michael, *All in the Family: Absolutism, Revolution, and Democracy in the Middle Eastern Monarchies* (New York: State University of New York Press, 1999).

Hertog, Steffen, *Princes, Brokers, and Bureaucrats: Oil and State in Saudi Arabia* (Ithaca: Cornell University Press, 2010).

Hobbes, Thomas, *The Leviathan* (1660).

Hopwood, Derek, *The Arabian Peninsula* (London: George Allen and Unwin, 1972).

Huntington, Samuel P., *Political Order in Changing Societies* (New Haven: Yale University Press, 1968).

Bin Huwaidin, Muhammed, *China's Relations with Arabia and the Gulf, 1949–1999* (London: Routledge, 2002).

Inglehart, Ronald and Welzel, Christian, *Modernization, Cultural Change, and Democracy* (Cambridge: Cambridge University Press, 2005).

Ismael, Jacqueline S., *Kuwait: Dependency and Class in a Rentier State* (Miami: University Press of Florida, 1993).

Ismael, Tareq Y., *The Communist Movement in the Arab World* (London: Routledge, 2005).

Kalra, Nidhi, *Recommended Research Priorities for the Qatar Foundation's Environment and Energy Research Institute* (Los Angeles: RAND Corporation, 2011).

Kamrava, Mehran, *The Modern Middle East: A Political History since the First World War* (Los Angeles: University of California Press, 2005).

———, 'Royal Factionalism and Political Liberalization in Qatar', *Middle East Journal*, Vol. 63, No. 3, 2009.

———— (ed.), *The Nuclear Question in the Middle East* (London: Hurst, 2012).

———— (ed.), *The Political Economy of the Persian Gulf* (London: Hurst, 2012).

Kamrava, Mehran and Babar, Zahra (eds.), *Migrant Labour in the Persian Gulf* (London: Hurst, 2012).

Katz, Mark, 'Assessing the Political Stability of Oman', *Middle East Review of International Affairs*, Vol. 8, No. 3, 2004.

Kéchichian, Joseph A., *Power and Succession in Arab Monarchies: A Reference Guide* (Boulder: Lynne Rienner, 2008).

Kerr, Malcolm, *The Arab Cold War, 1958–1970* (Oxford: Oxford University Press, 1971).

Khalaf, Sulayman, 'Gulf Societies and the Image of Unlimited Good', *Dialectical Anthropology*, Vol. 17, No. 1, 1992.

————, 'Poetics and Politics of Newly Invented Traditions in the Gulf: Camel Racing in the United Arab Emirates', *Ethnology*, Vol. 39, No. 3, 2000.

Kinninmont, Jane, 'Bahrain' in Davidson, Christopher M. (ed.), *Power and Politics in the Persian Gulf Monarchies* (London: Hurst, 2011).

————, *Bahrain: Beyond the Impasse* (London: Chatham House, 2012).

Lacroix, Stéphane, *Awakening Islam: The Politics of Religious Dissent in Contemporary Saudi Arabia* (Cambridge: Harvard University Press, 2011).

Ladwig, Walter C., 'Supporting Allies in Counterinsurgency: Britain and the Dhofar Rebellion', *Small Wars and Insurgencies*, Vol. 19, No. 1, 2008.

Lauterpacht, E., Greenwood, C. J. and Weller, Marc, 'The Determination of Boundaries between Iraq, Kuwait and Saudi Arabia (Najd)' in *The Kuwait Crisis: Basic Documents* (Cambridge: Cambridge University Press, 1991).

Lawson, Fred, *Bahrain: The Modernization of Autocracy* (Boulder: Westview Press, 1989).

Lee, Henry and Shalmon, Dan, 'Searching for Oil: China's Oil Initiatives in the Middle East' discussion paper published by the Environment and Natural Resources Program, Belfer Center for Science and International Affairs Discussion Paper, Harvard University, January 2007.

Lerner, Daniel, *The Passing of Traditional Society: Modernizing the Middle East* (New York: The Free Press, 1958).

Lipset, Seymour Martin, 'Some Social Requisites of Democracy: Economic Development and Political Legitimacy', *The American Political Science Review*, Vol. 53, No. 1, 1959.

————, *Political Man: The Social Bases of Politics* (Boston: Johns Hopkins University Press, 1960).

Locke, John, *Two Treatises of Government* (1689).

Lorimer, John G., *Gazetteer of the Persian Gulf, Oman, and Central Arabia* (London: Gregg International Publishers, 1970).

Louër, Laurence, *Transnational Shia Politics: Religious and Political Networks in the Gulf* (New York: Columbia University Press, 2008).

Lucas, Russell E., 'Monarchical Authoritarianism: Survival and Political Liberalization in a Middle Eastern Regime Type', *International Journal of Middle East Studies*, Vol. 36, No. 4, 2004.

Luomi, Mari, *The Gulf Monarchies and Climate Change: Abu Dhabi and Qatar in an Era of Natural Unsustainability* (London: Hurst, 2012).

Mahdavy, Hussein, 'The Patterns and Problems of Economic Development in Rentier States: The Case of Iran' in Cook, M. A. (ed.), *Studies in Economic History of the Middle East* (London: Oxford University Press, 1970).

Mahdavi, Parvis, *Gridlock: Labor, Migration, and Human Trafficking in Dubai* (Palo Alta: Stanford University Press, 2011).

See Metz, Helen (ed.), *Persian Gulf States: A Country Study* (Washington: GPO for the Library of Congress, 1993).

Mutawwa, Khalid, *The Arabic Falcon* (Sharjah, 2005) (*in Arabic*).

Al-Nabeh, Najat Abdullah, 'United Arab Emirates: Regional and Global Dimensions' (PhD thesis. Claremont Graduate School, 1984).

Al-Nahyan, Shamma bint Muhammad, *Political and Social Security in the United Arab Emirates* (Dubai: 2000).

Nakhleh, Emile, *Bahrain: Political Development in a Modernizing Society* (New York: Lexington Books, 2011).

Nelson, Caren, 'UAE National women at work in the private sector: conditions and constraints', Tanmia Labour Market Study, No. 20, 2004.

Nolan, Leigh, 'Managing Reform? Saudi Arabia and the King's Dilemma', Brookings Doha Center Policy Briefing, May 2011.

Nye, Joseph, *Soft Power: The Means to Success in World Politics* (New York: Public Affairs, 2004).

Obaid, Nawaf E., 'The Power of Saudi Arabia's Islamic Leaders', *Middle East Quarterly*, Vol. 6, No. 3, 1999.

Obaid, Nawaf E., *The Foreign Policy of the United Arab Emirates* (Beirut: Majd, 2004) (*in Arabic*).

Onley, James, *The Arabian Frontier of the British Raj: Merchants, Rulers, and the British in the Nineteenth Century Gulf* (Oxford, Oxford University Press, 2007).

Al-Otaibi, Manna Said, *Petroleum and the Economy of the United Arab Emirates* (Kuwait: Al-Qabas Press, 1977) (*in Arabic*).

Overton, J. L., 'Stability and Change: Inter-Arab Politics in the Arabian Peninsula and the Gulf' (PhD thesis. University of Maryland, 1983).

Peck, Malcolm, *The United Arab Emirates: A Venture in Unity* (Boulder: Westview, 1986).

Peterson, John E., *Oman's Insurgencies: The Sultanate's Struggle for Supremacy* (London: Saqi, 2008).

Pollin, Robert, 'Resurrection of the Rentier', *New Left Review*, Vol. 46, July–August 2007.

Purkis, S. and Riegl, B, 'Spatial and Temporal Dynamics of Arabian Gulf Coral

Assemblages Quantified from Remote-Sensing and in situ Monitoring Data (Jebel Ali, Dubai, UAE)', *Marine Ecology Progress Series*, No. 287, 2005.

Rabi, Uzi, *The Emergence of States in a Tribal Society: Oman Under Said bin Taimur, 1932–1970* (Brighton: Sussex Academic Press, 2011).

Al-Qasimi, Sultan bin Muhammad, *The Myth of Arab Piracy in the Gulf* (London: Croom Helm, 1986).

Al-Rasheed, Madawi, *A History of Saudi Arabia* (Cambridge: Cambridge University Press, 2002).

—— (ed.), *Kingdom Without Borders: Saudi Arabia's Political, Religious, and Media Frontiers* (London: Hurst, 2008).

Rizvi, S., 'From Tents to High Rise: Economic Development of the United Arab Emirates', *Middle Eastern Studies*, Vol. 29, No. 4, 1993.

Roberts, David, 'Kuwait' in Davidson, Christopher M. (ed.), *Power and Politics in the Persian Gulf Monarchies* (London: Hurst, 2011).

Ross, Michael, 'Does Oil Hinder Democracy', *World Politics*, Vol. 53, No. 3, 2001.

Rousseau, Jean-Jacques, *The Social Contract, or Principles of Political Right* (1762).

Roy, Olivier, *The Politics of Chaos in the Middle East* (London: Hurst, 2008).

Rush, Alan (ed.), *Ruling Families of Arabia: The United Arab Emirates* (Slough: Archive Editions 1991).

Al-Sagri, Saleh Hamad, 'Britain and the Arab Emirates, 1820–1956' (PhD thesis. University of Kent at Canterbury, 1988).

Salih, Kamal Eldin Osman, 'Kuwait Primary (Tribal) Elections 1975–2008: An Evaluative Study', *British Journal of Middle East Studies*, Vol. 38, No. 2, 2011.

Seznec, Jean-François, 'The Gulf Sovereign Wealth Funds: Myths and Reality', *Middle East Policy*, Vol. 15, No. 2, 2008.

Sharabi, Hisham, *Neopatriarchy: A Theory of Distorted Change in Arab Society* (Oxford: Oxford University Press, 1992).

Sigelman, Lee, 'Lerner's Model of Modernization: A Reanalysis', *Journal of Developing Areas*, Vol. 8, July 1974.

Spooner, Lysander, 'No Treason: The Constitution of No Authority' (1867).

Teitelbaum, Joshua, *The Rise and Fall of the Hashemite Kingdom of Arabia* (London: Hurst, 2001).

Von Thünen, Johann Heinrich, *The Isolated State* (1826).

——, 'Saudi Arabia' in Davidson, Christopher M. (ed.), *Power and Politics in the Persian Gulf Monarchies* (London: Hurst, 2011).

——, and Held, David (eds.), *The Transformation of the Gulf: Politics, Economics, and the Global Order* (London: Routledge, 2011).

Valbjørn, Morten, and Bank, André, 'Examining the Post in Post-Democratization: The Future of Middle Eastern Political Rule through Lenses of the Past', *Middle East Critique*, Vol. 19, No. 3, 2010.

Valeri, Marc, *Oman: Politics and Society in the Qaboos State* (London: Hurst, 2009).

————, 'Oman' in Davidson, Christopher M. (ed.), *Power and Politics in the Persian Gulf Monarchies* (London: Hurst, 2011).

Van der Meulen, Hendrik, 'The Role of Tribal and Kinship Ties in the Politics of the United Arab Emirates' (PhD thesis. The Fletcher School of Law and Diplomacy, 1997).

Weber, Max, 'Politics as a Vocation (*Politik als Beruf*)' (Munich, 1919).

Wheatcroft, Andrew, *With United Strength: Sheikh Zayed bin Sultan Al-Nahyan, the Leader and the Nation* (Abu Dhabi: Emirates Centre for Strategic Studies and Research, 2005).

White, Stephen, 'Economic Performance and Communist Legitimacy', *World Politics*, Vol. 38, No. 3, 1986.

Wilson, Graeme, *Rashid's Legacy: The Genesis of the Maktoum Family and the History of Dubai* (Dubai: Media Prima, 2006).

Wright, Steven, 'Qatar' in Davidson, Christopher M. (ed.), *Power and Politics in the Persian Gulf Monarchies* (London: Hurst, 2011).

Yetiv, Steve A., and Lu, Chunlong, 'China, Global Energy, and the Middle East', *Middle East Journal*, Vol. 61, No. 2, 2007.

INDEX

9/11 attacks, 14, 73, 80, 84, 106, 164,
    194, 270

Abdallah, Issam Muhammad Abu,
    272
Aberdeen University, 100
Abraj al-Bait Tower, 162
Abdulemam, Ali, 261
Abdul Nasser, Gamal, 3
Abdulemam, Ali, 261
Al-Abdulkarim, Muhammad, 262
Abu Dhabi Basic Industries
    Corporation, 45
Abu Dhabi Executive Council, 37
Abu Dhabi Fund for Arab Develop-
    ment, 81
Abu Dhabi Fund for Development,
    81
Abu Dhabi Future Energy Com-
    pany, 77–78
Abu Dhabi Investment Company,
    92
Abu Dhabi Investment Authority,
    43–44, 187, 247
Abu Dhabi National Consultative
    Council, 37
Abu Dhabi National Oil Company,
    41, 45, 117
Abu Dhabi Petroleum Exhibition,
    74

Abu Dhabi Polymers Company, 45,
    108
Abu Dhabi United Group for
    Development and Investment, 92
Abu Safah oilfield, 113
Aden, 31
Adopt-a-Camp, 66, 250
Advisory Council, of Qatar, 33–34,
    36, 226
Aegis cruisers, 167
Afghanistan, 73, 83–84, 86, 87,
    165–166, 170
Afghan National Army, 86
African Union, 89
Ahmadinejad, Mahmoud, 90, 172
Air Canada, 166
Airports, 122–123, 145, 165, 236,
    265
Alcohol, 29, 57, 121, 149, 157–158,
    162, 164
Alkhair, Waleed Abu, 234, 269
Allegiance Commission, of Saudi
    Arabia, 27, 189
Ajam, community, 261
Ajman, 22, 25, 244–245, 247
Arab Cold War, 3
Arab League, 3, 80, 82, 89, 239
Al-Arab, newspaper, 178
Arab Spring, 1–2, 14, 27, 36, 56, 73,

88, 111, 117, 134, 136, 146, 152,
    168, 170, 179, 192, 195, 199, 201–
    202, 204–205, 208, 212, 214, 216,
    220–222, 224–227, 232, 237
Arabian American Oil Company
    (Aramco), 25, 40, 106–107, 113
Arabian Canal, 124
Arabic language, 39, 59, 98–101,
    149, 161, 176, 178, 227
Arsenal, football club, 92
Asmara International Stadium, 83
Al-Assad, Bashar, 227
Al-Assad, Hafez, 13
Association of Tennis Professionals,
    93
Aston Martin, 93
Atlantic, The, magazine, 172
Attar, Ali Rida Sheikh, 90
Australia, 62–63, 102, 151–152, 166
Australia National University, 102
Avebury, Lord Eric, 261
Awwamiya, 213, 235
Al-Ayn, 123, 125, 181, 267
Al-Azhar University, 73–74

Bab al-Azizia compound, 129
Baghdad, 23, 165
Baharna, tribe, 261
Bahrain Independent Commission
    of Inquiry, 208
Bahrain Petroleum Company
    (Bapco), 40
Bahrain Centre for Human Rights,
    142, 146, 271
Bahrain Logistics Zone, 46
Baluchistan, 165, 261
Al-Bandar, Salah, 140, 144
Bandargate, 140, 146
Bangladesh, 65, 250
Bani Utub, 19–20, 139
Bank of Credit Commerce Interna-
    tional, 126

Banlieues, of Paris, 94
Barcelona Football Club, 91
Barwa Housing Project, of Qatar, 51
Al-Bashar, Omar, 89
Basic laws, 27, 33, 39, 175, 247
Basra, 19
Bassiouni, Cherif, 208, 232
Al-Bayan, newspaper, 176
Bedouin, 70–71
Al-Behar, yacht, 128
Beijing Automobile Works, 108
Beijing Foreign Studies University,
    109
Beirut, 88, 171–172
Bethany, 82
Bidoon, 134–139, 225
Bidoon Committee, 135
Big Ben, of London, 162
Bin Jbeil, 82
BlackBerry, 147, 150–151, 262
Blackwater, 224
Boeing, 168
Book World Prague, 96–97
Bombay, 19
Bond, James, 93
Borealis, 108
Borouge, see Abu Dhabi Polymers
    Company
Bosnia, 86
Brazil, 75, 256
Britain (contemporary power),
    92–94, 99–102, 105, 127, 150,
    165, 167, 184–185
British East India Company, 19–20
British Empire, 17–26, 28, 31–33,
    37–38, 40–41, 43, 68–69, 72, 99,
    139, 183, 229, 243
British Petroleum, 41, 244
British Society for Middle East
    Studies, 100
Bughnah, Feras, 272

Bulgaria, 88
Buraimi, 180–181
Burgan oilfield, 114
Burj Al-Arab, 46
Burj Dubai, 47
Burj Khalifa (formerly Burj Dubai),
    47, 122, 124, 185
Burns, William, 90
Bushire, 243

Cairo, 3, 206, 212, 228
Caltex, 40
Cambridge University, 100–101
Camel racing, 71
Camp Al-Jabar, 164
Camp Mirage, 166
Camp Ali Salem, 164
Camp Patriot, 164
Campagnie Française des Petroles,
    41–42
Canada, 63, 75, 102, 150, 166, 186,
    195
Capitalism, 6–8
Carlton Tower hotel, 92
Carnegie Mellon University, 104
Central Bank of the Gulf Co-opera-
    tion Council, 180
Central Bank of Lebanon, 82
Central Bank of Oman, 38
Central Bank of Qatar, 91
Central Intelligence Agency, of the
    United States, 164–165, 194
Central Mining and Investment, 41
Central System for Resolving Illegal
    Residents' Status, see Bidoon
    Committee
Chad, 89
Chamber of Commerce and
    Industry, of Qatar, 34
Chamber of Commerce and
    Industry, of Riyadh, 130

Chateau Fontainebleau, 96
Chelsea Barracks, 91
Cheney, Dick, 90
Chery Automobile, 108
Children's National Medical Center,
    in Washington DC, 94
China Islam Association, 109
China National Petroleum Corpora-
    tion, 107
China, People's Republic of, 3, 43,
    79, 85, 104–109, 150, 167
China Petroleum and Chemical
    Corporation, see Sinopec
China Plan, 107
Christianity, 75, 82, 95, 103
Christmas, 25, 158–159, 161
Chrysler Building, 92
Churches, 75, 82
Civil society, 7, 192, 201, 210,
    220–223
College of William and Mary, 103
Colombia, 23
Commonwealth Games, 92
Communism, 3
Consultative Council, of Oman,
    38–39, 211
Consultative Council, of Saudi
    Arabia, 27, 188
Co-operation Council for the Arab
    States of the Gulf, see Gulf
    Co-Operation Council
Cornell University, 53, 102–103
Cosmo Oil Company, 106
Council of Ministers, of Oman, 38
Council of Ministers, of Qatar, 33
Council of Ministers, of the United
    Arab Emirates, 35, 246
Council of Ministers, of Saudi
    Arabia, 26
Council of Saudi Chambers of
    Commerce and Industry, 119–120

Council of Senior Religious
Scholars, of Saudi Arabia, 26, 28,
213–215
Coups, 13, 27, 31, 38, 111, 124, 135,
145, 156, 182–184, 186, 188, 217,
231, 233, 235, 260, 266
Credit Suisse, 178
Crescent Petroleum, 174
Cuba, 3
Curzon, Lord George, 243
CyberTrust, 149

Dammam, 40
Darfur, 89
Darwish, Abdulsalam, 271
Al-Deraiwish, Hosam, 272
Desert Storm, Operation, 28
Dhafrah, airbase, 165–166
Al-Dhaheri, Hadef Jawan, 246
Dhahran, 40
Dhofar, 3–4, 38, 211
Dhofar Liberation Front, 3, 193
Dibba, 22, 25
Djibouti, 89
Doha, 20, 88–89, 133, 146, 153, 178,
226, 228, 237, 245, 251, 253
Doha Agreement, 88
Doha Centre for Media Freedom,
153, 228, 262
Doha Debates, 146, 237
Doha Summer Festival, 133
Dolphin pipeline, 114
Doosan, 263
Dow Chemicals, 45
Drones, 165, 168
Drugs, 121, 149, 162, 246
Dubai Air Show, 168
Dubai Healthcare City, 46
Dubai Holdings, 47, 159
Dubai Inc., 37, 63
Dubai International Airport,
164–165

Dubai International Capital, 92, 106
Dubai International Financial
Centre, 46
Dubai International Holy Koran
Award Committee, 74
Dubai Internet City, 46
Dubai Knowledge Village, 46, 103
Dubai Media City, 46, 147, 149
Dubai Oriental Finance Company,
108
Dubai Ports World, 43, 108, 164
Dubai School of Government, 200
Dubai World Trade Centre, 176
Durham University, 100–101

E-Government, 197, 267
Eastern Province, of Saudi Arabia,
18, 62, 143, 213–215, 233, 235,
272
Economic Development Board of
Bahrain, 33
Edinburgh University, 101
Education City, in Qatar, 104
Egypt, 3, 13, 18, 60, 65, 73, 89, 132,
189, 192, 199, 201–206, 221,
226–228
Electricity, 113–114, 116
Emarat, 116
Emirates airline, 92, 122–123, 158
Emirates Aluminium, 45
Emirates Centre for Human Rights,
237, 273
Emirates Foundation for Philan-
thropy, 100
Emirates National Oil Company,
117
Emirates Palace, hotel, 46, 159
Emirates Petroleum Products
Company, 117
Emirates Solidarity Project, 82
Emirates Stadium, in London, 92

Environmental Agency of Abu
  Dhabi, 77
Eid festivals, 158, 187
Eithad Airways, 92, 122–123
Eritrea, 83, 89
Essex Hotel, The, 254
Ethiopia, 89
Etisalat, 268, 270
Executive Affairs Authority, of Abu
  Dhabi, 92, 255
Exeter University, 99
Expatriates, 6, 8, 11–12, 46, 49–52,
  54–55, 58–59, 61–64, 72, 75–76,
  97, 104, 112, 115–116, 118–120,
  125–128, 130, 135, 137, 141,
  143–146, 149, 151, 155–157, 161,
  171–172, 175, 184, 194, 197, 229,
  241, 251, 257
External Aid Liaison Bureau, of the
  UAE, 81
Exxon-Mobil, 41

Facebook, 69, 197–198, 200, 212,
  222, 234, 237
Fakhro, Jamal, 271
Falconry, 68–71
Family Card, 137
Fanar, see Qatar Mosque
Al-Farooq Mosque, 74
Fateh offshore field, 244
Fatwas, 28, 213–214
Ferrari, 92
Feudalism, 7–8, 10
Fifth Fence, The, 217
Fihri, Al-Tayeb Al-Fassi, 268
First World War, 18–19
Foreign Direct Investment, 44–45,
  48, 58, 106, 156, 231
Federal National Council, of the
  United Arab Emirates, 36–37,
  224–246

Fédération International de Football
  Association, 93, 125
Fertil, 45
Financial Harbour, of Bahrain, 46
Finland, 77
Formula One, 92–93, 122, 206, 209
France, 23, 41, 88, 91, 96, 102, 158,
  166–168, 178, 182
Free trade agreements, 180
Friendship Bridge, 55
Fujairah, 25, 123, 130, 164, 244–245,
  247, 251
Fujian province, of China, 107
Fujian Petrochemical and Refining
  Company, 107
Futaisi Island, 128

Gaddafi, Muammar, 3, 13, 38, 129,
  226
Gang of the Dragon, 209
Gas to liquid fuels, 124
Gaza, 176–178
General Atomics Aeronautical
  Systems, 168
General Electrics, 263
Georgetown University, 103–104,
  255
Germany, 23, 41, 105, 128, 169
Al-Ghaddami, Abdullah, 242
Bin Ghayth, Nasser, 221
Ghubash, Said Ahmad, 258
Gillani, Yousaf Raza, 270
Globe Roundabout, in Sohar, 209
Goodrich Corporation, 168
Google Earth, 146
Grand Mosque, of Mecca, 163
Green March, of Oman, 209
Gross domestic products, 1, 45,
  47–48, 81, 131, 156, 167–168,
  226, 239
Grosvenor Square, 91

Guangdong province, of China, 107
Guangzhou Museum of Overseas
    History, 109
Guantanamo Bay, 270
Guggenheim, 96–97
Guiness Book of Records, The, 71
Gulf Air, 122–123
Gulf Civil Society Forum, 201
Gulf Co-operation Council, 156,
    179–182, 204–208, 211, 218, 231
Gulf News, newspaper, 176
Gwadar, 22, 37

Al-Habtoor, Khalaf, 268
Hail, 18
Haima, 210
Al-Haj, Youssef, 269
Halliburton, 46, 165
Halliday, Fred, 4–5
Hamas, 82
Hamdan bin Muhammad bin
    Rashid Sports Complex, 265
Al-Hamili, Muhammad bin Dhaen,
    244
Al-Hammadi, Hassan Muhammad
    Hassan, 268
Hamriyyah, 22, 25
Haq Movement for Liberty and
    Democracy, 141–142
Harrods, 90–91
Harvard Medical School, 46
Harvard University, 102–103, 149,
    177, 255
Al-Hasa, 18, 133, 261
Hashim, Husain Kazhim, 270
Hawar Islands, 55
Heineken International, 158
Hejaz, 18
Helmand Province, 86
Henjam oilfield, 174
Hezbollah, 88, 140, 144–145, 171

Hinduism, 75
Hitachi, 263
Hitler, Adolf, 172, 176
Ho Chi Minh City, 108
Hollywood, 92
Hong Kong, 47, 108
Hormuz, Strait of, 173
Horn of Africa, 83, 89
Horse-riding, 68–70, 159
House of Lords, of Britain, 142
Human immunodeficiency virus, 88
Hurricane Katrina, 94
Hussein bin Ali, Imam, 145
Hussein Mirza Najati, Ayatollah,
    245
Hussein, Saddam, 13, 28, 83, 89
Hussein, Sharif, of Mecca, 18
Hyundai, 263

Ibadism, 136, 143, 157, 179
Ibri, 210
IDB Holdings, 178
Islamic Front for the Liberation of
    Bahrain, 261
Independent, The, newspaper, 149
India, 19, 21–25, 64, 66, 75, 83, 157,
    243, 250
Indian Ocean, 22, 25
Indonesia, 84, 207, 214
Industrial and Commercial Bank of
    China, 106–107
Industries Qatar, 45
International Atomic Energy
    Agency, 173
International Covenant on Civil and
    Political Rights, 153
International Criminal Court, 89
International Defence Exhibition, of
    Abu Dhabi, 168
International Hunting and Eques-
    trian Exhibition, of Abu Dhabi,
    102

International Monetary Fund, 57
International Petroleum Investment
    Company, 44–45, 106, 248
International Prize for Arabic
    Fiction, 98
International Progress Organisation,
    265
International Renewable Energy
    Agency, 176
Internet, the, 46, 69, 133, 144–147,
    149, 151–153, 177, 192, 197–200,
    211, 214, 220, 262
Internet service providers, 177
Intifada, of Bahrain, 140
Intifada, of Dignity (Saudi Arabia),
    235
Intifada, of Palestine, 175
Investment Corporation of Dubai,
    43, 248
Investment Dar, 93
Iraq, 13, 19, 24, 28–29, 43, 56, 73,
    79, 82–83, 89–90, 135–136, 139,
    151–152, 164, 174, 179, 184, 194,
    233, 242–244, 250, 261
Iraqi Petroleum Company, 24–25
Iran, 6, 13, 29, 32, 41, 64, 79, 83, 90,
    137–140, 142–144, 151, 156, 160,
    166, 169–175, 179, 181–182,
    184–185, 187, 196, 202, 231–232,
    261, 263, 265, 271
Iran-Iraq War, 29, 174, 179
Al-Islah, 271
Islamic Arts Museum, of Qatar, 75
Islamic Front for the Liberation of
    Bahrain, 261
Islamic Jerusalem studies, 100
Islamic Revolution, of Iran, 29, 140
Islamic Umma Party, 213
Islamism, 14–15, 29, 73, 79, 139,
    194–196, 213, 225, 263
Israel, 3, 40, 75, 79, 82, 102, 156,

169, 175–179, 185, 187, 193, 228,
    231, 237, 265–266
Italy, 92, 128, 168
Al-Ittihad, newspaper, 176

Jahra, 19
Jamlaka, 13
Japan, 41, 93, 104–106, 173
Japan External Trade Organisation,
    106
Japan Oil Development Company,
    41
Al-Jazeera, news network, 84,
    152–153, 195, 208, 214, 226–228
Jazirah Al-Hamra, 271
Jebel Ali, 123, 164
Jebel Ali Free Zone, 46
Jebel Dhukan, 40
Jeddah, 102, 122, 233–234
Jenin Camp, 82
Jews, 75, 176, 237
Joint Arab Deterrent Force, 86
Jordan, 141, 184, 204–205, 207, 214
Jurists' Association, of the UAE, 225

Al-Kaabi, family, 26
Kabul, 165
Kafala system, 8, 58–59, 127
Kalba, 25, 185
Al-Kalbani, Muhammad Rashid,
    271
Kamel, Saleh, 258
Al-Kanjar, Abdulghani, 261
Kashgari, Hamza, 270
Kashmir, 84
Kenya, 83
Kerry, John, 272
Khal, Abdo, 98
Al-Khalaifi, Sultan, 272
Khalifa bin Zayed Al-Nahyan
    Foundation, 56

Khalifa bin Zayed Al-Nahyan
Mushaf, 74
Khalifa Committee for Social
Services and Commercial
Buildings, 53
Khalifa Port and Industrial Zone, 45
Al-Khalifa, Abdullah bin Ahmed,
20
Al-Khalifa, dynasty, 19–20, 32, 40,
62, 72, 139–140, 206
Al-Khalifa, Hamad bin Isa, 269
Al-Khalifa, Isa bin Salman, 30
Al-Khalifa, Khalid bin Ahmad, 269
Al-Khalifa, Khalifa bin Salman,
32–33, 41, 67, 269
Al-Khalifa, Salman bin Ahmed, 20
Al-Khalifa, Salman bin Hamad, 33
Khartoum, 89
Al-Khawaja, Abdulhadi, 269
Al-Khawaja, Maryam, 271
Al-Khoie, Abu Al-Qasem, 272
King Abdullah Economic City, 44
King Abdullah University of Science
and Technology, 53
King Khalid Military City, 180
Kingdom City, 122
Al-Kitbi, Fatima bint Mubarak, 266
Koran, the, 18, 59, 73–74, 86, 251
Korea, South, 105, 173
Kosovo, 85
Al-Kumaiti, Abdul Hamid, 262
Kuwait Airways, 122
Kuwait China Investment Com-
pany, 107
Kuwait Crisis, 27–28, 43, 83, 194,
244, 250
Kuwait Foundation for the
Advancement of Sciences,
101–102
Kuwait Fund for Arab Economic
Development, 81, 109

Kuwait Investment Authority, 43,
56, 106
Kuwait Oil Company, 40
Kuwait Petroleum Company,
106–107
Kuwait Projects Company, 55
Kuwaiti Bidoon Gathering, 136
Kuwaiti Journalists' Association, 218
Kuwaiti Lawyers' Society, 218

Bin Laden, Osama, 194
Las Vegas, 159
Lebanon, 82, 84, 86, 88, 144,
170–172, 200
Lebanese National Dialogue
Conference, 88
Leninism, 3–4
Libya, 3, 13, 88–89, 192, 226–227
Libya Contact Group, 226
Libyan National Transitional
Council, 226
Liquefied Natural Gas, 41
London, 18–19, 22, 24, 47, 85,
90–92, 97, 142, 162, 218, 236
London Eye, 92
London School of Economics and
Political Science, 100, 102
Louisiana, 94
Louvre, Le, 75, 95–96
Lowndes hotel, 92

Maaden, 44
Madame Tussauds, London, 92
Madinat Jumeirah, 71
Mahadha, 26
Malaysia, 207, 214–215
Manama, 142, 172, 205–206, 227,
239, 244
Manhatten, 92
Al-Makhdur, Nasser, 243
Maktoum bin Butti, 21

Al-Maktoum College, Dundee, 100
Al-Maktoum, dynasty, 21, 30, 63
Al-Maktoum Foundation, 95
Al-Maktoum, Hamdan bin
  Muhammad, 69
Al-Maktoum, Hamdan bin Rashid,
  102
Al-Maktoum, Maktoum bin
  Hasher, 21
Al-Maktoum, Rashid bin Maktoum,
  21
Al-Maktoum, Rashid bin Said, 30,
  68, 258
Al-Maktoum, Maktoum bin Rashid,
  30–31
Al-Maktoum, Muhammad bin
  Rashid, 31, 69, 127, 147, 242
Mamluk sultans, of Egypt, 73
Manama, 46, 142, 170, 172,
  205–206, 227
Al-Manasif, Fadhil Makki, 270
Manchester City Council, 94
Manchester City, football club, 92,
  94
Al-Mansoori, Muhammad, 271
Al-Mansuri, Sultan bin Said, 244
March 14 alliance, of Lebanon, 88
Marxism, 3–4, 6
Masdar City, 77–78
Masirah, 24
Mataams, 32, 245
McLaren Group, 93
McMaster University, 102
Mecca, 18, 22, 65, 73, 98, 162–163
Medina, 73, 98, 143
Ménard, Robert, 153
Mercenaries, 192, 105, 207, 214,
  218, 245
Mesaieed, 45
MGM Mirage Corporation, 159
Al-Misna, Moza bint Nasser, 75

Mohammed-Najjar, Mostafa, 266
Mongolia, 84–85
Morocco, 127, 204–205
Mozambique, 86
Al-Mualla, family, 22
Mubadala Development Company,
  44–45, 47, 55, 77–78, 92, 159,
  187, 242
Mubarak, Hosni, 13, 89, 202–203,
  212, 221, 228
Al-Mubarak, Khaldun Khalifa, 255
Al-Mubarak, Mustafa Al-Badr, 270
Muhabasher satellite television, 217
Muhammad, Prophet, 18, 215, 235,
  245
Muhammad bin Rashid Charitable
  and Humanitarian Establishment,
  85
Muhammad bin Rashid Housing
  Programme, of Dubai, 51
Muharraq, 20
Mumtalakat Holding Company, 43,
  93, 248
Municipal Council, of Qatar, 34
Municipal Council, of Saudi Arabia,
  27, 36
Al-Muqdad, Muhammed, 261
Musandam Peninsula, 173
Muscat, 3, 22, 26, 181, 209–210
Muslim Brotherhood, 14, 189, 194,
  203, 223, 267, 271
Al-Mustaqbal, newspaper, 217

Al-Nahyan, Ahmad bin Saif, 248
Al-Nahyan, Abdullah bin Zayed,
  268
Al-Nahyan, dynasty, 21, 30, 36
Al-Nahyan, Hamad bin Hamdan,
  128
Al-Nahyan, Khalifa bin Zayed, 30,
  47, 53, 90, 96, 100, 103, 127, 187,
  270

Al-Nahyan, Mansour bin Zayed, 92, 248
Al-Nahyan, Muhammad bin Hazza, 243
Al-Nahyan, Muhammad bin Zayed, 14, 30, 103, 172, 187, 242, 268
Al-Nahyan, Nahyan bin Mubarak, 261
Al-Nahyan, Shakhbut bin Sultan, 245
Al-Nahyan, Zayed bin Khalifa, 21, 243
Al-Nahyan, Zayed bin Saif, 243
Al-Nahyan, Zayed bin Sultan, 30, 52, 68, 74, 82, 100, 166
Najd, 18
Nakheel, 47, 92
Al-Naqi, Hamad, 272
Al-Nashiri, Abd Al-Rahim, 267
National, The, newspaper of Abu Dhabi, 148
National Action Charter, of Bahrain, 32, 139–140, 206
National Bonds Corporation, of the UAE, 263
National Consensus Dialogue, of Bahrain, 208
National Consultative Council, of Sharjah, 37
National fronts, 3, 193
National Human Resource Development and Employment Authority, of the UAE, see Tanmia
National Iranian Oil Company, 174
National Liberation Front, The, 239
National Media Council, 149
Naxalites, 250
Nepal, 65
Nevada, 159
New East Manchester, 94
New Orleans, 94

New York, 85, 92, 96, 104, 163
New York University, 104, 255
Nexter Corporation, 168
Nightclubs, 164
Al-Nimr, Nimr, 272
Non-governmental organisations, 56, 66 149
Nonoo, Houda Ezra Ebrahim, 251
North Atlantic Treaty Organisation, 171, 226
North Field, 41, 173
Northwestern University, 104, 255
Norway, 95
Al-Nouri, Said, 261
Al-Nuaimi, family, 22
Nuclear power, 79, 90, 94, 170–173, 175, 185, 255

Official development assistance, 81–83, 85
Olgiy, 85
Olayan Group, 178
Olympic Games, 93
Oman Air, 122
Omantel, 269
Omran, Muhammad, 268
Orange Movement, of Kuwait, 30
Organisation for Economic Co-operation and Development, 200
Organisation of the Petroleum Exporting Countries, 3, 115, 239
Al-Otaiba, Yousef, 263
Ottoman Empire, 18–20, 22, 73, 162, 242
Oxford Centre of Islamic Studies, 101
Oxford University, 101

Pakistan, 22, 38, 65–66, 83–84, 126, 141, 165, 207, 214, 222, 250, 261

Palestine, 64, 79, 81–82, 175
Palestinian Authority, 82
Palm Islands, 124
Paris, 75, 85, 91, 94–95, 153
Paris St. Germain, football club, 91
Partex, 42
Pashtun, 87
Pavilion de Flore, of Le Louvre, 95
Pearl, The, 162
Pearl diving, 23
Pearl Roundabout, in Manama, 206
Peninsula and Orient Steam
    Navigation Company, 43
Peninsula Shield Force, 180, 182,
    206
People's Daily newspaper, of China,
    109
Perpetual Maritime Truce, 20–21,
    116
Personal identification number, 150
Petitions, 27, 32, 36, 51, 71, 102,
    122–123, 139, 142–143, 152, 212,
    221–223, 225
Petrochemical Industries, of Kuwait,
    45
Petrochina, 107–108
Petroleum Concessions Ltd., 24
Petroleum Development Oman, 42
Philippines, 75
Pirates, 83
Planning Council, of Qatar, 57
Poetry, 69–70
Pope Benedict XVI, 268
Popular Bloc, of Bahrain, 38
Popular Front for the Liberation of
    the Occupied Arabian
Gulf, 3, 193
Port Rashid, 164
Port Zayed, 164, 166
Portugal, 22
Powell, Colin, 85

Predators, see Drones
Prince Sultan Airbase, 163
Princeton University, 103
Professional Golfers Association, of
    Europe, 93
Prostitution, 69, 159–162

Al-Qaeda, 80, 83, 172, 185, 194,
    196, 252
Al-Qaeda on the Arabian Peninsula,
    194, 252
Al-Qahtani, Muhammad, 9/11
    terrorist, 270
Al-Qahtani, Muhammad Fahad,
    Saudi human rights activist, 216,
    234
Al-Qasimi, Abul-Aziz bin Muham-
    mad, 31, 266
Al-Qasimi Building, Durham, 100,
    254
Al-Qasimi Building, Exeter, 100
Al-Qasimi, dynasty, 21–22
Al-Qasimi, Khalid bin Muhammad,
    31
Al-Qasimi, Khalid bin Saqr, 31, 266
Al-Qasimi, Saqr bin Muhammad,
    31
Al-Qasimi, Saqr bin Sultan, 31
Al-Qasimi, Saud bin Saqr, 31, 266
Al-Qasimi, Sultan bin Kayed, 271
Al-Qasimi, Sultan bin Muhammad,
    31, 100, 124, 236, 259
Qatar Airways, 122
Qatar Charity, 56–57
Qatar Environment and Energy
    Research Institute, 77
Qatar Financial Centre, 47
Qatar Foundation, 91, 104, 251
Qatar Holdings, 90–91
Qatar Investment Authority, 43, 91,
    178, 248

Qatar Mosque, 75
Qatar Petroleum Company, 41, 108
Qatar Primary Material Company, 45
Qatar Science and Technology Park, 46
Qatar Sports Investments, 91
Qatar Steel, 45
Qatar Television, 161
Qatar Tourism Authority, 133
Qatar University, 54, 72
Qatargas, 41, 257
Qatari-Eritrean Hall of Friendship, 83
Qatif, 213, 215, 261
Qilu, 106
Qingdao province, of China, 101–108
Queen Elizabeth 2 cruise liner, 92
Queen's Household Cavalry, 102

Ramadan, 57, 148, 157–158, 160
Ra's al-Khaimah, 21–22, 31–32, 35–36, 46, 123, 131–133, 184–186, 235–236, 247, 271
Ras Laffan, 45
Rasgas, 41
Al-Rashid, family, 18
Reach Out to Asia, 84
Red Sea, 44
Reform and Social Guidance Association, of the UAE, 225
Refusal Front, 175
Renaissance Day, of Oman, 38
Rentierism, 6–8, 11, 17, 25, 49–50, 57–58, 60–61, 63, 74, 76, 80, 229–230
Research and Development Corporation, 77
Research in Motion, 150
Revolution in Qatar, forum, 237
Revolutionary Guard, of Iran, 171

Rice, Condoleezza, 90
Riffa, 20
Rio Tinto, 248
Riyadh, 18, 28, 130, 180, 188–189, 214, 233–234
Riyadh Chamber of Commerce and Industry, 130
Al-Roken, Muhammad, 271
Rose of Dhofar, 211
Rotterdam, 95
Royal Air Force, 165
Royal Dutch Shell, 41–42, 114
Royal Mecca Clock Tower, 162
Ruling bargains, 10–11, 49–50, 66, 79, 229, 231, 241
Ruling Family Council, of Oman, 39, 186
Russia, 85, 150, 167–168, 256
Rutgers University, 103
Ruwais, 248
Rwanda, 86

Saadiyat island, 96–97
Al-Sabah, Abdullah, 19
Al-Sabah, Abdullah Al-Salim, 28
Al-Sabah, Ali Al-Khalifah Al-Athbi
Al-Sabah, dynasty, 18–19, 22, 29–30, 40, 260
Al-Sabah, Jabar Al-Ahmad Al-Jabar, 28, 89
Al-Sabah, Jabar Al-Mubarak Al-Hamad, 270
Al-Sabah, Meshaal Al-Malek, 272
Al-Sabah, Mubarak (the Great), 19, 29
Al-Sabah, Muhammad, 242
Al-Sabah, Nasser bin Muhammad, 29, 67, 101, 216
Al-Sabah, Saad Al-Abdullah, 28
Al-Sabah, Sabah Al-Ahmad Al-Jabar, 28, 127, 270
Al-Sabah, Salim Al-Ali, 260

Sahwa, awakening movement, 194
Bin Said, Abu Hilal Ahmed, 22
Al-Said, Azzam bin Qais, 22
Al-Said, dynasty, 22, 26, 38–39
Al-Said, Qaboos bin Said, 38–39, 59, 127–128, 186, 241, 269
Al-Said, Said bin Taimur, 38, 239
Al-Said, Sayyid Fahd bin Mahmoud, 250
Al-Said, Sayyid Haitham bin Tairq, 250
Al-Said, Sultan Said bin Sultan, 22
Al-Said, Tariq bin Taimur, 38, 266
Al-Said, Turki bin Said, 22
Al-Said, yacht, 128
Sainsburys, 90
Salalah, 24, 128
Salalah Free Zone, 46, 128, 210
Salmaniya Hospital, 54
Sanctions, against Iran, 169, 174
Sandhurst Academy, 101–102
SAMA (Saudi Arabian Monetary Authority), 43
Samsung, 263
Sarkozy, Nicolas, 89, 166, 182
Bin Saud, Abdul-Aziz, 18, 26–27, 189
Al-Saud, Abdullah bin Abdul-Aziz, 26–27, 127, 188–189, 244
Al-Saud, Ahmed bin Abdul-Aziz, 267
Al-Saud, Bandar bin Sultan, 270
Al-Saud, dynasty, 18–19, 22, 26–28, 30, 40–41, 68, 74, 189, 242
Al-Saud, Fahd bin Abdul-Aziz, 26–27, 244, 251
Al-Saud, Faisal bin Abdul-Aziz, 26, 103, 244
Al-Saud, Faisal bin Musaid, 244
Al-Saud, Khalid bin Abdul-Aziz, 26
Al-Saud, Nayef bin Abdul-Aziz, 188, 258

Al-Saud, Salman bin Abdul-Aziz, 189
Al-Saud, Saud bin Abdul-Aziz, 26
Al-Saud, Saud bin Faisal, 264
Al-Saud, Sultan bin Abdul-Aziz, 188
Al-Saud, Talal bin Abdul-Aziz, 189, 267
Al-Saud, Al-Waleed bin Talal, 83, 101, 122
Saudi Arabia Airlines, 122
Saudi Arabian Basic Industries Company, 44–45, 107
Saudi Arabia Royal Guard, 182
Saudi Joint Committee for the Relief of Kosovo, 85
Saudi Public Assistance for Pakistan Earthquake Victims, The, 84
Saudi Red Crescent Society, 85
Saudi Royal Air Force, 168
Sciences-Po, 102
Seeb, 128
SecDev Group, of Ottawa, 149
Seychelles, 127
Al-Shahed, newspaper, 151
Shah, of Iran, 6, 140, 171
Al-Shamsi base, 165
Shandong province, of China, 106
Sharia law, 27, 39, 213–214
Sharjah, 21–22, 24–26, 31–32, 36–37, 46, 66, 68, 100, 102, 114, 116, 123–124, 144, 162, 174, 183, 185, 203, 236, 245, 247, 250–251, 266
Sharm el-Sheikh, 89
Al-Sharqi, Muhammad bin Hamad, 244
Sharqiyin, tribe, 25
Al-Shehhi, Ahmed Mansour, 222, 242
Al-Shehhi tribe, 223

Al-Shehhi, Salim Hamdoon, 271
Sheikh Khalifa bin Zayed Mosque,
  in Palestine, 82
Sheikh Khalifa bin Zayed Al-
  Nahyan Mushaf, 74
Sheikh Zayed Grand Mosque, 74
Sheikh Zayed Housing Programme,
  of the UAE, 51
Sheikh Zayed Institute, 95
Sheikh Zayed Marriage Fund, of the
  UAE, 60
Al-Sheikh, Abdul-Aziz bin
  Abdullah, 26, 202, 268
Al-Sheikh, family, 26, 28
Shard, The, 91
Shia, of Islam, 32, 62, 72, 82, 112,
  134, 139–144, 170–171, 178, 185,
  196, 206, 208–209, 212–213, 230,
  232–234, 272
Shia Crescent, 170
Short message service, 210
Showa Shell Sekiyu, 106
Shuaiba Industrial Zone, 44
Sikh temples, 75
Al-Singace, Abduljalil, 261
Singapore, 47
Sino Arab Chemical Fertiliser
  Company, 106
Sinopec, 107
Al-Sistani, Ali, 272
Sitra, 131
Slavery, 22, 64
Soccer, 67, 91–94
Social contracts, 10–11, 13, 49, 112,
  229, 241
Social media, 130, 151, 161,
  198–201, 207, 217, 225, 231, 234,
  268
Socony-Vacuum Oil, 40
Sohar, 209–210
Somalia, 83, 86

Sony Corporation, 106
Sorbonne, La, 104
Souq al-Manakh crash, 56
South Africa, 62, 224
Sovereign wealth, 27, 42–43, 45,
  47–48, 90–93, 105–107, 125–126,
  167, 230
Sowwah island, 47
Spain, 41, 91, 127
Spying, 143, 182
Standard Oil of California, 40
Standard Oil of New Jersey, 40, 243
State Consultative Council, of Oman,
  38
State General Reserve Fund, of
  Oman, 43
Stockholm Environmental Institute,
  77
Al-Sudairi, Hassa bin Ahmed, 267
Sudairi Seven, 189, 267
Sudan, 83, 89, 140
Suez Canal, 202
Sultan Qaboos University, 54
Sunday Times, The, newspaper, 150
Sunni, of Islam, 18, 32, 82, 134,
  139–145, 170, 178, 185, 205–206,
  212, 233
Supreme Council for Family Affairs,
  of Qatar, 57
Supreme Council for Oil, of
  Bahrain, 40–41
Supreme Council of Rulers, of the
  United Arab Emirates, 35, 236
Supreme Council of the Armed
  Forces, of Egypt, 202
Supreme Petroleum Council, of Abu
  Dhabi, 37, 187
Al-Suwaidi, Issa Khalifa, 271
Sweden, 77
Switzerland, 88, 187
Syria, 2, 13, 60, 65, 88, 192, 199,
  227, 236, 271

Taleban, The, 86
Tahrir Square, 206, 212
Al-Tamim, Dahi Khalfan, 263, 268
Tan Thuan Industrial Promotion
   Company, 108
Tanmia, 55, 119
Taxation, 7, 11, 25, 46, 50, 57–58,
   63, 120, 130, 160, 241
Taweelah island, 45
Tawfiiq Islamic Centre, 95
Tehran, 160, 170, 174, 181–182,
   185, 202
Texas A&M University, 104
Texas Oil Company, 40
Thailand, 225
Thalin refinery project, in China,
   107
Al-Thani, Abdullah bin Jassim, 21
Al-Thani, Abdul-Aziz bin Khalifa,
   266
Al-Thani, Ahmad bin Ali, 30
Al-Thani, Ali bin Abdullah
Al-Thani, dynasty, 20, 30, 33, 56, 71
Al-Thani, Hamad bin Khalifa, 30,
   34, 87, 101, 127, 266, 271
Al-Thani, Hamad bin Jassim, 272
Al-Thani, Jabar bin Yusef bin Jassim,
   271
Al-Thani, Jassim bin Muhammad,
   20
Al-Thani, Khalifa bin Hamad, 30,
   257, 266
Bin Thani, Muhammad, 20
Thumrait, 165
Tianjin Port Group Company, 108
Tianjin province, of China, 107
Total, oil company, 41, 45
Tourism and Development Invest-
   ment Company, of Abu Dhabi,
   75, 96–97
Training and Rehabilitation Centre,
   in Dubai, 121

Tripoli, Libya, 227
Trucial States, 20–23, 25, 30–32, 40,
   137, 157, 243
Tunisia, 132, 192, 199, 201–203,
   206, 216, 221, 226, 227
Twitter, 69, 161, 197–198, 200, 217,
   225, 234–235

UAE Armed Forces, 35, 83, 86, 174,
   184
UAE Presidential Palace, 128
UAE Red Crescent Society, 82,
   84–85
Al-Udeid, airbase, 163–165
Umm al-Qawain, 22, 245, 247
Umm Shaif, 41
Union of Soviet Socialist Republics,
   3
United Kingdom, see Britain
United Nations, 28, 81–82, 140, 244
United Nations Children's Fund, 91
United Nations Education, Scien-
   tific, and Cultural Organisation,
   96
United Nations Relief and Works
   Agency, 82
United Nations Security Council,
   88, 90, 166
United Nations Working Group of
   Arbitrary Detention, 224
United States, of America, 14, 28,
   32, 41, 43, 63, 73–76, 79, 81–82,
   85, 87, 89–90, 92–94, 101–103,
   105, 108–109, 113, 126, 149, 150,
   161–169, 171–174, 176–178, 180,
   184, 188, 194, 228, 232, 237, 244,
   251
University College London, 104
University of Arkansas, 102
University of Connecticut, 102, 255
University of Southern California,
   103

University of Toronto, 149, 177
University of Wales in Lampeter,
    100
Uqair agreement, 242
US Central Command (CENT-
    COM), 164, 166, 172
US Congress, 94, 169, 173
US Fifth Fleet, 164
US Naval Support Activity Base,
    164
US Navy, 164, 173, 232
USS John Kennedy, 164

Value added tax, 57
Vanity Fair, 149–150
Vietnam, 65, 108
Virginia Commonwealth University,
    104

Al-Wahhab, Muhammab bin Abd,
    18, 26
Al-Wahhabi, Abdul-Aziz, 269
Wahhabism, 18–21, 26, 28, 73–74,
    180, 242
War on Terror, 1, 194–195
Washington DC, 94
Wa'ad, 44, 46
Web 2.0, 198–200
Al-Wefaq National Islamic Society,
    208
Weill Cornell Medical College, 104
Westinghouse, 263
Whisky, 158
Wilayet-e-faqih or rule by clerics,
    233
WinWinD, 77
Women, 27, 34, 36, 38, 59–61, 87,

98, 129, 160–162, 188, 212, 215,
    233–234, 258
World Athletics Championships, 93
World Bank, 76, 167
World Cup, 63, 93, 125, 262
World Food Programme, 83
World Trade Organisation, 176

Xingjiang province, of China, 109
Xingjiang University, 109
Xinhua News Agency, 109

Yacheng offshore gasfield, 106
Al-Yamanah arms deal, 169
Yemen, 3, 192, 199, 207, 261
Yemen, People's Democratic
    Republic of, 3
Yom Kippur War, 40
YouTube, 198, 208, 222, 233

Al-Zaabi, tribe, 271
Al-Zaman, newspaper, 211
Zanzibar, 22
Zayed bin Sultan Al-Nahyan
    Charitable and Humanitarian
    Foundation, 84
Zayed Centre for Co-ordination and
    Follow-Up, 102, 176, 265
Zayed City, in Afghanistan, 84
Zayed Future Energy Prize, 77
Zayed University of Afghanistan, 84
Zeitoun, Muannad, 261
Zhejian province, of China, 108
Zinat Al-Bihar, 182
Zionism, 175–177
Zoroastrianism, 75
Zubarah, 19–20